The Vascular Plants of Iowa

A Bur Oak Original

The Vascular Plants of Iowa

An Annotated Checklist and Natural History

Lawrence J. Eilers
Dean M. Roosa

University of Iowa Press Iowa City

University of Iowa Press, Iowa City 52242

Printed in the United States of America

The checklist and indexes in this book were printed from camera-ready copy prepared by Lawrence J. Eilers.

Printed on acid-free paper

Library of Congress Cataloging-in-Publication Data
Eilers, Lawrence J.
The vascular plants of Iowa: an annotated checklist and natural history / by Lawrence J. Eilers and Dean M. Roosa.
p. cm.—(A Bur oak original)
Includes bibliographical references (p.) and indexes.
ISBN 0-87745-463-9, ISBN 0-87745-464-7 (pbk.)
1. Botany—Iowa. I. Roosa, Dean M. II. Title. III. Series.
QK160.E35 1994
582.09777—dc20 94-21019
CIP

01 00 99 98 97 96 95 94 C 5 4 3 2 1
01 00 99 98 97 96 95 94 P 5 4 3 2 1

Contents

Preface and Acknowledgments

Individuals who work with the vascular plants of Iowa—researchers, conservationists, teachers, agricultural specialists, horticulturists, gardeners, etc.—and those who are simply interested in knowing more about the state's plants have long felt a need for a comprehensive flora of Iowa. This annotated checklist is designed to be a first step toward such a flora. It consists of a summary of the natural and vegetational history of the vascular plants of Iowa, including a description of the state's natural regions, a discussion of the origins of the Iowa flora by Dean M. Roosa, and an annotated checklist of the vascular plants of the state by Lawrence J. Eilers. The data were collected by both authors with the assistance of many other field botanists.

Previous Work

A more complete discussion of the history of field botanizing in Iowa can be found in Eilers (1975). Examples of early Euro-American explorations into Iowa are the Lewis and Clark expedition of 1804–1805, the Long expedition of 1819, and the Nicollet expedition of 1839. These exploratory expeditions usually included one or more naturalists whose duties were to observe and record what they could of the biological and physical features of the regions they passed through. Eilers summarizes this early work:

> Unfortunately, most of the records of Iowa plants in the reports of these travels were in the form of notes with indefinite localities, with the exception of a list of 11 plants from the Spirit Lake vicinity in the report of the Nicollet Expedition. (See Shimek [1915] for a more detailed account.) Although Zebulon Pike led an expedition up the Mississippi in 1805 (Pike, 1810), there are no

> specific references to Iowa plants in his report. Other botanists undoubtedly visited Iowa at an early time, e.g., Nuttall, Watson, and Gray, but, to my knowledge, they left no significant records of Iowa Plants.
>
> The earliest significant record of Iowa vascular plants appears to be the listing of 205 species from Iowa by Dr. C. C. Parry (1852) as a part of the report of D. D. Owens' geological survey of Wisconsin, Iowa, and Minnesota. The first effort toward a flora of Iowa was a partial checklist of vascular plants by Bessey (1871). Arthur published a catalogue of the phanerogamous plants in 1876 and a series of additions in 1877, 1878, 1882, and 1884. This was followed by an extensive series of papers on the vascular flora of Iowa by T. J. and M. F. L. Fitzpatrick beginning in 1897. Greene (1907) edited the only attempt at a flora of the entire plant kingdom native to Iowa. This was a joint effort by a number of prominent Iowa botanists, and included synoptic keys. Of the more than 3,000 species listed, 1,585 were vascular plants.
>
> The last attempt to publish a comprehensive vascular flora of the state was the annotated list of Cratty (1933) based on the collections in the Iowa State University herbarium. He listed 1,608 species, 1,315 of which are native. Goodman (1939, 1942) and Hayden (1940, 1945) added 75 additional species in supplementary lists. The keys in Conard's useful *Plants of Iowa* (1951) were based on Cratty's flora, with the addition of a number of cultivated plants and the elimination of the rare species. (Eilers 1975: 59–60)

In addition, a number of local checklists, county floras, and small and large revisions of plant groups are found in the literature from the early part of the century (see Eilers 1975 for a summary of these works). Other important early naturalists were L. H. Pammel, B. Shimek, T. H. Macbride, and H. S. Conard.

Present Status

In 1947 Gilly wrote that "no adequate flora of the state of Iowa can be prepared in the near future." Since that time, numerous specimens have been collected and stored in Iowa herbaria, and many articles have been published about Iowa's vascular flora. Much credit must be given to R. F. Thorne, taxonomist at the University of Iowa during the 1950s and early 1960s, for restimulating floristic study in Iowa. Thorne was an avid student of the Iowa flora (Thorne 1953, 1954, 1955, 1956, 1964). Also, seven of his Ph.D. students completed most of the floristic work in Iowa indicated by the shaded areas in map 1. In addition,

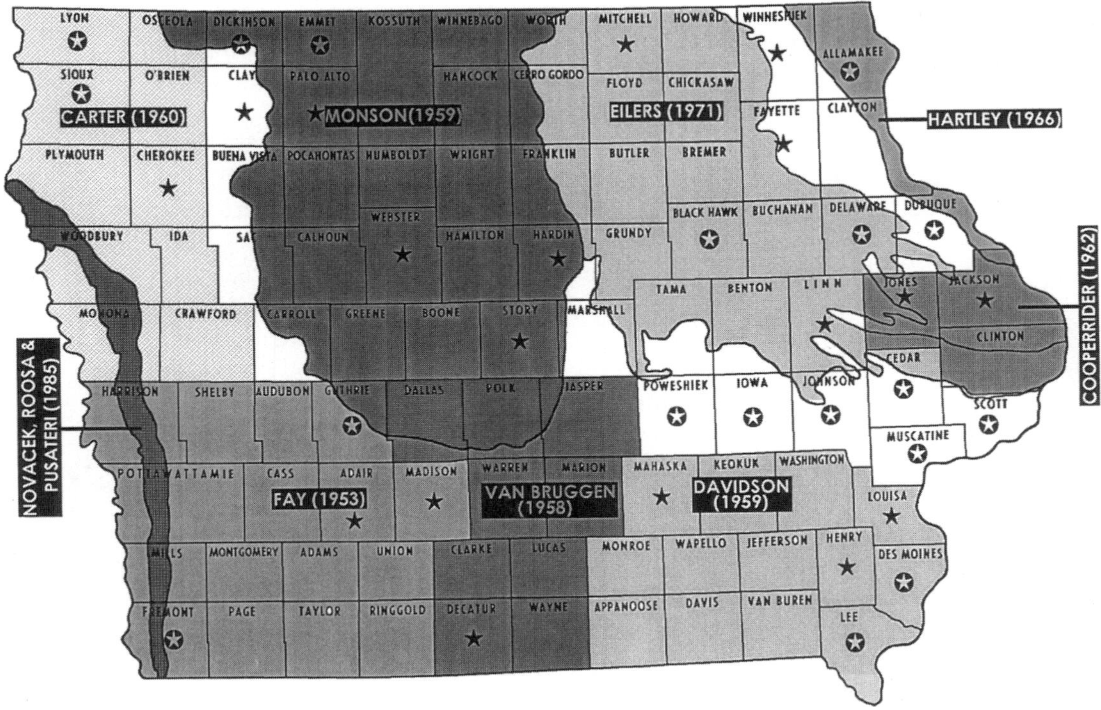

Map 1. Floristic surveys completed in Iowa. The various shaded areas indicate the regions studied by each author. The stars indicate additional county surveys (floras) conducted. ★ = County flora completed before 1950. ✪ = County flora completed between 1960 and the present.

P. H. Monson, a student of R. W. Pohl's at Iowa State University, completed a study of the Des Moines Lobe in north-central Iowa in 1959.

That this floristic momentum has continued since is illustrated by the county floras undertaken by master's students, county forays sponsored by the Department of Natural Resources (DNR), the field activities of Bureau of Preserves and Ecological Services personnel of the DNR, research instigated by the Nature Conservancy, and the individual studies of a number of dedicated field botanists. Map 1 summarizes the regional and county floras that have been completed in Iowa. Manuals, revisions of previous studies, and monographs based wholly or partly on Iowa taxa have also greatly expanded our knowledge of Iowa plants. In addition, the recently published state and regional checklists, floras, and manuals of this region have been most helpful. These include *Flora of the Great Plains* (Great Plains Flora Association 1986), *Guide to the Vascular Flora of Illinois* (Mohlenbrock 1986), *The Vascular Plants of South Dakota* (Van Bruggen 1985), the several parts of *Michigan Flora* (Voss 1972, 1985), *Vascular Plants of Minnesota* (Ownbey and Morley 1991), *A Synonymized Checklist of the*

Vascular Flora of the United States, Canada, and Greenland (Kartesz and Kartesz 1980), and *National List of Scientific Plant Names* (United States Department of Agriculture 1982a, 1982b).

Acknowledgments

Many individuals have contributed directly or indirectly to the development of this publication. To each, we offer our sincere thanks. We cannot thank each one of you here, of course, but that does not mean that we are not grateful for your assistance. Several have made significant contributions, beginning with James Peck, Carol Jacobs, and Margaret Oard, who spent much time pulling plant data together. We are grateful to John Pearson of the Bureau of Preserves and Ecological Services, Iowa Department of Natural Resources, and Mark Leoschke, formerly of that office, for a number of suggested additions, deletions, and modifications. William Pusateri of the Iowa Department of Transportation, Paul Christiansen of Cornell College, and William Watson also made significant contributions to this work. Jeffrey Nekola located several new species in Iowa and searched out a number of interesting habitats. We wish to thank Diana Horton of the Botany Department, the University of Iowa, for offering both corrections and encouragement. Her sharp-eyed assistant, Jennifer Bell, spotted several errors, and we appreciate her help. We owe a great debt to James Peck of the University of Arkansas and to Donald Farrar of Iowa State University for their reviews of the pteridophytes and to Duane Isely of Iowa State University for reviewing the legumes. They added significantly to the quality of the treatment of these taxa. Richard Baker of the University of Iowa reviewed the physical setting section and made important suggestions and corrections, for which we are grateful. We also want to express our gratitude to Douglas Ladd of the Nature Conservancy Office in Missouri, who carefully critiqued the checklist and offered a number of worthwhile suggestions for improving it.

John Downey, former head of the Biology Department at the University of Northern Iowa, suggested to the senior author that this work should be computerized. Because of this, the work has been greatly improved, but at the cost of countless hours learning how to do it! The curators of the herbaria at Iowa State University, Deborah Lewis, and the University of Iowa, Diana Horton, were most helpful with our herbarium research, for which we offer our sincere thanks. Much of this work was completed during summers spent at Iowa Lakeside Laboratory. Thanks are tendered to the successive directors of Lakeside Lab, Richard Bovbjerg and Robert Cruden, for their support and to Mark and Judy Wehrspahn, who made us comfortable while there. The senior author is grateful to John

Downey, Daryl Smith, and George Hoffman, successive heads of the Biology Department at the University of Northern Iowa, for continued support of this work. He is thankful for the unfailing encouragement of his wife, Charlotte. Also, we are grateful to all those, especially Lois Tiffany of Iowa State University, who gave us their support all along the way.

Financial Support

The senior author wishes to express his gratitude to the University of Northern Iowa for granting him a Professional Development Leave during the fall semester of 1983, for support for research during the summer of 1982, and for Faculty Research Awards for 1977–1978 and 1978–1979. He is also grateful for a research grant from the Iowa Science Foundation in 1985 and for grants from the Brenton Bank Foundation and Pioneer Hy-Bred International, Inc., to support a research leave during the spring of 1984. Finally, he wishes to thank the Department of Biology at the University of Northern Iowa for providing space, time, and assistance during the long course of this research.

The Vascular Plants of Iowa

Iowa and Its Flora

The Physical Setting

Location

Iowa lies near the center of the continental United States, between approximately 40° 35′ and 43° 30′ north latitude and between 90° and 96° 30′ west longitude, and encompasses an area of 56,290 square miles. It is located between two of the world's principal rivers, being bounded on the east by the Mississippi River and on the west by the Missouri River from the Missouri-Iowa border north to Sioux City. Running north from Sioux City, the Big Sioux River forms the remainder of the state's western boundary.

Climate

The climate of Iowa is characterized as extreme midcontinental (Reed 1941) or as humid continental, warm summer, with a small portion of northern and northeastern Iowa in the cool summer subtype (Espenshade 1964). These climatic types are characterized by warm or occasionally hot summers, with rainfall in the form of showers and thunderstorms. Iowa is subjected to seasonal extremes and frequent rapid local weather changes due to the convergence of cold dry arctic air, moist maritime air from the Gulf of Mexico, and Pacific air masses that have lost their moisture while crossing the Rocky Mountains. Summers are warm and humid due to the influence of relatively unstable maritime air masses. Hot winds and periods of high temperatures occasionally occur from May to September.

The average annual temperature ranges from 40°F along the northern border to 52°F in the southeast corner (Reed 1941). The mean July maximum temperatures range from 86°F to 90°F, with minima of 60°F to 66°F. The mean January maxima range from 24°F to 34°F, with minima of 4°F to 14°F. Winters are dominated by cold dry air masses from the Arctic, and there may be extended periods of subfreezing temperatures. Winter precipitation is of frontal origin and falls mostly in the form of snow. The lowest temperatures occur in the northern portion of the state, where minima of –20°F to –25°F are not uncommon. In southern Iowa, comparable lows of –10°F to –15°F occur. In the southeast, the January mean is 24°F; in the northwest, it is 13°F.

A considerable difference in the length of growing season can be found across Iowa (map 2). The extreme northwestern and northeastern portions average 135 days, which increases to 175 days in southern Lee County (Reed 1941). The statewide average is 158 days, from May 2 to October 7.

A gentle precipitation gradient exists generally from southeast to northwest (Reed 1941), with an average of over 34 inches in the extreme southeast and east to less than 26 inches in the northwest (map 3). This gradient is of importance in

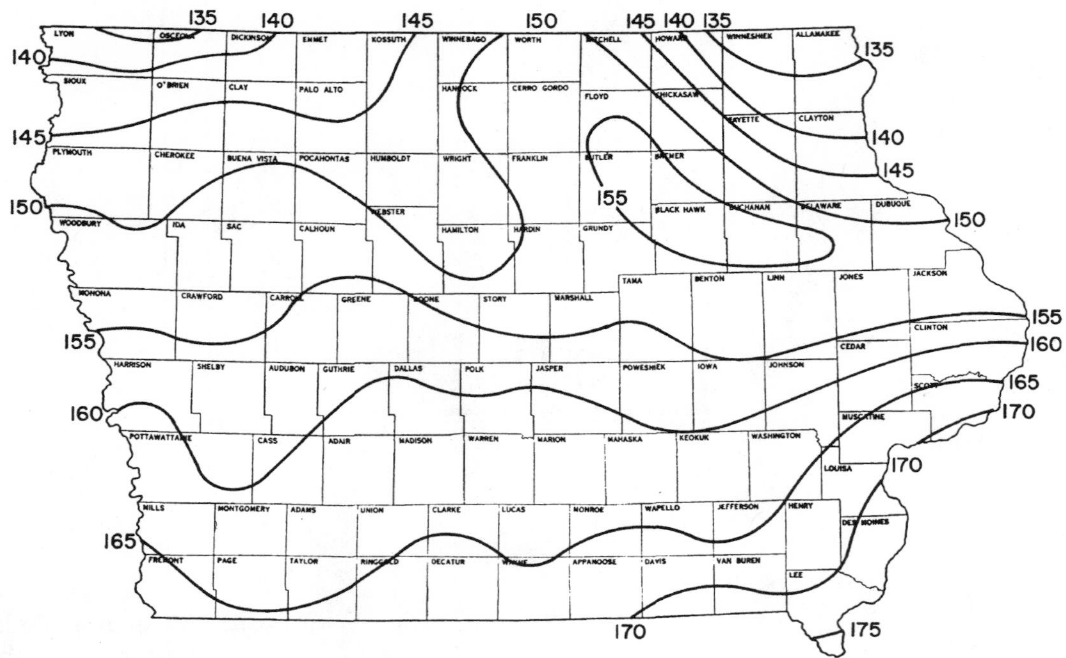

Map 2. Length of the growing season (in days).

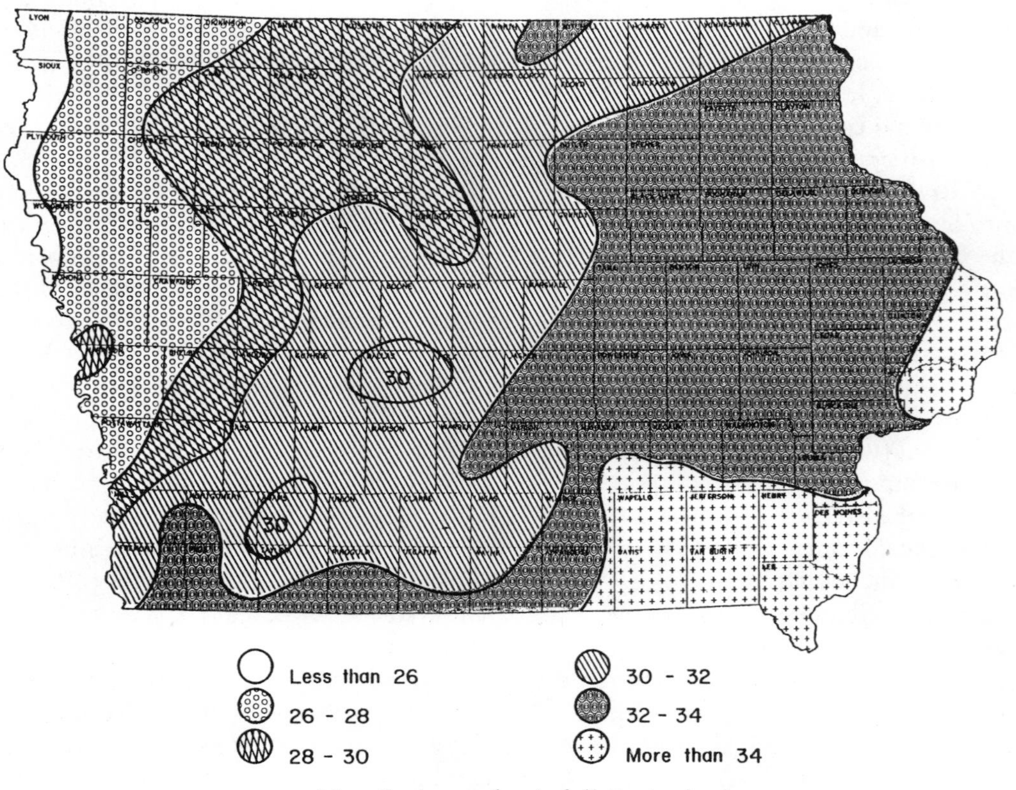

Map 3. Annual rainfall (in inches).

limiting the distribution of numerous plant species. The low rainfall of northwestern Iowa restricts woodlands to stream corridors and to some sparse or shrubby upland areas. The increased available moisture in eastern Iowa permits the growth of upland deciduous forests, an extension of the eastern deciduous forest. These interdigitate with the tallgrass prairie farther west.

About two-thirds of the state's precipitation falls from April to September, with a peak in late spring and early summer. An approximate twenty-year drought cycle occurs in Iowa. It may be of importance in limiting the occurrence of some prairie species and certain northern wetland species and, perhaps, is most critical in restricting woody species. The average annual daytime relative humidity of Iowa is 72 percent, ranging from 69 percent in the southwest to 78 percent in the northeast (Reed 1941).

The preceding factors, working in concert, have subtle but important effects on plant distributions. The longer growing season and high rainfall of southeastern Iowa allow certain southern species to enter that part of the state. On the other hand, the arid conditions of extreme western Iowa allow a number of Great Plains species to enter that part of the state.

Geology

Most of Iowa is underlain by sedimentary rocks such as shales, sandstones, limestones, and dolomites. These are generally deeply buried below glacial deposits and have little influence on plant distribution and abundance. Exceptions are in the northeast, where the bedrock is very near the surface and where many outcrops occur. In the extreme northwest, Sioux Quartzite is at the surface and provides habitat for some unusual plant species. Outcrops also occur along some of the major rivers where these rivers have cut into and exposed the underlying bedrock, such as at Ledges State Park, Boone County; at Dolliver State Park and Woodman Hollow State Preserve, Webster County; at Lacey-Keosauqua State Park on the Des Moines River in Van Buren County; along the Maquoketa River in Jones County; along the Upper Iowa River in Winneshiek County; at Palisades-Kepler State Park on the Cedar River in Linn County; and at many places along the Mississippi River. These outcrops extend the range of some northern and eastern plant species, especially certain species of ferns.

Glacial History

The influence of glaciers is of great importance in the distribution of Iowa vascular plants. There were repeated periods of ice cover: several in the Pre-Illinoian, followed by the Illinoian and the most recent, the Wisconsinan. The Pre-Illinoian, beginning over 2 million years before present, covered the entire state several times. Thin deposits of at least one of these glacial advances are present on the Paleozoic Plateau in northeastern Iowa. Deposits from this and other Pre-Illinoian advances can be found over the rest of the state but are buried by younger deposits on the Des Moines Lobe and in the Loess Hills. The next period of glacial advance in the state was the Illinoian, which entered from the east, causing an ice block that apparently impounded water in the Iowa–Cedar River basin, resulting in the formation of glacial Lake Calvin. The final Pleistocene event that affected Iowa was the Wisconsinan-age glacier. This last glacial episode occurred about 30,000 to 10,500 years ago. The plants present at that time either migrated south of the glacier or were extirpated. As the glacier retreated, it left a tongue-shaped area terminating at what is now the city of Des Moines. The young landscape is poorly drained and is dotted with lakes and prairie potholes. This final glacial event was followed by the present interglacial stage, when warmer conditions returned and plants were able to become reestablished in central Iowa.

As the glacier retreated or seasonally melted, the meltwater carried sediment in large volume which was deposited on the floodplains of the glacial rivers. When these streams dried at the approach of winter, prevailing westerly winds lifted the fine sediment and deposited it downwind on the Iowa landscape, forming a mantle on the land. This yellowish, flourlike material is termed loess and is today apparent in all except the north-central counties, which were covered by the Wisconsinan glacier at the time of the loess deposits. The hills adjacent to the floodplain of the Missouri River in far western Iowa, with loess de byits in excess of 150 feet deep in places, are a priceless scenic and biological heritage and are of great importance in plant distribution.

Vegetational History Since the Pleistocene

Iowa was covered by spruce-dominated forests from about 30,000 to 21,500 years ago. These forests were replaced by very open tundra and parkland during the last glacial maximum, about 21,500 to around 16,000 years ago. Spruce forests returned as the climate began to warm from 16,000 to 12,000 years ago, when they, in turn, were replaced by deciduous forests as the warming trend continued (Baker et al. 1990).

Prairies entered western Iowa about 9,000 years ago and extended to central Iowa by 8,500 years ago. The warmest and driest conditions prevailed about 6,300 years ago in western and central Iowa. However, in eastern Iowa, mesic deciduous forest prevailed until 5,500 years ago, when it finally was replaced by prairie. A sharp climatic and vegetational boundary must have extended north-south between eastern and central Iowa between 8,500 and 5,500 years ago, with prairie on the west and mesic forest on the east (Baker et al. 1990).

Between 4,000 and 3,000 years ago, oaks returned and became abundant in the state, apparently in oak savannas. This vegetation persisted until Euro-American settlers arrived (Baker et al. 1992).

Prairie fires, set by lightning and possibly by early Native Americans, retarded the advance of the forest and kept the prairie areas treeless. Evidence of the effectiveness of prairie fires comes from studies (e.g., McComb and Loomis 1944) showing forest-derived soils occurring principally on the eastern sides of streams, which provided breaks against the fires driven by the prevailing westerly winds. At the time of Euro-American settlement, approximately 85 percent of the state was covered by prairie (map 4; State Planning Board 1925). Extant prairies, when compared with photographs of the same sites from early in this century, show a great increase in forest invasion. Wetlands protected bur oak knobs from frequent fires; thus, these areas became savannas, of which degraded examples still exist. Today the prairie has been reduced to approximately 0.01 percent of its extent at the time of Euro-American settlement, the woodlands have decreased to about one-fourth of their former area (map 5; Thomson and Hertel 1981), and the wetlands have declined from around 1.5 million acres to perhaps as few as 27,000 acres (Bishop 1981). (This latter figure does not include sedge meadows, fens, or wet prairies.)

The Natural Regions of Iowa

As a result of the preceding factors, Iowa has a landscape which can be divided into biogeographical provinces or natural regions. These are shown in map 6 and are described in terms of their influence on the distribution of plants in Iowa. The regions were discussed in Prior (1991) and are expanded upon here to include additional information of a botanical nature.

Paleozoic Plateau

The Paleozoic Plateau in northeast Iowa is the most rugged part of the state and is often referred to as Little Switzerland. It is divided from the remainder of the state by the Silurian Escarpment. Deep valleys provide a variety of microhabitats that are necessary for the existence of many species of plants on the margins of their ranges. This portion of Iowa is of vital concern to botanists interested in the Iowa vascular plant flora because it contains many boreal species, disjuncts, and endangered or threatened species.

The Paleozoic Plateau occurs in the part of the state historically called the Driftless Area. It is a portion of a much larger multistate area of approximately 15,000 square miles. The majority of this area lies in Wisconsin, with smaller areas in Illinois, Iowa, and Minnesota. It is known to have escaped coverage during the Illinoian and Wisconsinan glacial advances into the upper Midwest and perhaps served as a refugium for plants during this time. In Iowa, the Paleozoic Plateau consists of an area of some 1,050 square miles, including portions of Allamakee, Clayton,

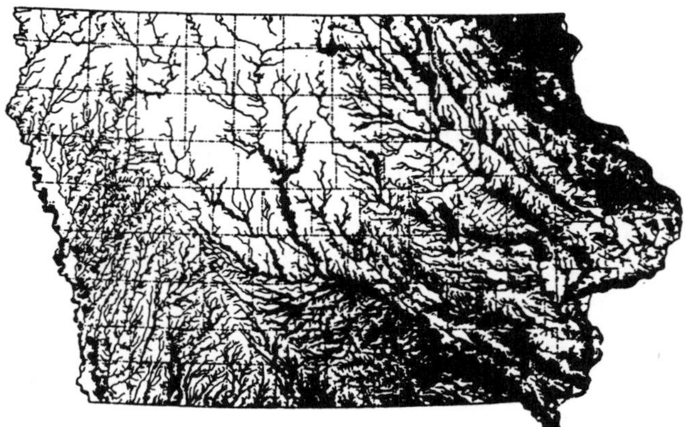

Map 4. Forested area at the time of Euro-American settlement, reconstructed from an original land survey conducted between 1832 and 1859 (Shimek 1948).

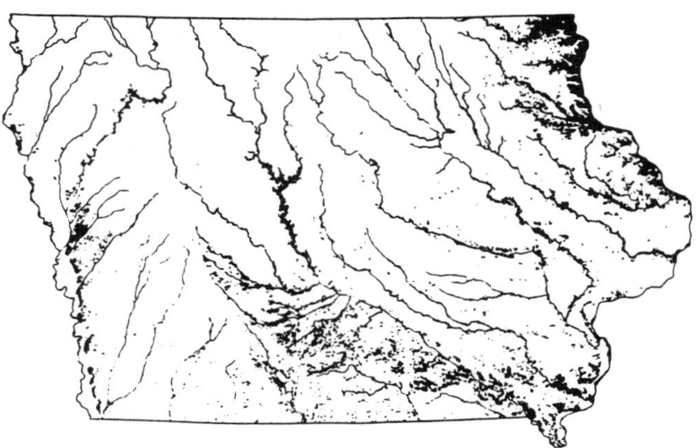

Map 5. Forested area in 1976, redrawn from remote-sensing satellite photography (Iowa Geological Survey 1976).

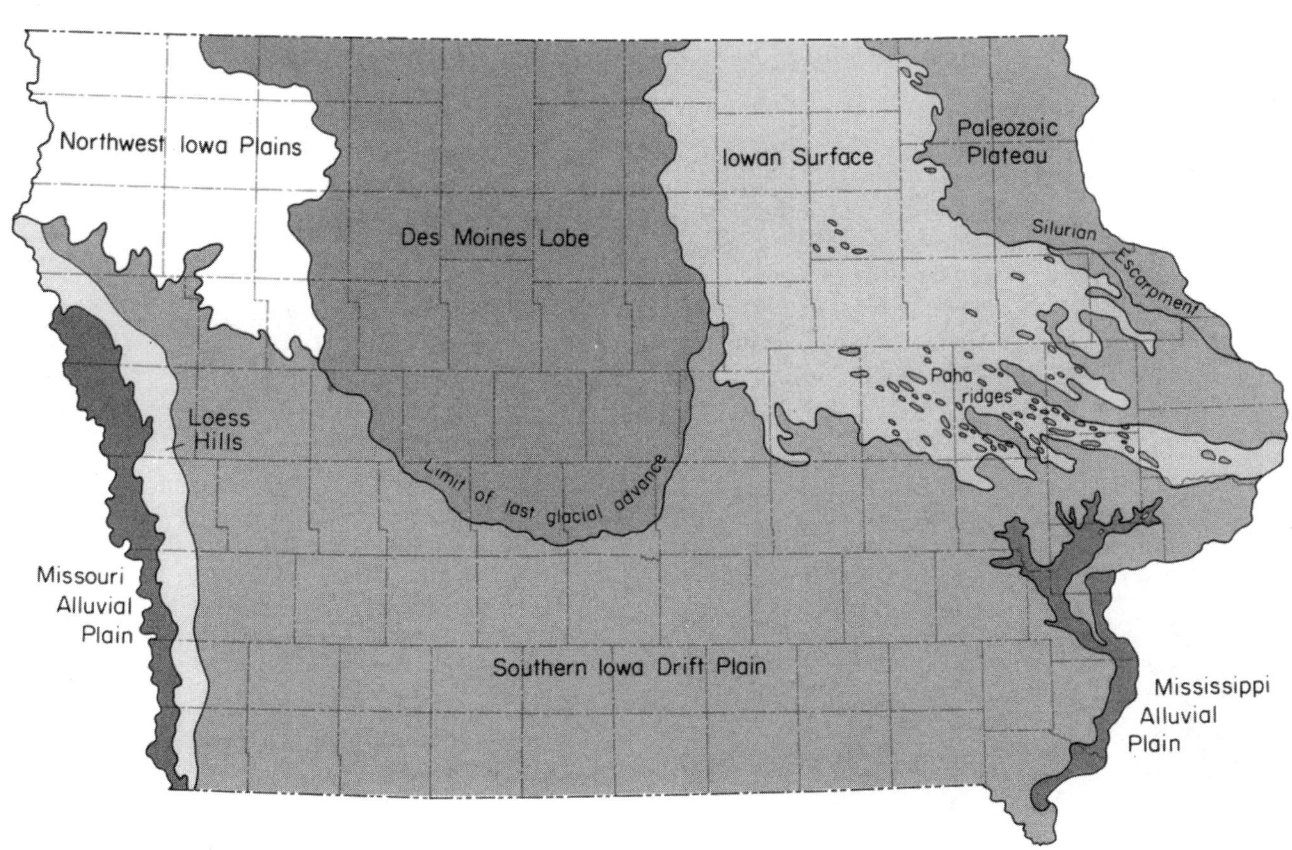

Map 6. Landform regions (Prior 1991).

Delaware, Dubuque, Howard, Jackson, and Winneshiek counties. Important references to this landform region are Hartley (1966), Cahayla-Wynne and Glenn-Lewin (1978), Peck (1982), Peck, Roosa, and Eilers (1980), and a special issue of the *Proceedings of the Iowa Academy of Science* (vol. 91, no. 1) devoted to the natural history of the Driftless Area.

Cliff-dwelling Plants

Bedrock controls the landscape of the Paleozoic Plateau and often outcrops to provide habitat for cliff-dwelling species such as:

Arabis hirsuta
A. lyrata
Campanula rotundifolia
Cheilanthes feei
Cryptogramma stelleri
Pellaea atropurpurea
P. glabella
Solidago sciaphila
Sullivantia sullivantii
Woodsia ilvensis
W. obtusa
W. oregana

Algific Talus Slope Plants

The north-facing, moss-covered talus slopes, with continuous cold air drainage, form habitat for a variety of plants, some of which are among Iowa's rarest. These slopes have recently been termed "algific talus slopes" by Frest (1981) and are briefly described by Glenn-Lewin, Laushman, and Whitson (1984) and Hartley (1966).

Hill prairie on the Paleozoic Plateau, Allamakee County.

Plants characteristic of this community include:

Abies balsamea
Acer spicatum
Aconitum noveboracense
Adoxa moschatellina
Betula alleghaniensis
Carex careyana
C. deweyana
C. media
C. peckii
Cerastium arvense
Chrysosplenium iowense
Circaea alpina
Cornus canadensis
Corylus cornuta
Cypripedium reginae
Equisetum scirpoides
Gymnocarpium dryopteris
G. robertianum
Linnaea borealis ssp. *americana*
Luzula acuminata
Mertensia paniculata
Poa paludigena
P. wolfii
Pyrola asarifolia
P. secunda
Ribes hudsonianum
Rosa acicularis
Rubus pubescens
Salix bebbiana
Sambucus racemosa ssp. *pubens*
Saxifraga forbesii
Streptopus roseus
Taxus canadensis
Viburnum trilobum
Viola renifolia

Plants of Cold, Spring-fed Streams

The following species occur in or along spring-fed streams mostly found in northeastern Iowa:

Nasturtium officinale
Potamogeton crispus
P. foliosus
Ranunculus aquatilis var. *capillaceus*
R. circinatus
Veronica americana
V. anagallis-aquatica
Zannichellia palustris

Algific talus slope on the Paleozoic Plateau, Clayton County.

Disjunct Populations

Populations which are disjunct from the more northern main portion of their ranges are found in the Paleozoic Plateau, including:

Abies balsamea
Aronia melanocarpa
Carex careyana
C. media
C. peckii
Chimaphila umbellata
Gymnocarpium robertianum
Mertensia paniculata
Oryzopsis pungens
Poa wolfii
Potentilla tridentata
Ribes hudsonianum
Vaccinium myrtilloides

Ken Formanek

Balsam fir stand, a relict community on the Paleozoic Plateau, Winneshiek County.

Very Rare Species

The only known Iowa stations for the following species are found in the Paleozoic Plateau:

Abies balsamea
Aconitum noveboracense
Arctostaphylos uva-ursi
Botrychium matricariifolium
Carex careyana
C. media
C. peckii
C. woodii
Chrysosplenium iowense
Conopholis americana
Corallorhiza maculata
Cornus canadensis
Dryopteris intermedia
Equisetum scirpoides
Gymnocarpium robertianum
Jeffersonia diphylla
Linnaea borealis ssp. *americana*
Lupinus perennis
Lycopodium dendroideum
Mitchella repens
Monotropa hypopithys
Oryzopsis pungens
Poa paludigena
Potentilla tridentata
Pyrola asarifolia
P. secunda
Ribes hudsonianum
Spiranthes lucida
Talinum rugospermum
Vaccinium myrtilloides
Viola renifolia
Woodsia ilvensis

Despite extensive plant collecting in this landform region in the past, new discoveries continue to occur. For example, the first Iowa stations for *Aureolaria pedicularia, Botrychium matricariifolium, Conopholis americana, Dryopteris X boottii, Hepatica nobilis* var. *obtusa, Pyrola asarifolia, Spiranthes lucida,* and *Viola adunca* were discovered here in recent years.

Hill Prairies

Relatively extensive hill prairies, described by Hartley (1966) and Ugarte (1987), are also in the Paleozoic Plateau. These were historically kept treeless by drying winds, fires, and very thin

Coldwater stream on the Paleozoic Plateau, Winneshiek County.

topsoil. Characteristic species include:

Andropogon gerardii
Anemone cylindrica
Bouteloua curtipendula
Bromus kalmii
Carex abdita
Castilleja sessiliflora
Ceanothus herbaceus var. *pubescens*
Juniperus communis var. *depressa*
J. virginiana
Liatris aspera
L. cylindracea
Lithospermum incisum
Pulsatilla patens var. *multifida*
Salix humilis
Schizachyrium scoparium
Sporobolus heterolepis
S. neglectus
S. vaginiflorus
Viola pedata

Oak-Juniper Glades

Hartley (1966) described juniper glades on the bluffs of the Mississippi River; Glenn-Lewin, Laushman, and Whitson (1984) called them oak-juniper glades and described them as assemblages of xerophytic species on dry, exposed, calcareous crags, cliffs, and bluffs having thin soil. These are dominated by *Quercus muhlenbergii, Q. macrocarpa, Q. ellipsoidalis, Juniperus virginiana*, and occasionally *J. communis* var. *depressa.*

Sandy Areas

Sandy wooded slopes, sand plains, and sand terraces occur in the northern portion of the Paleozoic Plateau. Sandy wooded slopes are present in Allamakee County along Bear Creek, Village Creek, and Yellow River. Plants normally associated with sandy areas include:

Brachyelytrum erectum
Carex deweyana
C. peckii
Diervilla lonicera
Equisetum pratense
E. scirpoides
Hamamelis virginiana
Luzula acuminata
Lycopodium digitatum
L. lucidulum
Maianthemum canadense
Sambucus pubens
Schizachne purpurascens
Viburnum trilobum

Sand plains can be found in northern Allamakee County along the Upper Iowa River and are a result of deposition by the river during the Pleistocene epoch. These are naturally nearly barren, but extensive pine planting has taken place on some. Plants characteristic of this habitat include:

Cyperus filiculmis
C. schweinitzii
Froelichia floridana var. *campestris*
Polygala polygama var. *obtusata*
Polygonella articulata
Polygonum douglasii
Talinum rugospermum

Sand terraces occur in Allamakee County along the Mississippi and Upper Iowa rivers. Some plants principally restricted to this habitat are:

Aureolaria pedicularia
Gaylussacia baccata
Lupinus perennis
Lycopodium digitatum
Vaccinium angustifolium
V. myrtilloides

Upland Woods

Upland woods in the Paleozoic Plateau were described by Hartley (1966) and by Cahayla-Wynne and Glenn-Lewin (1978). These woods exist in upland regions where the covering of loess soil still remains and may be very dry, dominated by oak and hickory. On deeper soils and protected slopes, the community may be mesic and may include such species as black walnut, red oak, hard maple, and basswood. Some characteristic species include:

Botrychium virginianum
Carex convoluta
C. sprengelii
Galearis spectabilis
Goodyera pubescens
Hystrix patula
Liparis liliifolia
Monotropa uniflora
Osmorhiza claytonii
Parthenocissus quinquefolia
Podophyllum peltatum
Polygonatum biflorum
Pyrola elliptica
Tilia americana
Ulmus rubra
Uvularia grandiflora
Viola sororia
Vitis aestivalis

Dry Sandstone Ledges and Talus

In the northern portion of the Paleozoic Plateau, in northern Allamakee and Winneshiek counties, are outcrops of dry sandstone, including the soft St. Peter sandstone. Among the characteristic or rare taxa here are:

Arabis lyrata
Aronia melanocarpa
Campanula rotundifolia
Juniperus communis var. *depressa*
Pellaea atropurpurea
P. glabella
Potentilla tridentata
Selaginella rupestris
Woodsia ilvensis
W. obtusa
W. oregana

Moist Limestone Ledges and Cliffs

Found in Allamakee, Clayton, Delaware, Dubuque, Fayette, and Winneshiek counties are moist limestone ledges and cliffs which support the following species:

Arabis hirsuta
Cryptogramma stelleri
Cystopteris bulbifera
Dodecatheon amethystinum
Sullivantia sullivantii

Iowan Surface

The Iowan Surface is a large landform region bounded on the east by the Niagaran Escarpment, on the south by the Southern Iowa Drift Plain, and on the west by the Des Moines Lobe. This landform encompasses all, or nearly all, of twenty-seven counties in northeastern Iowa. This region is somewhat tongue-shaped, with the long axis oriented in a north-northwest to south-southeast direction. The southern terminus is deeply lobed, the protrusions being upland areas between the valleys of the large rivers and streams (Eilers 1971).

The bedrock underlying the Iowan Surface dips from the northeast to southwest. The oldest system, the Silurian, outcrops as Niagaran dolomite along streams in Clayton, Jones, Cedar, and Fayette counties. Outcrops of Pennsylvanian sandstone along the Iowa River near Eldora are of interest because of the flora they support.

A prominent feature of the southern portion of the Iowan Surface are the paha, which are loess-capped knobs and ridges oriented west-northwest to east-southeast. These rise 50 feet or more above the existing landscape and have a nucleus of Pre-Illinoian (Kansan) till (Scholtes 1955). The most prominent paha are covered by oak-hickory woods.

The Iowan Surface is a botanically varied landscape, with plant communities such as wetlands, tallgrass prairie, loess-capped paha, fens, streams with submerged aquatic plants, and sand deposits. An important botanical reference to this erosional surface is Eilers (1971).

Wetlands

Wetlands, now often with stands of trembling aspen (*Populus tremuloides*), are of botanical interest because they provide an organically rich, usually moist humus for certain plants that need an acidic substrate. Species in this habitat include:

Angelica atropurpurea
Betula pumila var. *glandulifera*
Cypripedium calceolus var. *parviflorum*
C. calceolus var. *pubescens*
C. candidum
C. reginae
C. X *andrewsii*
Ophioglossum pusillum
Platanthera psycodes
Salix candida

Carol Thompson

Fen on the Iowan Surface, Cerro Gordo County.

Silver Lake Fen on the Des Moines Lobe, Dickinson County.

Fens

Throughout the Iowan Surface exists a special type of wetland or peatland which has developed in mineral-rich water. These are termed fens and may occur on hillsides where erosion has exposed a discharge area, where water is carried laterally through gravel deposits and discharges on the slope. Fens may occur on any portion of the slope face or as a mounded peat deposit on the nearly level ground in the drainageway. The latter type has long been called mound springs but differs little in its flora from other fens. Another peatland with a different developmental history is the type which develops in abandoned stream channels and undergoes succession through the centuries from an open-water habitat to a sedge mat with attendant peat deposition. Two classic examples of this type of peatland occur on the Iowan Surface: the renowned Buffalo Slough in Cerro Gordo County and Cutshall Access in Buchanan County. A complex of plant species, including the following, seems to be principally restricted to these two peatland types:

Betula pumila var. *glandulifera*
Eriophorum angustifolium
E. virginicum
Galium labradoricum
Gentianopsis crinita
G. procera
Lobelia kalmii
Mimulus glabratus var. *fremontii*
Muhlenbergia glomerata
Parnassia glauca
Rhynchospora capillacea
Salix candida
S. pedicellaris
Scleria verticillata
Triglochin maritimum

Sandy Areas

Extensive sandy areas exist on the Iowan Surface, particularly along the Cedar and Wapsipinicon rivers. These are mostly eolian deposits and may contain deflation basins and dunes, but most such dunes have been stabilized by vegetation. Some taxa which are principally restricted to these sandy areas include:

Anemone caroliniana
Astragalus distortus
Besseya bullii

Calamovilfa longifolia
Cycloloma atriplicifolium
Dalea villosa
Eragrostis trichodes
Froelichia floridana var. *campestris*
Geranium carolinianum
Hedyotis crassifolia
Hypericum gentianoides
Lycopodium inundatum
Monarda punctata var. *villicaulis*
Opuntia fragilis
Penstemon grandiflorus
Phlox bifida
Polygala cruciata
P. polygama var. *obtusata*
Polygonella articulata
Polygonum tenue
Rhus aromatica
Rumex acetosella
Selaginella rupestris
Strophostyles helvula
Tephrosia virginiana
Xyris torta

Prairie pothole on the Des Moines Lobe, Wright County.

Des Moines Lobe

The youngest landform region in Iowa is the Des Moines Lobe, a tongue-shaped area of approximately 12,000 square miles. It terminates at the city of Des Moines at the confluence of the Des Moines and Raccoon rivers. The Raccoon River forms the southern and western border of the lobe. This landform is poorly drained and is dotted with potholes, particularly in the northwestern portion. Glacial moraines form prominent features as, for example, Ocheyedan Mound in Osceola County, Pilot Knob in Hancock County, and Pilot Mound in Boone County. Large, open-water lakes such as Spirit Lake and Lake Okoboji in Dickinson County, Clear Lake in Cerro Gordo County, and Storm Lake in Buena Vista County are scattered throughout the landscape.

K. M. Madden

Tallgrass prairie on the Des Moines Lobe, Kossuth County.

The Des Moines Lobe once supported a prime example of the tallgass prairie biome, which has since been almost completely converted to agricultural crops. Nonetheless, this region contains some of Iowa's finest remnants of the tallgrass prairie. *Lespedeza leptostachya*, a plant endemic to the upper Midwest, is found on some of these remnants.

Savannas

In the northern part of the lobe, glacial knobs and ridges were partially or wholly surrounded by shallow marshes. The wetlands protected the ridges from frequent prairie fires and promoted the establishment of savannas. These are especially noticeable in the region of Pilot Knob State Preserve.

Peatlands

The Des Moines Lobe contained many peatlands and *Carex* swales. The peatlands contained *Drepanocladus* moss, unlike those of the more northern parts of the United States which are largely composed of *Sphagnum*. However, in this part of the lobe is found the state's only example of a *Sphagnum* bog (called by some researchers a "nutrient-poor fen" or "poor fen"), existing in Pilot Knob State Preserve. Recent palynological evidence indicates that this bog has been present since before Euro-American settlement and is probably a relict from conditions which prevailed at the end of the Pleistocene (R. Baker, personal communication). Somehow it escaped recognition until 1954 (Grant and Thorne 1955). A number of rare taxa, such as the following, are found on the floating mat:

Carex cephalantha
C. chordorrhiza
C. limosa
Drosera rotundifolia
Eriophorum gracile
Salix pedicellaris

In parts of the lobe are prominent end moraines which are dry and often gravelly. In central Iowa, good examples are found in the area of southwestern Wright County, southeastern Franklin County, and portions of Boone County. In the northwestern portion of the lobe, good examples of the characteristic swell and swale topography are found in the region of Lake Okoboji. Associated with this landscape are depressions termed kettleholes, where chunks of ice were covered by glacial till. As the glaciers melted, they left the concentric, cone-shaped kettleholes. One of the best examples of these is the Freda Haffner Kettlehole near Lake Okoboji. The plants of this preserve have recently been studied (Freese and Platt 1991). In close proximity to the potholes and marshes are found knobs and ridges caused by the relatively recent glacial activity.

Dry Knobs

On dry knobs are found, for example:

Bouteloua curtipendula
B. hirsuta
Koeleria macrantha
Pulsatilla patens var. *multifida*
Schizachyrium scoparium

Land-use practices are causing dry knobs to be highly modified, with some being mined for gravel.

Wet Depressions

In wet depressions are found an array of marsh plants. Most are at or near the southern terminus of their ranges and include:

Brasenia schreberi
Equisetum fluviatile
Eriophorum angustifolium
Hippuris vulgaris
Lysimachia thyrsiflora
Menyanthes trifoliata
Scirpus maritimus
Scolochloa festucacea

Fens

Fens are at or near the interface of the Des Moines Lobe and the older glacial surface to the west. Silver Lake Fen has long been state-owned; several other complexes have recently been acquired by the Nature Conservancy or Department of Natural Resources.

The northwestern portion of the Des Moines Lobe was thought until recently to be the only part of Iowa where fens existed. These fens have been studied by botanists for over a hundred years. Although similar in many respects to the fens on the Iowan Surface, some important differences exist. Des Moines Lobe fens are more likely to have a deposit of tufa (calcareous or siliceous rock deposits of springs or groundwater) at the surface; Des Moines Lobe fens are divided into distinctive vegetative zones; ferns do not normally occur on Des Moines Lobe fens, while Iowan Surface fens are much more likely to have trees and shrubs. Three rare shrubs, *Betula pumila* var. *glandulifera*, *Salix candida*, and *S. pedicellaris*, are not found on Des Moines Lobe fens.

Plants principally restricted to Des Moines Lobe fens include:

Berula erecta var. *incisum*
Eriophorum angustifolium
Gentianopsis procera
Lobelia kalmii
Platanthera hyperborea var. *huronensis*
Rhynchospora capillacea
Scleria verticillata
Spiranthes romanzoffiana
Triglochin maritimum
T. palustris
Utricularia minor

Northwest Iowa Plains

The Northwest Iowa Plains region is a largely treeless, gently rolling area that has the highest altitude and lowest rainfall in the state. Relief in this region is low, on the order of 10 to 30 feet. Because of this low relief, the region has been almost entirely converted to agricultural uses. This landform region is bordered on the west by the Big Sioux River, on the east by the Des Moines Lobe, and on the south by the Southern Iowa Drift Plain.

The area is not very well known botanically, as some of it fell between Carter's (1960) study of northwestern Iowa and Monson's (1959) study of the Des Moines Lobe. Hayden (1943) includes part of this section in her lakes area study. Native tallgrass prairie remnants are still found here but not in the abundance found by Hayden (1946). The upper reaches of the Little Sioux River provide the major source of drainage.

The western portion of this landform is of importance as habitat for Great Plains plant species and relict prairie areas. Peck et al. (1984) summarized and updated the flora of Lyon and Sioux counties.

Gravel Hills

The following uncommon species occur on the loess-capped or gravel hills along the Big Sioux River:

Artemisia frigida
Asclepias stenophylla
Lomatium orientale
Schedonnardus paniculatus
Sphaeralcea coccinea

Gravel Bluffs and Ridges

Extensive dry gravel bluffs and ridges along streams, especially in Cherokee and O'Brien counties, provide habitat for plants generally found farther west. Examples are:

Astragalus agrestis
Botrychium campestre
Lomatium foeniculaceum
Oxytropis lambertii
Potentilla pensylvanica
Stipa comata

Sioux Quartzite outcrops in extreme northwestern Iowa, Lyon County.

Sioux Quartzite Outcrops

A small, anomalous area occurs in the very northwestern part of the region. It is an outcrop of an ancient bedrock known as Sioux Quartzite. This is a pink to reddish stone dated at around 1.2 billion years before present. On the thin soil which covers portions of the quartzite, xeric conditions prevail, making excellent habitat for a number of rare species. Vernal pools on the edges of an old quarry provide another habitat for some rare taxa. Shimek (1896) and Vander Zee (1979) are important botanical references to this area. Taxa of restricted distribution in Iowa which occur in this habitat include:

Bacopa rotundifolia
Buchloe dactyloides
Heteranthera limosa
Heterotheca villosa
Marsilea vestita
Opuntia fragilis
Potentilla pensylvanica
Prunus besseyi
Schedonnardus paniculatus
Selaginella rupestris
Talinum parviflorum
Woodsia oregana

Southern Iowa Drift Plain

Most of the southern half of Iowa was last glaciated by the Pre-Illinoian glacier, approximately 600,000 years ago. This part of Iowa is a mature landscape, historically fairly heavily wooded. Today, the central portion still contains a significant proportion of Iowa's remaining woodlands.

Subtle changes in the landscape occur across this large area. The eastern portion is characterized by tabular uplands, which disappear as one travels westward. Loess mantles the entire area, decreasing from a thick blanket in the west to a thin layer on the flat uplands in the east. Through processes of erosion throughout the centuries, evidence of moraines or marshes has been lost.

Western Portion

The western portion of the Southern Iowa Drift Plain, exclusive of the Loess Hills, is relatively treeless. The tabular uplands have disappeared, and rolling uplands and broad valleys are characteristic. An important botanical reference to this landform region is Fay (1953). Probably no plant species are confined to this section, but the following are of restricted distribution in the state and are the most common here:

Asclepias stenophylla
Opuntia macrorhiza
Viola viarum

Central Portion

The landscape of the central portion of the Southern Iowa Drift Plain differs from that to the east by the near absence of flat uplands and a much more rolling character. It differs from that to the west by being more heavily forested, the loess mantle being thinner and the uplands more marked. An important botanical reference for this part of the landform is Van Bruggen (1958).

Perhaps no plant species are confined to this section, but the following are characteristic or occur here as their principal Iowa range:

Asclepias meadii
Carya laciniosa
Dasistoma macrophylla
Quercus marilandica
Q. stellata
Silphium integrifolium
Spiranthes lacera
Tripsacum dactyloides
Veratrum woodii

Eastern Portion

The eastern portion of the Southern Iowa Drift Plain is a large, fairly homogeneous area characterized by tabular uplands, with steep topography only along streams. Little forest cover remains, except in areas owned by the state of Iowa. Plant species restricted to this part of Iowa include:

Andropogon virginicus
Aristolochia serpentaria
Aster furcatus
Bacopa rotundifolia
Bidens bipinnata
Carex squarrosa
Carya illinoensis
Chelone obliqua var. *speciosa*
Eleocharis atropurpurea
Fraxinus quadrangulata
Leucospora multifida
Mimulus alatus
Oenothera pilosella
Penstemon pallidus
Sassafras albidum
Scirpus hallii
Thalictrum revolutum

The extreme eastern extension of the Southern Iowa Drift Plain is a rugged part of Iowa and is replete with flat uplands historically covered by prairie species, with scenic entrenched rivers, wooded ravines, and many rock outcrops. It is of importance botanically, and much of it was surveyed by Cooperrider (1962). In places, the Maquoketa River valley is a deep gorge with outcrops that provide habitats for many cliff-dwelling species normally found farther north. In recent years, algific talus slopes have been discovered in this portion of the Southern Iowa Drift Plain, and numerous plants have been documented farther south than previously suspected. Examples of these and other plants which have a narrow ecological tolerance include:

Aconitum noveboracense
Chrysosplenium iowense
Cypripedium reginae
Equisetum scirpoides
Gaylussacia baccata
Goodyera pubescens
Lycopodium lucidulum
Pinus strobus
Streptopus roseus
Taxus canadensis

Steep terrain which characterizes the Loess Hills of western Iowa, Monona County.

Loess Hills

Along the western edge of Iowa, a relatively narrow tract of deep deposits of wind-deposited loess parallels the floodplain of the Missouri River. These spectacular hills—steep, west-facing, and dry—are of singular biological significance for Iowa. Before Euro-American settlement, they were nearly treeless due to intermittent fires and extreme climatic conditions caused by exposure to drying winds and the hot afternoon sun. Great Plains plant species find suitable habitat in this landform region, and here the bulk of Iowa's remnant prairies remain. Important references to the Loess Hills of Iowa are Mutel (1991), two special issues of the *Proceedings of the Iowa Academy of Science* (vol. 92, no. 5, and vol. 93, no. 2), and Novacek, Roosa, and Pusateri (1983).

On the dry slopes and hilltops are found the following:

Agropyron cristatum
Andropogon hallii
Astragalus lotiflorus
A. missouriensis
Botrychium campestre
Carex saximontana
Dalea enneandra
Gaura coccinea
Lomatium foeniculaceum
Machaeranthera spinulosa
Mentzelia decapetela
Passerina annua
Schedonnardus paniculatus
Schrankia nuttallii
Sphaeralcea coccinea
Yucca glauca

Missouri River Alluvium Region

For centuries the Missouri River occupied a large floodplain, periodically flooding, changing course, and creating oxbows and annually depositing a layer of silt. Only recently has the river been channelized, straightened, diked, and "controlled." Now nearly entirely converted to agricultural uses, this floodplain once had extensive stands of low prairie species. Sand dune areas also exist in the floodplain, most with extensive growths of woody species. Many of these species became "stabilized," because a 1952 flood deposited a layer of silt that made it possible for succession to occur.

Oxbows

Remaining oxbows of the Missouri River contain a diverse array of aquatic species, including:

Alisma subcordatum
Ammannia coccinea
Calamagrostis canadensis
Ceratophyllum demersum
Cyperus esculentus
C. inflexus
C. rivularis
Echinodorus cordifolius
Eleocharis calva
E. obtusa
Eragrostis hypnoides
Heteranthera dubia
Juncus acuminatus
J. dudleyi
J. nodosus
Lindernia dubia
Najas guadalupensis
Nelumbo lutea
Phragmites australis
Polygonum coccineum
Potamogeton foliosus
P. nodosus
P. pectinatus
Sagittaria brevirostra
S. calycina
Salix amygdaloides

S. exigua ssp. *interior*
S. nigra
Scirpus acutus
S. americanus
S. atrovirens
Sparganium eurycarpum
Spartina pectinata
Typha latifolia
Utricularia vulgaris

Unusual but characteristic species which occur in this region include:

Dalea leporina
Hemicarpha micrantha
Lygodesmia rostrata
Psoralidium lanceolatum

Sand Dunes

Dry sand dunes are found near the Missouri River, especially in Harrison, Monona, and Woodbury counties. Although these are rapidly being overgrown by woody species, they still support a variety of plants, most of which are restricted to this habitat. These include:

Ambrosia psilostachya
Aristida oligantha
Cenchrus pauciflorus
Cycloloma atriplicifolium
Cyperus schweinitzii
Dichanthelium acuminatum var. *implicatum*
Eragrostis trichodes
Euphorbia maculata
Hedeoma hispidum
Juncus interior
Lithospermum incisum
Mollugo verticillata
Paspalum setaceum var. *ciliatifolium*
Plantago aristata
P. patagonica
Ruellia humilis
Strophostyles helvula
S. leiosperma

Riverine Systems

A Riverine System region was not recognized by Prior (1991) as a discrete landform because these corridors are part of each of the described landforms. The floodplains along streams contain what is perhaps the state's most endangered community—the floodplain forest. Because of the flat, rich character of this landform, most of it has been heavily logged, cleared for pastureland, or converted to agricultural use. In the valleys in the southeastern part of Iowa, an Ozarkian floristic element is apparent. In the wooded floodplains are found the following unusual or characteristic species which have migrated northward from the Ozark plateau:

Asimina triloba
Carya illinoensis
C. laciniosa
Diospyros virginiana
Fraxinus quadrangulata
Sassafras albidum

The Mississippi River forms the eastern border of Iowa. Oxbow of the river, Scott County.

Sand Provinces

Areas of pure sand occur along major rivers, principally the Mississippi, Cedar, and Wapsipinicon in eastern Iowa and along the Missouri River in western Iowa. Some of Iowa's rarest plants live in these sandy areas. Characteristic plants include:

Andropogon hallii
Aristida tuberculosa
Asclepias amplexicaulis
Astragalus distortus
Besseya bullii
Carex tonsa
C. umbellata
Commelina erecta var. *angustifolia*
Corydalis curvisiliqua ssp. *grandibracteata*

C. micrantha
Croton glandulosus var. *septentrionalis*
Cycloloma atriplicifolium
Cyperus filiculmis
C. schweinitzii
Dalea villosa
Diodia teres
Draba reptans
Eragrostis trichodes
Froelichia floridana var. *campestris*
F. gracilis
Hedyotis crassifolia
Heterotheca villosa
Hudsonia tomentosa
Krigia virginica
Leptoloma cognatum
Lygodesmia rostrata
Mollugo verticillata
Monarda punctata var. *villicaulis*
Opuntia humifusa
Paspalum setaceum var. *ciliatifolium*
Penstemon grandiflorus
Phlox bifida
Polanisia graveolens
Polygala polygama var. *obtusata*
Polygonella articulata
Polygonum douglasii
Rumex acetosella
Scirpus hallii
Selaginella rupestris
Stylisma pickeringii var. *pattersonii*
Talinum rugospermum
Tephrosia virginiana

Sand plain of the Big Sand Mound, Muscatine and Louisa counties.

Sand plain of aeolian origin, Black Hawk County.

Triplasis purpurea
Viola lanceolata
Xyris torta

Iowa still has a great diversity of native plant habitats containing many interesting and important species. Efforts are under way by state agencies and by private organizations to preserve as many representative native habitats as is possible. Unfortunately, these groups must work with limited resources. Thus, it is vitally important that each of us contribute what time and money we can to help the efforts succeed.

Origins of the Iowa Flora

Because of the midcontinental location of Iowa, its flora has affinities with the eastern deciduous forests, the boreal flora, the Great Plains prairies, and the Ozarkian woodlands. This makes Iowa a rewarding place to study phytogeography. Some of the elements that influence the state's total flora are given below.

Plants with Northern Affinities

Several regions of Iowa provide microhabitats similar to those somewhat farther north. Plants that are normally found in more northern latitudes often occur in these microhabitats. Habitats which harbor plants with northern affinities include the fens of the northwestern part of the Des Moines Lobe and the Iowan Surface; the cool, mossy, north-facing slopes of the Paleozoic

Plateau of northeastern Iowa; and the wetlands of northern Iowa. Some of the plants at or near the southern terminus of their ranges are:

Abies balsamea
Acer spicatum
Aconitum noveboracense
Arctostaphylos uva-ursi
Betula alleghaniensis
Brasenia schreberi
Chimaphila umbellata
Chrysosplenium iowense
Coeloglossum viride var. *virescens*
Cornus canadensis
Corylus cornuta
Cryptogramma stelleri
Equisetum fluviatile
E. scirpoides
Eriophorum angustifolium
E. gracile
Galium labradoricum
Hypericum boreale
Linnaea borealis ssp. *americana*
Liparis loeselii
Lycopodium dendroideum
L. digitatum
L. porophilum
Megalodonta beckii
Menyanthes trifoliata
Milium effusum
Oryzopsis pungens
O. racemosa
Pinus strobus
Platanthera hookeri
P. hyperborea var. *huronensis*
Potamogeton vaseyi
Potentilla palustris
Pyrola asarifolia
P. secunda
Rhamnus alnifolia
Salix candida
S. pedicellaris
Sambucus racemosa ssp. *pubens*
Spiranthes romanzoffiana
Taxus canadensis
Vaccinium angustifolium
V. myrtilloides
Viburnum trilobum

Eastern Deciduous Forests

In eastern Iowa occurs the western terminus of the Eastern Deciduous Forest biome. Plant species near the end of their range in this area are:

Acer saccharinum
A. saccharum
Carya ovata
Osmunda cinnamomea
O. regalis var. *spectabilis*
Platanthera psycodes
Podophyllum peltatum
Symplocarpus foetidus

Oak-Hickory Forest Region

The Oak-Hickory Association is centered on the Ozark Plateau and has spread from that refugium in postglacial times (Braun 1950; Curtis 1959) along protected corridors to southeastern and south-central Iowa and adjacent areas. The Mississippi and Missouri rivers and their tributaries acted as important migrational pathways. However, the existence of ecotypes and subspecies of Ozarkian species in Iowa is evidence that Iowa's oak-hickory forests have been separated from those in the Ozarks for a long enough time for evolutionary differentiation to occur.

Representative species of the Oak-Hickory Association in the upland woods are:

Adiantum pedatum
Amphicarpaea bracteata
Aralia racemosa
Aristolochia serpentaria
Aster sagittifolius
Athyrium filix-femina var. *angustum*
Botrychium virginianum
Carya cordiformis
C. ovata
Circaea lutetiana ssp. *canadensis*
Desmodium glutinosum
Fragaria virginiana
Galium concinnum
Geranium maculatum
Hystrix patula
Ostrya virginiana
Phryma leptostachya

Quercus alba
Q. macrocarpa
Q. muhlenbergii
Ranunculus abortivus

In the more mesic sites of the Oak-Hickory Association, the following occur:

Acer nigrum
Fraxinus americana
Osmunda claytoniana
Prunus serotina
Quercus borealis var. *maxima*
Q. imbricaria
Triosteum perfoliatum
Ulmus americana
U. rubra
Uvularia grandiflora
Veronicastrum virginicum
Vitis aestivalis

The lowland forests of Iowa can be found on alluvial soil, on the lower slopes of river valleys, and to a lesser extent on the old lake bed of glacial Lake Calvin. Representative species include:

Acer saccharinum
Aesculus glabra
Betula nigra
Boehmeria cylindrica
Fraxinus pennsylvanica
Gleditsia triacanthos
Gymnocladus dioica
Impatiens capensis
Laportea canadensis
Leersia virginica
Platanus occidentalis
Populus deltoides
Quercus bicolor
Salix nigra
Sambucus canadensis
Ulmus americana
Urtica dioica

The following plants usually occur on well-drained terraces above the floodplain:

Acer negundo
Arisaema dracontium
Carex grayi
C. typhina
Chaerophyllum procumbens
Cinna arundinacea
Cryptotaenia canadensis
Dentaria laciniata
Juglans nigra
Mertensia virginica
Muhlenbergia frondosa
Osmorhiza claytonii
Phlox divaricata
Rudbeckia laciniata
Sambucus canadensis
Sanicula gregaria
Scutellaria lateriflora
Teucrium canadense var. *occidentale*

Great Plains Species

Certain Great Plains species enter western Iowa where suitable growing conditions are found, especially on the dry blufftops and west-facing slopes of the Loess Hills. These include:

Agropyron cristatum
Asclepias stenophylla
A. viridiflora
Astragalus lotiflorus
A. missouriensis
A. striatus
Cleome serrulata
Dalea candida var. *oligophylla*
D. enneandra
D. multiflora
Gaura coccinea
Liatris punctata
Linum rigidum
Lomatium foeniculaceum
Lygodesmia juncea
Machaeranthera spinulosa
Mentzelia decapetala
Oxytropis lambertii
Pediomelum esculentum
Penstemon albidus
P. cobaea
P. gracilis
P. grandiflorus
Sphaeralcea coccinea
Stipa comata
Yucca glauca

Introduction to the Annotated Checklist

The data in this annotated checklist have been derived mostly from specimens in the major herbaria in Iowa, though for rare species we checked several of the smaller herbaria as well. The most complete information has been provided for rare plants and troublesome species. This checklist is a necessary step toward the publication of a state vascular flora with keys and species distribution maps.

The accepted species names are arranged alphabetically within major groups (Pteridophytes, Gymnosperms, Angiosperms: Dicotyledons, and Angiosperms: Monocotyledons). Contemporary synonyms are listed, common names are supplied for most species, and descriptions are given for the habitats, abundance and distribution, and origins of the plant species that inhabit Iowa.

Background

Scope

All known vascular plants (flowering plants, plus the ferns and cone-bearers) that grow and persist in Iowa without cultivation are included in the checklist. These are native plants, primarily, but there are a large number of foreign species that have been introduced, become established, and are widespread within the state. Many of these introduced plants are considered weeds. In addition, the checklist contains the major Iowa crop plants and some of the common garden plants, which, though not native, rarely escape or persist. Not all garden plants are listed, however. Many are rarely grown, and most do not escape from cultivation even if they do persist for a few years. We also included a few plants that are waiflike in nature, having been transported into the state by various means, and that grew for a season or two but have not been reported again in the state. It is possible, of course, that they will appear in Iowa again or that they still exist here without our knowledge.

Format

The format of the checklist was dictated by pragmatic considerations. We felt the need for a flora of the state, but time and money were controlling factors. We asked ourselves and others, "What information about the Iowa flora do we most need to know?" "Which data would be most useful to accumulate and publish now, and which can we add at a later time?" We agreed that, first, we needed factual data on the kinds of vascular plants and their distributions within the state. We believed that an accurate and up-to-date listing of Iowa's plant species names was essential, along with any synonyms for these names used by other authors in nearby states. We also agreed that we needed to know where these plants are found, in which habitats they occur, and how abundant they are around the state. Lastly, we thought that it would be useful to provide common names and the origin of each species (native or not native). Having this information, it should be much easier to identify correctly the plants of the state since the number of possibilities will have been reduced.

Identification Keys

Identification keys, though desirable to have, are not being provided at this time. Nearly all of Iowa's plant species can be identified by keys in the recent literature on the region. Species distribution maps are very time-consuming to construct, and we decided to delay providing them. However, general descriptions of distributions are provided for all species, and county names are given for very rare species.

Computerization

The information for the checklist was stored in a computer data bank (BIOBANK System). Alphabetizing the family, genus, and species names made it much easier to create and manage the data bank. The computer records are stored sequentially to limit spatial requirements. Information on the BIOBANK System can be obtained from Eilers (1979) or by contacting the author.

The Checklist Format

Organization

We have chosen traditional names for the major divisions. The sequence used for the Iowa vascular plants is: Pteridophytes, Gymnosperms, Angiosperms: Dicotyledons, and Angiosperms: Monocotyledons. Within these major groupings, families, genera, and species binomials are all arranged alphabetically for convenience.

Accepted Names (Binomials)

In general, we adopted a conservative approach for binomial plant names. We considered contemporary revisions, past and recent usage in Iowa, usage in manuals and floras of nearby areas, the familiar names in Fernald's *Gray's Manual of Botany* (1950) and in Gleason and Cronquist's *Manual of Vascular Plants of Northeastern United States and Adjacent Canada* (1963), and the names given in national checklists. We used older, more familiar names unless there were compelling reasons to adopt different ones. In any case, we attempted to supply enough synonyms so that the names we are using can be equated with those used in other recent (post-1950) publications.

Subspecific plant names are not given unless their usage in Iowa is well established. Some troublesome groups in the state have not been carefully studied and sorted into subspecific taxa. In these cases, the abbreviation "incl." precedes the names in question, which we have included under the binomial. In general, if a binomial is given without any subspecific names, it may be assumed that this binomial includes the type variety or subspecies.

Hybrids are cited in two different ways: *Dryopteris* X *bootii* = *D. cristata* X *D. intermedia.* Thus, the hybrid may have been given its own name—e.g., *bootii*, usually preceded with an "X"—or the two parental species names are joined by an "X" if the hybrid is unnamed. Two hybrid genera in the grasses (*Agrohordeum* and *Elyhordeum*) have an "X" preceding their names.

Authors' Names

The names we have used for the author(s) of the binomial may differ somewhat from those used in older publications. Most of these discrepancies are caused by a previous misunderstanding of how authors' names should be cited in short form when "in" or "ex" is a part of the full citation. Considerable effort was put into deriving the correct citations. Standard abbreviations are used except when the addition of only one character to an abbreviated name (Bessey, rather than Bess.) makes possible the citing of an author's complete name.

Synonyms

The citation of synonyms has been restricted to those names, different from ours, that are found in the current literature. Both taxonomic and nomenclatural synonyms are given, with no attempt to differentiate between them. If an incorrect name has been widely used for an Iowa species in the past, the citation of the name is followed by "misappl."

Common Names

Common names for vascular plants have not been adequately standardized. We have selected one or two common names for most plants, based on current usage. If no common name is given for the plant species, often a common name is given for the genus that applies to the whole group.

Habitats

The descriptive terms for habitats are those commonly used by biologists to describe habitats in Iowa. If several terms are listed, they are separated by semicolons. Special terms are defined in the "Natural Regions of Iowa" section.

Abundance and Distribution

The data presented here on abundance and distribution were derived from various publications. Most Iowa authors used the number of occurrences within some area as a scale for measuring abundance. They were not always consistent with each other in their use of terms to indicate either abundance or distribution. Consequently, though we have made extensive use of the existing literature, in some cases we have had to arrive at descriptions based on our own field experience.

Because plant species abundance often varies from area to area, the abundance and distribution data are combined. Thus, a particular species may be truly common throughout the state, or it may be common in one part of the state and rare in another area.

The following terms are used to indicate abundance:

- Common: Widely distributed and often found growing in large quantities in several different habitats.
- Freq: Widespread but not abundant and usually found in only one type of habitat.
- Infreq: Not widespread and often not found in places where it would be expected to occur.
- Rare: Found in only a few places and often in only one area of the state. If a species occurs in seven or fewer counties, the abbreviated county names (see pp. 26–27) are given in alphabetic order. If the collections for a county are older than 1950, the dates are given (n.d. = no date on specimen).
- Absent: Not reported for a given area. Assume this to be the case if a species is not listed in one or more areas of the state.
- Thr: Throughout the state.
- Elsewh: The remainder of the state not specifically mentioned.

The state is divided into nine geographical areas: c, wc, nw, nc, ne, ec, se, sc, sw. Map 7 shows which counties are included in each area. Other area designations include:

- w, e, n, s = 1/3 of state (e.g., the western 1/3 of Iowa).
- e 1/4, n 1/4, ne 1/4, etc. = 1/4 of state (e.g., the eastern 1/4 of Iowa).
- e 1/2, n 1/2, ne 1/2, etc. = 1/2 of state (e.g., the eastern 1/2 of Iowa).
- n 2/3, w 2/3, nw 2/3, etc. = 2/3 of state (e.g., the northern 2/3 of Iowa).
- n 3/4, w 3/4, nw 3/4, etc. = 3/4 of state (e.g., the northern 3/4 of Iowa).
- Extreme (w, e, ne, etc.) = the border counties (e.g., extreme western Iowa).

Specific area names, e.g., Loess Hills, are discussed in the "Iowa and Its Flora" chapter.

Origin

The origin of a species is the region of the world in which the species is native. For our purposes we have divided the plants of Iowa into three categories:

- Native: Plants occurring in Iowa before Euro-American settlement.
- Native of U.S., but not Iowa: Plants that have, since Euro-American settlement,

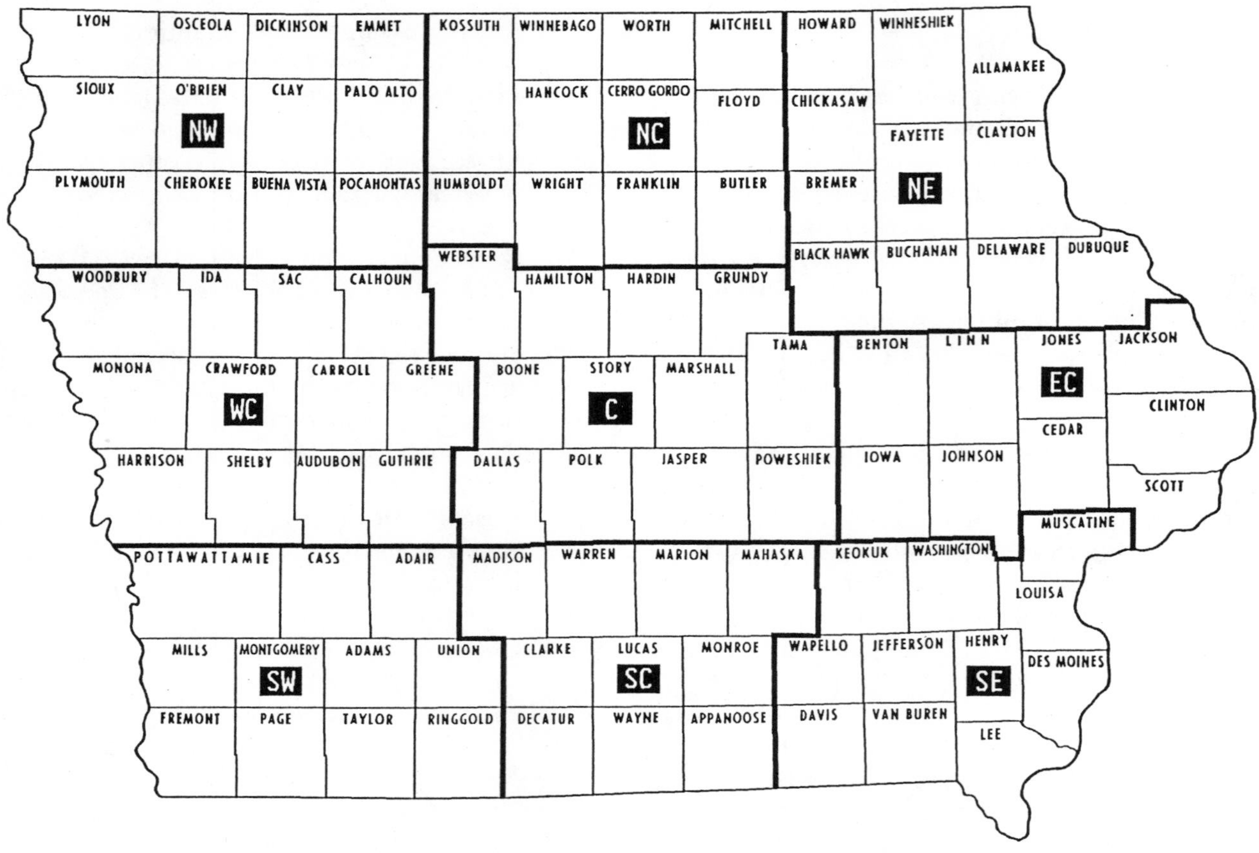

Map 7. Counties and geographical areas of Iowa.

migrated into the state from other regions of the United States.

- Not native: Plants that have migrated into Iowa from outside of the United States.

Any of the preceding plant species may succeed very well in Iowa; if so, they are called established. If they are only marginally successful at this time, they are often called adventive. No designation of origin is given when the plant is a hybrid of mixed origin.

Excluded Species

The species listed below were excluded from the checklist for several reasons. In many cases, we could find no specimen(s) to substantiate the report. In other instances, voucher specimens were located, but the specimens were either sterile or too incomplete or immature to identify accurately. Also, many of the reports were for plant species that do not occur naturally in Iowa (out of range). A number of reports resulted from misidentifications of other species.

- *Agrimonia rostellata* Wallr.: Unsubstantiated report from w counties.
- *Allium perdulce* S. V. Fraser: Unsubstantiated report; out of range.
- *Artemisia campestris* L. ssp. *borealis* (Pallas) Hall & Clem. [*A. canadensis* Michx.]: SUI specimen (Shimek, LYO, 1897) is depauperate. We agree with Davidson, who thought it was *A. caudata*.
- *Aster furcatus* Burgess X *A. umbellatus* P. Miller: SUI specimen (MUS, 1927) first named *A. macrophyllus* by Shimek. Guldner annotated as a hybrid. We agree with Davidson's annotation of *A. furcatus*.

- *Calla palustris* L.: LIN report. Specimen at IA; site information doubtful.
- *Carex castanea* Wahl.: Unsubstantiated report.
- *C. torta* Boott: Unsubstantiated report.
- *C. turgida* (Fern.) J. W. Moore: Invalid name in a report from GUT; specimen not located.
- *Chenopodium bonus-henricus* L.: WEB, 1904; fragmentary specimen.
- *Corispermem hyssopifolium* L.: Specimen was misidentified *C. nitidum.*
- *Cyperus houghtonii* Torrey: ALL; immature specimen.
- *Dalea multiflora* (Nutt.) Shinners [*Petalostemon m.* Nutt.]: PLY & WOO specimens were misidentified *D. candida* var. *oligophylla.*
- *Epilobium palustre* L.: BH specimen was misidentified *E. leptophyllum.*
- *Eupatorium fistulosum* Barratt: GUT report. Specimen at IA. Based on a specimen of *E. maculatum.*
- *Euphorbia vermiculata* Raf. [*Chamaesyce v.* (Raf.) House]: Unsubstantiated report.
- *Lespedeza intermedia* (S. Watson) Britton: Unsubstantiated reports in se.
- *Lycopus rubellus* Moench: IA specimen from EMM was misidentified *L. virginicus*; ILH specimen from DIC was misidentified *L. asper.*
- *Nothoscordum bivalve* (L.) Britton [*Allium bivalve* (L.) Kuntze]: Unsubstantiated SCO report; out of range.
- *Oenothera fruticosa* L. ssp. *fruticosa*: LIN report. Specimen at IA; site information doubtful.
- *Orontium aquaticum* L.: LIN report. Specimen at IA; site information doubtful.
- *Parnassia palustris* L.: LIN report. Specimen at IA; site information doubtful.
- *Penstemon alluviorum* Pennell: Unsubstantiated report; far out of range.
- *Prunus mahaleb* L.: LEE vouchers are sterile; identification questioned.
- *Quercus lyrata* Walter: Possibly cultivated; out of range.
- *Q. shumardii* Buckley: Out of range.
- *Rubus missouricus* Bailey, CLI; *R. semisetosus* Blanch., BRE; and *R. stipulatus* Bailey, SCO. These names are synonyms of *R. setosus*, which is out of range.
- *Rumex stenophyllus* Ledeb.: Unsubstantiated report.
- *Sisyrinchium albidum* Raf.: Unsubstantiated report.
- *Solidago bicolor* L.: Unsubstantiated report; extreme edge of range.
- *S. caesia* L.: Unsubstantiated report; extreme edge of range.
- *S. mollis* Bartl.: Misidentified MNN specimen, actually *S. canadensis* var. *gilvocanescens.*
- *S. rugosa* P. Miller [incl. ssp. *aspera* (Aiton) Cronq.]: Unsubstantiated report; out of range.
- *Spiraea* X *billiardii* Herincq: Unsubstantiated report.
- *Stachys germanica* L.: Scott Co.; unsubstantiated report; considerably out of range.
- *Thaspium trifoliatum* (L.) Gray: Unsubstantiated report.
- *Trillium erectum* L.: ILH specimen from DIC was misidentified *T. cernuum.*
- *Viola primulifolia* L.: Unsubstantiated report; out of range.

Summary Tables

Table 1 summarizes the number of vascular plant families, genera, and taxa in the Iowa flora.

Table 2 illustrates the number of vascular plants that occur in the major groups and also shows where they originated.

Table 3 shows the number of taxa in the twenty largest vascular plant families in Iowa and subdivides these figures by origin.

Table 1. Taxa in the Iowa Flora

Plant Families	141
Genera	673
Species (taxa)	1,958

Table 2. Numbers of Taxa in the Largest Plant Families and Their Origins

Group	Native	Native of U.S., Not Iowa	Not Native	Mixed-Origin Hybrid	Subtotal
Pteridophytes	69	0	1	0	70
Gymnosperms	6	0	1	0	7
Dicotyledons	982	36	328	1	1,347
Monocotyledons	459	1	74	0	534
Totals	1,516	37	404	1	1,958

Table 3. Largest Families and Their Origins

Family	Numbers of Species				
	Total	Native	Native of U.S., Not Iowa	Not Native	Mixed-Origin Hybrid
Asteraceae	238	170	12	56	0
Poaceae	213	150	1	62	0
Cyperaceae	161	160	0	1	0
Fabaceae	92	62	2	28	0
Rosaceae	77	64	0	13	0
Brassicaceae	71	27	2	42	0
Lamiaceae	56	37	0	19	0
Scrophulariaceae	55	41	0	14	0
Ranunculaceae	44	40	0	4	0
Liliaceae	37	30	0	7	0
Polygonaceae	34	21	1	12	0
Orchidaceae	31	31	0	0	0
Apiaceae	30	24	0	6	0
Aspleniaceae	30	30	0	0	0
Euphorbiaceae	30	24	1	5	0
Carophyllaceae	27	10	1	16	0
Salicaceae	26	17	0	8	1
Violaceae	26	25	0	1	0
Chenopodiaceae	25	9	1	15	0
Onagraceae	24	24	0	0	0

County Abbreviations

We have used the first three letters to abbreviate each county name, except for the following counties (as indicated by asterisks): Adair, Adams, Black Hawk, Buena Vista, Cerro Gordo, Clarke, Clay, Clayton, Des Moines, Hardin, Harrison, Marion, Marshall, Monona, Monroe, Montgomery, O'Brien, Palo Alto, Van Buren, Winnebago, and Winneshiek.

1	ADR	ADAIR*	sw
2	ADM	ADAMS*	sw
3	ALL	ALLAMAKEE	ne
4	APP	APPANOOSE	sc
5	AUD	AUDUBON	wc
6	BEN	BENTON	ec
7	BH	BLACK HAWK*	ne
8	BOO	BOONE	c
9	BRE	BREMER	ne
10	BUC	BUCHANAN	ne
11	BV	BUENA VISTA*	nw
12	BUT	BUTLER	nc
13	CAL	CALHOUN	wc
14	CAR	CARROLL	wc
15	CAS	CASS	sw
16	CED	CEDAR	ec
17	CG	CERRO GORDO*	nc
18	CHE	CHEROKEE	nw
19	CHI	CHICKASAW	ne
20	CLR	CLARKE*	sc
21	CLY	CLAY*	nw
22	CLT	CLAYTON*	ne
23	CLI	CLINTON	ec
24	CRA	CRAWFORD	wc
25	DAL	DALLAS	c
26	DAV	DAVIS	se
27	DEC	DECATUR	sc
28	DEL	DELAWARE	ne
29	DM	DES MOINES*	se
30	DIC	DICKINSON	nw
31	DUB	DUBUQUE	ne
32	EMM	EMMET	nw
33	FAY	FAYETTE	ne
34	FLO	FLOYD	nc
35	FRA	FRANKLIN	nc
36	FRE	FREMONT	sw
37	GRE	GREENE	wc
38	GRU	GRUNDY	c
39	GUT	GUTHRIE	wc

40	HAM	HAMILTON	c
41	HAN	HANCOCK	nc
42	HRD	HARDIN*	c
43	HRR	HARRISON*	wc
44	HEN	HENRY	se
45	HOW	HOWARD	ne
46	HUM	HUMBOLDT	nc
47	IDA	IDA	wc
48	IOW	IOWA	ec
49	JAC	JACKSON	ec
50	JAS	JASPER	c
51	JEF	JEFFERSON	se
52	JOH	JOHNSON	ec
53	JON	JONES	ec
54	KEO	KEOKUK	se
55	KOS	KOSSUTH	nc
56	LEE	LEE	se
57	LIN	LINN	ec
58	LOU	LOUISA	se
59	LUC	LUCAS	sc
60	LYO	LYON	nw
61	MAD	MADISON	sc
62	MAH	MAHASKA	sc
63	MRN	MARION*	sc
64	MRS	MARSHALL*	c
65	MIL	MILLS	sw
66	MIT	MITCHELL	nc
67	MNN	MONONA*	wc
68	MNR	MONROE*	sc
69	MNT	MONTGOMERY*	sw
70	MUS	MUSCATINE	se
71	OB	O'BRIEN*	nw
72	OSC	OSCEOLA	nw
73	PAG	PAGE	sw
74	PA	PALO ALTO*	nw
75	PLY	PLYMOUTH	nw
76	POC	POCAHONTAS	nw
77	POL	POLK	c
78	POT	POTTAWATTAMIE	sw
79	POW	POWESHIEK	c
80	RIN	RINGGOLD	sw
81	SAC	SAC	wc
82	SCO	SCOTT	ec
83	SHE	SHELBY	wc
84	SIO	SIOUX	nw
85	STO	STORY	c
86	TAM	TAMA	c
87	TAY	TAYLOR	sw
88	UNI	UNION	sw
89	VB	VAN BUREN*	se
90	WAP	WAPELLO	se
91	WAR	WARREN	sc
92	WAS	WASHINGTON	se
93	WAY	WAYNE	sc
94	WEB	WEBSTER	c
95	WNB	WINNEBAGO*	nc
96	WNS	WINNESHIEK*	ne
97	WOO	WOODBURY	wc
98	WOR	WORTH	nc
99	WRI	WRIGHT	nc

The Annotated Checklist

PTERIDOPHYTES

ADIANTACEAE

Adiantum L. Maidenhair ferns

A. pedatum L.
Com: Northern maidenhair fern
Hab: Moist woods; mesic rocky slopes
A&D: Rare nw; freq nc; common elsewh
Org: Native

Cheilanthes Sw. Lip ferns

C. feei Moore
Com: Slender lip fern
Hab: Exposed, dry, limestone cliffs
A&D: Infreq ne
Org: Native

Cryptogramma R. Br. Rockbrake ferns

C. stelleri (Gmelin) Prantl
Com: Slender rockbrake fern
Hab: Moist, cool ledges; rocky slopes
A&D: Rare nc; infreq ne
Org: Native

Pellaea Link Cliff-brake ferns

P. atropurpurea (L.) Link
Com: Purple cliff-brake
Hab: Dry, sandstone outcrops
A&D: Rare ne & se: ALL & VB
Org: Native

P. glabella Mett. ex Kuhn
Com: Smooth cliff-brake
Hab: Crevices; dry rock cliffs
A&D: Rare c; common ne
Org: Native

ASPLENIACEAE

Asplenium L. Spleenwort ferns

A. platyneuron (L.) Oakes ex D. C. Eaton
Com: Ebony spleenwort
Hab: Moist, rocky or sandy slopes
A&D: Infreq se; rare ne, ec & sc
Org: Native

A. rhizophyllum L.
Syn: *Camptosorus rhizophyllus* (L.) Link
Com: Walking fern
Hab: Humus-covered rocks in moist, wooded valleys
A&D: Common e; absent nw; rare elsewh
Org: Native

Athyrium Roth Lady ferns, spleenwort ferns

A. filix-femina (L.) Roth var. *angustum* (Willd.) Moore
Syn: *A. angustum* (Willd.) Presl
Com: Northern lady fern
Hab: Moist woods; forest margins; mesic prairie
A&D: Rare nw; freq to common elsewh
Org: Native

A. pycnocarpon (Sprengel) Tidestrom
Syn: *Diplazium pycnocarpon* (Sprengel) Broun
Com: Narrow-leaved spleenwort
Hab: Moist woods
A&D: Rare e
Org: Native

A. thelypterioides (Michx.) Desv.
Syn: *A. acrostichoides* (Sw.) Diels
Syn: *Deparia acrostichoides* (Sw.) M. Kato ined.
Com: Silvery spleenwort
Hab: Moist, wooded slopes
A&D: Infreq to freq e
Org: Native

Cystopteris Bernh. Fragile ferns, bladder ferns

C. bulbifera (L.) Bernh.
Com: Bulblet bladder fern
Hab: Dry, rocky woods; ravines; algific slopes
A&D: Rare c; freq to common e
Org: Native

C. fragilis (L.) Bernh.
Com: Fragile fern
Hab: Algific slopes; shaded sandstone & quartzite outcrops
A&D: Rare in Pal. Plateau, c & nw
Org: Native

C. X *laurentiana* (Weath.) Blasdell
Syn: *C. bulbifera* X *C. fragilis*
Com: Northern fragile fern
Hab: Shaded sandstone outcrops; n-facing, rocky slopes
A&D: Rare ne: ALL n.d., HOW & WNS
Org: Native

C. protrusa (Weath.) Blasdell
Syn: *C. fragilis* (L.) Bernh. var. *protrusa* Weath.
Com: Creeping fragile fern
Hab: Wooded slopes
A&D: Common s; freq nc; rare nw & ne
Org: Native

C. X *tennesseensis* Shaver
Syn: *C. bulbifera* X *C. protrusa*
Com: Southern bladder fern
Hab: Shaded rock ledges
A&D: Rare e 1/2
Org: Native

C. tenuis (Michx.) Desv.
Syn: *C. fragilis* (L.) Bernh. var. *mackayi* Lawson
Com: Fragile fern
Hab: Crevices of rocks in ravines; moist woods
A&D: Freq ne; absent w; infreq elsewh
Org: Native

Dryopteris Adanson Shield ferns, wood ferns

D. X *boottii* (Tuckerman) Underw.
Syn: *D. cristata* X *D. intermedia*
Com: Boott's wood fern
Hab: Wooded slopes, growing with parent species
A&D: Rare ne: ALL 1980
Org: Native

D. carthusiana (Vill.) H. P. Fuchs
Syn: *D. spinulosa* (O. F. Muell.) Watt
Com: Spinulose wood fern
Hab: Moist humus at base of n-facing slopes
A&D: Common ne; infreq se; rare c
Org: Native

D. cristata (L.) Gray
Com: Crested wood fern
Hab: Acid soil; calcareous seeps; marshes; fens; alder thickets
A&D: Rare e 1/2
Org: Native

D. goldiana (Hooker) Gray
Com: Goldie's wood fern
Hab: Moist, n-facing slopes
A&D: Freq ne; rare c & sc
Org: Native

D. intermedia (Willd.) Gray
Syn: *D. spinulosa* (O. F. Muell.) Watt var. *intermedia* (Muhl.) Underw.
Com: Glandular wood fern
Hab: Moist humus at base of n-facing slopes
A&D: Rare c & ne: ALL, CLT, DUB & WEB 1903
Org: Native

D. marginalis (L.) Gray
Com: Marginal shield fern
Hab: Moist humus at base of n-facing slopes
A&D: Rare c & ne: ALL, DUB 1922 & HRD
Org: Native

D. X *triploidea* Wherry
Syn: *D. intermedia* X *D. carthusiana*
Com: Hybrid wood fern
Hab: Wooded slopes, growing with parent species
A&D: Rare ne: ALL, CLT & DUB; discovered 1979
Org: Native

D. X *uliginosa* (A. Br.) Druce
Syn: *D. cristata* X *D. carthusiana*
Hab: Backwater marsh of Mississippi R., growing with parent species
A&D: Rare ec: JAC 1980
Org: Native

Gymnocarpium Newman Oak ferns

G. dryopteris (L.) Newman
Com: Oak fern
Hab: Cool, moist talus on n-facing, wooded slopes
A&D: Rare in Pal. Plateau & in c & ec: HRD & JOH 1892
Org: Native

G. robertianum (Hoffm.) Newman
Com: Limestone oak fern
Hab: Cool, moist algific talus slopes
A&D: Rare ne: ALL, CLT, DUB & WNS
Org: Native

Matteuccia Todaro Ostrich ferns

M. struthiopteris (L.) Todaro var. *pensylvanica* (Willd.) Morton
Syn: *Pteretis pennsylvanica* (Willd.) Fern.
Com: Ostrich fern
Hab: Wooded alluvium; moist, wooded slopes
A&D: Infreq to freq e; rare elsewh
Org: Native

Onoclea L. Sensitive ferns

O. sensibilis L.
Com: Sensitive fern
Hab: Fens; sedge meadows; moist, sandy areas
A&D: Freq to common e; infreq w
Org: Native

Polystichum Roth Holly ferns

P. acrostichoides (Michx.) Schott
Com: Christmas fern
Hab: Often sandy or rocky moist, wooded slopes
A&D: Freq se; rare ne
Org: Native

Thelypteris Schmidel Marsh ferns, beech ferns

T. hexagonoptera (Michx.) Weath.
Syn: *Phegopteris hexagonoptera* (Michx.) Fee
Com: Broad beech fern
Hab: Moist humus on wooded slopes
A&D: Rare to infreq e; rare c: HRD 1901
Org: Native

T. palustris Schott var. *pubescens* (Lawson) Fern.
Syn: *Dryopteris thelypteris* Gray
Com: Marsh fern
Hab: Wet, sandy slopes; seeps; sedge meadows; fens
A&D: Freq ne; infreq c & se
Org: Native

T. phegopteris (L.) Slosson in Rydb.
Syn: *Phegopteris connectilis* (Michx.) Watt
Com: Long beech fern
Hab: Moist, wooded, rocky slopes
A&D: Rare ne & se: ALL, DEL 1878, JON & MUS 1897
Org: Native

Woodsia R. Br. Cliff ferns

W. ilvensis (L.) R. Br.
Com: Rusty woodsia
Hab: Dry, exposed rock ledges & crevices
A&D: Rare ne: ALL & WNS
Org: Native

W. obtusa (Sprengel) Torrey
Com: Blunt-lobed woodsia
Hab: Exposed rock crevices; dry woods
A&D: Infreq to freq e; rare c & sc
Org: Native

W. oregana D. C. Eaton
Com: Oregon woodsia
Hab: Exposed Sioux Quartzite; sandstone outcrops
A&D: Rare nw & ne: ALL, LYO & WNS
Org: Native

AZOLLACEAE

Azolla Lam. Mosquito ferns

A. mexicana Presl
Com: Mosquito fern
Hab: Stagnant water; shallow, sandy ponds
A&D: Common to infreq along Mississippi R.; rare ec & sw: BEN, CED, FRE 1906, JOH & LIN
Org: Native

DENNSTAEDTIACEAE

Pteridium Gleditsch ex Scop. Bracken ferns

P. aquilinum (L.) Kuhn var. *latiusculum* (Desv.) Underw. ex Heller
Com: Bracken fern
Hab: Moist, often sandy, woods & roadsides
A&D: Common ne to rare c & se
Org: Native

EQUISETACEAE

Equisetum L. Scouring-rushes, horsetails

E. arvense L.
Com: Common horsetail
Hab: Disturbed, moist, open areas
A&D: Common thr
Org: Native

E. X *ferrissii* Clute
Syn: *E. hyemale* X *E. laevigatum*
Com: Hybrid scouring-rush
Hab: Moist prairies; roadsides
A&D: Common nw & nc; infreq to freq elsewh
Org: Native

E. fluviatile L.
Com: Swamp horsetail
Hab: Marshes; pond edges; seeps
A&D: Rare ne half
Org: Native

E. hyemale L. var. *affine* (Engelm.) A. A. Eaton
Com: Common scouring-rush
Hab: Roadsides; moist banks; lowland woods
A&D: Freq to common thr
Org: Native

E. laevigatum A. Br.
Syn: *E. kansanum* Schaffner
Com: Smooth scouring-rush
Hab: Dry prairies; roadsides
A&D: Infreq e; common elsewh
Org: Native

E. X *litorale* Kuhl. ex Rupr.
Syn: *E. arvense* X *E. fluviatile*
Com: Hybrid shore horsetail
Hab: Marshes; backwaters
A&D: Rare n & e: ALL, CLI, DM, DIC, JAC & MIT
Org: Native

E. pratense Ehrh.
Com: Meadow horsetail
Hab: Seeps; algific talus slopes; sandy woods
A&D: Freq ne; rare c & ec
Org: Native

E. scirpoides Michx.
Com: Dwarf scouring-rush
Hab: Moist talus slopes in woodland openings
A&D: Rare ne & ec: ALL, CLT, DEL, DUB, JAC & WNS
Org: Native

E. sylvaticum L.
Com: Woodland horsetail
Hab: Seeps; wooded areas; sandy places; prairie swales
A&D: Rare c, ne & ec
Org: Native

ISOETACEAE

Isoetes L. Quillworts

I. melanopoda Gay & Dur.
Com: Black-footed quillwort
Hab: Moist, sandy soil; standing, shallow water
A&D: Rare ec: CLI
Org: Native

LYCOPODIACEAE

Lycopodium L. Clubmosses

L. X *bartleyi* Cusick
Syn: *L. lucidulum* X *L. porophilum*
Hab: Moist, wooded, n-facing slopes; sandstone cliffs
A&D: Rare ne: ALL & CLT
Org: Native

L. clavatum L.
Com: Ground pine
Hab: Sandy, moist, n-facing, wooded slopes
A&D: Rare ne & ec: ALL, IOW & JOH
Org: Native

L. dendroideum Michx.
Syn: *L. obscurum* L. var. *dendroideum* (Michx.) D. C. Eaton
Com: Tree clubmoss
Hab: Moist, n-facing, wooded talus slopes
A&D: Rare ne: ALL, CLT & DUB
Org: Native

L. digitatum A. Br.
Syn: *L. complanatum* L. var. *flabelliforme* Fern.
Syn: *L. flabelliforme* (Fern.) Blanch.
Com: Ground cedar
Hab: Wooded, sandy, well-drained slopes
A&D: Rare ne & ec
Org: Native

L. inundatum L.
Com: Bog clubmoss
Hab: Wet, open sand
A&D: Rare ne: BUC
Org: Native

L. lucidulum Michx.
Com: Shining clubmoss
Hab: Moist, wooded, n-facing slopes; sandstone cliffs
A&D: Rare c, ne & ec
Org: Native

L. porophilum Lloyd & Underw.
Syn: *L. selago* L. var. *patens* (Lloyd and Underw.) Clute
Com: Rock clubmoss
Hab: Moist, shaded, n-facing sandstone cliffs
A&D: Rare ne: ALL, CLT & DEL 1930
Org: Native

MARSILEACEAE

Marsilea L. Water-clover ferns

M. quadrifolia L.
Com: European water-clover
Hab: Shallow margins of lakes
A&D: Rare se & sc: DEC & VB
Org: Not native

M. vestita Hooker & Grev.
Syn: *M. mucronata* A. Br.
Com: Hairy water-clover
Hab: Vernal pools adjacent to Sioux Quartzite rocks
A&D: Rare nw: LYO
Org: Native

OPHIOGLOSSACEAE

Botrychium Sw. Grape ferns, rattlesnake ferns

B. campestre Wagner & Farrar
Com: Prairie moonwort
Hab: Open areas on steep loess hills; gravel prairies
A&D: Rare w; discovered in 1982
Org: Native

B. dissectum Sprengel f. *dissectum*
Com: Dissected grape fern
Hab: Acid soils; mesic woods
A&D: Rare e half
Org: Native

B. dissectum Sprengel f. *obliquum* (Muhl.) Fern.
Syn: *B. dissectum* Sprengel var. *obliquum* (Muhl.) Clute
Com: Oblique grape fern
Hab: Acid soils; sandy shores
A&D: Infreq e half
Org: Native

B. matricariifolium A. Br.
Com: Daisy-leaved moonwort
Hab: N-facing, wooded slopes
A&D: Rare ne: ALL
Org: Native

B. multifidum (Gmelin) Rupr.
Syn: *B. multifidum* (Gmelin) Rupr. var. *intermedium* (D. C. Eaton) Farw.
Com: Leathery grape fern
Hab: Sandy, upland woods; moist sand; sedge meadows
A&D: Rare ne: ALL, BUC, CLT, DUB, FAY 1893, LIN & WNS
Org: Native

B. simplex E. Hitchc.
Com: Little grape fern
Hab: Open, moist, sandy areas
A&D: Rare c, ne & ec: BH, LIN & MRS
Org: Native

B. virginianum (L.) Sw.
Com: Rattlesnake fern
Hab: Alluvial woods; moist, wooded slopes; uplands
A&D: Common e; freq w
Org: Native

Ophioglossum L. Adder's-tongue ferns

O. pusillum Raf.
Syn: *O. vulgatum* L. var. *pseudopodum* (Blake) Farw.
Com: Northern adder's-tongue
Hab: Sandy woods; sedge meadows; calcareous seeps
A&D: Rare c, ne & ec
Org: Native

OSMUNDACEAE

Osmunda L. Royal ferns

O. cinnamomea L.
Com: Cinnamon fern
Hab: Seeps; sandy, wooded slopes
A&D: Rare e: CLT 1945, DEL, HEN 1938, JAC 1905 & MUS
Org: Native

O. claytoniana L.
Com: Interrupted fern
Hab: Moist humus of wooded, n-facing slopes; dry woods
A&D: Freq e; infreq c
Org: Native

O. regalis L. var. *spectabilis* (Willd.) Gray
Com: Royal fern
Hab: Sandy marshes; seeps; fens
A&D: Rare e: ALL, CED, CLI, DEL, JON & MUS
Org: Native

POLYPODIACEAE

Polypodium L. Rockcap ferns

P. virginianum L.
Syn: *P. vulgare* L. var. *virginianum* (L.) A. Eaton
Com: Common polypody fern
Hab: Crevices in shaded, rocky slopes
A&D: Absent sw & s; rare to infreq elsewh
Org: Native

SELAGINELLACEAE

Selaginella Beauv.   Spikemosses

S. eclipes Buck
Syn: *S. apoda* (L.) Fern., misappl.
Com: Meadow spikemoss
Hab: Edges of sandy seeps in open pastures; sandy margins of fens
A&D: Rare se: MUS & WOR
Org: Native

S. rupestris (L.) Spring
Com: Rock spikemoss
Hab: Exposed limestone ridges; open rock outcrops; sandy prairies
A&D: Rare extreme nw, ne & se
Org: Native

GYMNOSPERMS

CUPRESSACEAE

Juniperus L.

J. communis L. var. *depressa* Pursh
Com: Common juniper
Hab: Dry, wooded bluffs; rocky slopes
A&D: Infreq ne; rare c: HRD
Org: Native

J. horizontalis Moench
Com: Creeping juniper
Hab: Dry, calcareous, prairie bluffs
A&D: Rare nc & ne: ALL & FLO
Org: Native

J. virginiana L.
Com: Red cedar
Hab: Dry, open woods; rocky bluffs; pastures
A&D: Common e 1/2; infreq to freq w
Org: Native

Thuja L.

T. occidentalis L.
Com: Arbor vitae, eastern white cedar
Hab: Cult, occasionally becoming established in plantations
A&D: Rare: scattered populations
Org: Not native

PINACEAE

Abies P. Miller

A. balsamea (L.) Miller
Com: Balsam fir
Hab: Steep, n-facing bluffs
A&D: Rare ne: ALL, CLT, HOW & WNS
Org: Native

Pinus L.

P. strobus L.
Com: Eastern white pine
Hab: Often sandy or rocky, steep, wooded slopes & ledges
A&D: Rare e 1/2; freq in Pal. Plateau
Org: Native

TAXACEAE

Taxus L.

T. canadensis Marsh.
Com: American yew
Hab: Steep, moist, wooded calcareous slopes, often with talus
A&D: Infreq to freq ne & e; rare se
Org: Native

ANGIOSPERMS: DICOTYLEDONS

ACANTHACEAE

Justicia Houst. ex L.

J. americana (L.) Vahl
Com: Water willow
Hab: Muddy shores; shallow water
A&D: Rare se: DM, HEN, JEF 1935 & LEE 1931
Org: Native

Ruellia L.

R. humilis Nutt. [incl. var. *frondosa* Fern.; var. *longiflora* (Gray) Fern.; var. *expansa* Fern.]
Com: Wild petunia
Hab: Prairies; open, dry sand; dry woods
A&D: Freq to common s 1/2; infreq to rare n 1/2
Org: Native

R. strepens L.
Com: Smooth ruellia
Hab: Alluvial woods
A&D: Infreq to rare s 1/2
Org: Native

ACERACEAE

Acer L.

A. ginnala Maxim.
Com: Amur maple
Hab: Disturbed areas
A&D: Infreq escape from cult
Org: Not native

A. negundo L.
Com: Box elder
Hab: Alluvial woods; moist, disturbed habitats
A&D: Common thr
Org: Native

A. nigrum Michx. f.
Com: Black maple
Hab: Moist woods; wooded slopes
A&D: Common e 2/3, except rare se
Org: Native

A. rubrum L.
Com: Red maple
Hab: Wooded bluff
A&D: Rare ne: ALL; widely cultivated
Org: Native

A. saccharinum L.
Com: Silver maple
Hab: Alluvial woods
A&D: Common thr
Org: Native

A. saccharum Marsh.
Com: Sugar maple
Hab: Moist woods; wooded slopes
A&D: Common e
Org: Native

A. spicatum Lam.
Com: Mountain maple
Hab: Steep, moist, n- & e-facing, wooded slopes; algific talus slopes
A&D: Rare ne: ALL, CLT, DUB & WNS
Org: Native

ADOXACEAE

Adoxa L.

A. moschatellina L.
Com: Moschatel, muskroot
Hab: Moist, shaded soil around ledges on n-facing, wooded slopes
A&D: Rare c, ne & ec
Org: Native

AIZOACEAE

Mollugo L.

M. verticillata L.
Com: Carpetweed
Hab: Dry, open sand; waste areas; roadsides
A&D: Freq to common thr
Org: Not native

AMARANTHACEAE

Amaranthus L. Pigweed, amaranth

A. albus L.
Com: Pigweed
Hab: Disturbed areas; roadsides
A&D: Rare nw; freq to common elsewh
Org: Native

A. arenicola I. M. Johnston
Syn: *A. torreyi* (Gray) Bentham, misappl.
Hab: Dry, often sandy areas
A&D: Rare wc, nw & se: GUT, MUS 1895 & PA 1935
Org: Native

A. graecizans L.
Syn: *A. blitoides* S. Watson
Com: Prostrate pigweed
Hab: Disturbed or waste ground
A&D: Rare in Iowan Surface; freq to common elsewh
Org: Native of U.S., but not Iowa

A. hybridus L.
Com: Green amaranth
Hab: Waste ground; disturbed soil
A&D: Rare ne & sw; infreq se
Org: Not native

A. powellii S. Watson
Com: Smooth pigweed
Hab: Disturbed ground
A&D: Rare nw: CLY & PA
Org: Native of U.S., but not Iowa

A. retroflexus L.
Com: Pigweed
Hab: Waste areas; disturbed ground
A&D: Freq to common thr
Org: Not native

A. rudis Sauer
Syn: *A. tamariscinus* Nutt.
Hab: Marshy ground; shores; moist, disturbed areas
A&D: Infreq to freq thr
Org: Native

A. spinosus L.
Com: Spiny pigweed
Hab: Waste ground
A&D: Rare se: KEO & LEE 1925
Org: Not native

A. tuberculatus (Moq.) Sauer
Syn: *Acnida altissima* (Riddell) Moq.
Com: Water hemp
Hab: Wet ground; margins of marshes & sandbars
A&D: Freq to common se; infreq nc & ne; rare sc
Org: Native

Froelichia Moench

F. floridana (Nutt.) Moq. var. *campestris* (Small) Fern.
Com: Cottonweed
Hab: Open, sandy soil
A&D: Common se; freq ne
Org: Native

F. gracilis (Hooker) Moq.
Com: Cottonweed
Hab: Open, sandy soil
A&D: Rare c, e & sc
Org: Native

ANACARDIACEAE

Rhus L.

R. aromatica Aiton [incl. var. *serotina* (Greene) Rehder; var. *illinoensis* (Greene) Rehder; var. *arenaria* (Greene) Fern.]
Syn: *R. trilobata* Nutt. var. *arenaria* (Greene) Barkley
Com: Fragrant sumac
Hab: Sandy, open areas; rocky bluffs
A&D: Common se; rare ne
Org: Native

R. copallina L.
Com: Dwarf sumac
Hab: Dry woodland edges & openings
A&D: Rare se & sc: DAV 1943, MAD 1930 & VB 1940
Org: Native

R. glabra L.
Com: Smooth sumac
Hab: Woodland openings; edges of woods; disturbed areas
A&D: Common thr
Org: Native

R. typhina L.
Com: Staghorn sumac
Hab: Dry openings in woods; woodland edges; rocky slopes
A&D: Common in Pal. Plateau; rare remainder of ne; freq extreme ec
Org: Native

Toxicodendron P. Miller

T. radicans (L.) Kuntze ssp. *negundo* (Greene) Gillis
Syn: *Rhus radicans* L.
Syn: *Rhus toxicodendron* L., misappl.
Com: Poison ivy
Hab: Moist woodlands; fencerows; open, sandy areas; disturbed ground
A&D: Common thr
Org: Native

T. rydbergii (Small ex Rydb.) Greene
Syn: *Rhus radicans* L. var. *rydbergii* (Small) Rehder
Com: Rydberg's poison ivy
Hab: Disturbed woods; waste places; fencerows; dry, open sand
A&D: Freq to common n 1/2
Org: Native

ANNONACEAE

Asimina Adanson

A. triloba (L.) Dunal
Com: Paw paw
Hab: Wooded alluvium; wooded slopes
A&D: Rare ec, se & sw: CLI, DM, FRE, JAC, LEE, LOU, TAY & VB
Org: Native

APIACEAE (UMBELLIFERAE)

Angelica L.

A. atropurpurea L.
Com: Angelica
Hab: Marshes; seeps; sedge meadows; fens
A&D: Rare nc & e
Org: Native

Berula Koch

B. erecta (Hudson) Cov. var. *incisum* (Torrey) Cronq.
Syn: *B. incisa* (Torrey) G. N. Jones
Syn: *B. pusilla* (Nutt.) Fern.
Com: Water parsnip
Hab: Fens; springs
A&D: Rare nw & sw: CHE, CLY, DIC, EMM 1949, PA 1936 & POT 1853
Org: Native

Chaerophyllum L.

C. procumbens (L.) Crantz
Com: Chervil
Hab: Alluvial woods
A&D: Freq nc & se; rare ne & extreme e
Org: Native

Cicuta L.

C. bulbifera L.
Com: Bulblet water hemlock
Hab: Marshes; wet ditches; fens
A&D: Freq in lakes area; rare e 1/2
Org: Native

C. maculata L.
Com: Water hemlock
Hab: Marshes; wet prairies
A&D: Freq to common thr most of state; rare w
Org: Native

Conium L.

C. maculatum L.
Com: Poison hemlock
Hab: Roadsides; waste ground; disturbed alluvium
A&D: Infreq s 1/2; rare n 1/2; not reported from Pal. Plateau
Org: Not native

Cryptotaenia DC.

C. canadensis (L.) DC.
Com: Honewort
Hab: Moist woods
A&D: Common thr
Org: Native

Daucus L.

D. carota L.
Com: Queen Anne's lace
Hab: Roadsides; fields; waste places
A&D: Freq to common thr
Org: Not native

Eryngium L.

E. yuccifolium Michx.
Com: Rattlesnake master
Hab: Prairie remnants
A&D: Infreq to freq thr most of state; rare in western tier of counties
Org: Native

Falcaria Bernh.

F. sioides (Wibel) Ascherson
Syn: *F. vulgaris* Bernh.
Com: Sickleweed
Hab: Waste ground
A&D: Rare wc: GUT 1931
Org: Not native

Heracleum L.

H. lanatum Michx.
Syn: *H. maximum* Bartram
Syn: *H. spondylium* L. ssp. *montanum* (Schl.) Briq.
Com: Cow parsnip
Hab: Alluvial woods; woodland edges; moist prairies
A&D: Freq nc; infreq w 1/2; rare e
Org: Native

Lomatium Raf.

L. foeniculaceum (Nutt.) Coulter & Rose
Hab: Loess bluffs
A&D: Rare nw & sw: FRE, LYO & SIO
Org: Native

L. orientale Coulter & Rose
Hab: Gravel hills; dry prairies; loess bluffs
A&D: Rare nw & sw: CHE, CLY 1942, EMM, LYO, O'B, SIO & UNI 1926
Org: Native

Osmorhiza Raf.

O. claytonii (Michx.) C. B. Clarke
Com: Sweet cicely
Hab: Moist, upland woods; wooded slopes
A&D: Common e 1/2; infreq w 1/2
Org: Native

O. longistylis (Torrey) DC. [incl. var. *villicaulis* Fern.; var. *brachycoma* Blake]
Com: Anise root
Hab: Moist woods; wooded slopes
A&D: Infreq sw; freq to common elsewh
Org: Native

Oxypolis Raf.

O. rigidior (L.) Raf.
Com: Cowbane
Hab: Moist prairie remnants; fens
A&D: Rare w, nw & s; infreq elsewh
Org: Native

Pastinaca L.

P. sativa L.
Com: Wild parsnip
Hab: Roadsides; along railroads; alluvial woods; waste places
A&D: Common thr
Org: Not native

Polytaenia DC.

P. nuttallii DC.
Com: Prairie parsley
Hab: Prairies; borders of upland woods
A&D: Infreq ne & sc; rare elsewh
Org: Native

Sanicula L.

S. canadensis L.
Com: Black snakeroot
Hab: Upland woods
A&D: Freq to common thr
Org: Native

S. gregaria Bickn.
Com: Common snakeroot
Hab: Moist woods
A&D: Infreq nw; common elsewh
Org: Native

S. marilandica L.
Com: Black snakeroot
Hab: Moist, upland woods; wooded slopes
A&D: Common in Pal. Plateau & se; infreq to rare n 1/2
Org: Native

S. trifoliata Bickn.
Com: Large-fruited black snakeroot
Hab: Moist, wooded, calcareous hillsides
A&D: Common in Pal. Plateau; absent elsewh
Org: Native

Sium L.

S. suave Walter
Com: Water parsnip
Hab: Marshes
A&D: Common in lakes area; freq to infreq s 1/2; rare elsewh
Org: Native

Spermolepis Raf.

S. inermis (Nutt.) Math. & Const.
Hab: Open sandy areas
A&D: Rare c, ne & se: DUB, LEE, MRS 1929 & MUS
Org: Not native

Taenidia (Torrey & Gray) Drude

T. integerrima (L.) Drude
Com: Yellow pimpernel
Hab: Wooded, calcareous slopes & bluffs; dry, upland prairies
A&D: Infreq to rare thr
Org: Native

Thaspium Nutt.

T. barbinode (Michx.) Nutt.
Com: Meadow parsnip
Hab: Moist prairies; open, wooded slopes
A&D: Freq e 1/2; rare nw 1/4
Org: Native

Torilis Adanson

T. arvensis (Hudson) Link
Syn: *T. japonica* (Houtt.) DC.
Com: Hedge parsley
Hab: Waste ground
A&D: Infreq thr
Org: Not native

Zizia Koch

Z. aptera (Gray) Fern.
Com: Heart-leaved meadow parsnip
Hab: Prairie remnants
A&D: Infreq to rare n 1/2; not reported elsewh
Org: Native

Z. aptera (Gray) Fern. X *Z. aurea* (L.) Koch
Hab: Prairie remnants
A&D: Rare nw & ne: DEL & EMM
Org: Native

Z. aurea (L.) Koch
Com: Golden alexanders
Hab: Prairie remnants; sedge meadows
A&D: Freq to common thr
Org: Native

APOCYNACEAE

Apocynum L. Dogbane

A. androsaemifolium L.
Com: Spreading dogbane
Hab: Woodland openings; woodland borders; upland prairies
A&D: Common ne; rare nw; infreq elsewh
Org: Native

A. cannabinum L. [incl. var. *pubescens* (Mitchell) A. DC.]
Com: Indian hemp
Hab: Moist, disturbed areas
A&D: Freq to common thr
Org: Native

A. X *medium* Greene
Syn: *A. androsaemifolium* X *A. sibiricum*
Com: Intermediate dogbane
Hab: Roadsides; along railroads; prairie remnants
A&D: Freq se
Org: Native

A. sibiricum Jacq. [incl. var. *cordigerum* (Greene) Fern.]
Syn: *A. cannabinum* L. var. *hypericifolium* Gray
Hab: Disturbed, open areas
A&D: Freq to infreq thr
Org: Native

Vinca L.

V. minor L.
Com: Common periwinkle
Hab: Roadsides; waste ground
A&D: Rare escape from cult
Org: Not native

AQUIFOLIACEAE

Ilex L.

I. verticillata (L.) Gray
Com: Winterberry
Hab: Sandy woods; streamsides
A&D: Rare nc, ne & ec: ALL, BRE, HOW, LIN & MIT
Org: Native

ARALIACEAE

Aralia L.

A. nudicaulis L.
Com: Wild sarsaparilla
Hab: Moist, wooded slopes
A&D: Freq to common nc & ne; infreq to rare elsewh
Org: Native

A. racemosa L.
Com: Spikenard
Hab: Moist woods; rocky, wooded slopes
A&D: Freq e 1/2; infreq to rare w 1/2
Org: Native

Panax L.

P. quinquefolius L.
Com: Ginseng
Hab: Moist woods
A&D: Freq ne & ec; infreq se; rare w 1/2
Org: Native

ARISTOLOCHIACEAE

Aristolochia L.

A. serpentaria L.
Com: Virginia snakeroot
Hab: Moist woods
A&D: Rare se: HEN, LEE, & MUS 1897
Org: Native

Asarum L.

A. canadense L. [incl. var. *acuminatum* Ashe; var. *reflexum* (Bickn.) B. L. Robinson]
Com: Wild ginger
Hab: Moist, wooded slopes
A&D: Common e 2/3; freq sw; rare nw
Org: Native

ASCLEPIADACEAE

Asclepias L.

A. amplexicaulis Smith
Com: Sand milkweed
Hab: Dry, open, sandy soil; mesic prairies
A&D: Freq e; rare to infreq elsewh
Org: Native

A. engelmanniana Woodson
Syn: *A. auriculata* (Engelm.) Holz.
Com: Eared milkweed
Hab: Dry loess bluffs
A&D: Rare wc & sw: MNN & POT
Org: Native

A. exaltata L.
Com: Poke milkweed
Hab: Moist, upland woods; woodland borders
A&D: Freq in Pal. Plateau; rare elsewh
Org: Native

A. hirtella (Pennell) Woodson
Com: Tall green milkweed
Hab: Usually sandy, dry to mesic prairie remnants
A&D: Not reported c & w; infreq to rare elsewh
Org: Native

A. incarnata L.
Com: Swamp milkweed
Hab: Marsh edges; prairie swales; wet ditches
A&D: Freq to common thr
Org: Native

A. lanuginosa Nutt.
Syn: *A. nuttalliana* Torrey
Syn: *A. otarioides* Fourn., misappl.
Com: Wooly milkweed
Hab: Dry, sandy, hillside prairies
A&D: Rare n 1/2 & MUS
Org: Native

A. meadii Torrey ex Gray
Com: Mead's milkweed
Hab: Dry to mesic prairies
A&D: Rare ec & s: ADM 1899, ADR, CLR, DEC, SCO 1889 & WAR
Org: Native

A. ovalifolia Dcne.
Com: Oval milkweed
Hab: Dry, upland prairies
A&D: Rare to infreq n
Org: Native

A. purpurascens L.
Com: Purple milkweed
Hab: Woodland openings; dry to mesic, sandy prairies
A&D: Infreq to rare thr
Org: Native

A. quadrifolia Jacq.
Com: Whorled milkweed
Hab: Dry to mesic, upland woods
A&D: Rare c & sc; infreq se
Org: Native

A. speciosa Torrey
Com: Showy milkweed
Hab: Prairies; woodland openings
A&D: Infreq to rare w 1/2
Org: Native

A. stenophylla Gray
Com: Narrow-leaved milkweed
Hab: Dry, loess or gravel prairies
A&D: Rare wc & nw: GUT, PLY & SIO
Org: Native

A. sullivantii Engelm. ex Gray
Com: Prairie milkweed
Hab: Mesic prairies
A&D: Infreq to rare thr most of state; apparently absent ne & ec
Org: Native

A. syriaca L.
Com: Common milkweed
Hab: Disturbed, open ground
A&D: Common thr
Org: Native

A. tuberosa L. ssp. *interior* Woodson
Com: Butterfly weed
Hab: Prairie remnants
A&D: Infreq to freq thr
Org: Native

A. verticillata L.
Com: Whorled milkweed
Hab: Open, dry soil
A&D: Common thr
Org: Native

A. viridiflora Raf.
Com: Green milkweed
Hab: Dry, often sandy prairies; loess bluffs
A&D: Freq to common w 1/2; infreq to rare e 1/2
Org: Native

Cynanchum L.

C. laeve (Michx.) Pers.
Syn: *Ampelamus albidus* (Nutt.) Britton
Com: Bluevine
Hab: Alluvial woods; moist, sandy soil
A&D: Freq sw; rare se: LEE & LOU in late 1800's
Org: Native

ASTERACEAE (COMPOSITAE)

Achillea L.

A. millefolium L. ssp. *lanulosa* (Nutt.) Piper
Syn: *A. lanulosa* Nutt.
Com: Western yarrow
Hab: Disturbed ground; prairie remnants; dry, open, sandy areas
A&D: Common thr
Org: Native

Agoseris see ***Nothocalais***

Ambrosia L.

A. artemisiifolia L. [incl. var. *elatior* (L.) Descourt.]
Com: Common ragweed
Hab: Dry, disturbed, open ground
A&D: Common thr
Org: Native

A. bidentata Michx.
Hab: Fields; waste ground
A&D: Rare se & sc: JEF, MNR 1949 & VB
Org: Native

A. psilostachya DC. [incl. var. *coronopifolia* (T. & G.) Farw.]
Com: Western ragweed
Hab: Roadsides; dry, sandy soil; loess bluffs
A&D: Common sw & in Loess Hills; infreq to rare elsewh
Org: Native

A. trifida L.
Com: Giant ragweed
Hab: Open alluvium; disturbed soil
A&D: Common thr
Org: Native

Anaphalis DC.

A. margaritacea (L.) Bentham & Hooker
Com: Pearly everlasting
Hab: Dry, open places
A&D: Rare ne & ec: BH 1892, CLT 1924, FAY ca. 1897 & LIN 1933
Org: Native

Antennaria Gaertner

A. neglecta Greene
Com: Pussytoes
Hab: Dry prairies; loess bluffs; dry, open, upland woods
A&D: Infreq sw; freq to common elsewh
Org: Native

A. plantaginifolia (L.) Richardson
Com: Ladies'-tobacco
Hab: Prairies; pastures; dry, open woods
A&D: Rare to infreq sw; common elsewh
Org: Native

Anthemis L.

A. arvensis L.
Com: Field chamomile
Hab: Disturbed habitats
A&D: Rare c: POW & WEB 1903
Org: Not native

A. cotula L.
Com: Dog fennel
Hab: Farmyards; pastures; roadsides; other disturbed habitats
A&D: Freq to common thr
Org: Not native

A. tinctoria L.
Hab: Roadside escape from cult
A&D: Rare ne: CLT 1929
Org: Not native

Arctium L.

A. lappa L.
Com: Great burdock
Hab: Disturbed, wooded areas
A&D: Rare nc & se: DM & FLO
Org: Not native

A. minus Bernh.
Com: Common burdock
Hab: Disturbed ground; roadsides; pastures
A&D: Freq to common thr
Org: Not native

A. tomentosum Miller
Hab: Waste area
A&D: Rare nw: EMM 1923
Org: Not native

Artemisia L.

A. abrotanum L.
Hab: Old gardens; around dwellings
A&D: Rare se: MUS 1892
Org: Not native

A. absinthium L.
Hab: Disturbed prairies
A&D: Rare nw: SIO
Org: Not native

A. annua L.
Com: Annual wormwood
Hab: Disturbed soil
A&D: Rare se & sc
Org: Not native

A. biennis Willd.
Com: Biennial wormwood
Hab: Moist, disturbed soil
A&D: Infreq to rare thr
Org: Native of U.S., but not Iowa

A. campestris L. ssp. *caudata* (Michx.) Hall & Clem.
Syn: *A. caudata* Michx.
Com: Western sagewort
Hab: Moist, disturbed soil
A&D: Rare to infreq w & s; freq to common elsewh
Org: Native

A. dracunculus L.
Syn: *A. dracunculoides* Pursh
Syn: *A. glauca* Pallas
Com: False tarragon
Hab: Sandy plains; dry soils
A&D: Infreq to rare thr
Org: Native

A. frigida Willd.
Com: Prairie sagewort
Hab: Low, gravelly ridge
A&D: Rare nw: LYO
Org: Native

A. ludoviciana Nutt. [incl. var. *gnaphalodes* (Nutt.) T. & G.]
Syn: *A. gnaphalodes* Nutt.
Com: White sage
Hab: Sandy prairie remnants
A&D: Freq to common thr
Org: Native

A. serrata Nutt.
Hab: Edges of marshes; wet ditches; alluvium
A&D: Rare e 2/3
Org: Native

A. vulgaris L.
Com: Common mugwort
Hab: Roadsides; disturbed ground; pastures
A&D: Rare ne & ec: DEL, SCO late 1800's
Org: Not native

Aster L. see also ***Solidago***

A. X *amethystinus* Nutt.
Syn: *A. ericoides* X *A. novae-angliae*
Hab: Prairies; ditches
A&D: Rare nc & ec: BUT, FLO & SCO
Org: Native

A. azureus Lindley
Syn: *A. oolentangiensis* Riddell
Com: Sky-blue aster
Hab: Dry, open woods; dry prairies; roadsides
A&D: Freq to common se 2/3
Org: Native

A. brachyactis Blake
Syn: *Brachyactis ciliata* (Ledeb.) Ledeb.
Com: Rayless aster
Hab: Edges of marshes; low prairies
A&D: Rare nc & in lakes area
Org: Native

A. cordifolius L.
Com: Blue wood aster
Hab: Dry, upland woods
A&D: Common sw; freq e 1/2
Org: Native

A. drummondii Lindley
Syn: *A. sagittifolius* Wedem. var. *drummondii* (Lindley) Shinners
Com: Drummond's aster
Hab: Dry to mesic woods; wooded slopes; disturbed areas in open woods
A&D: Freq se; infreq to rare n & sc
Org: Native

A. dumosus L.
Com: Ricebutton aster
Hab: Moist, sandy soil
A&D: Rare e & sc: DEC 1903, DEL, JOH, LOU & MRN 1920
Org: Native

A. ericoides L.
Com: Heath aster, frost weed
Hab: Prairie remnants; roadsides
A&D: Freq to common thr
Org: Native

A. falcatus Lindley ssp. *commutatus* (T. & G.) A. Gray
Hab: Marshes; lakeshores
A&D: Rare nw: CLY 1936 & PA 1936
Org: Native

A. furcatus Burgess
Com: Forked aster
Hab: Sandy, wooded slopes; dry woods
A&D: Rare se & sc: MAD 1917 & MUS
Org: Native

A. junciformis Rydb.
Syn: *A. borealis* (T. & G.) Prov.
Com: Rush aster
Hab: Marshes; fens
A&D: Rare n
Org: Native

A. laevis L.
Com: Smooth blue aster
Hab: Roadsides; prairies; dry, open soil
A&D: Freq to common thr
Org: Native

A. lanceolatus Willd. [incl. ssp. *simplex* (Willd.) A. G. Jones; ssp. *interior* (Wiegand) A. G. Jones]
Syn: *A. simplex* Willd.
Syn: *A. simplex* Willd. var. *ramossimus* (T. & G.) Cronq.
Syn: *A. interior* Wieg.
Com: Panicled aster
Hab: Moist shores; low prairies; open woods
A&D: Rare to infreq thr
Org: Native

A. lateriflorus (L.) Britton
Syn: *A. vimineus* Lam.
Com: Side-flowered aster
Hab: Woods; prairie openings; pastures; loess bluffs
A&D: Common se; freq ne; infreq sw
Org: Native

A. linariifolius L.
Com: Flax-leaved aster
Hab: Dry soil; sandy, open woods
A&D: Rare ec & se: CLI, LOU 1927 & MUS 1896
Org: Native

A. macrophyllus L.
Com: Big-leaved aster
Hab: Moist, upland woods
A&D: Rare ne: WNS
Org: Native

A. novae-angliae L.
Com: New England aster
Hab: Prairie swales; other moist habitats
A&D: Freq to common thr
Org: Native

A. oblongifolius Nutt.
Com: Aromatic aster
Hab: Dry, sandy soil; dry, rocky bluffs
A&D: Common sw; freq to infreq elsewh
Org: Native

A. ontarionis Wieg.
Com: Ontario aster
Hab: Alluvial woods; low, moist woods
A&D: Freq to common thr
Org: Native

A. parviceps (Burgess) Mack. & Bush
Hab: Prairie remnants; dry, sandy soil; roadsides
A&D: Freq to infreq sw; rare ne
Org: Native

A. pilosus Willd.
Com: Hairy aster
Hab: Prairie remnants; woodland openings; roadsides
A&D: Rare n 1/2; common s 1/2
Org: Native

A. praealtus Poiret
Com: Willow aster
Hab: Moist woods; moist, open soil
A&D: Freq to infreq e 1/2 of state
Org: Native

A. praealtus Poiret var. *nebraskensis* (Britton) Wieg.
Syn: *A. nebraskensis* Britton
Syn: *A. woldeni* Rydb.
Hab: Roadsides
A&D: Rare nw: EMM 1942
Org: Native

A. prenanthoides Muhl. ex Willd.
Com: Crooked stem aster
Hab: Wooded ravines; moist, disturbed woods
A&D: Rare to infreq e 2/3 of state
Org: Native

A. pubentior Cronq.
Syn: *A. umbellatus* Miller var. *pubens* Gray
Hab: Shores of lakes; marshes
A&D: Rare c: JAS
Org: Native

A. puniceus L. [incl. var. *lucidulus* Gray]
Syn: *A. lucidulus* (Gray) Wieg.
Com: Swamp aster
Hab: Marshy ground; fens
A&D: Infreq in DM Lobe & in Iowan Surface; rare se & sc: DEC 1903 & MUS 1927
Org: Native

A. sagittifolius Willd.
Syn: *A.* X *sagittifolius* Willd.
Com: Arrow-leaved aster
Hab: Dry, upland woods
A&D: Common s 1/2; freq ne; rare nc
Org: Native

A. schreberi Nees
Com: Schreber's aster
Hab: Sandy, moist, wooded slopes
A&D: Rare ec & se: MUS & SCO 1932
Org: Native

A. sericeus Vent.
Com: Silky aster
Hab: Dry, rocky prairies; loess bluffs
A&D: Common w; freq to infreq e
Org: Native

A. shortii Lindley
Hab: Upland woods; moist, wooded slopes
A&D: Common ne; infreq se; rare nc
Org: Native

A. turbinellus Lindley
Hab: Prairies; dry, open woods; woodland edges
A&D: Rare se: LEE
Org: Native

A. umbellatus Miller
Com: Flat-topped aster, white aster
Hab: Marshes; fens; moist, sandy prairies
A&D: Rare to infreq thr
Org: Native

Bidens L. see also ***Megalodonta***
Stick-tight

B. aristosa (Michx.) Britton
Com: Swamp marigold
Hab: Moist, disturbed areas
A&D: Rare c, ec & se: DM, IOW 1928, JEF, KEO, MUS, POW, SCO & WAS
Org: Native

B. bipinnata L.
Syn: *Cosmos bipinnatus* Cav.
Com: Spanish needles
Hab: Moist, sandy, open habitats; wooded bluffs
A&D: Rare se: LEE & LOU
Org: Not native

B. cernua L.
Com: Nodding bur marigold
Hab: Mud flats; lakeshores; streambanks
A&D: Freq to common thr
Org: Native

B. connata Muhl. ex Willd.
Hab: Marshes; lake margins; moist, sandy, disturbed areas
A&D: Common se; rare to freq elswhere
Org: Native

B. coronata (L.) Britton
Syn: *B. trichosperma* (Michx.) Fern.
Com: Tickseed sunflower
Hab: Marshes; streambanks; alluvial woods
A&D: Common sw; freq to infreq elsewh
Org: Native

B. discoidea (T. & G.) Britton
Com: Swamp beggar-ticks
Hab: Open, moist soil; marsh edges; moist, pastured woods
A&D: Rare e 1/4
Org: Native

B. frondosa L.
Com: Beggar-ticks
Hab: Marshes; streambanks; prairie swales
A&D: Common nc & in lakes area; rare to infreq elsewh
Org: Native

B. polylepis Blake
Syn: *B. aristosa* (Michx.) Nutt. var. *retrorsa* (Sherff) Wunderlin
Hab: Wet depressions; roadsides; waste ground; alluvium
A&D: Common sw; rare ne; infreq elsewh
Org: Native

B. tripartita L.
Syn: *B. comosa* (Gray) Wieg.
Hab: Marshes; lake margins; moist, sandy, disturbed areas
A&D: Common se; rare to infreq elsewh
Org: Native

B. vulgata Greene
Com: Tall beggar-ticks
Hab: Moist lowlands; ditches; along lakeshores
A&D: Rare nw & ne; freq to common elsewh
Org: Native

Boltonia L'Her.

B. asteroides (L.) L'Her. [incl. var. *recognita* (Fern. & Grisc.) Cronq.; var. *latisquama* (Gray) Cronq.]
Com: False aster
Hab: Marshes; prairie swales; sandy areas
A&D: Common nc; infreq to freq s, also DIC
Org: Native

Brickellia Ell.

B. eupatorioides (L.) Shinners [incl. var. *corymbulosa* (T. & G.) Shinners]
Syn: *Kuhnia eupatorioides* L.
Com: False boneset
Hab: Dry prairies; roadsides; railroad ballast
A&D: Freq to common thr
Org: Native

Cacalia L.

C. atriplicifolia L.
Syn: *Arnoglossum atriplicifolium* (L.) H. Robinson
Com: Indian plantain
Hab: Moist woods; moist ditches; sandy, open areas
A&D: Infreq to freq s 1/2
Org: Native

C. muhlenbergii (Sch.-Bip.) Fern.
Syn: *Arnoglossum reniforme* (Hooker) H. Robinson
Com: Great Indian plantain
Hab: Moist alluvial woods; algific slopes
A&D: Rare ne (except freq in Pal. Plateau), & in se & sw: MUS & CAS
Org: Native

C. plantaginea (Raf.) Shinners
Syn: *C. tuberosa* Nutt.
Syn: *Arnoglossum plantagineum* Raf.
Com: Prairie Indian plantain
Hab: Prairie remnants; loess bluffs
A&D: Common sw; infreq elsewh
Org: Native

C. suaveolens L.
Syn: *Hasteola suaveolens* (L.) Pojark.
Com: Sweet Indian plantain
Hab: Wooded streambanks; marshes; fens
A&D: Rare e 1/2 & sw
Org: Native

Carduus L.

C. acanthoides L.
Com: Plumeless thistle
Hab: Disturbed ground; fields
A&D: Rare s 1/2; infreq nw
Org: Not native

C. nutans L.
Com: Musk thistle
Hab: Roadsides; fallow fields; overgrazed pastures
A&D: Freq to common w 1/2; rare e 1/2
Org: Not native

Centaurea L.

C. calcitrapa L.
Hab: Disturbed areas
A&D: Rare c: STO
Org: Not native

C. cyanus L.
Com: Bachelor's button, cornflower
Hab: Disturbed, open ground
A&D: Rare escape from cult
Org: Not native

C. diffusa Lam.
Hab: Adventive along roadsides
A&D: Rare nw: SIO
Org: Not native

C. jacea L.
Hab: Disturbed areas
A&D: Rare nw: CHE 1924
Org: Not native

C. maculosa Lam.
Syn: *C. biebersteinii* DC.
Com: Star thistle
Hab: Disturbed soil; roadsides
A&D: Infreq to rare thr
Org: Not native

C. moschata L.
Hab: Disturbed areas
A&D: Rare c: POL 1928
Org: Not native

C. nigra L.
Com: Black knapweed
Hab: Disturbed soil
A&D: Rare wc: CAL 1911
Org: Not native

C. repens L.
Hab: Disturbed areas
A&D: Rare wc & nw: SIO 1933, WOO
Org: Not native

C. scabiosa L.
Hab: Disturbed areas
A&D: Rare wc & nw: O'B 1944, SAC
Org: Not native

C. solstitialis L.
Com: Yellow star thistle
Hab: Fields; disturbed ground
A&D: Rare sc & sw
Org: Not native

Chrysanthemum see ***Leucanthemum***

Chrysopsis see ***Heterotheca***

Cichorium L.

C. intybus L.
Com: Chicory
Hab: Roadsides; farmyards
A&D: Rare ne; common elsewh
Org: Not native

Cirsium P. Miller Thistle

C. altissimum (L.) Sprengel
Syn: *C. iowense* (Pammel) Fern.
Com: Tall thistle
Hab: Pastures; open woods; prairie remnants; roadsides
A&D: Rare ne; infreq nw; common elsewh
Org: Native

C. arvense (L.) Scop.
Com: Canada thistle
Hab: Weed of cult fields; pastures; roadsides; waste places
A&D: Freq to common thr
Org: Not native

C. discolor (Muhl. ex Willd.) Sprengel
Com: Field thistle
Hab: Open woods; roadsides; moist prairie remnants; disturbed ground
A&D: Freq to common thr
Org: Native

C. flodmanii (Rydb.) Arthur
Hab: Moist prairies; dry upland pastures; roadsides
A&D: Common nw; freq w; rare ne
Org: Native

C. hillii (Canby) Fern.
Syn: *C. pumilum* (Nutt.) Sprengel
Hab: Sandy prairies; dry prairies
A&D: Not reported w & s; rare to infreq elsewh
Org: Native

C. muticum Michx.
Com: Swamp thistle
Hab: Edges of marshes & lakes; prairie swales; fens
A&D: Rare ne 2/3
Org: Native

C. undulatum (Nutt.) Sprengel
Hab: Dry prairies
A&D: Rare c, nw, ec, se & sw
Org: Native

C. vulgare (Savi) Tenore
Syn: *C. lanceolatum* Hill, misappl.
Com: Bull thistle
Hab: Pastures; disturbed ground; roadsides
A&D: Freq to common thr
Org: Not native

Conyza Less.

C. canadensis (L.) Cronq.
Syn: *Erigeron canadensis* L.
Com: Horseweed, muletail
Hab: Open, disturbed soil; pastures; fields
A&D: Common thr
Org: Native

C. ramosissima Cronq.
Syn: *Erigeron divaricatum* (Michx.) Raf.
Com: Low horseweed
Hab: Sandy pastures; farmyards; roadsides; disturbed soil
A&D: Rare to infreq thr
Org: Native

Coreopsis L.

C. grandiflora Hogg ex Sweet
Com: Large-flowered coreopsis
Hab: Prairie remnants; roadsides; open, dry uplands
A&D: Rare escape from cult
Org: Native of U.S., but not Iowa

C. lanceolata L.
Com: Tickseed coreopsis
Hab: Prairie remnants; roadsides; open, dry uplands
A&D: Rare se
Org: Native of U.S., but not Iowa

C. palmata Nutt.
Com: Tickseed, prairie coreopsis
Hab: Prairie remnants; open woods
A&D: Infreq se; freq to common elsewh
Org: Native

C. tinctoria Nutt.
Com: Golden coreopsis
Hab: Railroad ballast; dry waste places
A&D: Rare escape from cult, also adventive from west
Org: Native of U.S., but not Iowa

C. tripteris L.
Com: Tall tickseed
Hab: Prairie remnants; margins of upland woods
A&D: Infreq s 1/2
Org: Native

Crepis L.

C. runcinata (James) T. & G.
Com: Hawksbeard
Hab: Lakeshores; waste ground
A&D: Rare nw & ne: BH 1921 & OSC 1912
Org: Native of U.S., but not Iowa

C. tectorum L.
Hab: Disturbed areas near human dwellings
A&D: Rare escape from cult in wc & c
Org: Not native

Dyssodia Cav.

D. papposa (Vent.) A. S. Hitchc.
Com: Fetid marigold
Hab: Loess bluffs; disturbed, open areas; prairies; roadsides
A&D: Infreq nw & s 1/2 of state
Org: Native

Echinacea Moench

E. angustifolia DC.
Syn: *E. pallida* Nutt. var. *angustifolia* (DC.) Cronq.
Com: Purple coneflower
Hab: Loess bluffs; dry prairies
A&D: Common in Loess Hills of w; rare in w & s
Org: Native

E. pallida Nutt.
Com: Pale coneflower
Hab: Loess bluffs; dry prairies; roadsides
A&D: Common w; infreq elsewh
Org: Native

E. purpurea (L.) Moench
Com: Purple coneflower
Hab: Woodland borders; prairie remnants
A&D: Rare in se & sc
Org: Native

Echinops L.

E. sphaerocephalus L.
Com: Globe thistle
Hab: Roadsides; disturbed areas
A&D: Rare nw & ne: BRE & CLY 1923
Org: Not native

Eclipta L.

E. alba (L.) Hassk.
Syn: *E. prostrata* (L.) L.
Com: Yerbo-de-Tajo
Hab: Floodplains; muddy shores; moist, disturbed areas
A&D: Freq e 1/2; rare nc
Org: Native

Erechtites Raf.

E. hieracifolia (L.) Raf. ex DC.
Com: Fireweed
Hab: Marshes; shores; moist ditches
A&D: Freq to common s 1/2; rare nc
Org: Native

Erigeron L.

E. annuus (L.) Pers.
Com: Annual fleabane
Hab: Roadsides; pastures; upland openings
A&D: Common thr
Org: Native

E. philadelphicus L.
Com: Fleabane
Hab: Moist woods & shores; moist, sandy areas
A&D: Common nc; freq elsewh
Org: Native

E. pulchellus Michx.
Com: Robin's plantain
Hab: Open woods
A&D: Common in Pal. Plateau; rare elsewh
Org: Native

E. strigosus Muhl. ex Willd.
Com: Daisy fleabane
Hab: Open woods; prairie remnants; roadsides
A&D: Common thr
Org: Native

Eupatorium L.

E. altissimum L.
Syn: *Ageratina altissima* (L.) King & H. Robinson
Com: Tall thoroughwort
Hab: Lower portions of loess bluffs; prairie remnants; dry, open woods
A&D: Freq s; rare to infreq n
Org: Native

E. maculatum L. [incl. var. *bruneri* (Gray) Breitung]
Syn: *Eupatoriadelphus maculatus* (L.) King & H. Robinson
Com: Spotted Joe-pye-weed
Hab: Fens; open marshy places
A&D: Common in Pal. Plateau; freq in Iowan Surface; infreq nc & sc
Org: Native

E. perfoliatum L.
Com: Boneset
Hab: Edges of marshes; fens; prairie swales; open alluvium
A&D: Infreq se; freq elsewh
Org: Native

E. purpureum L.
Syn: *Eupatoriadelphus purpureus* (L.) King & H. Robinson
Com: Purple Joe-pye-weed
Hab: Moist woods
A&D: Freq to common thr
Org: Native

E. rugosum Houtt.
Syn: *Ageratina altissima* (L.) King & H. Robinson, in part
Com: White snakeroot
Hab: Woodlands
A&D: Common thr
Org: Native

E. serotinum Michx.
Com: Late boneset
Hab: Moist, open woods; alluvium
A&D: Freq se; rare sw
Org: Native

E. sessilifolium L. var. *brittonianum* Porter
Com: Upland boneset
Hab: Dry, wooded slopes
A&D: Rare ne & ec: ALL, CLT, FAY 1926 & JON 1948
Org: Native

Euthamia Ell.

E. graminifolia (L.) Nutt. ex Cass.
Syn: *E. gymnospermoides* Greene
Syn: *Solidago graminifolia* (L.) Salisb. [incl. var. *gymnospermoides* (Greene) Croat; var. *major* (Michx.) Fern.; var. *media* (Greene) Harris]
Hab: Low, moist prairies; sandy, open places; fens
A&D: Rare extreme w; absent ne; freq to infreq elsewh
Org: Native

Gaillardia Foug.

G. pulchella Foug.
Com: Blanket flower, rose-ring gaillardia
Hab: Disturbed prairies
A&D: Rare wc & nw: EMM 1954, WOO
Org: Native of U.S., but not Iowa

Galinsoga Ruiz & Pavon

G. parviflora Cav.
Com: Peruvian daisy
Hab: Waste places
A&D: Rare escape from gardens
Org: Not native

G. quadriradiata Ruiz & Pavon
Syn: *G. ciliata* (Raf.) Blake
Com: Peruvian daisy
Hab: Weed of waste places & cult soil, especially in urban areas
A&D: Freq sw; infreq se; rare nc
Org: Not native

Gnaphalium L.

G. obtusifolium L.
Com: Everlasting
Hab: Disturbed prairies; grassy & sandy uplands
A&D: Common e 1/2 & sc; rare nc
Org: Native

G. purpureum L.
Syn: *Gamochaeta purpurea* (L.) Cabrera
Com: Early cudweed
Hab: Railroad ballast; disturbed lowlands
A&D: Rare se & sc: DEC, LEE 1931 & WAR
Org: Native

Grindelia Willd.

G. squarrosa (Pursh) Dunal
Com: Gum plant
Hab: Loess bluffs; disturbed, sandy soil; dry prairies
A&D: Freq to common w, especially in Loess Hills; infreq to rare elsewh
Org: Native

Gutierrezia Lag.

G. dracunculoides (DC.) Blake
Com: Broomweed
Hab: Pastures
A&D: Rare sw: RIN
Org: Native of U.S., but not Iowa

Haplopappus see ***Machaeranthera***; ***Prionopsis***

Helenium L.

H. amarum (Raf.) H. Rock.
Com: Bitterweed
Hab: Sandy fields; waste ground
A&D: Rare ec: JON
Org: Native

H. autumnale L.
Com: Sneezeweed
Hab: Marshes; moist prairies; fens; sedge meadows
A&D: Freq to common thr
Org: Native

Helianthus L.

H. annuus L.
Com: Common sunflower
Hab: Roadsides; fields; along railroads; disturbed, open ground
A&D: Common w 1/2; freq e 1/2
Org: Native

H. decapetalus L.
Com: Pale sunflower
Hab: Moist, upland woods; wooded slopes
A&D: Infreq to rare ne 1/4 & s 1/2
Org: Native

H. divaricatus L.
Com: Woodland sunflower
Hab: Dry, open woods
A&D: Rare extreme e
Org: Native

H. giganteus L.
Com: Tall sunflower
Hab: Moist prairies; sandy pond margins; low woods
A&D: Rare se & sc
Org: Native

H. grosseserratus Martens
Com: Saw-tooth sunflower
Hab: Moist, open ground; roadsides; disturbed soil; sandy prairie remnants
A&D: Freq to common thr
Org: Native

H. hirsutus Raf.
Com: Bristly sunflower
Hab: Open woods; woodland margins
A&D: Rare nc, se & sw
Org: Native

H. maximiliani Schrader
Com: Maximillian's sunflower
Hab: Prairie remnants; roadsides; disturbed soil
A&D: Common nc; infreq w
Org: Native

H. mollis Lam.
Hab: Dry prairies; disturbed soil along railroads
A&D: Rare se & sc: DEC & MUS 1896
Org: Not native

H. occidentalis Riddell
Com: Western sunflower
Hab: Dry prairies; dry, open sand
A&D: Common in Pal. Plateau; infreq remainder of e
Org: Native

H. petiolaris Nutt.
Com: Petioled sunflower
Hab: Dry, open, sandy soil; roadsides; disturbed ground
A&D: Rare sc & sw; freq se
Org: Native

H. rigidus (Cass.) Desf.
Syn: *H. laetiflorus* Pers.
Com: Prairie sunflower
Hab: Sandy or dry, upland prairies; dry loess bluffs
A&D: Common w 1/2; infreq e 1/2
Org: Native

H. rigidus (Cass.) Desf. ssp. *subrhomboideus* (Rydb.) Heiser
Hab: Sandy or dry, upland prairies; dry loess bluffs
A&D: Common w; infreq e
Org: Native

H. strumosus L.
Syn: *H. trachelifolius* Miller
Com: Pale-leaved sunflower
Hab: Open woods; prairie remnants; open, disturbed areas
A&D: Rare nw; freq elsewh
Org: Native

H. tuberosus L.
Com: Jerusalem artichoke
Hab: Moist prairies; roadsides; disturbed areas
A&D: Infreq n; freq to common s
Org: Native

Heliopsis Pers.

H. helianthoides (L.) Sweet [incl. var. *scabra* (Dunal) Fern.]
Com: Ox-eye
Hab: Prairies; roadsides; loess bluffs
A&D: Freq to common thr
Org: Native

Heterotheca Cass.

H. villosa (Pursh) Shinners [incl. var. *angustifolia* (Rydb.) Harms; var. *camporum* (Greene) Wunderlin; var. *hispida* (Hooker) Harms]
Syn: *Chrysopsis villosa* Nutt. ex DC.
Syn: *H. camporum* (Greene) Shinners
Hab: Sandy alluvium
A&D: Rare nw & ec: CLI, JAC & LYO
Org: Native

Hieracium L.

H. aurantiacum L.
Com: King-devil
Hab: Fields; roadsides; pastures
A&D: Rare nc & ne: ALL, CLT 1935 & MIT
Org: Not native

H. canadense Michx. [incl. var. *fasciculatum* (Pursh) Fern.]
Com: Hawkweed
Hab: Dry, wooded hillsides
A&D: Rare n, & in ec & se: LIN, MUS & SCO late 1800's
Org: Native

H. longipilum Torrey
Com: Hawkweed
Hab: Dry prairies; sandy soils
A&D: Infreq in Pal. Plateau; rare remainder of e 1/2
Org: Native

H. scabrum Michx.
Com: Rough hawkweed
Hab: Open, upland woods; upland prairies
A&D: Freq s & in Pal. Plateau; rare to infreq elsewh
Org: Native

H. umbellatum L.
Hab: Prairie remnants; open, upland woods
A&D: Common in Pal. Plateau; infreq remainder of n; rare se
Org: Not native

Inula L.

I. helenium L.
Com: Elecampane
Hab: Open woods
A&D: Rare e: JOH, MUS & WNS
Org: Not native

Iva L.

I. annua L.
Syn: *I. ciliata* Willd.
Com: Sumpweed
Hab: Moist sand
A&D: Rare se & sw: DM, JEF 1935 & POT 1898
Org: Native

I. xanthifolia Nutt.
Com: Marsh elder
Hab: Disturbed prairies; moist waste places
A&D: Freq to infreq w 1/2 & nc; rare se: MUS 1892
Org: Native

Krigia Schreber

K. biflora (Walter) Blake
Com: False dandelion
Hab: Prairie remnants; openings in woods
A&D: Rare n; freq e
Org: Native

K. dandelion (L.) Nutt.
Hab: Moist, open, sandy areas
A&D: Rare sw: UNI
Org: Native of U.S., but not Iowa

K. virginica (L.) Willd.
Com: Dwarf dandelion
Hab: Sandy plains or dunes
A&D: Rare ec & se: DM, CLI, JAC, LOU & MUS
Org: Native

Kuhnia see ***Brickellia***

Lactuca L.

L. biennis (Moench) Fern.
Com: Tall blue lettuce
Hab: Roadsides; disturbed ground
A&D: Common in lakes area; rare nc, & in ne & ec: JON & WNS
Org: Native

L. canadensis L. [incl. var. *longifolia* (Michx.) Farw.; var. *obovata* Wieg.; var. *latifolia* Kuntze]
Com: Wild lettuce
Hab: Roadsides; along railroads; open, sandy areas
A&D: Infreq nw; common elsewh
Org: Native

L. floridana (L.) Gaertner [incl. var. *villosa* (Jacq.) Cronq.]
Com: Blue lettuce
Hab: Moist woods & alluvium; woodland margins
A&D: Freq to common s 1/2; infreq to rare n 1/2
Org: Native

L. ludoviciana (Nutt.) Riddell
Com: Prairie lettuce
Hab: Prairie remnants; open, wooded bluffs
A&D: Infreq to freq w 1/2; rare or absent e 1/2
Org: Native

L. saligna L.
Hab: Disturbed habitats
A&D: Rare sw: PAG
Org: Not native

L. serriola L.
Syn: *L. scariola* L.
Com: Prickly lettuce
Hab: Weed of waste ground & disturbed places
A&D: Common sw 2/3; infreq to rare elsewh
Org: Not native

L. tatarica (L.) C. A. Meyer ssp. *pulchella* (Pursh) Stebbins
Syn: *L. oblongifolia* Nutt.
Syn: *L. pulchella* (Pursh) DC.
Hab: Loess bluffs; roadsides; sandy shores
A&D: Common w; freq to infreq nc & sc
Org: Native

Leontodon L. Fall dandelion

L. autumnalis L.
Hab: Open, disturbed sites
A&D: Rare sw: PAG
Org: Not native

Leucanthemum P. Miller

L. vulgare Lam.
Syn: *Chrysanthemum leucanthemum* L.
Com: Ox-eye daisy
Hab: Roadsides; along railroads; pastures; rocky alluvium
A&D: Freq to common sw, sc & in Pal. Plateau; infreq to rare remainder of ne & se
Org: Not native

Liatris Gaertner ex Schreber
Blazing star, gay-feather

L. aspera Michx.
Com: Blazing star
Hab: Prairie remnants
A&D: Common e 2/3; infreq elsewh
Org: Native

L. cylindracea Michx.
Com: Blazing star
Hab: Dry, rocky or sandy prairies
A&D: Rare ne 1/3; freq in Pal. Plateau
Org: Native

L. ligulistylis (A. Nelson) K. Schum.
Com: Blazing star
Hab: Prairies; roadsides; along railroads
A&D: Rare nc & ne
Org: Native

L. punctata Hooker
Hab: Loess bluffs; prairies; gravel hills
A&D: Freq to common nw; infreq rest of w 1/2
Org: Native

L. pycnostachya Michx.
Com: Prairie blazing star
Hab: Moist prairies; roadsides; along railroads
A&D: Rare or infreq extreme w; freq to common elsewh
Org: Native

L. squarrosa (L.) Michx. [incl. var. *hirsuta* (Rydb.) Gaiser; var. *glabrata* (Rydb.) Gaiser]
Hab: Prairies; woodland openings
A&D: Infreq w 1/2; rare se
Org: Native

Lygodesmia D. Don

L. juncea (Pursh) D. Don
Com: Skeletonweed
Hab: Open, disturbed soil of loess bluffs; dry, gravelly prairies
A&D: Common in Loess Hills; freq to infreq nw
Org: Native

L. rostrata Gray
Syn: *Shinneroseris rostrata* (Gray) Tomb
Com: Annual skeletonweed
Hab: Sandy plains
A&D: Rare wc & nw: HRR & PLY 1927
Org: Native

Machaeranthera Nees

M. spinulosa Greene
Syn: *Haplopappus spinulosus* (Pursh) DC.
Syn: *M. pinnatifida* (Hooker) Shinners
Hab: Loess bluffs; gravel hills; dry prairies
A&D: Common sw; freq wc & nw
Org: Native

Madia Molina

M. sativa Molina var. *congesta* T. & G.
Com: Tarweed
Hab: Open, dry, sandy soils
A&D: Rare waif from western plains in nw & sc: EMM & MAH 1930's
Org: Native of U.S., but not Iowa

Matricaria L.

M. chamomilla L.
Syn: *Chamomilla recuita* (L.) Raushert
Com: Wild chamomile
Hab: Dry, disturbed soil
A&D: Rare ec & se: JOH 1927 & MUS 1895, SCO
Org: Not native

M. maritima L.
Hab: Disturbed alluvium
A&D: Rare se: MUS 1925
Org: Not native

M. matricarioides (Less.) Porter
Syn: *Chamomilla suaveolens* (Pursh) Rydb.
Com: Pineapple weed
Hab: Roadsides; paths; pastures; other disturbed habitats
A&D: Freq to common ne 2/3; infreq w
Org: Not native

Megalodonta Greene

M. beckii (Torrey ex Sprengel) Greene
Syn: *Bidens beckii* Torrey ex Sprengel
Com: Water marigold
Hab: Shallow, clear water of lakes
A&D: Rare nw & nc: CG 1901 & DIC
Org: Native

Microseris see ***Nothocalais***

Nothocalais (Gray) Greene

N. cuspidata (Pursh) Greene
Syn: *Agoseris cuspidata* (Pursh) Raf.
Syn: *Microseris cuspidata* (Pursh) Sch.-Bip.
Com: Prairie dandelion
Hab: Dry prairies; gravel hills; loess bluffs
A&D: Freq nw & nc; infreq wc & sw
Org: Native

Onopordum L.

O. acanthium L.
Com: Scotch thistle
Hab: Disturbed ground
A&D: Rare c & ne: FAY 1929, HRD 1939
Org: Not native

Parthenium L.

P. integrifolium L.
Com: Feverfew, wild quinine
Hab: Prairies
A&D: Infreq to rare e 1/2
Org: Native

Picris L.

P. echiodes L.
Com: Ox-tongue
Hab: Fields; roadsides; waste ground
A&D: Rare sc: CLR 1924
Org: Not native

Polymnia L.

P. canadensis L.
Com: Leafcup
Hab: Moist, alluvial woods; wooded slopes; algific talus slopes
A&D: Freq extreme e; infreq to rare remainder of e 1/2
Org: Native

Prenanthes L.

P. alba L.
Com: Rattlesnake-root, white lettuce
Hab: Moist woods; prairie remnants; roadsides
A&D: Freq to common thr most of state; not reported from nw
Org: Native

P. aspera Michx.
Com: Rough white lettuce
Hab: Prairies
A&D: Freq to infreq w; rare elsewh
Org: Native

P. racemosa Michx. [incl. ssp. *multiflora* Cronq.]
Com: Glaucous white lettuce
Hab: Prairies
A&D: Freq to common nc & in lakes area; infreq to rare elsewh
Org: Native

Prionopsis Nutt.

P. ciliata Nutt.
Syn: *Haplopappus ciliatus* (Nutt.) DC.
Hab: Dry, sandy prairie along railroads
A&D: Rare c & se: HAR & MUS
Org: Native of U.S., but not Iowa

Pyrrhopappus DC.

P. carolinianus (Walter) DC.
Com: False dandelion
Hab: Dry woods; prairies
A&D: Rare ec, se & sw: JEF 1934, PAG & SCO
Org: Native of U.S., but not Iowa

Ratibida Raf.

R. columnifera (Nutt.) Wooton & Standley
Com: Long-headed coneflower
Hab: Dry prairies; loess bluffs; sandy areas
A&D: Common nw; rare remainder of w 1/2
Org: Native

R. pinnata (Vent.) Barnh.
Com: Gray-headed coneflower
Hab: Prairie remnants; loess bluffs; roadsides
A&D: Freq to common thr most of state
Org: Native

Rudbeckia L.

R. hirta L. [incl. var. *pulcherrima* Farw.]
Syn: *R. serotina* Nutt.
Com: Black-eyed Susan
Hab: Prairie remnants; roadsides
A&D: Common thr most of state; rare nw
Org: Native

R. laciniata L.
Com: Tall coneflower
Hab: Alluvial woods
A&D: Common nc & in Pal. Plateau; freq to infreq elsewh
Org: Native

R. subtomentosa Pursh
Com: Fragrant coneflower
Hab: Moist prairies; open grasslands
A&D: Apparently absent wc & nw; rare to infreq elsewh
Org: Native

R. triloba L.
Com: Brown-eyed Susan
Hab: Alluvial or moist woods
A&D: Freq to common e 2/3; infreq sw
Org: Native

Senecio L.

S. aureus L.
Com: Golden ragwort
Hab: Moist prairies; woodland openings
A&D: Freq nc & in Pal. Plateau; rare elsewh
Org: Native

S. congestus (R. Br.) DC.
Syn: *S. palustris* (L.) Hooker, misappl.
Com: Marsh fleabane
Hab: Prairie swales
A&D: Rare nc, ne & in lakes area
Org: Native

S. glabellus Poiret
Com: Butterweed
Hab: Moist woods; moist, shaded ground along streams
A&D: Rare sw: FRE
Org: Native of U.S., but not Iowa

S. integerrimus Nutt.
Hab: Moist prairies; open woods; shores; algific talus slopes
A&D: Rare nc & in lakes area
Org: Native

S. pauperculus Michx.
Com: Prairie ragwort
Hab: Moist prairies
A&D: Freq nc & se; rare ne
Org: Native

S. plattensis Nutt.
Com: Prairie ragwort
Hab: Prairies; woodland openings
A&D: Infreq sw; freq to common elsewh
Org: Native

S. pseudaureus Rydb. var. *semicordatus* (Mack. & Bush) T. Barkley
Syn: *S. semicordatus* Mack. & Bush
Hab: Edges of moist, wooded slopes; Loess Hills
A&D: Rare c, wc & n: CLY 1936, DIC 1949, EMM 1882, HAN, MNN, STO 1907, & WNS
Org: Native

S. vulgaris L.
Com: Common groundsel
Hab: Moist, disturbed soil
A&D: Rare c: BOO
Org: Not native

Silphium L.

S. integrifolium Michx.
Com: Rosinweed
Hab: Prairie remnants; old pastures; open, sandy soil
A&D: Freq to common s 1/2; infreq to rare ne 1/4
Org: Native

S. laciniatum L.
Com: Compass plant
Hab: Prairie remnants; roadsides; along railroads
A&D: Common w 1/2; freq to infreq e 1/2
Org: Native

S. perfoliatum L.
Com: Cup plant
Hab: Moist alluvial woods & woodland edges; prairie swales; roadsides
A&D: Freq to common thr most of state; infreq nw
Org: Native

S. terebinthinaceum Jacq.
Com: Prairie dock
Hab: Prairies; along railroads
A&D: Rare ne & ec: DUB & JAC
Org: Native

Solidago L. see also ***Euthamia***

S. canadensis L. [incl. var. *gilvocanescens* Rydb.; var. *hargeri* Fern.; var. *scabra* (Muhl.) T. & G.]
Syn: *S. altissima* L.
Com: Tall goldenrod
Hab: Roadsides; disturbed prairies; open woods
A&D: Freq to common thr
Org: Native

S. flexicaulis L.
Syn: *S. latifolia* L.
Com: Zig-zag goldenrod
Hab: Moist woods & wooded slopes
A&D: Not reported from nw; infreq in Iowan Surface; freq to common elsewh
Org: Native

S. gigantea Aiton [incl. var. *serotina* (Kuntze) Cronq.]
Com: Smooth goldenrod
Hab: Woodland borders; roadsides; loess bluffs; moist, open habitats
A&D: Freq to common thr
Org: Native

S. hispida Muhl. ex Willd.
Syn: *S. bicolor* L. var. *concolor* T. & G.
Hab: Dry, rocky woods
A&D: Rare in Pal. Plateau & extreme e
Org: Native

S. missouriensis Nutt. [incl. var. *fasciculata* Holz.]
Com: Missouri goldenrod
Hab: Upland prairie remnants; loess bluffs
A&D: Common w 2/3; infreq to rare e
Org: Native

S. nemoralis Aiton [incl. var. *longipetiolata* (Mack. & Bush) Palmer & Steyerm.]
Syn: *S. decemflora* DC.
Syn: *S. longipetiolata* Mack. & Bush
Com: Field goldenrod
Hab: Open woods; fields; prairie remnants
A&D: Freq to common thr most of state; infreq nw
Org: Native

S. patula Muhl. ex Willd.
Hab: Wooded, sandy soil; fens
A&D: Rare se: MUS
Org: Native

S. ptarmicoides (Nees) Boivin
Syn: *Aster ptarmicoides* (Nees) T. & G.
Hab: Often sandy or rocky, dry prairies
A&D: Absent sc; infreq to rare elsewh
Org: Native

S. riddellii Frank ex Riddell
Com: Riddell's goldenrod
Hab: Marshes; moist calcareous prairies; sedge meadows; fens
A&D: Freq nc & in lakes area; rare ne, & in se: MUS 1895
Org: Native

S. rigida L. [incl. var. *humilis* Porter]
Com: Stiff goldenrod
Hab: Prairies; loess bluffs
A&D: Infreq se; freq to common elsewh
Org: Native

S. sciaphila Steele
Com: Cliff goldenrod
Hab: Algific talus slopes; rock cliffs; ledges
A&D: Freq to common in Pal. Plateau; rare ec: JAC & CLI
Org: Native

S. speciosa Nutt. [incl. var. *jejunifolia* (Steele) Cronq.; var. *rigidiuscula* T. & G.]
Com: Showy goldenrod
Hab: Prairies; open woods; loess bluffs
A&D: Common nc; rare se; freq to infreq elsewh
Org: Native

S. uliginosa Nutt.
Com: Swamp goldenrod
Hab: Fens
A&D: Rare ne: ALL
Org: Native

S. ulmifolia Muhl. ex Willd.
Com: Elm-leaved goldenrod
Hab: Open, upland woods
A&D: Rare nw; common elsewh
Org: Native

Sonchus L.

S. arvensis L. [incl. ssp. *uliginosus* (Bieb.) Nyman]
Syn: *S. uliginosus* Bieb.
Com: Perennial sow thistle
Hab: Roadsides; disturbed soil
A&D: Rare e 1/4; infreq elsewh
Org: Not native

S. asper (L.) Hill
Com: Spiny-leaved sow thistle
Hab: Waste places; roadsides; fields; disturbed soil
A&D: Infreq to rare e 1/4; freq to common elsewh
Org: Not native

S. oleraceus L.
Com: Common sow thistle
Hab: Waste places; fields; woodland borders
A&D: Freq s 1/2, nc & in lakes area; rare extreme e
Org: Not native

Tanacetum L.

T. vulgare L.
Com: Tansy
Hab: Roadsides; pastures; waste places
A&D: Rare escape from cult
Org: Not native

Taraxacum Wiggers

T. laevigatum (Willd.) DC.
Syn: *T. erythrospermum* Andrz.
Com: Red-seeded dandelion
Hab: Weed of lawns; alluvial woodlands; disturbed prairie
A&D: Infreq to freq thr
Org: Not native

T. officinale Weber
Com: Common dandelion
Hab: Weed of lawns; fields; roadsides; other disturbed habitats
A&D: Common thr
Org: Not native

Tragopogon L.

T. dubius Scop. [incl. ssp. *major* (Jacq.) Voll.]
Syn: *T. major* Jacq.
Com: Goat's-beard
Hab: Roadsides; along railroads; pastures; disturbed prairies
A&D: Infreq ne; common elsewh
Org: Not native

T. porrifolius L.
Com: Salsify, oyster plant
Hab: Roadsides; along railroads; other disturbed habitats
A&D: Rare nc & se
Org: Not native

T. pratensis L.
Com: Goat's-beard
Hab: Disturbed woods; roadsides; waste places
A&D: Rare nw & ne; infreq elsewh
Org: Not native

Verbesina L.

V. alternifolia (L.) Britton
Com: Wingstem
Hab: Alluvial woods
A&D: Common sc; freq se; rare nc
Org: Native

V. encelioides (Cav.) Bentham & Hooker f. ex Gray ssp. *exauriculata* (B. L. Robinson & Greenman) Coleman
Hab: Disturbed habitats
A&D: Rare c, wc & nw: EMM 1934, HRR 1942, PA 1934 & STO 1934
Org: Not native

Vernonia Schreber

V. baldwinii Torrey [incl. var. *interior* (Small) Schub.]
Com: Baldwin's ironweed
Hab: Prairie remnants; open woods; pastures
A&D: Freq to common s 1/2; rare nc
Org: Native

V. fasciculata Michx. [incl. ssp. *corymbosa* (Schwein. ex Keating) S. B. Jones]
Com: Ironweed
Hab: Moist prairies; roadsides; other open, moist habitats
A&D: Infreq nw & sc; freq to common elsewh
Org: Native

V. gigantea (Walter) Trel. ex Branner & Cov.
Syn: *V. altissima* Nutt.
Com: Tall ironweed
Hab: Low woods; open ground
A&D: Freq to infreq sw 1/4
Org: Native

V. missurica Raf.
Com: Missouri ironweed
Hab: Prairie remnants; open, grazed woods; pastures
A&D: Freq se; rare nw
Org: Native

Xanthium DC.

X. spinosum L.
Com: Spiny cocklebur
Hab: Fields; disturbed soil
A&D: Rare c: STO & DAL
Org: Not native

X. strumarium L. [incl. var. *canadensis* (P. Miller) T. & G.; var. *glabratum* (DC.) Cronq.]
Com: Cocklebur
Hab: Roadsides; fields; pastures; other disturbed habitats
A&D: Freq to common thr
Org: Not native

BALSAMINACEAE

Impatiens L.

I. capensis Meerb.
Syn: *I. biflora* Walter
Com: Spotted touch-me-not
Hab: Alluvial woods; moist, wooded slopes; marsh edges
A&D: Freq to common thr
Org: Native

I. pallida Nutt.
Com: Pale touch-me-not, jewel weed
Hab: Alluvial woods; moist, wooded slopes
A&D: Infreq nw & nc; freq to common elsewh
Org: Native

BERBERIDACEAE

Berberis L.

B. thunbergii DC.
Com: Japanese barberry
Hab: Pastures; woods
A&D: Rare escape from cult
Org: Not native

B. vulgaris L.
Com: European barberry
Hab: Edges of woods; open, disturbed ground
A&D: Rare escape from cult
Org: Not native

Caulophyllum Michx.

C. thalictroides (L.) Michx.
Com: Blue cohosh
Hab: Moist woods
A&D: Common nc & ne; infreq nw & se; rare sw
Org: Native

Jeffersonia Barton

J. diphylla (L.) Pers.
Com: Twinleaf
Hab: Moist, wooded slopes
A&D: Rare ne: ALL, CLT, DUB & FAY
Org: Native

Podophyllum L.

P. peltatum L.
Com: Mayapple
Hab: Open woods; woodland edges; moist, upland woods
A&D: Common e 2/3
Org: Native

BETULACEAE

Alnus P. Miller

A. rugosa (Du Roi) Sprengel
Syn: *A. incana* (L.) Moench ssp. *rugosa* (Du Roi) Clausen
Com: Speckled alder
Hab: Sandy soil in alluvial woods; streamsides; seeps
A&D: Rare ne
Org: Native

Betula L.

B. alleghaniensis Britton
Syn: *B. lutea* Michx. f.
Com: Yellow birch
Hab: N-facing, rocky, wooded slopes; algific talus slopes
A&D: Rare c, nc & ne: ALL, CLT, DEL, DUB, FAY, HRD, MIT & WNS
Org: Native

B. nigra L.
Com: River birch
Hab: Alluvial woods; stream margins
A&D: Common e; infreq to freq c; rare sw
Org: Native

B. papyrifera Marsh.
Syn: *B. alba* L., misappl.
Com: Paper birch, canoe birch
Hab: Steep, sheltered, rocky bluffs; n-facing slopes
A&D: Common in Pal. Plateau; rare in Iowan Surface, & in c & ec: HRD, JOH
Org: Native

B. pumila L. var. *glandulifera* Regel
Syn: *B. glandulosa* Michx. var. *glandulifera* (Regel) Gl.
Com: Swamp birch
Hab: Fens; sedge meadows; mesic prairies
A&D: Rare nc & ne: ALL, BH, BRE, CHI, CLT, HOW & MIT
Org: Native

B. pumila X *Betula nigra*
Hab: Fen
A&D: Rare ne: CHI
Org: Native

Carpinus L.

C. caroliniana Walter
Com: Blue beech
Hab: Moist, often rocky, wooded slopes
A&D: Common ne; infreq nc & se
Org: Native

Corylus L.

C. americana Walter
Com: Hazelnut
Hab: Woodland openings & borders
A&D: Infreq nw; common elsewh
Org: Native

C. cornuta Marsh.
Syn: *C. rostrata* Aiton
Com: Beaked hazel
Hab: N-facing wooded slopes; algific talus slopes
A&D: Freq in Pal. Plateau; infreq rest of ne 1/4
Org: Native

Ostrya Scop.

O. virginiana (P. Miller) K. Koch
Com: Ironwood, hop hornbeam
Hab: Upland woods; wooded slopes
A&D: Freq to common thr
Org: Native

BIGNONIACEAE

Campsis Lour.

C. radicans (L.) Seem. ex Bureau
Com: Trumpet creeper
Hab: Open, wooded bluffs; fencerows
A&D: Infreq escape from cult
Org: Native of U.S., but not Iowa

Catalpa Scop.

C. bignonioides Walter
Com: Common catalpa
Hab: Disturbed areas near human habitation
A&D: Rare escape from cult
Org: Native of U.S., but not Iowa

C. speciosa Warder
Com: Cigar tree
Hab: Plantations; disturbed areas near human habitation
A&D: Infreq thr
Org: Native of U.S., but not Iowa

BORAGINACEAE

Anchusa L.

A. azurea Miller
Com: Alkanet
Hab: Roadsides
A&D: Rare wc & nw: CAR, DIC 1928
Org: Not native

Cynoglossum L.

C. officinale L.
Com: Hound's-tongue
Hab: Open pastures; pastured woods
A&D: Freq in Pal. Plateau; infreq to rare elsewh
Org: Not native

Echium L.

E. vulgare L.
Com: Blueweed
Hab: Dry fields; roadsides
A&D: Rare sw
Org: Not native

Hackelia Opiz

H. deflexa (Wahl.) Opiz var. *americana* (Gray) Fern. & I. M. Johnston
Syn: *H. americana* (Gray) Fern.
Com: Stickseed
Hab: Wooded, rocky slopes; talus slopes
A&D: Freq e; infreq to rare nc & ne
Org: Native

H. virginiana (L.) I. M. Johnston
Syn: *Lappula virginiana* (L.) Greene
Com: Stickseed
Hab: Open woods; alluvium
A&D: Common in Pal. Plateau & e; infreq to freq elsewh
Org: Native

Lappula Fabr.

L. echinata Gilib.
Syn: *L. squarrosa* (Retz.) Dumort.
Com: Beggar's-lice
Hab: Disturbed areas; dry prairies; loess bluffs
A&D: Common nw; infreq to rare elsewh
Org: Not native

L. redowskii (Hornem.) Greene [incl. var. *texana* (Scheele) Brand]
Syn: *L. texana* (Scheele) Britton
Hab: Open, dry places; railroad ballast; disturbed areas
A&D: Rare thr
Org: Not native

Lithospermum L.

L. arvense L.
Syn: *Buglossoides arvense* (L.) I. M. Johnston
Com: Corn-gromwell
Hab: Sandy, disturbed habitats
A&D: Rare se & sc: DM 1937, LEE, MAH 1938 & MUS 1892
Org: Not native

L. canescens (Michx.) Lehm.
Com: Hoary puccoon
Hab: Prairie remnants; sandy, open ground; open, upland woods
A&D: Common thr
Org: Native

L. caroliniense (Walter) MacM.
Syn: *L. croceum* Fern.
Com: Hairy puccoon
Hab: Dry, sandy soil
A&D: Freq to infreq ne; rare to infreq s 1/2
Org: Native

L. incisum Lehm.
Com: Fringed puccoon
Hab: Loess bluffs; sandy prairies; sandy alluvium
A&D: Common n 1/2 & sw; rare elsewh
Org: Native

L. latifolium Michx.
Com: American gromwell
Hab: Moist woods
A&D: Freq ne 1/4; infreq to rare elsewh
Org: Native

Mertensia Roth

M. paniculata (Aiton) G. Don
Com: Northern lungwort
Hab: Mossy, calcareous talus slopes
A&D: Rare ne: ALL, CLT, FAY, HOW & WNS
Org: Native

M. virginica (L.) Pers. ex Link
Com: Bluebell
Hab: Moist woods; bottomlands
A&D: Freq to infreq e 1/2; rare w 1/2
Org: Native

Myosotis L.

M. micrantha Pallas
Hab: Disturbed river terrace
A&D: Rare ne: DUB
Org: Not native

M. verna Nutt.
Syn: *M. virginica* (L.) BSP., misappl.
Com: Forget-me-not
Hab: Open, sandy, alluvial woods
A&D: Infreq to rare se 2/3
Org: Native

Onosmodium Michx.

O. molle Michx. var. *hispidissimum* (Mack.) Cronq.
Syn: *O. molle* ssp. *hispidissimum* (Mack.) Cochrane
Syn: *O. hispidissimum* Mack.
Com: False gromwell
Hab: Dry, rocky prairies; sandy, alluvial woods
A&D: Rare ne & se
Org: Native

O. molle Michx. var. *occidentale* (Mack.) I. M. Johnston
Syn: *O. molle* ssp. *occidentale* (Mack.) Cochrane
Syn: *O. occidentale* Mack.
Com: False gromwell
Hab: Low, sandy or gravelly prairies; loess bluffs; roadsides
A&D: Freq to common w; rare e
Org: Native

BRASSICACEAE (CRUCIFERAE)

Alliaria Heist. ex Fabr.

A. petiolata (Bieb.) Cavara & Grande
Syn: *A. officinalis* Andrz. ex Bieb.
Com: Garlic mustard
Hab: Upland & lowland woods; wooded slopes; roadsides
A&D: Rare: scattered localities, rapidly increasing its range
Org: Not native

Alyssum L.

A. alyssoides (L.) L.
Hab: Waste areas; disturbed soil
A&D: Rare wc, nw & ec: EMM 1927, DIC, JOH 1919 & MNN 1932
Org: Not native

Arabis L. see also ***Sibara*** Rock cress

A. canadensis L.
Com: Sickle pod, rock cress
Hab: Upland woods; ravines; algific talus slopes
A&D: Common in Pal. Plateau; infreq to freq elsewh
Org: Native

A. divaricarpa A. Nelson
Com: Purple rock cress
Hab: Sandy or rocky woods
A&D: Rare c, nw, ne & ec: DEL 1919, DUB 1922, EMM 1927, JOH, JON & WEB 1903
Org: Native

A. drummondii Gray
Com: Rock cress
Hab: Prairies; openings in woods
A&D: Infreq e; rare sc
Org: Native

A. glabra (L.) Bernh.
Com: Tower mustard
Hab: Prairies; sandy roadsides
A&D: Rare ne, extreme e & sc
Org: Native

A. hirsuta (L.) Scop. [incl. var. *pycnocarpa* (M. Hopk.) Roll.; var. *adpressipilis* (M. Hopk.) Roll.]
Hab: Wooded, rocky bluffs
A&D: Infreq to rare thr
Org: Native

A. laevigata (Muhl. ex Willd.) Poiret
Hab: Rocky, wooded slopes; shaded sandstone & limestone ledges
A&D: Infreq ne 1/4; rare se
Org: Native

A. lyrata L.
Hab: Sandstone or limestone cliffs & ledges; algific talus slopes
A&D: Common in Pal. Plateau; infreq to rare rest of ne, e & sc
Org: Native

A. missouriensis Greene
Syn: *A. viridis* Harger var. *deamii* M. Hopk.
Hab: Rocky, wooded slopes
A&D: Rare ne: ALL
Org: Native

A. shortii (Fern.) Gl.
Syn: *A. perstellata* E. L. Br. var. *shortii* Fern.
Com: Rock cress
Hab: Wooded talus slopes; alluvium; shaded bluffs
A&D: Infreq to rare thr
Org: Native

Armoracia Gaertner, Meyer & Schreber

A. aquatica (Eaton) Wieg.
Syn: *A. lacustris* (Gray) Al-Shehbaz & V. Bates
Com: Lake cress
Hab: Marshes; quiet streams
A&D: Rare ec, se & sw: MUS 1894, SCO pre-1900 & UNI 1882
Org: Native

A. rusticana (Lam.) Gaertner, Meyer & Schreber
Syn: *A. lapathifolia* Gilib.
Com: Horseradish
Hab: Disturbed ground near human habitation
A&D: Rare escape from cult thr
Org: Not native

Barbarea R. Br.

B. vulgaris R. Br. [incl. var. *arcuata* (Opiz) Fries]
Com: Yellow rocket
Hab: Weed of roadsides; waste places
A&D: Rare nw; common elsewh
Org: Not native

Berteroa DC.

B. incana (L.) DC.
Com: Hoary alyssum
Hab: Roadsides; disturbed soil; sandy, open areas
A&D: Rare ne & sc; freq to infreq elsewh
Org: Not native

Brassica L. see also ***Sinapis***

B. campestris L.
Syn: *B. rapa* L. ssp. *olifera* DC.
Com: Field mustard
Hab: Fields; waste places
A&D: Rare escape from cult
Org: Not native

B. juncea (L.) Czern.
Com: Chinese mustard
Hab: Weed of roadsides; cultivated fields
A&D: Common sw; infreq elsewh
Org: Not native

B. Kaber (DC.) Wheeler
Hab: Cultivated fields
A&D: Rare sw: PAG
Org: Native

B. napus L.
Com: Turnip
Hab: Disturbed areas
A&D: Rare escape from cult
Org: Not native

B. nigra (L.) W. D. J. Koch
Com: Black mustard
Hab: Weed of roadsides; disturbed areas
A&D: Absent nw; freq to common elsewh
Org: Not native

B. oleracea L.
Com: Wild cabbage
Hab: Disturbed areas
A&D: Rare escape from cult
Org: Not native

Camelina Crantz

C. microcarpa Andrz. ex DC.
Com: Small-fruited false flax
Hab: Fields; waste places
A&D: Infreq to rare thr
Org: Not native

C. sativa (L.) Crantz
Com: False flax
Hab: Waste ground; disturbed soil
A&D: Rare nc, ne & sw
Org: Not native

Capsella Medicus

C. bursa-pastoris (L.) Medicus
Com: Shepherd's purse
Hab: Lawns; disturbed soil; along roads
A&D: Common thr
Org: Not native

Cardamine L.

C. bulbosa (Schreber) BSP.
Com: Spring cress
Hab: Shallow water; marshes; prairie potholes; fens
A&D: Common ne; rare w; infreq elsewh
Org: Native

C. douglassii (Torrey) Britton
Com: Purple cress
Hab: Moist, wooded ravine bottoms
A&D: Rare se 1/4
Org: Native

C. parviflora L. var. *arenicola* (Britton) Schulz
Com: Small-flowered bitter cress
Hab: Open, sandy soil
A&D: Rare in Iowan Surface
Org: Native

C. pensylvanica Muhl. ex Willd.
Com: Bitter cress
Hab: Wet ground at marsh edges; along streams
A&D: Freq to infreq ne 2/3; rare sc: DEC
Org: Native

Cardaria Desv.

C. chalapensis (L.) Handel-Mazzetti
Hab: Roadsides; pastures
A&D: Rare sw: PAG
Org: Not native

C. draba (L.) Desv.
Com: Hoary cress
Hab: Roadsides; open, sandy areas; field edges
A&D: Infreq nc & sw; rare nw & sc
Org: Not native

Chorispora R. Br.

C. tenella (Pallas) DC.
Hab: Roadsides; waste ground; disturbed areas
A&D: Rare c, wc, nw & ne: CLY, DUB, PLY, SAC, STO & WOO 1930
Org: Not native

Conringia Link

C. orientalis (L.) Dum.
Com: Hare's-ear mustard
Hab: Weed of waste places
A&D: Infreq to rare thr
Org: Not native

Dentaria L.

D. laciniata Muhl. ex Willd.
Syn: *Cardamine concatenata* (Michx.) O. Schwartz
Com: Toothwort
Hab: Moist, wooded slopes; bottomland woods
A&D: Not reported from nw; freq to common elsewh
Org: Native

Descurainia Webb & Berth. Tansy mustard

D. pinnata (Walter) Britton var. *brachycarpa* (Richardson) Fern.
Com: Tansy mustard
Hab: Dry, usually sandy, habitats
A&D: Rare sw; freq to common elsewh
Org: Native

D. sophia (L.) Webb ex Prantl
Hab: Dry, sandy, disturbed areas; fields
A&D: Freq nw; rare sw, & in se: MUS 1890
Org: Not native

Diplotaxis DC.

D. muralis (L.) DC.
Com: Wall rocket
Hab: Waste ground; other disturbed habitats
A&D: Rare c & n
Org: Not native

Draba L.

D. nemorosa L.
Hab: Sandy river terraces
A&D: Rare ne: DUB
Org: Native of U.S., but not Iowa

D. reptans (Lam.) Fern. [incl. var. *micrantha* (Nutt.) Fern.]
Com: Whitlow grass
Hab: Open, sandy or gravelly soil; loess
A&D: Freq in sandy places thr
Org: Native

D. verna L.
Syn: *Erophila verna* (L.) Chev.
Com: Vernal whitlow grass
Hab: Sandy, alluvial terrace
A&D: Rare ne: BUC
Org: Not native

Eruca P. Miller

E. sativa P. Miller
Syn: *E. vesicaria* (L.) Cav. ssp. *sativa* (P. Miller) Thell.
Com: Garden rocket
Hab: Disturbed soil; waste ground
A&D: Rare escape from cult
Org: Not native

Erucastrum Presl

E. gallicum (Willd.) Schulz
Com: Dog mustard
Hab: Waste ground
A&D: Rare wc & ne: DEL, WNS & WOO
Org: Not native

Erysimum L. Treacle mustard

E. asperum (Nutt.) DC.
Com: Western wallflower
Hab: Sandy prairies
A&D: Rare c, wc & se: IDA 1925, TAM 1895 & VB 1940
Org: Native of U.S., but not Iowa

E. cheiranthoides L.
Com: Wormseed mustard
Hab: Open woods; roadsides; waste places
A&D: Freq to infreq n 1/2; infreq to rare s 1/2
Org: Not native

E. inconspicuum (S. Watson) MacM.
Hab: Dry, sandy or gravelly places
A&D: Rare w 1/2, & in c, nw & ne: CHI 1926, EMM 1926, WEB 1906
Org: Native

E. repandum L.
Hab: Waste places
A&D: Rare c, nw & s: DEC, FRE, JEF 1933, LEE, PAG & STO
Org: Not native

Hesperis L.

H. matronalis L.
Com: Dame's rocket
Hab: Roadsides; waste ground near human habitation
A&D: Infreq to rare w 1/2 & e
Org: Not native

Iberis L.

I. umbellata L.
Com: Candy tuft
Hab: Waste places
A&D: Rare escape from cult in sc: MAD 1942
Org: Not native

Iodanthus Torrey & Gray ex Steudel

I. pinnatifidus (Michx.) Steudel
Com: Purple rocket
Hab: Moist, sandy, alluvial woods
A&D: Rare to infreq s 1/2 & ne
Org: Native

Lepidium L.

L. campestre (L.) R. Br.
Com: Field cress
Hab: Roadsides; along railroads; disturbed ground
A&D: Freq to infreq s 1/2; rare nc & se
Org: Not native

L. densiflorum Schrader
Com: Peppergrass
Hab: Roadsides; pastures; waste places
A&D: Common n 1/2; freq e & sc; rare se & sw
Org: Native

L. perfoliatum L.
Com: Perfoliate peppergrass
Hab: Disturbed ground along railroads
A&D: Rare c & nw: CHE 1931 & STO
Org: Not native

L. virginicum L.
Com: Poor-man's pepper
Hab: Waste ground; fields; roadsides
A&D: Rare nw; freq to common elsewh
Org: Native

Lesquerella S. Watson

L. ludoviciana (Nutt.) S. Watson
Com: Silvery bladder-pod
Hab: Sandy soil
A&D: Rare c & ne: BH 1921 & HRD 1905
Org: Native

Lobularia Desv.

L. maritima (L.) Desv.
Com: Sweet alyssum
Hab: Roadsides
A&D: Rare escape from cult in c, nc & ec: CG, LIN 1937, POW, TAM 1895
Org: Not native

Nasturtium R. Br.

N. officinale R. Br.
Syn: *Rorippa nasturtium-aquaticum* (L.) Hayek
Com: Watercress
Hab: Cold streams; springs
A&D: Common ne; widely distributed
Org: Not native

Neslia Desv.

N. paniculata (L.) Desv.
Com: Ball mustard
Hab: Abandoned fields
A&D: Rare c, ec & sw: JOH 1908, LIN 1949, MIL 1925 & WEB 1906
Org: Not native

Raphanus L.

R. raphanistrum L.
Com: Wild radish
Hab: Roadsides; old fields
A&D: Rare thr
Org: Not native

R. sativus L.
Com: Radish
Hab: Disturbed ground
A&D: Rare escape from cult thr
Org: Not native

Rorippa Scop. Yellow cress

R. austriaca (Crantz) Besser
Com: Austrian field cress
Hab: Roadsides; disturbed ground
A&D: Rare c & w: EMM 1932, IDA, PAG & STO
Org: Not native

R. palustris (L.) Besser [incl. ssp. *fernaldiana* (Butters & Abbe) Jonsell; ssp. *glabra* (Schulz) R. Stuckey; ssp. *hispida* (Desv.) Jonsell]
Syn: *R. islandica* (Oeder) Borbas var. *fernaldiana* Butters & Abbe
Syn: *R. islandica* (Oeder) Borbas var. *hispida* (Desv.) Butters & Abbe
Com: Marsh cress
Hab: Shallow water; shores
A&D: Infreq to common thr
Org: Native

R. prostrata (Bergeret) Schintz & Thell.
Hab: Disturbed soil of floodplains
A&D: Rare nw: EMM
Org: Not native

R. sessiliflora (Nutt.) A. S. Hitchc.
Hab: Moist, sandy soil
A&D: Freq to infreq thr most of state; rare in Pal. Plateau
Org: Native

R. sinuata (Nutt.) A. S. Hitchc.
Hab: Sandy shores
A&D: Rare w, & in ne, se & sc: BH 1929, FRE 1888, HRR 1907, HEN 1928, LYO, MRN 1898,& PAG
Org: Native

R. sylvestris (L.) Besser
Com: Creeping yellow cress
Hab: Wet, often sandy, bottomlands
A&D: Rare thr most of state; absent nw & sc
Org: Not native

Sibara Greene

S. virginica (L.) Roll.
Syn: *Arabis virginica* (L.) Poiret
Hab: Marshy area
A&D: Rare ne: WNS
Org: Native

Sinapis L.

S. alba L.
Syn: *Brassica hirta* Moench
Com: White mustard
Hab: Fields
A&D: Rare c & ne: CHI 1926 & STO 1894
Org: Not native

S. arvensis L.
Syn: *Brassica kaber* (DC.) L. C. Wheeler
Com: Charlock
Hab: Roadsides; fields; disturbed places
A&D: Common w; rare in Pal. Plateau; infreq to freq elsewh
Org: Not native

Sisymbrium L. Tumble mustard

S. altissimum L.
Com: Tumble mustard
Hab: Fields; roadsides; waste places
A&D: Freq to common s 1/2; freq nc; infreq to rare elsewh
Org: Not native

S. loeselii L.
Hab: Waste areas
A&D: Rare c & w: EMM 1925, IDA, MNN, PAG, PLY, STO & WOO
Org: Not native

S. officinale (L.) Scop.
Hab: Weed of roadsides; pastures; fields; waste places
A&D: Freq to common s 1/2; freq to infreq n 1/2
Org: Not native

Thlaspi L.

T. arvense L.
Com: Penny cress
Hab: Weed of roadsides; fields; disturbed ground
A&D: Freq to common thr
Org: Not native

CACTACEAE

Opuntia P. Miller

O. fragilis (Nutt.) Haw.
Com: Little prickly pear
Hab: Thin soils on Sioux Quartzite; sand barrens
A&D: Rare c, nw & ne: BUC, HRD & LYO
Org: Native

O. humifusa (Raf.) Raf.
Syn: *O. compressa* (Salisb.) J. P. Macbr.
Com: Eastern prickly pear
Hab: Dry, sandy soil
A&D: Rare e & s
Org: Native

O. macrorhiza Engelm.
Com: Prickly pear
Hab: Sandy prairie
A&D: Rare sw, wc, c, & ne: ALL, GUT MNT, PAG & POL
Org: Native

CALLITRICHACEAE

Callitriche L. Water-starwort

C. heterophylla Pursh
Hab: Wet shores; shallow water
A&D: Rare: scattered thr
Org: Native

C. verna L.
Syn: *C. palustris* L.
Hab: Wet shores; shallow water
A&D: Rare in lakes area & in Pal. Plateau
Org: Native

CAMPANULACEAE

Campanula L. Bellflower

C. americana L.
Com: Tall bellflower
Hab: Moist, alluvial woods
A&D: Common thr
Org: Native

C. aparinoides Pursh
Syn: *C. uliginosa* Rydb.
Com: Marsh bellflower
Hab: Moist prairies; shores; marshes; fens
A&D: Freq nc; rare to absent elsewh
Org: Native

C. rapunculoides L.
Hab: Roadsides; waste ground near cemeteries
A&D: Rare escape from cult
Org: Not native

C. rotundifolia L.
Com: Harebell
Hab: Rocky prairies; limestone ledges; algific talus slopes
A&D: Common extreme e & in Pal. Plateau; rare c
Org: Native

Lobelia L.

L. cardinalis L.
Com: Cardinal flower
Hab: Moist, alluvial woods; moist, open areas
A&D: Freq ne & se; infreq sc; rare nc
Org: Native

L. inflata L.
Com: Indian tobacco
Hab: Open, often disturbed, woods & roadsides
A&D: Freq to common se 2/3
Org: Native

L. kalmii L.
Com: Kalm's lobelia
Hab: Fens
A&D: Rare n: CG, CLT 1921, CLY, DIC, EMM, HOW & PA
Org: Native

L. siphilitica L.
Com: Great lobelia
Hab: Moist, open places; sandy soil
A&D: Infreq nw; freq to common elsewh
Org: Native

L. spicata Lam. [incl. var. *hirtella* Gray; var. *campanulata* Mcvaugh; var. *leptostachya* (A. DC.) Mack. & Bush]
Com: Spiked lobelia
Hab: Moist prairies
A&D: Common n & e; freq to infreq elsewh
Org: Native

Triodanis Raf.

T. leptocarpa (Nutt.) Nieuw.
Syn: *Specularia leptocarpa* (Nutt.) A. Gray
Hab: Disturbed, sandy areas
A&D: Rare: PAG
Org: Native

T. perfoliata (L.) Nieuw.
Syn: *Specularia perfoliata* (L.) A. DC.
Com: Venus' looking-glass
Hab: Open woods; roadsides; dry, sandy soil
A&D: Common se; infreq to rare nw 1/2
Org: Native

CAPPARIDACEAE

Cleome L.

C. serrulata Pursh
Com: Stinking clover
Hab: Loess Hills; dry soil; roadsides
A&D: Rare, persisting only in nw
Org: Native

Cristatella see ***Polanisia***

Polanisia Raf. Clammy weed

P. dodecandra (L.) DC.
Syn: *P. graveolens* Raf.
Com: Clammy weed
Hab: Dry, open, sandy or gravelly soil; loess
A&D: Freq to common nc, se & sc; infreq elsewh
Org: Native

P. dodecandra (L.) DC. ssp. *trachysperma* (T. & G.) Iltis
Syn: *P. trachysperma* T. & G.
Com: Clammy weed
Hab: Dry, open, sandy or gravelly soil; loess
A&D: Common nc; freq to infreq elsewh
Org: Native

P. jamesii (T. & G.) Iltis
Syn: *Cristatella jamesii* T. & G.
Hab: Disturbed sand dunes; sandy banks; bluff tops
A&D: Rare ec & se: CED, JAC & MUS
Org: Native

CAPRIFOLIACEAE

Diervilla P. Miller

D. lonicera Miller
Com: Bush honeysuckle
Hab: Moist, wooded slopes; shaded sandstone or limestone ledges; talus slopes
A&D: Common in Pal. Plateau; rare rest of ne & se
Org: Native

Linnaea L.

L. borealis L. ssp. *americana* (Forbes) Hulten
Syn: *L. americana* Forbes
Com: Twinflower
Hab: Algific talus slopes
A&D: Rare ne: CLT & WNS
Org: Native

Lonicera L.

L. dioica L. var. *glaucescens* (Rydb.) Butters
Com: Wild honeysuckle
Hab: Open, wooded, rocky slopes & bluffs
A&D: Common nc, e & in Pal. Plateau; freq sw; infreq to rare elsewh
Org: Native

L. morrowi Gray
Com: Morrow's honeysuckle
Hab: Open, disturbed areas
A&D: Rare escape from cult thr
Org: Not native

L. prolifera (Kirchner) Rehder
Syn: *L. sullivantii* Gray
Com: Wild honeysuckle
Hab: Dry, wooded, rocky slopes
A&D: Common nc & ne; infreq to freq se & sc; rare sw
Org: Native

L. sempervirens L.
Com: Trumpet honeysuckle
Hab: Roadsides; waste places
A&D: Rare escape in ne & sc: DEL 1891, MAH late 1800's
Org: Not native

L. tatarica L.
Com: Tartarian honeysuckle
Hab: Dry woods; woodland edges
A&D: Freq escape from cult
Org: Not native

Sambucus L.

S. canadensis L.
Com: Elderberry, common elder
Hab: Edges of moist woods; shorelines; fencerows
A&D: Common thr
Org: Native

S. racemosa L. ssp. *pubens* (Michx.) House
Syn: *S. pubens* Michx.
Com: Red-berried elder
Hab: Steep, n-facing, wooded talus slopes
A&D: Rare ne & ec
Org: Native

Symphoricarpos Duhamel

S. albus (L.) Blake
Com: Snowberry
Hab: Dry limestone; sandstone ledges or bluffs
A&D: Rare ne: native in ALL, rare escape from cult elsewh
Org: Native

S. occidentalis Hooker
Com: Wolfberry, buckbrush
Hab: Dry prairies
A&D: Common nw, nc & sw; infreq to rare elsewh
Org: Native

S. orbiculatus Moench
Com: Coralberry, buckbrush
Hab: Dry prairies; dry, disturbed areas
A&D: Common s; rare to infreq n
Org: Native

Triosteum L. Horse gentian, feverwort

T. aurantiacum Bickn. [incl. var. *illinoense* (Wieg.) Palmer & Steyerm.]
Syn: *T. perfoliatum* L. var. *aurantiacum* (Bickn.) Wieg.
Hab: Upland woods
A&D: Infreq to rare e 1/2, except common ne
Org: Native

T. perfoliatum L.
Hab: Upland woods; woodland openings
A&D: Infreq nw; freq to common elsewh
Org: Native

Viburnum L.

V. dentatum L.
Com: Southern arrowwood
Hab: Borders of dry, upland woods
A&D: Infreq sw 1/4
Org: Native

V. lentago L.
Com: Nannyberry
Hab: Upland woods
A&D: Freq to infreq s 1/2; rare nw; common elsewh
Org: Native

V. molle Michx.
Com: Arrowwood
Hab: Bluffs; rocky woods
A&D: Rare se & sw: HEN, JEF, POT & VB
Org: Native

V. opulus L.
Com: Guelder-rose
Hab: Woodland edges
A&D: Rare escape from cult
Org: Not native

V. prunifolium L.
Com: Black haw
Hab: Woodland borders
A&D: Rare c, ec, se & sw: JAC, JOH, LEE, POW, TAY & VB
Org: Native

V. rafinesquianum Schultes [incl. var. *affine* (Bush) House]
Com: Downy arrowwood
Hab: Upland woods or rocky, wooded bluffs
A&D: Common ne; freq se; infreq to rare w 1/2
Org: Native

V. trilobum Marsh.
Syn: *V. opulus* L. var. *americanum* (P. Miller) Aiton
Com: Highbush cranberry
Hab: Moist, n-facing, wooded slopes
A&D: Freq in Pal. Plateau
Org: Native

CARYOPHYLLACEAE

Agrostemma L.

A. githago L.
Com: Corn cockle
Hab: Grain fields; waste ground
A&D: Rare weed in e 2/3; last collected in 1925
Org: Not native

Arenaria L. see also ***Moehringia*** & ***Minuartia***

A. serpyllifolia L.
Com: Thyme-leaved sandwort
Hab: Disturbed soil or waste ground
A&D: Rare nw: EMM 1929
Org: Not native

Cerastium L.

C. arvense L.
Syn: *C. velutinum* Raf.
Com: Field chickweed
Hab: Algific talus slopes
A&D: Rare ne & ec: ALL, CLT, DEL, DUB, FAY, JAC, HOW & WNS
Org: Native

C. glomeratum Thuill.
Syn: *C. viscosum* L., misappl.
Com: Clammy chickweed
Hab: Open, sandy alluvium; thin soil on Sioux Quartzite
A&D: Rare nw & e: BUC, CED, JON, LIN 1896, LYO, MUS & SCO 1895
Org: Not native

C. nutans Raf.[incl. var. *brachypodum* Engelm. ex Gray]
Syn: *C. brachypodum* (Engelm. ex Gray)B. L. Robinson
Com: Nodding chickweed
Hab: Wooded slopes; open, sandy or rocky habitats
A&D: Common sw; freq e; infreq nc & sc
Org: Native

C. vulgatum L.
Syn: *C. fontanum* Baumg.
Com: Mouse-ear chickweed
Hab: Open, moist, disturbed habitats
A&D: Freq e 1/2; infreq nc
Org: Not native

Dianthus L.

D. armeria L.
Com: Deptford pink
Hab: Disturbed prairies; waste areas
A&D: Infreq to rare s 1/2
Org: Not native

Holosteum L.

H. umbellatum L.
Com: Jagged chickweed
Hab: Disturbed, sandy areas
A&D: Rare wc, ne & se: DM, DUB & WOO
Org: Not native

Lychnis see ***Silene***

Minuartia L.

M. michauxii (Fern.) Farw.
Syn: *Arenaria stricta* Michx.
Com: Rock sandwort
Hab: Rock crevices on dry prairie remnants; limestone bluffs
A&D: Rare ne & ec: ALL, CLI, DEL, DUB, JAC, JON & WNS 1899
Org: Native

Moehringia L.

M. lateriflora (L.) Fenzl
Syn: *Arenaria lateriflora* L.
Com: Sandwort
Hab: Moist, upland woods & slopes
A&D: Freq in Pal. Plateau & in Iowan Surface; infreq se
Org: Native

Myosoton Moench

M. aquaticum (L.) Moench
Syn: *Stellaria aquatica* (L.) Scop.
Com: Giant chickweed
Hab: Moist, disturbed soil
A&D: Rare nc, ne & ec
Org: Not native

Paronychia P. Miller

P. canadensis (L.) Wood
Com: Tall forked chickweed
Hab: Woods & openings; dry, often sandy, uplands
A&D: Rare to infreq n & sw; freq se
Org: Native

P. fastigiata (Raf.) Fern.
Com: Low forked chickweed
Hab: Dry, often sandy, upland woods & woodland openings
A&D: Infreq se & sc
Org: Native

Saponaria L. see also ***Vaccaria***

S. officinalis L.
Com: Bouncing Bet, soapwort
Hab: Roadsides; waste places
A&D: Freq to common thr
Org: Not native

Silene L.

S. antirrhina L.
Com: Sleepy catchfly
Hab: Sandy soil; waste ground
A&D: Infreq to freq n; freq to common s
Org: Native

S. cserei Baumg.
Hab: Weed along railroads
A&D: Rare e 1/2; rare to infreq nw
Org: Not native

S. dichotoma Ehrh.
Com: Catchfly
Hab: Upland prairies; waste places
A&D: Freq nc; rare s 1/2
Org: Not native

S. nivea (Nutt.) Otth
Hab: Moist woods; open, grassy places
A&D: Infreq in Pal. Plateau; rare elsewh
Org: Native

S. noctiflora L.
Com: Night-flowering catchfly
Hab: Disturbed soil; roadsides; waste ground
A&D: Infreq escape from cult thr; common in some areas
Org: Not native

S. pratensis (Rafn) Gren. & Godron
Syn: *Lychnis alba* P. Miller
Syn: *S. alba* (P. Miller) Krause
Syn: *S. latifolia* Poiret
Com: White campion
Hab: Disturbed, open places; prairies
A&D: Infreq sc & sw; freq to common elsewh
Org: Not native

S. stellata (L.) Aiton f.
Com: Starry campion
Hab: Upland woods; shores; moist prairies
A&D: Common nw & nc; freq s; rare ne
Org: Native

S. virginica L.
Com: Firepink
Hab: Escapes from cult to roadsides
A&D: Rare ne & c: BH 1949 & BOO 1989
Org: Native of U.S., but not Iowa

S. vulgaris (Moench) Garcke
Syn: *S. cucubalus* Wibel
Com: Bladder campion
Hab: Disturbed soil; waste ground
A&D: Freq nc; rare sc
Org: Not native

Stellaria L.

S. graminea L.
Com: Common stitchwort
Hab: Moist, disturbed soil
A&D: Rare c, nw & e: ALL, EMM 1923, HRD, JEF 1935, JOH, LOU & POW
Org: Not native

S. longifolia Muhl. ex Willd.
Com: Stitchwort
Hab: Sedge meadows; marsh edges; moist woods; fens
A&D: Infreq nc & sc; rare ne & se
Org: Native

S. media (L.) Vill.
Com: Common chickweed
Hab: Open woods; disturbed ground; waste places
A&D: Rare ne; common elsewh
Org: Not native

Vaccaria Moench

V. pyramidata Medicus
Syn: *Saponaria vaccaria* L.
Syn: *V. segetalis* (Neck.) Garcke
Com: Cowherb, cow cockle
Hab: Roadsides; fields
A&D: Infreq sw; rare nc
Org: Not native

CELASTRACEAE

Celastrus L.

C. orbiculatus Thunb.
Com: Round-leaved bittersweet
Hab: Open woods; thickets
A&D: Rare escape in ne & sc: DEL & MAH
Org: Not native

C. scandens L.
Com: Bittersweet
Hab: Woodland edges; woodland openings; fencerows
A&D: Infreq nw; common elsewh
Org: Native

Euonymus L.

E. alatus (Thunb.) Sieb.
Com: Winged wahoo, burning bush
Hab: Woodlands
A&D: Rare c, ec & wc: LIN, WEB & WOO
Org: Not native

E. atropurpureus Jacq.
Com: Wahoo, burning bush
Hab: Moist woods
A&D: Infreq w; rare ne; freq elsewh
Org: Native

CERATOPHYLLACEAE

Ceratophyllum L.

C. demersum L.
Com: Coontail, hornwort
Hab: Shallow water of lakes; ponds
A&D: Freq s & in lakes area; rare to infreq n
Org: Native

CHENOPODIACEAE

Atriplex L.

A. patula L. [incl. var. *hastata* (L.) Gray]
Com: Spearscale, common orach
Hab: Often sandy, disturbed areas
A&D: Infreq to rare nw, e & s 1/2
Org: Native

A. rosea L.
Com: Red orach
Hab: Waste places; roadsides
A&D: Rare c, nw & sw: CAS 1927, EMM 1932, POL 1911 & SIO 1931
Org: Not native

Chenopodium L. Goosefoot, pig weed

C. album L. [incl. var. *lanceolatum* (Muhl.) Cosson & Germ.]
Com: Lamb's quarters
Hab: Disturbed soil; fields; waste ground
A&D: Freq in Pal. Plateau; common elsewh
Org: Not native

C. ambrosioides L.
Com: Mexican tea
Hab: Disturbed soil; waste ground
A&D: Rare s 1/2 & nc
Org: Not native

C. berlandieri Moq. [incl. var. *zschackei* (Murr) Murr]
Hab: Prairie remnants; disturbed, open areas
A&D: Common nc; rare ec & se: JOH & HEN
Org: Native

C. botrys L.
Com: Jerusalem oak
Hab: Disturbed soil; waste ground
A&D: Infreq c; rare ne & se
Org: Not native

C. bushianum Aellen
Hab: Wet, disturbed areas
A&D: Common nc; rare extreme e
Org: Not native

C. capitatum (L.) Ascherson
Com: Strawberry blite
Hab: Freshly disturbed ground
A&D: Rare ne & ec: ALL 1939 & JOH 1907
Org: Not native

C. desiccatum A. Nelson
Syn: *C. leptophyllum* (Moq.) Nutt. ex S. Watson var. *oblongifolium* S. Watson
Syn: *C. pratericola* Rydb. ssp. *desiccatum* (A. Nelson) Aellen
Com: Narrow-leaved goosefoot
Hab: Open, dry, sandy soil; roadsides; grazed woods
A&D: Freq s 1/2; infreq nw & ne; rare nc
Org: Native

C. foggii H. A. Wahl
Hab: Floodplain forest
A&D: Rare c, ec & se: DM, IOW 1928 & STO 1907
Org: Native

C. glaucum L.
Hab: Disturbed soil; waste places
A&D: Rare wc, nc, ec, se, & sw
Org: Not native

C. hybridum L. [incl. var. *gigantospermum* (Aellen) Rouleau]
Syn: *C. gigantospermum* Aellen
Com: Maple-leaved goosefoot
Hab: Disturbed woods; waste places
A&D: Freq sw; infreq ne; rare nw: DIC
Org: Native

C. missouriensis Aellen
Hab: Waste areas
A&D: Rare c & se: LEE, LOU, STO & TAM
Org: Native

C. murale L.
Hab: Waste ground
A&D: Rare nw, nc & se
Org: Not native

C. polyspermum L.
Com: Many-seeded goosefoot
Hab: Waste ground
A&D: Rare weed in nw & ec: EMM & JOH 1902
Org: Not native

C. rubrum L.
Com: Coast blite
Hab: Sandy or muddy shores
A&D: Rare nw: CLY 1936, DIC, EMM 1922 & PA 1935
Org: Native

C. standleyanum Aellen
Syn: *C. boscianum* Moq., misappl.
Com: Woodland goosefoot
Hab: Moist woods; moist, open, sandy soil
A&D: Freq nc, se & sc; infreq nw & ne
Org: Native

C. strictum Roth var. *glaucophyllum* (Aellen) H. A. Wahl
Hab: Waste ground
A&D: Common nc
Org: Not native

C. urbicum L.
Hab: Waste places; wooded, rocky bluffs
A&D: Rare weed thr
Org: Not native

Corispermum L.

C. nitidum Kit. ex Schultes
Hab: Sandy alluvium along Missouri River
A&D: Rare wc: HRR 1952
Org: Not native

Cycloloma Moq.

C. atriplicifolium (Sprengel) Coulter
Com: Winged pigweed
Hab: Open, dry, sandy soil
A&D: Freq to common se; infreq extreme e & sc; rare elsewh
Org: Native

Kochia Roth

K. scoparia (L.) Schrader
Com: Summer cypress
Hab: Dry, sandy soil; waste ground
A&D: Common nc & sw; rare e 1/2; infreq elsewh
Org: Not native

Monolepis Schrader

M. nuttalliana (Roemer & Schultes) Greene
Hab: Disturbed urban area
A&D: Rare sw & c: PAG & STO 1917
Org: Native of U.S., but not Iowa

Salsola L.

S. collina Pallas
Hab: Disturbed ground along railroad
A&D: Rare c: STO
Org: Not native

S. iberica Sennen & Pau
Syn: *S. kali* L. var. *tenuifolia* Tausch
Com: Russian thistle
Hab: Sandy shores; roadsides; field edges; waste ground
A&D: Common nc & extreme w; rare to infreq elsewh
Org: Not native

CISTACEAE

Helianthemum P. Miller Frost weed

H. bicknellii Fern.
Com: Rockrose
Hab: Sandy, upland prairies; woodland openings
A&D: Freq to common s 1/2 & ne; infreq nc & in lakes area
Org: Native

H. canadense (L.) Michx.
Hab: Sandy prairies; open woods
A&D: Common ne; freq sw; rare se
Org: Native

Hudsonia L.

H. tomentosa Nutt.
Com: False heather
Hab: Disturbed sand dunes
A&D: Rare ec: JAC
Org: Native

Lechea L. Pin weed

L. intermedia Leggett
Hab: Dry, sandy prairies; sandy, upland woods; open sandstone ledges
A&D: Rare wc, ec & ne: ALL, BEN, DUB, GUT & WNS
Org: Native

L. racemulosa Michx.
Hab: Dry soil
A&D: Rare: old c (WEB) collection, n.d.
Org: Native

L. stricta Leggett
Hab: Sandy prairie remnants; wooded sandstone bluffs
A&D: Freq to infreq ne; rare elsewh
Org: Native

L. tenuifolia Michx.
Com: Slender-leaved pinweed
Hab: Open, dry, sandy areas; open, sandy woods
A&D: Infreq sc & se; rare nc & ne
Org: Native

L. villosa Ell.
Syn: *L. mucronata* Raf.
Com: Hairy pinweed
Hab: Prairie openings; upland, dry, sandy woods
A&D: Rare e: JEF 1946, JON, LEE 1923 & WNS 1932
Org: Native

CONVOLVULACEAE

Calystegia R. Br. Morning glory, bindweed

C. sepium (L.) R. Br. [incl. var. *americana* (Sims) Matsuda; var. *fraterniflora* (Mack. & Bush) Shinners]
Syn: *Convolvulus sepium* L.
Syn: *Convolvulus americanus* (Sims) Greene
Syn: *Convolvulus repens* L.
Syn: *C. macounii* (Greene) Brummitt
Hab: Roadsides; fencerows; railroad ballast; woodland edges
A&D: Common thr
Org: Native

C. spithamaea (L.) Pursh
Syn: *Convolvulus spithamaeus* L.
Com: Low bindweed
Hab: Dry, sandy or rocky, upland woods
A&D: Rare e
Org: Native

Convolvulus L. see also ***Calystegia***

C. arvensis L.
Com: Creeping Jenny, European bindweed
Hab: Fields; roadsides
A&D: Rare se; freq to common elsewh
Org: Not native

Cuscuta L. Dodder

C. cephalanthii Engelm.
Hab: Parasitic on ***Salix***, ***Solidago***, ***Aster*** & ***Ribes***
A&D: Infreq to rare thr, except not reported sw
Org: Native

C. coryli Engelm.
Hab: Moist woods; moist thickets
A&D: Infreq c & nc
Org: Native

C. cuspidata Engelm.
Hab: Alluvial woods; moist habitats
A&D: Infreq to rare thr
Org: Native

C. glomerata Choisy
Hab: Along roads; disturbed borders of woods
A&D: Common nc; infreq se; infreq to rare w 1/2
Org: Native

C. gronovii Willd.
Hab: Alluvial woods; moist habitats
A&D: Infreq to rare e 2/3; rare nw: DIC, EMM & LYO
Org: Native

C. indecora Choisy
Hab: Cult fields; sandy shores
A&D: Rare w & ec: CLI, HRR, LIN, LYO & POT
Org: Native

C. pentagona Engelm.
Hab: Moist, disturbed areas
A&D: Infreq nc; rare in c, nw, se & sc: BOO, DAL 1919, LEE 1925, LYO 1896 & MAH
Org: Native

C. polygonorum Engelm.
Hab: Moist habitats; parasitic on *Polygonum*
A&D: Infreq se; rare elsewh
Org: Native

Ipomoea L. Morning glory

I. coccinea L.
Syn: *Quamoclit coccinea* (L.) Moench
Com: Red morning glory
Hab: Waste areas
A&D: Rare escape from cult
Org: Not native

I. hederacea (L.) Jacq.
Syn: *I. nil* (L.) Roth, misappl.
Hab: Cult fields; along railroads
A&D: Freq sw; infreq to rare elsewh
Org: Not native

I. lacunosa L.
Hab: Wooded alluvium
A&D: Rare sw & se: DM, FRE, MUS 1891 & PAG
Org: Native

I. pandurata (L.) G. F. W. Meyer
Com: Wild sweet potato
Hab: Woods; woodland borders
A&D: Freq se; rare nw, ne, ec & sc: CLT 1920, DEC 1898, JOH 1933, LIN 1902, LYO 1896 & WNS
Org: Native

I. purpurea (L.) Roth
Com: Annual morning glory
Hab: Roadsides; edges of fields; disturbed soil
A&D: Freq nc & sc; infreq to rare elsewh
Org: Not native

Stylisma Raf.

S. pickeringii (Torrey ex M. A. Curtis) Gray var. *pattersonii* (Fern. & Schub.) Myint
Syn: *Breweria pickeringii* (Torrey) Gray var. *pattersonii* Fern. & Schub.
Hab: Sandy soil
A&D: Rare se: MUS
Org: Native

CORNACEAE

Cornus L.

C. alternifolia L. f.
Com: Alternate-leaved dogwood, pagoda dogwood
Hab: Moist, upland woods
A&D: Freq to common ne 2/3; rare s; absent nw & sw
Org: Native

C. amomum P. Miller ssp. *obliqua* (Raf.) J. S. Wilson
Syn: *C. obliqua* Raf.
Syn: *C. purpusi* Koehne
Com: Silky dogwood
Hab: Wet thickets; low woods; wet prairies
A&D: Common in ne 1/4; infreq thr most of state
Org: Native

C. canadensis L.
Com: Bunchberry, dwarf cornel
Hab: Algific talus slopes; moist, sandstone outcrops
A&D: Rare ne: ALL, CLT, DEL & WNS
Org: Native

C. drummondii C. A. Meyer
Syn: *C. asperifolia* Michx., misappl.
Com: Rough-leaved dogwood
Hab: Moist woods; along wooded streams; woodland borders
A&D: Freq to common thr most of state; rare in Pal. Plateau & extreme n
Org: Native

C. foemina P. Miller ssp. *racemosa* (Lam.) J. S. Wilson
Syn: *C. racemosa* Lam.
Com: Gray dogwood
Hab: Upland woods
A&D: Common thr most of state; rare nw
Org: Native

C. rugosa Lam.
Com: Speckled dogwood, round-leaved dogwood
Hab: Rich, upland woods; n-facing, wooded slopes
A&D: Common in Pal. Plateau; infreq to rare elsewh
Org: Native

C. stolonifera Michx.
Syn: *C. sericea* L.
Com: Red-osier dogwood
Hab: Shores; lake & pond margins; fens
A&D: Rare in northern tier of counties; absent or rare escape from cult elsewh
Org: Native

CRASSULACEAE

Sedum L. Stonecrop

S. acre L.
Com: Mossy stonecrop
Hab: Sandy river terrace
A&D: Rare ne: DUB
Org: Not native

S. ternatum Michx.
Com: Wild stonecrop
Hab: Moist, wooded ravines near rivers
A&D: Rare ec: CED 1950
Org: Native

CUCURBITACEAE

Cucurbita L.

C. foetidissima HBK.
Com: Missouri gourd
Hab: Railroad embankments; railroad ballast
A&D: Rare s 1/2
Org: Native

Echinocystis Torrey & Gray

E. lobata (Michx.) T. & G.
Com: Wild balsam apple, wild cucumber
Hab: Low, moist woods
A&D: Freq nw; infreq to rare elsewh
Org: Native

Sicyos L.

S. angulatus L.
Com: Bur-cucumber
Hab: Alluvial woods; shorelines; moist roadsides
A&D: Freq se & e; infreq to rare w 2/3 of state
Org: Native

DIPSACACEAE

Dipsacus L.

D. laciniatus L.
Com: Cut-leaved teasel
Hab: Roadsides; disturbed soil; waste ground
A&D: Infreq s; rare ne & ec: CLI, DEL, JAC & JON
Org: Not native

D. sylvestris Hudson
Syn: *D. fullonum* L.
Com: Common teasel
Hab: Roadsides; waste ground
A&D: Rare escape from cult s 1/2
Org: Not native

DROSERACEAE

Drosera L.

D. rotundifolia L.
Com: Sundew
Hab: Sphagnum fen
A&D: Rare nc: HAN
Org: Native

EBENACEAE

Diospyros L.

D. virginiana L.
Com: Persimmon
Hab: Sandstone bluffs
A&D: Rare se & sc: LEE, LOU, MRN & WAY; possibly only the LEE population is native
Org: Native

ELAEAGNACEAE

Elaeagnus L.

E. angustifolia L.
Com: Russian olive
Hab: Disturbed woods
A&D: Infreq escape from cult thr
Org: Not native

E. umbellata Thunb.
Com: Autumn olive
Hab: Sandy areas; railroad ballast
A&D: Occasional escape from cult
Org: Not native

Shepherdia Nutt.

S. argentea (Pursh) Nutt.
Com: Buffalo berry
Hab: Dry uplands; loess bluffs; prairie-woodland edges
A&D: Rare wc & nw: EMM, HRR, MNN, PLY & WOO
Org: Native

ELATINACEAE

Elatine L.

E. triandra Schkuhr
Com: Waterwort
Hab: Shallow water of pothole
A&D: Rare nw: DIC
Org: Native

ERICACEAE

Arctostaphylos Adanson

A. uva-ursi (L.) Sprengel
Com: Bearberry
Hab: Limestone bluffs; outcrops of St. Peter sandstone
A&D: Rare ne: FAY & WNS 1930
Org: Native

Chimaphila Pursh Pipsissewa, wintergreen (Some authors place in Pyrolaceae)

C. umbellata (L.) Bartram
Com: Prince's pine
Hab: Moist, upland woods
A&D: Rare ne & ec: ALL, FAY 1895, JAC 1896, LIN 1911 & WNS
Org: Native

Gaylussacia HBK.

G. baccata (Wang.) K. Koch
Com: Black huckleberry
Hab: Sandy soil in open woods
A&D: Rare ne, ec & se: ALL, CED, CLI, LIN & MUS
Org: Native

Monotropa L. (Some authors place in Pyrolaceae)

M. hypopithys L.
Syn: *Hypopithys monotropa* Crantz
Com: Pine-sap
Hab: Loamy, upland woods
A&D: Rare ne, se & sc: ALL, APP, CLT 1921, DUB, LEE & WNS 1903
Org: Native

M. uniflora L.
Com: Indian pipe
Hab: Moist woods
A&D: Infreq to rare thr most of state
Org: Native

Pyrola L. (Some authors place in Pyrolaceae)

P. asarifolia Michx.
Com: Pink pyrola
Hab: Algific talus slopes
A&D: Rare ne: ALL & WNS
Org: Native

P. elliptica Nutt.
Com: Shinleaf
Hab: Wooded slopes
A&D: Common in ne 1/4; infreq e; formerly found in nc & se
Org: Native

P. secunda L.
Syn: *Orthilia secunda* (L.) House
Com: One-sided pyrola
Hab: Algific talus slopes
A&D: Rare nw & ne: ALL, DEL, EMM 1928, WNS
Org: Native

Vaccinium L.

V. angustifolium Aiton
Com: Low sweet blueberry
Hab: Dry, sandstone ledges; sandy woodlands
A&D: Rare ne & ec: ALL, CLT & JON
Org: Native

V. myrtilloides Michx.
Com: Velvet-leaf blueberry
Hab: Dry, sandstone ledges; sandy woods
A&D: Rare ne: ALL & CLT
Org: Native

EUPHORBIACEAE

Acalypha L.

A. gracilens Gray [incl. var. *monococca* Engelm.]
Syn: *A. monococca* (Engelm. ex Gray) Miller
Hab: Dry, sandy pastures
A&D: Rare e: BEN, BUC, JON, LEE, MUS & WAP 1938
Org: Native

A. ostryifolia Riddell
Com: Three-seeded mercury
Hab: Streambanks; roadsides; fields
A&D: Rare sw: FRE 1940 & POT 1949
Org: Native

A. rhomboidea Raf.
Com: Three-seeded mercury
Hab: Edges of ponds & marshes; lowland prairies
A&D: Common e, nc & sc; infreq elsewh
Org: Native

A. virginica L.
Hab: Disturbed soil
A&D: Common s; infreq e; rare nw
Org: Native

Croton L.

C. capitatus Michx.
Hab: Sandy soil; dry loess bluffs
A&D: Infreq to rare s; loess bluffs in nw & sw
Org: Native

C. glandulosus L. var. *septentrionalis* Mueller-Arg.
Hab: Sandy pond margins
A&D: Freq se 1/4; rare ne: CLT
Org: Native

C. monanthogynus Michx.
Com: Prairie tea
Hab: Dry, sandy soil; loess bluffs
A&D: Rare c, wc & se: DAV, LEE 1917, MNN, VB 1954 & WAP 1940
Org: Native

C. texensis (Kl.) Mueller-Arg. ex DC.
Com: Texas croton
Hab: Dry, disturbed soil
A&D: Rare se: MUS 1897
Org: Not native

Crotonopsis Michx.

C. elliptica Willd.
Hab: Pastures
A&D: Rare sw: RIN
Org: Native

Euphorbia L. Spurge

E. commutata Engelm.
Com: Wood spurge
Hab: Moist, sandy soil
A&D: Rare ne: WNS 1933
Org: Native

E. corollata L.
Com: Flowering spurge
Hab: Prairie remnants; roadsides; loess bluffs
A&D: Infreq nw; common elsewh
Org: Native

E. cyathophora Murray
Syn: *E. heterophylla* L.
Syn: *Poinsettia cyathophora* (Murray) Kl. & Garcke
Com: Wild poinsettia
Hab: Open, sandy soil; woodland margins; loess
A&D: Freq to infreq thr
Org: Native

E. cyparissias L.
Com: Cypress spurge
Hab: Waste places, especially near cemeteries; spreading from cult
A&D: Freq to infreq thr
Org: Not native

E. dentata Michx.
Syn: *Poinsettia dentata* (Michx.) Kl. & Garcke
Com: Toothed spurge
Hab: Roadsides; along railroads; loess bluffs; disturbed prairie remnants
A&D: Freq to common nw & s 1/2 ; infreq to rare elsewh
Org: Native

E. esula L.
Syn: *E. podperae* Croizat
Com: Leafy spurge
Hab: Weed of roadsides; waste places; prairies
A&D: Freq nw; infreq to rare elsewh
Org: Not native

E. falcata L.
Com: Falcate spurge
Hab: Mesic to dry mesic open areas
A&D: Rare in Loess Hills: MNN
Org: Not native

E. geyeri Engelm.
Syn: *Chamaesyce geyeri* (Engelm.) Small
Hab: Sandy fields; roadsides
A&D: Infreq to rare e 1/2
Org: Native

E. glyptosperma Engelm.
Syn: *Chamaesyce glyptosperma* (Engelm.) Small
Hab: Open, sandy soil; loess bluffs
A&D: Freq to common w 1/2; infreq to rare e 1/2
Org: Native

E. hexagona Nutt. ex Sprengel
Hab: Open, sandy soil; moist, sandy alluvium
A&D: Rare w 1/2; infreq e
Org: Native

E. maculata L.
Syn: *Chamaesyce maculata* (L.) Small
Syn: *E. supina* Raf., misappl.
Com: Carpet spurge
Hab: Low, sandy prairie remnants; roadsides; gardens; yards
A&D: Infreq wc, nw & nc; common elsewh
Org: Native

E. marginata Pursh
Com: Snow-on-the-mountain
Hab: Waste places; heavily grazed pastures; loess bluffs
A&D: Common w, especially in Loess Hills; infreq to rare se & sc
Org: Native

E. missurica Raf.
Hab: Along railroads
A&D: Rare c & wc: HRR & STO 1880's
Org: Native

E. nutans Lag.
Syn: *E. maculata* L., misappl.
Syn: *Chamaesyce nutans* (Lag.) Small
Syn: *E. preslii* Guss.
Com: Nodding spurge
Hab: Dry loess prairies; roadsides; disturbed areas
A&D: Infreq nc; freq to common elsewh
Org: Native

E. obtusata Pursh
Com: Blunt-leaved spurge, warty spurge
Hab: Woods
A&D: Rare s 2/3, & in nw: LYO 1897
Org: Native

E. peplus L.
Com: Petty spurge
Hab: Dry, disturbed soil
A&D: Rare se: MUS 1891
Org: Not native

E. prostrata Aiton
Hab: Dry, disturbed soil
A&D: Rare wc & sw: HRR, MIL & PAG
Org: Native

E. serpens HBK.
Syn: *Chamaesyce serpens* (HBK.) Small
Hab: Moist, sandy soil
A&D: Infreq to rare w 1/2
Org: Native

E. serpyllifolia Pers.
Syn: *Chamaesyce serpyllifolia* (Pers.) Small
Hab: Sandy alluvium; moist habitats; dry, loess bluffs
A&D: Infreq nw & nc; rare sw
Org: Native of U.S., but not Iowa

E. spathulata Lam.
Syn: *E. dictyosperma* Fischer & Meyer
Hab: Moist sand; alluvium
A&D: Rare thr most of state
Org: Native

E. stictospora Engelm.
Syn: *Chamaesyce stictospora* (Engelm.) Small
Hab: Disturbed loess prairies; pastures
A&D: Rare wc & nw: MNN, PLY & WOO
Org: Native

FABACEAE (LEGUMINOSAE)

Amorpha L.

A. canescens Pursh
Com: Lead plant
Hab: Prairie remnants; loess bluffs; dry, sandy, open habitats
A&D: Common thr
Org: Native

A. fruticosa L. [incl. var. *angustifolia* Pursh]
Com: Indigo bush, false indigo
Hab: Alluvium; marsh edges; streambanks; prairie swales
A&D: Freq to common thr most of state
Org: Native

A. nana Nutt.
Syn: *A. microphylla* Pursh
Com: Fragrant false indigo
Hab: Low, mesic prairies
A&D: Rare c, n, & sc
Org: Native

Amphicarpaea Ell. ex Nutt. (***Amphicarpa***)

A. bracteata (L.) Fern. [incl. var. *comosa* (L.) Fern.]
Com: Hog peanut
Hab: Woods; woodland edges; shores
A&D: Freq to common thr
Org: Native

Anthyllis L.

A. vulneraria L.
Hab: Fields & waste ground
A&D: Rare c & nc: STO & WRI, last collected in 1935
Org: Not native

Apios Fabr.

A. americana Medicus
Com: Ground-nut
Hab: Alluvial woods; streambanks; moist prairies
A&D: Absent nw; rare in Iowan Surface; freq to common elsewh
Org: Native

Astragalus L. Milk vetch

A. adsurgens Pallas var. *robustior* Hooker
Syn: *A. striatus* Nutt.
Hab: Gravelly prairie remnants
A&D: Rare nw: DIC & OSC
Org: Native

A. agrestis Douglas ex D. Don
Syn: *A. goniatus* Nutt.
Hab: Dry, gravelly, prairie remnants
A&D: Rare in nw & nc
Org: Native

A. canadensis L.
Com: Milk vetch
Hab: Prairies; roadsides; woodland borders
A&D: Common w 1/2; infreq to freq e 1/2
Org: Native

A. crassicarpus Nutt.
Syn: *A. caryocarpus* Ker
Com: Ground plum
Hab: Dry, gravelly or sandy prairies; loess prairies
A&D: Common nw & nc; infreq ne, sc & sw; rare or absent elsewh
Org: Native

A. distortus T. & G.
Com: Bent milk vetch
Hab: Sandy prairies; alluvium; open sandy soil
A&D: Infreq to rare e
Org: Native

A. flexuosus (Hooker) G. Don
Hab: Dry prairies
A&D: Rare nw: LYO
Org: Native

A. lotiflorus Hooker
Hab: Dry, gravelly prairies; loess bluffs
A&D: Common nw; rare nc & sw
Org: Native

A. missouriensis Nutt.
Hab: W-facing loess bluffs
A&D: Rare wc & nw: PLY & WOO
Org: Native

Baptisia Vent.

B. australis (L.) R. Br. var. *minor* (Lehm.) Fern.
Syn: *B. minor* Lehm.
Com: Blue wild indigo
Hab: Prairie remnants; roadsides
A&D: Rare nw, sc & sw: ADR, DEC & PAG
Org: Native

B. bracteata Muhl. ex Ell. var. *glabrescens* (Larisey) Isely
Syn: *B. leucophaea* Nutt.
Com: Cream wild indigo
Hab: Upland prairies; roadsides; open woods
A&D: Infreq to freq thr much of state; rare nw & extreme e
Org: Native

B. lactea (Raf.) Thieret
Syn: *B. leucantha* T. & G.
Syn: *B. alba* (L.) R. Br. var. *macrophylla* (Larisey) Isely
Com: White wild indigo
Hab: Prairie remnants; open, sandy soil; roadsides
A&D: Infreq to freq thr much of state; rare nw & extreme ne
Org: Native

B. tinctoria (L.) R. Br. [incl. var. *crebra* Fern.]
Com: Yellow wild indigo
Hab: Sandy woods
A&D: Rare sc: MAD 1917
Org: Native

Caragana Fabr.

C. arborescens Lam.
Com: Siberian pea tree
Hab: Spring
A&D: Rare ne: DUB
Org: Not native

Cassia L.

C. marilandica L.
Com: Wild senna
Hab: Moist alluvial, or open upland woods
A&D: Infreq s 1/2; rare ne & ec
Org: Native

Cercis L.

C. canadensis L.
Com: Redbud
Hab: Wooded ravines; wooded bluffs; alluvium
A&D: Common se; infreq sc & sw; adventive ne
Org: Native

Chamaecrista (L.) Moench

C. fasciculata (Michx.) Greene
Syn: *Cassia fasciculata* Michx.
Com: Partridge pea
Hab: Prairie remnants; dry, open habitats; roadsides; sandy areas
A&D: Freq to common thr
Org: Native

Coronilla L.

C. varia L.
Com: Crown vetch
Hab: Roadsides
A&D: Common, planted along highways thr
Org: Not native

Crotalaria L.

C. sagittalis L.
Com: Rattle box
Hab: Prairie remnants; woodland openings; dry, sandy soil
A&D: Infreq to freq n 1/2; rare s 1/2
Org: Native

Dalea L. ex Juss.

D. candida Willd.
Syn: *Petalostemon candidum* (Willd.) Michx.
Com: White prairie clover
Hab: Prairies
A&D: Common w 1/2; freq e 1/2; absent from Loess Hills
Org: Native

D. candida Willd. var. *oligophylla* (Torrey) Shinners
Syn: *Petalostemon occidentale* (Heller) Fern.
Hab: Dry loess bluffs; prairies
A&D: Infreq nw; rare sw
Org: Native

D. enneandra Nutt.
Syn: *D. laxiflora* Pursh
Hab: Dry loess bluffs; prairies
A&D: Common sw; infreq nw
Org: Native

D. leporina (Aiton) Bullock
Syn: *D. alopecuroides* Willd.
Com: Foxtail dalea
Hab: Sandy alluvium; sandy lake margins; moist prairies
A&D: Infreq s 1/2; rare nw & e; freq on Missouri R. floodplain
Org: Native

D. purpurea Vent.
Syn: *Petalostemon purpureum* (Vent.) Rydb.
Com: Purple prairie clover
Hab: Prairies; loess bluffs; gravelly hills
A&D: Freq to common thr
Org: Native

D. villosa (Nutt.) Sprengel
Syn: *Petalostemon villosum* Nutt.
Com: Silky prairie clover
Hab: Sandy prairies
A&D: Rare ne: BH
Org: Native

Desmanthus Willd.

D. illinoensis (Michx.) MacM. ex B. L. Robinson & Fern.
Com: Prairie mimosa, Illinois bundle flower
Hab: Loess bluffs; sandy alluvium
A&D: Common sw in loess; infreq to rare elsewh
Org: Native

Desmodium Desv. Tick-trefoil, tick clover

D. canadense (L.) DC.
Com: Showy tick-trefoil
Hab: Dry, open woods; roadsides; prairies
A&D: Common nw, ne & s; infreq to freq elsewh
Org: Native

D. canescens (L.) DC.
Com: Hoary tick-trefoil
Hab: Dry or clay soil; upland woodland openings
A&D: Infreq to rare thr
Org: Native

D. cuspidatum (Muhl. ex Willd.) Loudon [incl. var. *longifolium* (T. & G.) Schub.]
Com: Bracted tick-trefoil
Hab: Sandy or rocky woods; alluvium
A&D: Common ne; infreq to rare elsewh
Org: Native

D. glutinosum (Muhl. ex Willd.) Wood
Com: Pointed tick-trefoil
Hab: Moist woods
A&D: Freq to common thr most of state; rare nw
Org: Native

D. illinoense Gray
Com: Illinois tick-trefoil
Hab: Dry prairie remnants
A&D: Freq to common s 1/2 & e; rare elsewh
Org: Native

D. nudiflorum (L.) DC.
Com: Bare-stemmed tick-trefoil
Hab: Open, upland woods
A&D: Infreq in Pal. Plateau; rare remainder of e 1/2
Org: Native

D. paniculatum (L.) DC.
Syn: *D. dillenii* Darl.
Syn: *D. paniculatum* var. *dillenii* (Darl.) Isely
Syn: *D. perplexum* Schub.
Com: Panicled tick-trefoil
Hab: Sandy, alluvial woods; upland woodland openings
A&D: Common se; infreq to rare sc & sw; rare n 1/2
Org: Native

D. sessilifolium (Torrey) T. & G.
Com: Sessile-leaved tick-trefoil
Hab: Dry, upland woods; alluvial sand flats
A&D: Rare c, ne & se: BH 1895, DM, LEE & POW
Org: Native

Gleditsia L.

G. triacanthos L.
Com: Honey locust
Hab: Alluvial woods; old pastures; sandy prairies
A&D: Common thr most of state; infreq nw
Org: Native

Glycine L.

G. max (L.) Merr.
Com: Soybean
Hab: Fields; disturbed ground; roadsides
A&D: Common, widely cult, not persisting
Org: Not native

Glycyrrhiza L.

G. lepidota Pursh
Com: Wild licorice
Hab: Prairie remnants; loess bluffs; pastures
A&D: Freq to common w 1/2; waif along railroads in e 1/2
Org: Native

Gymnocladus Lam.

G. dioica (L.) K. Koch
Com: Kentucky coffee tree
Hab: Moist, wooded ravines; alluvium
A&D: Freq to infreq thr
Org: Native

Kummerowia Schindl.

K. stipulacea (Maxim.) Makino
Syn: *Lespedeza stipulacea* Maxim.
Com: Korean clover
Hab: Dry, open soil; roadsides; pastures; disturbed areas
A&D: Common se; infreq sc; rare ne
Org: Not native

K. striata (Thunb.) Schindl.
Syn: *Lespedeza striata* (Thunb.) H. & A.
Com: Japanese clover
Hab: Sandy prairie
A&D: Rare se: MUS
Org: Not native

Lathyrus L.

L. ochroleucus Hooker
Com: Wild pea, vetchling
Hab: Upland woods; n-facing, wooded talus slopes
A&D: Freq nc; rare ne & in Pal. Plateau
Org: Native

L. palustris L.
Com: Marsh vetchling
Hab: Moist prairie remnants; marshy shores
A&D: Common nc; infreq to rare elsewh
Org: Native

L. tuberosus L.
Hab: Roadsides; fencerows
A&D: Rare se, & in sw: CAS & ADM 1947
Org: Not native

L. venosus Muhl. ex Willd.
Com: Veiny pea
Hab: Dry, upland prairies; roadsides
A&D: Common nw & nc; infreq to absent elsewh
Org: Native

Lespedeza Michx. See also ***Kummerowia*** Bush clover

L. capitata Michx.
Com: Round-headed bush clover
Hab: Prairies; loess bluffs; dry, open, sandy soil
A&D: Common thr
Org: Native

L. cuneata (Dum.-Cours.) G. Don
Com: Silky bush clover
Hab: Roadsides; disturbed ground
A&D: Rare s 1/2
Org: Not native

L. daurica (Laxm.) Schindl.
Hab: Dry, open sand
A&D: Rare se: LOU
Org: Not native

L. leptostachya Engelm.
Com: Prairie bush clover
Hab: Prairie remnants; dry, gravelly prairies
A&D: Rare c, n & sc
Org: Native

L. repens (L.) Barton
Com: Creeping bush clover
Hab: Open woods
A&D: Rare se & sc: HEN 1897, MAH 1921 & VB 1932
Org: Native

L. violacea (L.) Pers.
Com: Violet bush clover
Hab: Open, upland woods; prairie remnants; exposed rocky ledges; gravelly soil
A&D: Common se; infreq c & sc; rare ne & sw
Org: Native

L. virginica (L.) Britton
Com: Slender bush clover
Hab: Woodland edges; open, upland woods; prairie remnants
A&D: Freq se; rare sc & sw
Org: Native

Lotus L.

L. corniculatus L.
Com: Bird's-foot trefoil
Hab: Roadsides; waste places
A&D: Infreq to rare thr
Org: Not native

L. purshianus Clem. & Clem.
Syn: *L. americanus* (Nutt.) Bisch.
Hab: Dry prairies; woodland openings; sandy soil
A&D: Rare nw, nc & se; no records since 1926
Org: Native

Lupinus L.

L. perennis L. [incl. var. *occidentalis* S. Watson]
Com: Wild lupine
Hab: Dry, sandy prairies; sandy openings in woods
A&D: Rare ne: ALL & WNS 1893
Org: Native

Medicago L.

M. falcata L.
Syn: *M. sativa* L. ssp. *falcata* (L.) Arcangeli
Com: Yellow alfalfa
Hab: Waste places; field edges; roadsides
A&D: Rare c & w: LYO, MRS, PAG, SAC & SIO
Org: Not native

M. lupulina L.
Com: Black medic
Hab: Roadsides; along railroads; other waste places
A&D: Freq to common thr
Org: Not native

M. sativa L.
Com: Alfalfa
Hab: Fields; roadsides; disturbed soil
A&D: Common escape from cult
Org: Not native

Melilotus P. Miller

M. alba Medicus
Com: White sweet clover
Hab: Roadsides; disturbed soil; fields
A&D: Common thr
Org: Not native

M. officinalis (L.) Pallas
Com: Yellow sweet clover
Hab: Roadsides; disturbed soil; fields
A&D: Common thr
Org: Not native

Orbexilum Raf.

O. onobrychis (Nutt.) Rydb.
Syn: *Psoralea onobrychis* Nutt.
Hab: Moist woods; woodland openings
A&D: Rare se: DM & LEE 1931
Org: Native

Oxytropis DC.

O. lambertii Pursh
Com: Locoweed, Lambert's crazy weed
Hab: Loess bluffs; dry, gravelly hillsides
A&D: Infreq w except common in Loess Hills
Org: Native

Pediomelum Rydb.

P. argophyllum (Pursh) Grimes
Syn: *Psoralea argophylla* Pursh
Com: Silvery scurf-pea
Hab: Dry prairies; loess bluffs
A&D: Freq to common w 1/2; rare ne
Org: Native

P. esculentum (Pursh) Rydb.
Syn: *Psoralea esculenta* Pursh
Com: Prairie turnip
Hab: Dry, upland prairies; loess bluffs
A&D: Freq to common w, especially in Loess Hills; infreq to rare nc & sc
Org: Native

Petalostemon see ***Dalea***

Psoralea See ***Orbexilum***, ***Pediomelum***, or ***Psoralidium***

Psoralidium Rydb.

P. batesii Rydb.
Syn: *Psoralea tenuiflora* Pursh var. *floribunda* (Nutt.) Rydb.
Com: Scurfy pea
Hab: Dry prairies; openings in woods
A&D: Rare to infreq s 1/2 & nc
Org: Native

P. lanceolatum (Pursh) Rydb.
Syn: *Psoralea lanceolata* Pursh
Hab: Dry, sandy soil
A&D: Rare w: HRR, MNN, POT, SIO & WOO
Org: Native

Robinia L.

R. pseudoacacia L.
Com: Black locust
Hab: Disturbed woodlands; open hillsides
A&D: Freq to common thr most of state; often escaping from cult
Org: Native of U.S., but not Iowa

Schrankia Willd.

S. nuttallii (DC. ex Britton & Rose) Standley
Syn: *S. uncinata* Willd., misappl.
Com: Sensitive brier
Hab: Sandy soil; loess bluffs
A&D: Rare c, wc & sw: HRR 1926, MIL, TAM 1895
Org: Native

Strophostyles Ell. Wild bean

S. helvula (L.) Ell.
Hab: Dry, open, mostly sandy soil
A&D: Common se & sw; freq to infreq elsewh
Org: Native

S. leiosperma (T. & G.) Piper
Hab: Dry, sandy, upland woods
A&D: Freq to common s 1/2; infreq to rare n 1/2
Org: Native

Tephrosia Pers.

T. virginiana (L.) Pers.
Com: Goat's-rue
Hab: Dry, sandy soil; loess bluffs
A&D: Infreq e; rare nw & ne
Org: Native

Trifolium L. Clover

T. arvense L.
Com: Rabbit-foot clover
Hab: Disturbed soil; roadsides; pastures
A&D: Rare thr
Org: Not native

T. aureum Pollich
Syn: *T. agrarium* L.
Com: Hop-clover
Hab: Roadsides; disturbed prairies
A&D: Rare e & sw
Org: Not native

T. campestre Schreber
Syn: *T. procumbens* L., misappl.
Com: Low hop-clover
Hab: Disturbed, open habitats
A&D: Freq to common nc & sc; infreq to rare e 1/2
Org: Not native

T. dubium Sibth.
Com: Little hop-clover
Hab: Disturbed places
A&D: Rare ec & se: CED, JEF 1935 & WAS
Org: Not native

T. hybridum L.
Com: Alsike clover
Hab: Disturbed soil; field edges
A&D: Freq to common thr
Org: Not native

T. incarnatum L.
Com: Crimson clover
Hab: Disturbed soil; waste ground
A&D: Rare c, ne & ec: DAL 1924, FAY 1898 & IOW 1903
Org: Not native

T. pratense L.
Com: Red clover
Hab: Fields; roadsides; disturbed soil
A&D: Common thr
Org: Not native

T. reflexum L.
Com: Buffalo clover
Hab: Sandy soil; upland prairies
A&D: Rare ec & s
Org: Native

T. repens L.
Com: White clover
Hab: Lawns; roadsides; pastures
A&D: Common thr
Org: Not native

T. resupinatum L.
Com: Persian clover
Hab: Lawns; disturbed soil
A&D: Rare se: JEF 1935
Org: Not native

Vicia L. Vetch

V. americana Muhl. ex Willd.
Com: Vetch
Hab: Prairie remnants; loess bluffs; roadsides
A&D: Freq to common n 1/2; infreq to rare s 1/2
Org: Native

V. americana Muhl. ex Willd. var. *minor* Hooker
Hab: Prairie remnants; loess bluffs; roadsides
A&D: Rare w
Org: Native

V. cracca L.
Com: Cow vetch
Hab: Disturbed soil
A&D: Rare nw: CLY 1945
Org: Not native

V. sativa L.
Syn: *V. angustifolia* Reichard var. *segetalis* (Thuill.) Seringe
Com: Common vetch
Hab: Roadsides; fields
A&D: Rare ec: SCO
Org: Not native

V. sativa L. var. *nigra* L.
Syn: *V. angustifolia* Reichard
Com: Narrow-leaved vetch
Hab: Roadsides; pastures; margins of upland woods
A&D: Freq in Pal. Plateau; rare remainder of ne & nc
Org: Not native

V. villosa Roth
Hab: Roadsides; old fields; sandy soil
A&D: Infreq to rare thr most of state
Org: Not native

Wisteria Nutt.

W. frutescens (L.) Poiret
Hab: Floodplains
A&D: Rare escape from cult in c: BOO & HRD
Org: Native of U.S., but not Iowa

FAGACEAE

Castanea P. Miller

C. dentata (Marsh.) Borkh.
Com: American chestnut
Hab: Open ground near human habitation
A&D: Rare: scattered trees persisting from cult
Org: Native of U.S., but not Iowa

Quercus L.

Q. alba L.
Com: White oak
Hab: Upland woods; dry slopes
A&D: Rare sw; absent nw; common elsewh
Org: Native

Q. X *bebbiana* Schneider
Syn: *Q. alba* X *Q. macrocarpa*
Hab: Dry soil
A&D: Rare se: MUS 1895
Org: Native

Q. bicolor Willd.
Com: Swamp white oak
Hab: Alluvial woods
A&D: Infreq to freq e 2/3
Org: Native

Q. borealis Michx. f. var. *maxima* (Marsh.) Ashe
Syn: *Q. rubra* L. nom. ambig.
Com: Northern red oak
Hab: Moist, upland woods
A&D: Rare nw; freq to common elsewh
Org: Native

Q. X *bushii* Sarg.
Syn: *Q. marilandica* X *Q. velutina*
Hab: Dry, often sandy, woods
A&D: Freq se & sc
Org: Native

Q. X *deamii* Trel.
Syn: *Q. alba* X *Q. muhlenbergii*
Hab: Upland forest
A&D: Rare se: DM 1929
Org: Native

Q. ellipsoidalis E. J. Hill
Com: Hill's oak, northern pin oak
Hab: Open, sandy, upland woods
A&D: Freq to common ne; infreq extreme e
Org: Native

Q. X *exacta* Trel.
Syn: *Q. imbricaria* X *Q. palustris*
Hab: Floodplain forest
A&D: Rare se: DM
Org: Native

Q. X *fernowii* Trel.
Syn: *Q. alba* X *Q. stellata*
Hab: Upland woods
A&D: Rare se: LEE
Org: Native

Q. X *hawkinsii* Sudw.
Syn: *Q. borealis* X *Q. velutina*
Hab: None given
A&D: Rare sc: APP 1906
Org: Native

Q. imbricaria Michx.
Com: Shingle oak
Hab: Bottomlands; dry hillsides
A&D: Common in extreme se; infreq in southern tier of counties
Org: Native

Q. X *leana* Nutt.
Syn: *Q. imbricaria* X *Q. velutina*
Hab: Low, sandy woods
A&D: Rare se: DM & KEO
Org: Native

Q. macrocarpa Michx.
Com: Bur oak
Hab: Dry uplands; slopes
A&D: Freq to common thr
Org: Native

Q. marilandica Muench.
Com: Blackjack oak
Hab: Upland woods
A&D: Rare se
Org: Native

Q. muhlenbergii Engelm.
Syn: *Q. prinoides* Willd. var. *acuminata* (Michx.) Gl.
Com: Chinquapin oak, yellow chestnut oak
Hab: Exposed bluffs; rocky slopes
A&D: Common e & sw; freq se & sc; rare c
Org: Native

Q. palustris Muench.
Com: Pin oak
Hab: Alluvial woods
A&D: Common se; infreq e; rare sc & sw
Org: Native

Q. X *paleolithicola* Trel.
Syn: *Q. ellipsoidalis* X *Q. velutina*
Hab: Grazed woods
A&D: Rare se: KEO
Org: Native

Q. prinoides Willd.
Com: Dwarf chinquapin oak
Hab: Dry ridges; rocky bluffs
A&D: Rare sc & sw
Org: Native

Q. X *schuettei* Trel.
Syn: *Q. bicolor* X *Q. macrocarpa*
Syn: *Q.* X *hillii* Trel.
Hab: Sandy, alluvial woods
A&D: Rare ne: BRE
Org: Native

Q. stellata Wang.
Com: Post oak
Hab: Dry, open, upland woods
A&D: Rare se & sc: APP, DEC, HEN 1941, LEE & VB 1941
Org: Native

Q. velutina Lam.
Com: Black oak
Hab: Upland woods; sandy, alluvial flats
A&D: Common se 2/3; freq c; rare nw
Org: Native

GENTIANACEAE

Gentiana L.

G. alba Muhl.
Syn: *G. flavida* Gray
Com: Pale gentian, yellow gentian
Hab: Open, upland woods; rocky slopes; prairie remnants
A&D: Infreq to rare thr most of state; not reported nw
Org: Native

G. andrewsii Griseb.
Com: Bottle gentian, closed gentian
Hab: Moist prairie remnants
A&D: Freq in Iowan Surface & c; infreq to rare e & sc
Org: Native

G. X *billingtonii* Farw.
Syn: *G. andrewsii* X *G. puberulenta*
Syn: *G. saponaria* L., misappl.
Com: Soapwort gentian
Hab: Moist prairie remnants; sandy woods
A&D: Rare nc, ne, ec & sc: DEC, DUB & JOH
Org: Native

G. puberulenta J. Pringle
Syn: *G. puberula* Michx., misappl.
Com: Downy gentian
Hab: Upland woods; prairie remnants
A&D: Infreq to rare thr most of state; freq nc
Org: Native

Gentianella Moench

G. quinquefolia (L.) Small ssp. *occidentalis* (A. Gray) J. Gillett
Syn: *Gentiana quinquefolia* L. var. *occidentalis* (A. Gray) A. S. Hitchc.
Com: Stiff gentian
Hab: Prairie openings; algific talus slopes; wooded slopes
A&D: Infreq to rare ne 1/2
Org: Native

Gentianopsis Ma

G. crinita (Froel.) Ma
Syn: *Gentiana crinita* Froel.
Com: Fringed gentian
Hab: Mesic prairies; sandy lowlands; fens
A&D: Rare nc, ne & in lakes area
Org: Native

G. procera (Holm) Ma
Syn: *Gentiana procera* Holm.
Com: Small fringed gentian
Hab: Fens
A&D: Rare n, & in c: MRS 1902
Org: Native

Sabatia Adanson

S. campestris Nutt.
Com: Prairie rose gentian
Hab: Moist, upland woods; prairies
A&D: Rare ec & se: JAC 1924 & LEE 1931
Org: Native

GERANIACEAE

Erodium L'Her. ex Aiton

E. cicutarium (L.) L'Her.
Com: Pin clover, stork's bill
Hab: Fields; disturbed ground
A&D: Rare c & nw: BV 1920, CHE 1924 & STO 1914
Org: Not native

Geranium L.

G. bicknellii Britton
Com: Northern cranesbill
Hab: Sandy woods; fields
A&D: Rare c, nw & ne: EMM 1922, FAY 1893 & WEB 1905
Org: Native

G. carolinianum L. [incl. var. *confertifolium* Fern.]
Syn: *G. sphaerospermum* Fern. in part
Com: Cranesbill
Hab: Sandy prairies; alluvial flats
A&D: Freq to rare sw; infreq to rare elsewh
Org: Native

G. maculatum L.
Com: Wild geranium
Hab: Moist, wooded slopes; sandy prairies
A&D: Not reported nw; common elsewh
Org: Native

HALORAGIDACEAE

Myriophyllum L.

M. exalbescens Fern.
Com: American milfoil
Hab: Shallow water of marshes & lakes
A&D: Infreq nc, in Iowan Surface & in lakes area; rare sc & sw
Org: Native

M. heterophylum Michx.
Com: Water milfoil
Hab: Shallow lakes; marshes; ponds
A&D: Rare c, nw & nc: CLY 1895, DIC 1901, EMM, PA 1938, WEB 1905 & WNB
Org: Native

M. pinnatum (Walter) BSP.
Com: Rough water milfoil
Hab: Muddy shores; shallow water
A&D: Rare ne & s: DEC 1899, DUB 1900, FRE, LEE, LUC, MUS & RIN 1898
Org: Native

M. spicatum L.
Com: Spiked water milfoil
Hab: Shallow standing water
A&D: Rare: HAN
Org: Not native

M. verticillatum L.
Hab: Shallow water
A&D: Rare c, nw & ne: BH, DIC, EMM, PA 1938 & WEB 1906
Org: Native

Proserpinaca L.

P. palustris L. [incl. var. *creba* Fern. & Griseb.]
Com: Mermaid weed
Hab: Shallow water; muddy shores
A&D: Rare ec & se: CLI & MUS
Org: Native

HAMAMELIDACEAE

Hamamelis L.

H. virginiana L.
Com: Witch hazel
Hab: Moist, wooded, n-facing slopes
A&D: Infreq extreme e, except common in Pal. Plateau
Org: Native

HIPPOCASTANACEAE

Aesculus L.

A. glabra Willd. [incl. var. *arguta* (Buckley) Robinson]
Com: Ohio buckeye
Hab: Moist, or sandy, lowland woods
A&D: Common se & sc; infreq sw; infreq escape from cult nc
Org: Native

A. hippocastanum L.
Com: Horse chestnut
Hab: Moist woods
A&D: Occasional escape from cult thr
Org: Not native

HIPPURIDACEAE

Hippuris L.

H. vulgaris L.
Com: Mare's-tail
Hab: Muddy shores; shallow, standing water of marshes or ponds
A&D: Rare nw & nc: CG 1903, CLY 1936 & DIC 1948
Org: Native

HYDROPHYLLACEAE

Ellisia L.

E. nyctelea L.
Com: Waterpod, wild tomato
Hab: Wooded alluvial flats; disturbed woods
A&D: Freq to common thr
Org: Native

Hydrophyllum L.

H. appendiculatum Michx.
Com: Appendaged waterleaf
Hab: Low, moist woods
A&D: Freq in Pal. Plateau; infreq s 1/2, ec & se; rare elsewh
Org: Native

H. virginianum L.
Com: Virginia waterleaf
Hab: Moist, wooded slopes & alluvium
A&D: Common nw 1/2; freq se 1/2
Org: Native

HYPERICACEAE

Hypericum L. (Some authors place in Guttiferae) St. John's wort

H. boreale (Britton) Bickn.
Com: Northern St. John's wort
Hab: Sandy margins of marshes
A&D: Rare ec: LIN
Org: Native

H. canadense L.
Com: Canadian St. John's wort
Hab: Moist, prairie lowlands
A&D: Rare ne: WNS 1933
Org: Native

H. drummondii (Grev. & Hooker) T. & G.
Com: Nits and lice
Hab: Dry, wooded slopes
A&D: Rare se: VB 1933
Org: Native

H. gentianoides (L.) BSP.
Com: Pineweed
Hab: Open, sandy soil
A&D: Rare e & sc: BUC, CLI 1932, MAD 1917 & MUS pre-1900
Org: Native

H. majus (Gray) Britton
Hab: Marsh margins; prairie swales
A&D: Infreq to rare thr most of state
Org: Native

H. mutilum L.
Com: Weak St. John's wort
Hab: Seepage slopes; margins of marshes & ponds
A&D: Freq se; infreq sc; rare ne 1/4
Org: Native

H. perforatum L.
Com: Common St. John's wort
Hab: Dry roadsides; sandy fields; disturbed prairies
A&D: Freq sw; infreq to rare elsewh
Org: Not native

H. prolificum (Spach) Steudel
Syn: *H. spathulatum* (Spach) Steudel
Com: Shrubby St. John's wort
Hab: Rocky streambanks; pastures
A&D: Freq se; rare sc & sw
Org: Native

H. punctatum Lam.
Syn: *H. maculatum* Walter
Com: Spotted St. John's wort
Hab: Open woods; prairie remnants
A&D: Freq to common s & in Iowan Surface; rare nc & in Pal. Plateau
Org: Native

H. pyramidatum Aiton
Syn: *H. ascyron* L.
Com: Giant St. John's wort
Hab: Marshes; riverbanks
A&D: Freq to infreq n 1/2; infreq to rare s 1/2
Org: Native

H. sphaerocarpum Michx.
Com: Round-fruited St. John's wort
Hab: Prairie remnants; moist, usually sandy ground
A&D: Freq to common e 1/2; rare nw & sw: FRE 1890, PA 1939
Org: Native

Triadenum Raf.

T. fraseri (Spach) Gl.
Syn: *T. virginicum* (L.) Raf.
Syn: *Hypericum virginicum* L. var. *fraseri* (Spach) Fern.
Com: Marsh St. John's wort
Hab: Sandy shores; low, sandy woods; marshes; sedge meadows
A&D: Rare n & e
Org: Native

JUGLANDACEAE

Carya Nutt.

C. cordiformis (Wang.) K. Koch
Com: Bitternut hickory
Hab: Upland woods; wooded slopes; bluffs
A&D: Infreq nw & nc; common elsewh
Org: Native

C. illinoensis (Wang.) K. Koch
Syn: *C. pecan* (Marsh.) Engelm. & Graebn.
Com: Pecan
Hab: Alluvial woods
A&D: Rare se 1/4, ne (DUB); introduced in nc (KOS)
Org: Native

C. laciniosa (Michx. f.) Loudon
Com: Kingnut hickory
Hab: Alluvial woods
A&D: Rare se 1/4
Org: Native

C. ovata (P. Miller) K. Koch
Com: Shagbark hickory
Hab: Dry, upland woods; bluffs
A&D: Rare nw; common elsewh
Org: Native

C. tomentosa (Poiret) Nutt.
Syn: *C. alba* K. Koch, misappl.
Com: Mockernut hickory
Hab: Dry, upland woods; slopes
A&D: Infreq se; rare elsewh in s
Org: Native

Juglans L.

J. cinerea L.
Com: Butternut
Hab: Moist, wooded slopes; alluvial woods
A&D: Common e & nc; infreq sw
Org: Native

J. nigra L.
Com: Black walnut
Hab: Moist woodlands, especially alluvial woods
A&D: Common thr
Org: Native

LAMIACEAE (LABIATAE)

Agastache Clayton ex Gronovius

A. foeniculum (Pursh) Kuntze
Com: Blue giant-hyssop
Hab: Upland woods; dry, wooded slopes
A&D: Rare c, nw & ne: CLY, CLT 1933, DIC, EMM, LYO & STO 1948
Org: Native

A. nepetoides (L.) Kuntze
Com: Yellow giant-hyssop
Hab: Open, upland woods; alluvium; woodland edges
A&D: Freq sc; infreq to rare elsewh
Org: Native

A. scrophulariifolia (Willd.) Kuntze
Com: Purple giant-hyssop
Hab: Woodlands; edges of woods
A&D: Common nc; infreq to rare elsewh
Org: Native

Ballota L.

B. nigra L.
Com: Black horehound
Hab: Dry, disturbed habitats
A&D: Rare sw: MIL
Org: Not native

Blephilia Raf.

B. ciliata (L.) Bentham
Com: Pagoda plant
Hab: Open woods; fields
A&D: Rare se & sc: APP 1902, DAV 1939, DM, HEN n.d., JEF 1934, LEE & VB
Org: Native

B. hirsuta (Pursh) Bentham
Com: Wood mint
Hab: Moist woods; wooded slopes; shaded alluvium
A&D: Not reported from nw; rare nc & in Iowan Surface; infreq elsewh
Org: Native

Dracocephalum L.

D. parviflorum Nutt.
Syn: *Moldavica parviflora* (Nutt.) Britton
Com: Dragonhead
Hab: Dry, often sandy or rocky, soils
A&D: Rare n, ec & sc
Org: Native

Galeopsis L.

G. tetrahit L.
Com: Hemp nettle
Hab: Moist, open or alluvial woods
A&D: Rare wc, ne & sw
Org: Not native

Glechoma L.

G. hederacea L. [incl. var. *micrantha* Moric.]
Com: Creeping Charlie, ground ivy
Hab: Moist woods; shaded alluvium; roadsides; yards
A&D: Rare nw; infreq sw; freq to common elsewh
Org: Not native

Hedeoma Pers.

H. hispidum Pursh
Com: Rough pennyroyal
Hab: Dry soil; rocky woods; prairies
A&D: Freq to common thr
Org: Native

H. pulegioides (L.) Pers.
Com: American pennyroyal
Hab: Open, upland woods; prairies; roadsides
A&D: Common se; infreq to rare extreme e, sc & sw
Org: Native

Isanthus see ***Trichostema***

Lamium L.

L. amplexicaule L.
Com: Dead nettle, henbit
Hab: Naturalized in waste areas
A&D: Infreq s & nc; rare nw & ne: PA & WNS
Org: Not native

L. purpureum L.
Com: Purple dead nettle
Hab: Fields; disturbed ground
A&D: Rare c, ec & se: DM, JOH & STO
Org: Not native

Leonurus L. Motherwort

L. cardiaca L.
Com: Motherwort
Hab: Disturbed woods; shaded, disturbed areas
A&D: Freq to common thr
Org: Not native

L. marrubiastrum L.
Hab: Moist, grassy areas; along railroads
A&D: Freq in sw; rare nc, ne & ec: CED, JOH, WNS & WRI
Org: Not native

L. sibiricus L.
Hab: Waste ground; disturbed soil
A&D: Rare c: POW
Org: Not native

Lycopus L. Water horehound

L. americanus Muhl. ex Barton
Com: Water horehound
Hab: Marshes; muddy shores
A&D: Rare in Pal. Plateau; infreq nw & extreme e; common elsewh
Org: Native

L. asper Greene
Hab: Alluvium; margins of lakes & marshes
A&D: Infreq w; rare in lakes area & extreme e
Org: Native

L. uniflorus Michx.
Com: Northern bugleweed
Hab: Wet ground of lake edges & marshes
A&D: Freq n 1/2; rare elsewh
Org: Native

L. virginicus L.
Hab: Open, wet ground; alluvium; stream margins
A&D: Not reported nw; infreq to rare elsewh
Org: Native

Marrubium L. Horehound

M. vulgare L.
Hab: Weed of fields; waste places
A&D: Infreq s & ec
Org: Not native

Mentha L. Mint

M. arvensis L. [incl. var. *villosa* (Bentham) Stewart; var. *glabrata* (Bentham) Fern.]
Com: Wild mint
Hab: Marshes; prairie swales; shallow water
A&D: Rare nw; infreq in Iowan Surface; freq to common elsewh
Org: Native

M. X *gentilis* L.
Syn: *M. arvensis* X *M. spicata*
Syn: *M. cardiaca* Gerarde ex Baker
Hab: Moist, disturbed soil
A&D: Freq cult, occasionally escaping or persisting
Org: Not native

M. X *piperita* L.
Syn: *M. aquatica* X *M. spicata*
Com: Peppermint
Hab: Alluvial woods
A&D: Freq cult, occasionally escaping or persisting
Org: Not native

M. spicata L.
Com: Spearmint
Hab: Moist ground or disturbed soil
A&D: Freq cult, occasionally escaping or persisting
Org: Not native

Monarda L.

M. didyma L.
Com: Oswego tea
Hab: Disturbed ground; roadsides
A&D: Rare e: ALL 1922, LEE 1924 & SCO 1880's
Org: Not native

M. fistulosa L. [incl. var. *mollis* (L.) Bentham]
Com: Wild bergamot, horsemint
Hab: Prairies; roadsides; other dry, open habitats
A&D: Common thr
Org: Native

M. punctata L. var. *villicaulis* (Pennell) Shinners
Com: Spotted horsemint
Hab: Dry, sandy prairies
A&D: Freq to common e & in Pal. Plateau; rare sc, sw & in Iowan Surface
Org: Native

Nepeta L.

N. cataria L.
Com: Catnip
Hab: Disturbed, dry, open ground
A&D: Freq to common thr
Org: Not native

Perilla L.

P. frutescens (L.) Britton
Com: Beefsteak plant
Hab: Woodland edges
A&D: Rare c, ec & se: CLI, DAV 1940, JOH, JON 1948 & STO
Org: Not native

Physostegia Bentham

P. parviflora Nutt. ex Gray
Syn: *Dracocephalum nuttallii* Bentham
Com: Obedient plant, small-flowered false dragonhead
Hab: Streambanks; open, moist habitats
A&D: Freq to common ne 1/2; infreq se & sw
Org: Native

P. virginiana (L.) Bentham
Syn: *P. speciosa* Sweet
Com: False dragonhead
Hab: Moist-to-mesic woods; prairies
A&D: Rare nw; infreq elsewh
Org: Native

Prunella L.

P. vulgaris L.
Com: Self heal
Hab: Lawns; waste ground
A&D: Rare w; occasional elswh
Org: Not native

P. vulgaris L. var. *lanceolata* (Bartram) Fern.
Com: Self heal
Hab: Disturbed, open woods; moist, open habitats
A&D: Rare nw; common elsewh
Org: Native

Pycnanthemum Michx. Mountain mint

P. pilosum Nutt.
Com: Hairy mountain mint
Hab: Dry woods & prairies
A&D: Freq se; rare nw: EMM 1923
Org: Native

P. tenuifolium Schrader
Syn: *P. flexuosum* (Walter) BSP., misappl.
Com: Slender mountain mint
Hab: Moist prairies
A&D: Freq to common s 1/2; infreq to rare n 1/2
Org: Native

P. virginianum (L.) Dur. & Jackson
Com: Common mountain mint
Hab: Prairies; along railroads; roadsides
A&D: Common e 2/3; infreq to rare w
Org: Native

Salvia L.

S. nemorosa L.
Syn: *S. sylvestris* L., misappl.
Hab: Roadsides; waste ground
A&D: Rare wc & nw: DIC, EMM & GUT
Org: Not native

S. pitcheri Torrey ex Bentham
Syn: *S. azurea* Lam.
Com: Pitcher's sage
Hab: Dry prairies
A&D: Rare w & ec: CLY, FRE, HRR & LIN
Org: Native

S. reflexa Hornem.
Syn: *S. lanceolata* Willd.
Com: Rocky mountain sage, lance-leaved salvia
Hab: Dry soil of roadsides; railroad ballast; waste ground
A&D: Freq to common w 1/2; infreq to rare se 1/4
Org: Native

S. sylvestris L.
Hab: Waste ground
A&D: Rare nw: DIC 1920
Org: Not native

Satureja L.

S. vulgaris (L.) Fritsch
Syn: *Clinopodium vulgare* L.
Com: Basil
Hab: Dry soil near dwellings
A&D: Rare ne & ec: ALL & JOH 1907
Org: Not native

Scutellaria L. Skullcap

S. galericulata L.
Syn: *S. epilobiifolia* A. Hamilton
Hab: Marshes
A&D: Common in lakes area; infreq to rare elsewh
Org: Native

S. incana Biehler
Com: Downy scullcap
Hab: Dry woods & openings
A&D: Rare se: LOU 1892
Org: Native

S. lateriflora L.
Com: Mad-dog skullcap
Hab: Marshes; shores; alluvial bottoms
A&D: Common ne 2/3; freq sc & sw; rare nw
Org: Native

S. leonardii Epling
Syn: *S. parvula* Michx. var. *leonardii* (Epling) Fern.
Hab: Dry, sandy prairies; rocky soil; moist, wooded slopes
A&D: Infreq to freq thr
Org: Native

S. nervosa Pursh [incl. var. *calvifolia* Fern.]
Hab: Open alluvial woods
A&D: Rare ec & se: JEF 1930 & LIN
Org: Native

S. ovata Hill [incl. var. *versicolor* (Nutt.) Fern.]
Hab: Moist-to-dry calcareous woods
A&D: Freq se; infreq to rare ne, ec & in Pal. Plateau
Org: Native

S. parvula Michx.
Hab: Dry, sandy prairies; rocky soil; occasionally on wooded slopes
A&D: Common in Pal. Plateau; infreq nw; freq elsewh
Org: Native

Stachys L. Hedge nettle

S. aspera Michx.
Syn: *S. hyssopifolia* Michx. var. *ambigua* Gray
Hab: Marshy shores
A&D: Rare ne, ec & sc: CLT, JOH & MAH
Org: Native

S. palustris L. [incl. var. *pilosa* (Nutt.) Fern.; var. *homotricha* Fern.; var. *phaneropoda* Weath.]
Com: Woundwort
Hab: Marshes; moist ground
A&D: Infreq nw; freq to common elsewh
Org: Native

S. tenuifolia Willd. [incl. var. *hispida* (Pursh) Fern.]
Syn: *S. hispida* Pursh
Hab: Alluvial woods; marshes; moist prairies
A&D: Common e; infreq to rare elsewh
Org: Native

Teucrium L.

T. canadense L. [incl. var. *virginicum* (L.) Eaton]
Com: American germander
Hab: Low woods; wet prairies; wet ditches
A&D: Freq to common thr
Org: Native

T. canadense L. var. *boreale* (Bickn.) Shinners
Syn: *Teuchrium canadense* L. var. *occidentale* (Gray) McCl. & Epling
Com: Wood sage, germander
Hab: Alluvial woods; marshes; moist prairies
A&D: Infreq nw; common elsewh
Org: Native

Trichostema L. Bluecurls

T. brachiatum L.
Syn: *Isanthus brachiatus* (L.) BSP.
Com: False pennyroyal
Hab: Dry prairies; loess bluffs
A&D: Common extreme e; infreq to rare elsewh
Org: Native

T. dichotomum L.
Com: Blue curls
Hab: Margins of woods & fields
A&D: Rare: MAD 1917
Org: Native

LAURACEAE

Sassafras Trew

S. albidum (Nutt.) Nees
Com: Sassafras
Hab: Dry crest of bluff
A&D: Rare se: a single station in LEE
Org: Native

LENTIBULARIACEAE

Utricularia L.

U. gibba L.
Com: Humped bladderwort
Hab: Shallow, standing water; muddy shores
A&D: Rare ec & se: JOH & MUS 1878
Org: Native

U. intermedia Hayne
Com: Flat-leaved bladderwort
Hab: Shallow, standing water
A&D: Rare nw: CLY 1939 & EMM 1904
Org: Native

U. minor L.
Com: Small bladderwort
Hab: Shallow water of fens
A&D: Rare nw & nc: CG, DIC, EMM 1880 & HAN
Org: Native

U. vulgaris L.
Syn: *U. macrorhiza* Le Conte
Com: Common bladderwort
Hab: Shallow water of ponds & marshes
A&D: Freq nw & nc; infreq to rare elsewh
Org: Native

LIMNANTHACEAE

Floerkea Willd.

F. proserpinacoides Willd.
Com: False mermaid
Hab: Shaded seepage areas
A&D: Rare ne: DUB
Org: Native

LINACEAE

Linum L.

L. medium (Planchon) Britton var. *texanum* (Planchon) Fern.
Com: Wild flax
Hab: Dry, open woods
A&D: Rare se: DM 1925, JEF 1933 & LEE 1928
Org: Native

L. perenne L.
Com: Flax
Hab: Waste ground; field edges
A&D: Rare escape from cult
Org: Not native

L. rigidum Pursh [incl. var. *compactum* (A. Nelson) Rogers]
Com: Stiff flax
Hab: Dry loess bluffs
A&D: Freq to rare w
Org: Native

L. sulcatum Riddell
Com: Wild flax
Hab: Dry prairies; sandy soil; loess bluffs
A&D: Common sw; rare se; freq to infreq elsewh
Org: Native

L. usitatissimum L.
Com: Cultivated flax
Hab: Roadsides; fencerows; railroad ballast; fields
A&D: Rare escape from cult, not persisting
Org: Not native

LOASACEAE

Mentzelia L.

M. decapetala (Pursh) Urban & Gilg
Com: Sand lily
Hab: Crests of dry loess bluffs; roadcuts
A&D: Rare wc & nw: HRR, PLY & WOO
Org: Native

LYTHRACEAE

Ammannia L.

A. coccinea Rottb.
Com: Toothcup
Hab: Moist, often sandy habitats; marsh edges
A&D: Common sw; infreq to rare elsewh; no records from Pal. Plateau
Org: Native

A. robusta Heer & Regel
Hab: Moist, often sandy habitats; marsh edges
A&D: Rare s
Org: Not native

Cuphea P. Br.

C. viscosissima Jacq.
Syn: *C. petiolata* (L.) Koehne
Com: Waxweed
Hab: Upland woodland margins; gravelly hills
A&D: Rare se: DAV, JEF 1935 & LEE 1917
Org: Native

Decodon J. F. Gmelin

D. verticillatus (L.) Ell.
Com: Swamp loosestrife
Hab: Marsh edges; moist, sandy, pond margins
A&D: Rare ne & ec: ALL & SCO 1890
Org: Native

Didiplis Raf.

D. diandra (DC.) Wood
Syn: *Peplis diandra* (DC.) Nutt.
Com: Water purslane
Hab: Shallow, standing water
A&D: Rare e 1/2
Org: Native

Lythrum L. Purple loosestrife

L. alatum Pursh
Syn: *L. dacotanum* Nieuw.
Com: Winged loosestrife
Hab: Marsh edges; wet prairies; fens
A&D: Common in lakes area; infreq to rare elsewh
Org: Native

L. salicaria L.
Com: Purple loosestrife
Hab: Marshes; lakeshores; streambanks
A&D: Rare thr, escaping from cult & spreading rapidly
Org: Not native

Rotala L.

R. ramosior (L.) Koehne
Com: Toothcup
Hab: Margins of ponds, streams & marshes
A&D: Rare n, c & e
Org: Native

MAGNOLIACEAE

Liriodendron L.

L. tulipifera L.
Com: Tulip tree, yellow poplar
Hab: Cult situations
A&D: Commonly planted in se; a population is reproducing in LEE
Org: Native of U.S., but not Iowa

MALVACEAE

Abutilon P. Miller

A. theophrasti Medicus
Com: Velvet leaf
Hab: Weed of cult fields
A&D: Common thr
Org: Not native

Alcea L.

A. rosea L.
Syn: *Althaea rosea* (L.) Cav.
Com: Hollyhock
Hab: Roadsides; disturbed ground near human habitation
A&D: Common thr most of state
Org: Not native

Callirhoe Nutt. Poppy mallow

C. alcaeoides (Michx.) Gray
Hab: Prairies
A&D: Rare nw & sw: DIC, PAG
Org: Native

C. bushii Fern.
Hab: Roadside prairies
A&D: Rare sw: PAG
Org: Native

C. involucrata (Nutt. ex T. & G.) Gray
Com: Purple poppy mallow
Hab: Roadsides; disturbed ground
A&D: Rare nw & s 1/2
Org: Native

C. triangulata (Leavenw.) Gray
Com: Clustered loosestrife
Hab: Dry, sandy plains & prairies
A&D: Rare e: ALL, CLI & DAV (early 1900's)
Org: Native

Hibiscus L.

H. laevis All.
Syn: *H. militaris* Cav.
Com: Halberd-leaved rose mallow
Hab: Wet, alluvial bottoms; pond & marsh shores
A&D: Freq to infreq ec, se & sc; rare nc, sw & in Pal. Plateau
Org: Native

H. trionum L.
Com: Flower-of-an-hour
Hab: Field edges; roadsides
A&D: Rare ne; freq to common elsewh
Org: Not native

Malva L. Mallow

M. neglecta Wallr.
Com: Cheeses
Hab: Waste ground
A&D: Common sw 1/2; infreq to rare elsewh
Org: Not native

M. parviflora L.
Com: Little mallow
Hab: Disturbed soil
A&D: Rare nw: EMM
Org: Not native

M. rotundifolia L.
Com: Round-leaved mallow
Hab: Waste ground; farmyards; roadsides
A&D: Freq to common thr
Org: Not native

M. sylvestris L.
Com: High mallow
Hab: Waste ground; roadsides
A&D: Rare escape from cult, no records since 1924
Org: Not native

M. verticillata L.
Hab: Disturbed soil; waste ground
A&D: Rare escape from cult, last record in 1929
Org: Not native

Malvastrum Gray

M. hispidum (Pursh) Hochr.
Syn: *M. angustum* Gray
Syn: *Sidopsis hispida* (Pursh) Rydb.
Hab: Streambanks
A&D: Rare ec & se: MUS 1895 & SCO 1898
Org: Native

Napaea L.

N. dioica L.
Com: Glade mallow
Hab: Moist, alluvial woods
A&D: Rare nc & ne: ALL, BH, BUT, FAY, FLO n.d., HOW & WNS
Org: Native

Sida L.

S. spinosa L.
Com: Prickly mallow
Hab: Waste or disturbed ground
A&D: Infreq to freq s 1/2
Org: Not native

Sphaeralcea St. Hil.

S. coccinea (Nutt.) Rydb.
Syn: *Malvastrum coccineum* (Nutt.) Gray
Com: Scarlet mallow
Hab: Crests of dry loess bluffs
A&D: Rare wc, nw & sw: HRR, PLY & POT
Org: Native

MARTYNIACEAE

Proboscidea Schmidel

P. louisianica (P. Miller) Thell.
Com: Unicorn plant
Hab: Riverbanks; sandy habitats
A&D: Rare nw, ec, se & sc: DIC 1912, EMM 1883, KEO 1897, MAD 1910, MUS 1884 & SCO
Org: Native of U.S., but not Iowa

MELASTOMATACEAE

Rhexia L.

R. virginica L.
Com: Meadow beauty
Hab: Moist, sandy soil
A&D: Rare ec & se: CED, CLI & MUS
Org: Native

MENISPERMACEAE

Menispermum L.

M. canadense L.
Com: Moonseed
Hab: Woods; woodland borders
A&D: Freq to common thr
Org: Native

MENYANTHACEAE

Menyanthes L.

M. trifoliata L.
Com: Buckbean
Hab: Shallow water of fens & marshes
A&D: Rare n 1/2, & in se: MUS
Org: Native

MORACEAE

Cannabis L. (Some authors place in Cannabaceae)

C. sativa L.
Com: Hemp, marijuana
Hab: Wide variety of disturbed habitats; waste ground
A&D: Common thr
Org: Not native

Humulus L. (Some authors place in Cannabaceae)

H. japonicus Sieb. & Zucc.
Com: Japanese hops
Hab: Waste ground; roadsides; moist woods
A&D: Freq sw; infreq to rare e 2/3
Org: Not native

H. lupulus L.
Com: Common hops
Hab: Floodplains; low, open woods
A&D: Infreq to freq thr most of state
Org: Native

Maclura Nutt.

M. pomifera (Raf. ex Sarg.) Schneider
Com: Osage orange, hedge apple
Hab: Roadsides; fencerows; successional fields; once planted for fencerows
A&D: Common escape from cult, especially in s 1/2
Org: Native of U.S., but not Iowa

Morus L.

M. alba L.
Com: Chinese mulberry, white mulberry
Hab: Woods; roadsides; riverbanks; loess bluffs
A&D: Common thr
Org: Not native

M. rubra L.
Com: Red mulberry
Hab: Moist alluvial woods; wooded slopes
A&D: Infreq to freq sw 1/2
Org: Native

NYCTAGINACEAE

Mirabilis L.

M. albida (Walter) Heimerl
Syn: *Oxybaphus albidus* (Walter) Sweet
Com: Pale four-o'clock
Hab: Dry prairies; gravelly hills
A&D: Rare nw, nc & sc
Org: Native

M. hirsuta (Pursh) MacM.
Syn: *Oxybaphus hirsutus* (Pursh) Sweet
Com: Hairy four-o'clock
Hab: Dry prairies; loess bluffs; gravel hills
A&D: Freq to infreq w 1/2
Org: Native

M. nyctaginea (Michx.) MacM.
Syn: *Oxybaphus nyctagineus* (Michx.) Sweet
Com: Wild four-o'clock
Hab: Dry sandy or gravelly soil; roadsides; along railroads
A&D: Common thr
Org: Native

NYMPHAEACEAE

Brasenia Schreber (Some authors place in Cabombaceae)

B. schreberi J. F. Gmelin
Com: Watershield
Hab: Shallow, standing water
A&D: Rare in scattered localities thr
Org: Native

Nelumbo Adanson (Some authors place in Nelumbonaceae)

N. lutea (Willd.) Pers.
Com: American lotus
Hab: Shallow water; backwaters of rivers
A&D: Freq to rare in Mississippi R. basin; rare along Missouri R.; introduced into a few interior lakes
Org: Native

Nuphar Sm.

N. luteum (L.) Sibth. & Smith ssp. *variegatum* (Engelm. ex Dur.) E. O. Beal
Syn: *N. advena* (Aiton) Aiton f.
Syn: *N. variegatum* Engelm. ex Dur.
Com: Yellow water lily
Hab: Shallow water of ponds & marshes
A&D: Not reported from sw; infreq to rare elsewh
Org: Native

Nymphaea L.

N. tuberosa Paine
Syn: *N. odorata* Aiton
Com: White water lily
Hab: Shallow, standing water of marshes & ponds
A&D: Freq in lakes area; infreq to rare elsewh
Org: Native

OLEACEAE

Fraxinus L.

F. americana L.
Com: White ash
Hab: Upland woods
A&D: Infreq nc; absent nw; freq to common elsewh
Org: Native

F. nigra Marsh.
Com: Black ash
Hab: Moist, wooded slopes; alluvium
A&D: Absent w; infreq to rare se & sc; freq to common elsewh
Org: Native

F. pennsylvanica Marsh.
Com: Red ash
Hab: Alluvial or low, moist woods
A&D: Common sw; rare elsewh
Org: Native

F. pennsylvanica Marsh. var. *lanceolata* (Borkh.) Sarg.
Syn: *F. lanceolata* Borkh.
Syn: *F. pennsylvanica* Marsh. var. *subintegerrima* (Vahl) Fern.
Com: Green ash
Hab: Edges of low, moist woods
A&D: Freq to common thr
Org: Native

F. quadrangulata Michx.
Com: Blue ash
Hab: Rocky bluffs
A&D: Rare se: DM & LEE
Org: Native

Syringa L.

S. vulgaris L.
Com: Lilac
Hab: Disturbed ground around old dwelling sites
A&D: Freq persists from cult
Org: Not native

ONAGRACEAE

Calylophus Spach

C. serrulatus (Nutt.) Raven
Syn: *Oenothera serrulata* Nutt.
Com: Toothed evening primrose
Hab: Sandy or gravelly prairies; dry uplands
A&D: Common nw & nc; freq to infreq rest of nw 1/2
Org: Native

Circaea L.

C. alpina L.
Com: Enchanter's nightshade
Hab: Moist, shaded, sandstone cliffs; algific talus slopes
A&D: Freq in Pal. Plateau; rare se: MUS 1896
Org: Native

C. lutetiana L. ssp. *canadensis* (L.) Ascherson & Magnus
Syn: *C. quadrisulcata* (Maxim.) Franch. & Sav. var. *canadensis* (L.) Hara
Com: Enchanter's nightshade
Hab: Moist woods
A&D: Freq to common thr
Org: Native

Epilobium L. Willow herb

E. angustifolium L.
Com: Fireweed
Hab: Dry roadsides; open woods; talus slopes
A&D: Infreq ne 1/4; rare nc
Org: Native

E. ciliatum Raf.
Syn: *E. adenocaulon* Hassk.
Syn: *E. glandulosum* Lehm. var. *adenocaulon* (Hassk.) Fern.
Hab: Marshes; sedge meadows
A&D: Common sw; infreq to rare elsewh
Org: Native

E. coloratum Biehler
Com: Cinnamon willowherb
Hab: Marshes; moist woods
A&D: Freq to common thr; not reported from extreme w
Org: Native

E. leptophyllum Raf.
Syn: *E. densum* L., misappl.
Syn: *E. lineare* L., misappl.
Com: Bog willowherb
Hab: Margins of marshes; sedge meadows; fens
A&D: Freq in lakes area; otherwise rare to infreq n 1/2
Org: Native

E. strictum Muhl.
Hab: Fens
A&D: Rare ne: BH, BRE, BUC & CHI
Org: Native

E. X *wisconsinense* Ugent
Syn: *E. ciliatum* X *E. coloratum*
Hab: Margins of marshes
A&D: Rare nw: LYO 1910
Org: Native

Gaura L.

G. biennis L. [incl. var. *pitcheri* T. & G.]
Syn: *G. longiflora* Spach
Syn: *G. filiformis* Small
Hab: Prairie remnants; open, sandy areas; roadsides
A&D: Freq to common s 1/2; infreq to rare ne 1/4; rare nw: EMM
Org: Native

G. coccinea Pursh
Hab: Dry loess bluffs
A&D: Freq in Loess Hills
Org: Native

G. parviflora Douglas
Hab: Crests of loess bluffs; dry, upland prairies
A&D: Infreq in Loess Hills of sw; rare se, & in c & ec: IOW 1940 & STO 1892
Org: Native

Ludwigia L. False loosestrife

L. alternifolia L.
Com: Seedbox
Hab: Marsh shores; moist, sandy habitats
A&D: Infreq se & sc
Org: Native

L. palustris (L.) Ell.
Com: Water purslane
Hab: Marshes; wet sand
A&D: Rare e
Org: Native

L. peploides (HBK.) Raven ssp. *glabrescens* (Kuntze) Raven
Syn: *Jussiaea repens* L. var. *glabrescens* Kuntze
Hab: Shallow water; muddy shores
A&D: Rare s: FRE, LOU & LUC
Org: Native

L. polycarpa Short & Peter
Com: False loosestrife
Hab: Marshes; shallow, standing water
A&D: No records from wc; rare nw & sw; infreq to freq elsewh
Org: Native

Oenothera L. Evening primrose

O. biennis L. ssp. *centralis* Munz
Hab: Sandy roadsides; disturbed prairie remnants
A&D: Infreq to rare e 1/2
Org: Native

O. laciniata Hill
Com: Ragged evening primrose
Hab: Sandy soil; prairie remnants; along railroads
A&D: Freq to infreq se 1/3; rare nw, sc & sw
Org: Native

O. parviflora L.
Syn: *O. cruciata* Nutt.
Hab: Marshes; alluvial woods; clearings
A&D: Rare c, nc, ne & se
Org: Native

O. perennis L.
Com: Small sundrops
Hab: Moist prairies
A&D: Rare ne & ec: DEL, FAY, HOW, LIN & WNS
Org: Native

O. pilosella Raf.
Com: Prairie sundrops
Hab: Prairie remnants; open, sandy soil; margins of fens
A&D: Infreq se 1/2
Org: Native

O. rhombipetala Nutt. ex T. & G.
Syn: *O. clelandii* D. Dietr. & Raven
Com: Sand primrose
Hab: Dry, sandy soil
A&D: Freq e; infreq to rare c & sc
Org: Native

O. speciosa Nutt.
Com: Showy evening primrose
Hab: Roadsides; along railroads
A&D: Rare nc & s: CLR, FRE, KOS & VB
Org: Native

O. villosa Thunb.
Syn: *O. biennis* L. var. *canescens* T. & G.
Syn: *O. strigosa* (Rydb.) Mack. & Bush
Com: Gray evening primrose
Hab: Prairie remnants; open, alluvial woods
A&D: Common thr
Org: Native

OROBANCHACEAE

Conopholis Wallr.

C. americana (L.) Wallr.
Com: Cancer-root, squaw-root
Hab: Parasitic on roots of oak trees
A&D: Rare ne: ALL
Org: Native

Orobanche L.

O. fasciculata Nutt.
Com: Clustered broomrape
Hab: Parasitic on roots of *Artemesia* spp. & paper birch
A&D: Rare nw & ne: ALL & DIC 1933
Org: Native

O. ludoviciana Nutt.
Com: Broomrape
Hab: Parasitic on roots of Asteraceae
A&D: Rare nw: LYO 1896
Org: Native

O. uniflora L.
Com: One-flowered cancer-root
Hab: Moist woods; parasitic on various species
A&D: Rare se 1/3, & in wc: GUT
Org: Native

OXALIDACEAE

Oxalis L.

O. dillenii Jacq.
Syn: *O. stricta* L., misappl.
Com: Yellow wood sorrel
Hab: Sandy fields; prairies
A&D: Infreq to rare e & sc
Org: Native

O. stricta L.
Syn: *O. europaea* Jordan
Com: Yellow wood sorrel, lady's sorrel
Hab: Roadsides; moist, open ground; disturbed soil
A&D: Freq s 1/2; infreq extreme e & nw; common ne
Org: Native

O. violacea L.
Com: Violet wood sorrel
Hab: Prairie remnants; loess bluffs; dry, sparsely-wooded ridges
A&D: Infreq sw 1/4; freq to common elsewh
Org: Native

PAPAVERACEAE

Adlumia Raf. ex DC. (Some authors place in Fumariaceae)

A. fungosa (Aiton) Greene
Hab: Wooded bluff
A&D: Rare ec: BEN 1910
Org: Not native

Argemone L.

A. albiflora Hornem.
Syn: *A. intermedia* Sweet, misappl.
Com: Prickly poppy
Hab: Sandy, disturbed ground
A&D: Rare wc, ec & se: IOW 1927, LOU & SAC 1923
Org: Not native

A. mexicana L.
Com: Mexican poppy
Hab: Waste ground
A&D: Rare se: HEN 1897 & MUS 1896
Org: Not native

A. polyanthemos (Fedde) G. Ownbey
Hab: Dry pasture in loess bluffs
A&D: Rare nw: PLY
Org: Native of U.S., but not Iowa

Chelidonium L.

C. majus L.
Com: Swallow-wort, celandine
Hab: Moist woods; open alluvium
A&D: Rare escape from cult: ALL, BH, CHE, IOW, JOH & WNS
Org: Not native

Corydalis Vent. (Some authors place in Fumariaceae)

C. aurea Willd.
Com: Golden corydalis
Hab: Dry, rocky hillsides
A&D: Rare in scattered localities thr
Org: Native

C. curvisiliqua Engelm. ssp. *grandibracteata* (Fedde) G. Ownbey
Hab: Open, sandy soil
A&D: Rare se & sc: HEN, LEE, LOU, MAH & MUS
Org: Native

C. micrantha (Engelm.) Gray
Com: Slender fumewort
Hab: Dry, sandy soil
A&D: Freq se & sc; infreq sw; infreq to rare nc & ne
Org: Native

C. sempervirens (L.) Pers.
Com: Pink corydalis
Hab: Dry or rocky wooded slopes
A&D: Rare ne: ALL
Org: Native

Dicentra Bernh. (Some authors place in Fumariaceae)

D. canadensis (Goldie) Walp.
Com: Squirrel corn
Hab: Moist, n- & e-facing, wooded slopes
A&D: Freq ne 1/4; absent w; infreq elsewh
Org: Native

D. cucullaria (L.) Bernh.
Com: Dutchman's breeches
Hab: Moist, wooded slopes
A&D: Freq nw; common elsewh
Org: Native

Fumaria L. (Some authors place in Fumariaceae)

F. officinalis L.
Com: Fumitory
Hab: Disturbed areas; railroad tracks
A&D: Rare sc & sw: adventive in WAY & PAG
Org: Not native

Sanguinaria L.

S. canadensis L.
Com: Bloodroot
Hab: Upland woods; ravines
A&D: Freq to common thr
Org: Native

PHRYMACEAE

Phryma L. (Some authors place in Verbenaceae)

P. leptostachya L.
Com: Lopseed
Hab: Woods
A&D: Freq to common thr
Org: Native

PHYTOLACCACEAE

Phytolacca L.

P. americana L.
Com: Pokeweed
Hab: Alluvial woods; fencerows; old pastures; sandy, waste areas
A&D: Freq se; infreq sc; rare nc, ne & sw
Org: Native

PLANTAGINACEAE

Plantago L. Plantain

P. aristata Michx.
Com: Bracted plantain
Hab: Dry, open habitats
A&D: Common s 1/2; infreq elsewh
Org: Native

P. cordata Lam.
Hab: Along wooded streams
A&D: Rare ec: SCO (an 1847 collection by Parry from near Davenport)
Org: Native

P. indica L.
Hab: Along railroad tracks
A&D: Rare se: JEF 1933
Org: Not native

P. lanceolata L.
Com: Buckhorn plantain
Hab: Dry, disturbed areas
A&D: Rare ne; infreq extreme e; freq to common elsewh; spreading rapidly
Org: Not native

P. major L.
Hab: Yards; pastures; waste places
A&D: Common w; infreq to rare elsewh
Org: Not native

P. patagonica Jacq.
Syn: *P. purshii* R. & S.
Hab: Roadsides; dry, sandy prairies; loess bluffs; waste ground
A&D: Common w; infreq elsewh
Org: Native

P. rugelii Dcne.
Com: Common plantain, Rugel's plantain
Hab: Yards; open woods; disturbed soil; waste ground
A&D: Common thr
Org: Native

P. virginica L.
Hab: Dry, open places, usually sandy
A&D: Freq se; infreq sc; rare sw
Org: Native

PLATANACEAE

Platanus L.

P. occidentalis L.
Com: Sycamore
Hab: Alluvial woods
A&D: Freq to common s 1/2 & e; rare in Pal. Plateau
Org: Native

POLEMONIACEAE

Collomia Nutt.

C. linearis Nutt.
Hab: Dry, or sandy, prairies; along railroads
A&D: Rare: adventive in n, ec & sc
Org: Not native

Ipomopsis Michx.

I. rubra (L.) Wherry
Syn: *Gilia rubra* (L.) Heller
Com: Standing cypress
Hab: Sandy soil
A&D: Rare escape from cult in nc, ec & sw: CG, FRE & JOH
Org: Not native

Navarretia R. & P.

N. intertexta (Bentham) Hooker
Hab: Vernal pools
A&D: Rare nw, & in sw: PAG 1920
Org: Native of U.S., but not Iowa

Phlox L.

P. bifida Beck
Com: Cleft phlox
Hab: Dry, open sand; sand prairies
A&D: Rare e 1/2
Org: Native

P. divaricata L. [incl. ssp. *laphamii* (Wood) Wherry]
Com: Sweet William, blue phlox
Hab: Moist woods
A&D: Infreq nw; freq to common elsewh
Org: Native

P. maculata L.
Hab: Prairie swales; moist roadsides; fens
A&D: Freq ne; infreq nc; rare ec, & in sc: WAR
Org: Native

P. paniculata L.
Com: Garden phlox
Hab: Roadsides; disturbed soil near dwellings
A&D: Infreq to rare escape from cult thr
Org: Native of U.S., but not Iowa

P. pilosa L. [incl. ssp. *fulgida* (Wherry) Wherry]
Com: Prairie phlox
Hab: Prairie remnants; open, sandy plains
A&D: Infreq se; freq to common elsewh
Org: Native

P. subulata L.
Com: Moss-pink
Hab: Sandy or gravelly soil near dwellings
A&D: Rare escape from cult
Org: Not native

Polemonium L.

P. reptans L.
Com: Jacob's ladder
Hab: Open woods; woodland edges; wet prairies; fens
A&D: Common e 1/2; infreq to rare w 1/2
Org: Native

POLYGALACEAE

Polygala L.

P. cruciata L.
Com: Milkwort
Hab: Dry, usually sandy soil; vernal pools
A&D: Rare ne & se: BUC & MUS 1898
Org: Native

P. incarnata L.
Com: Pink milkwort
Hab: Dry, sandy soil
A&D: Rare e & sw
Org: Native

P. polygama Walter var. *obtusata* Chodat
Com: Purple milkwort
Hab: Sandy plains; sand blowouts
A&D: Rare e: ALL, BUC, CLI, JAC, LIN & WAP 1941
Org: Native

P. sanguinea L.
Syn: *P. viridescens* L.
Com: Field milkwort
Hab: Prairie remnants; openings in woods; sandy, moist places
A&D: Freq to infreq e 2/3
Org: Native

P. senega L. [incl. var. *latifolia* T. & G.]
Com: Seneca snakeroot
Hab: Dry, rocky soil; sparsely wooded slopes; openings on bluffs
A&D: Freq in Iowan Surface; infreq in Pal. Plateau; rare c & se
Org: Native

P. verticillata L. [incl. var. *isocycla* Fern.; var. *sphenostachya* Pennell; var. *ambigua* (Nutt.) Wood]
Com: Whorled milkwort
Hab: Dry slopes; prairie remnants
A&D: Freq sw; rare nc; infreq elsewh
Org: Native

POLYGONACEAE

Fagopyrum P. Miller

F. esculentum Moench
Syn: *F. sagittatum* Gilib.
Com: Buckwheat
Hab: Roadsides; fencerows; disturbed soil near dwellings
A&D: Rare escape from cult thr, not persisting
Org: Not native

Polygonella Michx.

P. articulata (L.) Meisner
Hab: Sand dunes; blowouts; dry, open habitats
A&D: Rare c & e: ALL, BUC, CLI, HRD 1902, JAC, LOU 1910, MUS & WNS
Org: Native

Polygonum L. Smartweed

P. achoreum Blake
Hab: Open, disturbed areas
A&D: Freq to common thr
Org: Native

P. amphibium L. var. *emersum* Michx.
Syn: *P. coccineum* Muhl.
Com: Water smartweed
Hab: Muddy shores; standing water of marshes
A&D: Common nc, sc & sw; infreq nw & ec; rare in Pal. Plateau
Org: Native

P. amphibium L. var. *stipulaceum* (Coleman) Fern.
Syn: *P. fluitans* Eaton
Syn: *P. natans* Eaton
Hab: Edges of marshes & ponds; shallow, standing water
A&D: Common nc, sc, & in lakes area
Org: Native

P. aviculare L.
Syn: *P. arenastrum* Jordan ex Boreau
Com: Knotweed
Hab: Yards; dry, disturbed areas
A&D: Freq to common thr
Org: Not native

P. cespitosum Blume var. *longisetum* (DeBruyn) Stewart
Com: Creeping smartweed
Hab: Roadsides; disturbed, moist soil
A&D: Rare sw: MIL
Org: Not native

P. convolvulus L.
Com: Black bindweed
Hab: Roadsides; alluvial woods; waste places
A&D: Freq to common thr
Org: Not native

P. cuspidatum Sieb. & Zucc.
Com: Japanese bamboo
Hab: Roadsides
A&D: Infreq e; rare elsewh
Org: Not native

P. douglasii Greene
Hab: Sandy or gravelly soil
A&D: Rare ne: ALL
Org: Native

P. erectum L.
Hab: Roadsides; dry, disturbed soil
A&D: Infreq to rare e
Org: Native

P. hydropiper L.
Hab: Shallow water; marshes; stream margins
A&D: Not reported from extreme nw counties; freq to common elsewh
Org: Native

P. hydropiperoides Michx.
Hab: Shallow water; shores; marshes
A&D: Rare c, ec, se & sc
Org: Native

P. lapathifolium L.
Hab: Alluvial woods; shores; waste ground
A&D: Common w 1/2 & in Pal. Plateau; freq elsewh
Org: Native

P. orientale L.
Hab: Moist, disturbed soil; waste places
A&D: Infreq s & e
Org: Not native

P. pensylvanicum L. var. *laevigatum* Fern.
Syn: *P. bicorne* Raf.
Syn: *P. longistylum* Small
Hab: Fields; marshes; ponds; open, wet habitats
A&D: Common thr
Org: Native

P. persicaria L.
Com: Lady's thumb
Hab: Open, wet habitats
A&D: Infreq to rare ne 1/4; freq to common elsewh
Org: Not native

P. punctatum Ell. [incl. var. *confertiflorum* (Meisner) Fassett]
Syn: *P. acre* HBK.
Com: Water smartweed
Hab: Open, wet ground; marsh edges; prairie swales
A&D: Rare nw; freq to common elsewh
Org: Native

P. ramosissimum Michx.
Syn: *P. prolificum* (Small) B. L. Robinson
Com: Bushy knotweed
Hab: Moist, usually sandy soil
A&D: Common sw; freq nc; infreq e 1/2
Org: Native

P. sagittatum L.
Com: Tearthumb
Hab: Open, marshy ground
A&D: Freq ne 1/4; infreq se & sc
Org: Native

P. scandens L. [incl. var. *cristatum* (Engelm. & Gray) Gl.; var. *dumetorum* (L.) Gl.]
Com: Climbing false buckwheat
Hab: Roadsides; fencerows; alluvial woods
A&D: Common nc & sw; freq e 1/2; rare nw
Org: Native

P. tenue Michx.
Hab: Dry, open, sandy habitats; Sioux Quartzite outcrops
A&D: Freq in Pal. Plateau; infreq to rare elsewh
Org: Native

P. virginianum L.
Syn: *Tovara virginianum* (L.) Raf.
Com: Jumpseed
Hab: Moist, wooded slopes & ravines
A&D: Common nc & ec; infreq nw; freq elsewh
Org: Native

Rumex L. Dock

R. acetosella L.
Com: Red sorrel
Hab: Dry, sandy soil or waste ground
A&D: Infreq sc; freq to common elsewh
Org: Not native

R. altissimus Wood
Hab: Prairie remnants; open, alluvial woods
A&D: Infreq in Pal. Plateau; freq to common elsewh
Org: Native

R. crispus L.
Com: Curly dock
Hab: Open, moist, often disturbed, habitats
A&D: Infreq sc & sw; freq to common elsewh
Org: Not native

R. maritimus L. var. *fueginus* (Phil.) Dusen
Syn: *R. persicarioides* L., misappl.
Hab: Shores; marshes; wet sand
A&D: Freq nc & in lakes area; rare elsewh
Org: Not native

R. mexicanus Meisner
Syn: *R. triangulivalvis* (Danser) Rech. f.
Hab: Moist, open soil; disturbed ground
A&D: Not reported sw; infreq to rare elsewh
Org: Native

R. obtusifolius L.
Com: Bitter dock
Hab: Roadsides; sandy marshes; moist lowlands
A&D: Infreq to rare thr
Org: Not native

R. occidentalis S. Watson
Hab: Moist lowlands
A&D: Rare ne: ALL
Org: Native

R. orbiculatus Gray
Hab: Pond margins; marshes; prairie swales; fens
A&D: Infreq to rare thr
Org: Native

R. patientia L.
Hab: Moist roadsides; alluvium; sandy soil
A&D: Infreq n & e
Org: Not native

R. venosus Pursh
Hab: Roadsides; railroads
A&D: Rare ne & se: DM, DUB 1936
Org: Native of U.S., but not Iowa

R. verticillatus L.
Hab: Lake margins; marshes; low, moist ground
A&D: Freq e 1/2
Org: Native

PORTULACACEAE

Claytonia L.

C. virginica L.
Com: Spring beauty
Hab: Moist, wooded slopes
A&D: Freq to common thr
Org: Native

Montia L.

M. chamissoi (Ledeb. ex Sprengel) Greene
Hab: Shaded, wet, sandstone ledges
A&D: Rare ne: FAY 1898
Org: Native

Portulaca L.

P. grandiflora Hooker
Com: Moss-rose
Hab: Waste ground; disturbed sites
A&D: Widely cult, rarely escapes, not persisting
Org: Not native

P. oleracea L.
Com: Common purslane
Hab: Waste ground; yards; disturbed habitats
A&D: Common thr
Org: Not native

Talinum Adanson

T. parviflorum Nutt. ex T. & G.
Com: Prairie fameflower
Hab: Thin soil over Sioux Quartzite rock outcrops
A&D: Rare nw: LYO
Org: Native

T. rugospermum Holz.
Com: Fameflower
Hab: Blowouts in sandy plains
A&D: Rare ne: ALL
Org: Native

PRIMULACEAE

Anagallis L.

A. arvensis L.
Hab: Disturbed ground
A&D: Rare c & ec: JOH, SCO 1886 & STO
Org: Not native

Androsace L.

A. occidentalis Pursh
Com: Rock jasmine
Hab: Dry, often sandy, open habitats
A&D: Freq nc & extreme e; infreq to rare elsewh
Org: Native

Dodecatheon L.

D. amethystinum Fassett
Syn: *D. pulchellum* (Raf.) Merr.
Syn: *D. radicatum* Greene
Com: Jeweled shooting star
Hab: Limestone & sandstone cliffs & ledges
A&D: Rare ne & ec: ALL, CLT, DUB, JAC & WNS
Org: Native

D. meadia L. [incl. var. *brachycarpum* (Small) Fassett]
Com: Shooting star
Hab: Prairie remnants; open, upland, wooded bluffs
A&D: Common in Iowan Surface; infreq se; rare in DM lobe & in Pal. Plateau
Org: Native

Lysimachia L. Loosestrife

L. ciliata L.
Com: Fringed loosestrife
Hab: Moist, lowland woods; low prairies; marsh edges
A&D: Infreq to common thr
Org: Native

L. clethroides Duby
Hab: Disturbed soil
A&D: Rare escape from cult
Org: Not native

L. hybrida Michx.
Syn: *L. lanceolata* Walter var. *hybrida* (Michx.) Gray
Hab: Alluvial woods, shores & marshy ground
A&D: Rare c & nw; freq to common elsewh
Org: Native

L. lanceolata Walter
Hab: Moist woods; bottomlands; edges of wooded streams
A&D: Freq to infreq n 1/2
Org: Native

L. nummularia L.
Com: Moneywort
Hab: Alluvial woods; open, moist habitats; moist, disturbed soil
A&D: Freq ne 1/4; infreq nc; rare se & sc
Org: Not native

L. punctata L.
Hab: Roadsides; woodland edges; disturbed sites
A&D: Rare escape from cult
Org: Not native

L. quadriflora Sims
Hab: Low, moist ground; alluvium; marsh edges
A&D: Common nc; freq ne 1/4; infreq to rare nw, ec & se
Org: Native

L. terrestris (L.) BSP.
Com: Swamp loosestrife, swamp candle
Hab: Marshes; low prairies; wet, sandy ground
A&D: Not reported from nw; infreq to rare elsewh
Org: Native

L. thyrsiflora L.
Hab: Marshes, often in standing, shallow water
A&D: Infreq nc & in lakes area; rare ne & se
Org: Native

Primula L.

P. mistassinica Michx.
Com: Bird's-eye primrose
Hab: Seeps; wet limestone or sandstone cliffs
A&D: Rare c: HRD 1921
Org: Native

RANUNCULACEAE

Aconitum L.

A. noveboracense Gray
Syn: *A. uncinatum* L. ssp. *noveboracense* (Gray) Hardin
Com: Northern wild monkshood
Hab: Moist limestone or sandstone cliffs; algific talus slopes
A&D: Rare c, ne & ec: ALL, CLT, DEL, DUB, HRD & JAC
Org: Native

Actaea L.

A. pachypoda Ell.
Syn: *A. alba* (L.) Miller
Com: White baneberry
Hab: Upland woods; wooded slopes
A&D: Freq to common e 1/2 & c; rare sw
Org: Native

A. rubra (Aiton) Willd.
Com: Red baneberry
Hab: Upland woods; wooded slopes
A&D: Rare se & sc; freq to common elsewh
Org: Native

Anemone L. see also ***Pulsatilla***

A. canadensis L.
Com: Canada anemone
Hab: Moist prairies; roadsides; alluvium
A&D: Freq extreme e & sc; common elsewh
Org: Native

A. caroliniana Walter
Com: Carolina anemone
Hab: Dry, usually sandy, open places
A&D: Freq in DM lobe; infreq to rare elsewh
Org: Native

A. cylindrica Gray
Com: Windflower, thimbleweed
Hab: Prairie remnants; dry, sandy soil; loess bluffs
A&D: Common nw 1/2; infreq to rare elsewh
Org: Native

A. quinquefolia L. [incl. var. *interior* Fern.]
Com: Wood anemone
Hab: Open, upland woods; wooded slopes
A&D: Common ne & in Pal. Plateau; infreq extreme e & c; rare se & sc
Org: Native

A. virginiana L.
Com: Tall anemone
Hab: Wooded slopes; woodland openings; woodland edges; prairie remnants
A&D: Freq sc; infreq nw; common elsewh
Org: Native

Anemonella see ***Thalictrum***

Aquilegia L.

A. canadensis L. [incl. var. *coccinea* (Small) Munz]
Com: Columbine
Hab: Moist, wooded slopes, often on rocky or sandy soil; limestone & sandstone outcrops
A&D: Freq sc & sw; common elsewh
Org: Native

Caltha L.

C. palustris L.
Com: Marsh marigold
Hab: Marshes; springs; seeps; fens
A&D: Freq nc & ne 1/4; rare nw, se & sw
Org: Native

Cimicifuga Wernischeck

C. racemosa (L.) Nutt.
Com: Bugbane
Hab: Lowland woods; wooded slopes
A&D: Rare wc: WOO 1938
Org: Native

Clematis L.

C. occidentalis (Hornem.) DC.
Syn: *C. verticillaris* DC.
Hab: Steep, rocky, n- or e-facing, talus slopes; algific slopes
A&D: Rare ne: ALL, CLT, DUB & WNS
Org: Native

C. pitcheri T. & G.
Com: Leather flower
Hab: Openings in woods; sandy alluvium; occasionally on prairies
A&D: Common se; freq sc; infreq to rare elsewh
Org: Native

C. virginiana L.
Com: Virgin's bower
Hab: Disturbed, open, alluvial woods
A&D: Freq to common n 1/2; infreq s 1/2
Org: Native

Consolida (DC.) S. F. Gray

C. ambigua (L.) Ball & Heywood
Syn: *Delphinium ajacis* L.
Hab: Disturbed ground; exposed soil; roadsides
A&D: Rare escape from cult s
Org: Not native

Delphinium L. see also ***Consolida***

D. carolinianum Walter
Hab: Often sandy, dry soil
A&D: Rare c, se & sc: LEE, MAH & POW
Org: Native

D. tricorne Michx.
Com: Dwarf larkspur
Hab: Wooded slopes; banks; bluffs
A&D: Infreq to rare s 1/2
Org: Native

D. virescens Nutt. [incl. var. *penardii* (Huth.) Perry]
Syn: *D. carolinianum* Walter ssp. *virescens* (Nutt.) R. E. Brooks
Com: Prairie larkspur
Hab: Dry, upland prairies
A&D: Infreq sc; rare se; freq to common elsewh
Org: Native

Hepatica P. Miller

H. nobilis P. Miller var. *acuta* (Pursh) Steyerm.
Syn: *H. acutiloba* DC.
Com: Liverleaf
Hab: Wooded, rocky hillsides
A&D: Common e & nc; freq sc; rare nw
Org: Native

H. nobilis P. Miller var. *obtusa* (Pursh) Steyerm.
Syn: *H. americana* (DC.) Ker-Gawl.
Com: Round-lobed liverleaf
Hab: Sandy, wooded ravines
A&D: Rare ne & se: ALL & HEN 1942
Org: Native

Hydrastis Ellis

H. canadensis L.
Com: Golden seal
Hab: Moist, loamy, wooded slopes
A&D: Rare ne & ec
Org: Native

Isopyrum L.

I. biternatum (Raf.) T. & G.
Syn: *Enemion biternatum* Raf.
Com: False rue anemone
Hab: Moist, wooded slopes; low woods; alluvial flats
A&D: Freq to common c & ne; infreq to rare elsewh
Org: Native

Myosurus L.

M. minimus L.
Com: Mousetail
Hab: Sandy shores of rivers, ponds or lakes
A&D: Infreq ec & s
Org: Native

Pulsatilla P. Miller

P. patens (L.) P. Miller ssp. *multifida* (Pritz.) Zamels
Syn: *Anemone patens* L. var. *wolfgangiana* (Besser) K. Koch
Syn: *Anemone patens* L.
Syn: *P. nuttalliana* (DC.) Bercht. & J. S. Presl
Com: Pasque flower
Hab: Dry, sandy or gravelly, prairie knolls; hillsides; loess bluffs
A&D: Common nw; infreq in Iowan Surface; rare in Pal. Plateau
Org: Native

Ranunculus L. Buttercup, crowfoot

R. abortivus L.
Com: Small-flowered crowfoot
Hab: Moist woods; moist, open places
A&D: Common thr
Org: Native

R. acris L.
Hab: Sparsely wooded or rocky pastures; moist woods
A&D: Rare thr
Org: Not native

R. aquatilis L. var. *capillaceus* (Thuill.) DC.
Syn: *R. trichophyllus* Chaix
Hab: Spring-fed streams
A&D: Freq in Pal. Plateau
Org: Native

R. circinatus Sibth. var. *subrigidus* (Drew) Benson
Syn: *R. subrigidus* Drew
Hab: Shallow, standing water
A&D: Rare nw: CLY 1936, & LYO 1899
Org: Native

R. cymbalaria Pursh
Com: Seaside crowfoot
Hab: Muddy shores; marsh edges
A&D: Freq nc & in lakes area; infreq to rare rest of w 1/2
Org: Native

R. fascicularis Muhl. [incl. var. *apricus* (Greene) Fern.]
Com: Early buttercup
Hab: Prairie openings; open, sandy places
A&D: Common ec; freq in ne; rare c & se
Org: Native

R. flabellaris Raf.
Com: Yellow water crowfoot
Hab: Muddy shores & shallow water of marshes
A&D: Common in lakes area; infreq c & extreme e; rare sc
Org: Native

R. gmelinii DC. var. *hookeri* (D. Don) Benson
Syn: *R. purshii* Richardson
Hab: Shallow, standing water
A&D: Rare nw: DIC 1950
Org: Native

R. longirostris Godron
Syn: *R. circinatus* Sibth., misappl.
Com: White water crowfoot
Hab: Lakes; ponds; streams
A&D: Common in lakes area; infreq c, e & in Pal. Plateau; rare elsewh
Org: Native

R. pensylvanicus L. f.
Com: Bristly crowfoot
Hab: Marshes; lake margins
A&D: Common in lakes area; infreq nc & ne; rare s 1/2
Org: Native

R. recurvatus Poiret
Com: Hooked buttercup
Hab: Moist, wooded slopes; upland woods
A&D: Infreq extreme e; not reported from nw; rare elsewh
Org: Native

R. repens L.
Com: Creeping buttercup
Hab: Wet ditches; meadows
A&D: Rare c, ec & se: DM, JOH 1909, SCO & TAM
Org: Not native

R. rhomboideus Goldie
Com: Prairie buttercup
Hab: Dry, open soil; prairies
A&D: Infreq to rare n
Org: Native

R. sceleratus L.
Com: Cursed crowfoot
Hab: Sandy lowlands; pond margins
A&D: Freq in lakes area; infreq to rare elsewh
Org: Native

R. septentrionalis Poiret
Syn: *R. hispidus* Michx. var. *nitidus* (Ell.) Duncan
Com: Swamp buttercup
Hab: Low, moist woods
A&D: Rare nw; freq to common elsewh
Org: Native

R. testiculatus Crantz
Syn: *Ceratocephalus testiculatus* (Crantz) Roth
Hab: Campgrounds
A&D: Rare ec & sw: CAS & JOH
Org: Not native

Thalictrum L.

T. dasycarpum Fischer & Ave-Lall.
Com: Purple meadow-rue
Hab: Moist prairie remnants; roadside ditches; open woods; moist alluvium
A&D: Common thr
Org: Native

T. dioicum L.
Com: Early meadow-rue
Hab: Moist woods
A&D: Freq to common n 1/2; rare in Pal. Plateau & sc
Org: Native

T. revolutum DC.
Com: Waxy meadow-rue
Hab: Prairies; open woods
A&D: Rare ec & se: DM, JOH 1913, LEE & SCO
Org: Native

T. thalictroides (L.) Eames & Boivin
Syn: *Anemonella thalictroides* (L.) Spach
Com: Rue anemone
Hab: Moist, wooded slopes
A&D: Freq to common thr
Org: Native

RESEDACEAE

Reseda L.

R. luteola L.
Com: Dyer's rocket
Hab: Dry, disturbed areas
A&D: Rare c, & in wc: HRR 1930, IDA & MNN 1931
Org: Not native

RHAMNACEAE

Ceanothus L.

C. americanus L. var. *pitcheri* T. & G.
Com: New Jersey tea
Hab: Prairie remnants; woodland edges; openings in dry woods
A&D: Freq nw; infreq sc; common elsewh
Org: Native

C. herbaceus Raf. var. *pubescens* (T. & G.) Shinners
Syn: *C. ovatus* Desf., misappl.
Com: Redroot
Hab: Dry hillsides; sandy plains; loess ridges
A&D: Common nw & extreme ne; freq sw; infreq c
Org: Native

Rhamnus L. Buckthorn

R. alnifolia L'Her.
Com: Alder buckthorn
Hab: Algific talus slopes
A&D: Rare in Pal. Plateau
Org: Native

R. cathartica L.
Com: Common buckthorn
Hab: Escape from cult to woodlands
A&D: Freq n 1/2; rare se
Org: Not native

R. davurica Pallas
Hab: Along gravel roads
A&D: Rare ne: WNS
Org: Not native

R. frangula L.
Com: Glossy buckthorn
Hab: Escape from cult to low, sandy woods
A&D: Rare escape from cult
Org: Not native

R. lanceolata Pursh [incl. var. *glabrata* Gl.]
Com: Lance-leaved buckthorn
Hab: Upland woods; open, wooded hillsides; woodland edges; rocky bluffs
A&D: Freq to common s 1/2 & extreme e; rare or absent elsewh
Org: Native

ROSACEAE

Agrimonia L. Agrimony

A. eupatoria L.
Hab: Dry pasture
A&D: Rare c: STO 1907
Org: Not native

A. gryposepala Wallr.
Com: Tall agrimony
Hab: Dry woods; woodland borders
A&D: Infreq s 1/2 & nc; freq to common elsewh
Org: Native

A. parviflora Aiton
Com: Swamp agrimony
Hab: Moist, open woods; alluvium
A&D: Freq se; infreq sc
Org: Native

A. pubescens Wallr.
Com: Soft agrimony
Hab: Upland woods; moist, wooded slopes
A&D: Infreq nw & nc; freq to common elsewh
Org: Native

A. striata Michx.
Hab: Dry, upland or low, moist woods
A&D: Infreq to rare thr
Org: Native

Amelanchier Medicus   Shadbush

A. alnifolia Nutt.
Hab: Thickets; margins of lakes
A&D: Rare nw & nc: DIC, EMM, HAN & LYO
Org: Native

A. arborea (Michx. f.) Fern.
Syn: *A. canadensis* L., misappl.
Syn: *A. laevis* Wieg.
Com: Serviceberry
Hab: Moist, wooded slopes; rocky, wooded slopes
A&D: Infreq ne 1/4; absent nw; freq elsewh
Org: Native

A. humilis Wieg.
Syn: *A. spicata* (Lam.) K. Koch, in part
Syn: *A. stolonifera* Wieg., in part
Hab: Dry, sandy prairies; rocky bluffs
A&D: Freq nc & in Pal. Plateau; rare in Iowan Surface
Org: Native

A. interior Nielsen
Syn: *A.* X *wiegandii* Nielsen
Hab: Dry sandstone ledges
A&D: Freq in Pal. Plateau; rare extreme e
Org: Native

A. sanguinea (Pursh) DC.
Hab: Sandstone ledges; algific slopes
A&D: Rare n, c & ec
Org: Native

Aronia Medicus

A. melanocarpa (Michx.) Ell.
Syn: *Pyrus melanocarpa* (Michx.) Willd.
Com: Black chokeberry
Hab: Dry sandstone ledges
A&D: Rare ne: WNS
Org: Native

Aruncus Schaeffer

A. dioicus (Walter) Fern. [incl. var. *pubescens* (Rydb.) Fern.]
Com: Goat's beard
Hab: Rocky, wooded slopes
A&D: Rare e: CLI, DM, DUB, JAC, LEE & MUS
Org: Native

Crataegus L.   Hawthorn

C. calpodendron (Ehrh.) Medicus
Hab: Prairie openings in upland woods; woodland edges
A&D: Infreq to rare thr
Org: Native

C. chrysocarpa Ashe
Syn: *C. rotundifolia* Moench, in part
Hab: Lake margins; wet sand
A&D: Rare n; all records before 1950
Org: Native

C. coccinea L.
Syn: *C. chrysocarpa* Ashe of authors
Syn: *C. pedicellata* Sarg.
Hab: Moist, open alluvium; upland woods
A&D: Rare c & e: DUB, HRD, LEE, LIN & WAP
Org: Native

C. crus-galli L.
Com: Cockspur hawthorn
Hab: Open, upland woods; pastures
A&D: Infreq sw & extreme e; freq remainder of s 1/2
Org: Native

C. disperma Ashe
Syn: *C. cuneiformis* (Marsh.) Eggleston
Hab: Open woods; pastures
A&D: Rare sc & se: DAV 1940, DEC 1940 & WAP 1940
Org: Native

C. margaretta Ashe
Syn: *C. chrysocarpa* Ashe in part
Hab: Upland woods; slopes; open alluvial woods
A&D: Infreq to freq e 1/2
Org: Native

C. mollis (T. & G.) Scheele
Hab: Open, upland woods; sandy alluvium; prairie openings
A&D: Infreq in Pal. Plateau; freq to common elsewh
Org: Native

C. pruinosa (Wendl. f.) K. Koch
Syn: *C. mackenzii* Sarg.
Hab: Thickets; rocky woods
A&D: Rare c & se: BOO 1940 & WAP 1929
Org: Native

C. punctata Jacq.
Hab: Open woods; pastures
A&D: Rare nw & se; freq to infreq elsewh
Org: Native

C. succulenta Schrader ex Link
Hab: Open woods; woodland edges
A&D: Infreq nw; rare thr much of state
Org: Native

Filipendula P. Miller

F. rubra (Hill) B. L. Robinson
Com: Queen of the prairie
Hab: Wet prairies
A&D: Rare ne & se: FAY & MUS
Org: Native

Fragaria L.

F. vesca L. var. *americana* Porter
Syn: *F. americana* (Porter) Britton
Com: Woodland strawberry
Hab: Wooded, calcareous slopes; upland woods
A&D: Rare se; freq to common elsewh
Org: Native

F. virginiana Duchesne [incl. var. *illinoense* (Prince) Gray; var. *glauca* S. Watson]
Com: Wild strawberry
Hab: Prairie remnants; open woods
A&D: Common thr
Org: Native

Geum L.

G. aleppicum Jacq. var. *strictum* (Aiton) Fern.
Syn: *G. strictum* Aiton
Com: Yellow avens
Hab: Low woods; woodland seeps; fens
A&D: Infreq to rare ne, & in nw: DIC
Org: Native

G. canadense Jacq. [incl. var. *camporum* (Rydb.) Fern. & Weath.]
Com: White avens
Hab: Moist woods; prairies; alluvial woods
A&D: Common thr
Org: Native

G. laciniatum Murray [incl. var. *trichocarpum* Fern.]
Com: Rough avens
Hab: Marshes; lakeshores; wet, disturbed sites
A&D: Rare nw; freq to infreq s & e
Org: Native

G. triflorum Pursh
Syn: *G. ciliatum* Pursh
Syn: *Sieversia triflorum* (Pursh) R. Br.
Com: Prairie smoke, purple avens
Hab: Prairie remnants; roadsides
A&D: Infreq ne; rare nw: DIC
Org: Native

G. vernum (Raf.) T. & G.
Com: Spring avens
Hab: Moist, upland woods
A&D: Rare nw & s: JEF 1928, MAH 1938, PAG, TAY & WAP 1939
Org: Native

Malus P. Miller

M. ioensis (Wood) Britton
Syn: *M. coronaria* (L.) P. Miller, misappl.
Syn: *Pyrus ioensis* (Wood) Carruth
Com: Wild crab
Hab: Dry, brushy uplands; open woods; prairie remnants
A&D: Freq to common thr
Org: Native

M. sylvestris (L.) P. Miller
Syn: *Pyrus malus* L.
Com: Apple
Hab: Alluvial flats
A&D: Rarely escaping from cult
Org: Not native

Physocarpus (Camb.) Maxim.

P. opulifolius (L.) Maxim.
Com: Ninebark
Hab: Wooded, rocky hillsides; rocky ledges
A&D: Freq to infreq e & sc; rare nc
Org: Native

Potentilla L. Cinquefoil

P. anserina L.
Com: Silverweed
Hab: Fens & wet soils at wetland margins
A&D: Rare c, nw & nc: DIC, EMM, HAM 1886, HRD ca. 1900 & WRI 1904
Org: Native

P. argentea L.
Hab: Open, sandy soil; sandy alluvium
A&D: Rare c & e, & in nw: DIC & EMM 1930
Org: Not native

P. arguta Pursh
Hab: Dry prairies; sandy soil
A&D: Rare ne; freq to infreq elsewh
Org: Native

P. fruticosa L.
Com: Shrubby cinquefoil
Hab: Limestone ledges; bluffs
A&D: Rare ne & ec: ALL, JAC, JON & WNS
Org: Native

P. intermedia L.
Hab: Sandy soil
A&D: Rare ne: BH
Org: Not native

P. norvegica L.
Com: Norwegian cinquefoil
Hab: Roadsides; pastures; shores; alluvium; waste places
A&D: Common thr
Org: Native

P. palustris (L.) Scop.
Com: Marsh cinquefoil
Hab: Marshes; fens
A&D: Rare in n part of DM lobe, & in nc, ne & ec: BH, BRE, BUC, CG & JON
Org: Native

P. paradoxa Nutt. ex T. & G.
Syn: *P. nicolletii* (S. Watson) Sheldon
Com: Bushy cinquefoil
Hab: Sandy or muddy shores of lakes & marshes
A&D: Freq in n part of DM lobe; infreq nw; rare sw
Org: Native

P. pensylvanica L.
Hab: Gravelly prairies; Sioux Quartzite
A&D: Rare nw: LYO & O'B
Org: Native

P. recta L.
Com: Sulphur cinquefoil
Hab: Dry roadsides; along railroads; pastures; waste ground
A&D: Freq to infreq thr most of state
Org: Not native

P. rivalis Nutt. [incl. var. *millegrana* (Engelm.) S. Watson; var. *pentandra* (Engelm.) S. Watson]
Com: Brook cinquefoil
Hab: Lake margins; sandy marshes
A&D: Rare n & e
Org: Native

P. simplex Michx. [incl. var. *calvescens* Fern.]
Com: Common cinquefoil
Hab: Woodland openings; sandy prairie remnants ; woodland edges
A&D: Common e 1/2; infreq to rare w 1/2
Org: Native

P. tridentata (Solander) Aiton
Com: Three-toothed cinquefoil
Hab: Sandstone ledges
A&D: Rare ne: ALL & WNS
Org: Native

Prunus L. Plum

P. americana Marsh.
Com: Wild plum
Hab: Fencerows; along railroads; woodland edges; open woods
A&D: Common thr
Org: Native

P. besseyi Bailey
Syn: *P. pumila* L. var. *besseyi* (Bailey) Gl.
Com: Dwarf cherry
Hab: Crevices in Sioux Quartzite
A&D: Rare nw: LYO
Org: Native

P. hortulana Bailey
Com: Hortulan plum
Hab: Road cuts; low woods
A&D: Rare se: LEE & VB
Org: Native

P. mexicana S. Watson
Com: Big-tree plum
Hab: Roadsides; fencerows
A&D: Infreq thr
Org: Native

P. nigra Aiton
Com: Canada plum
Hab: Steep, n- or e-facing, wooded slopes
A&D: Rare c, nw & ne: ALL, BOO 1936, CLY 1934, CLT & WNS
Org: Native

P. pensylvanica L. f.
Com: Pin cherry
Hab: Woods; clearings
A&D: Common in Pal. Plateau; freq nc; rare in Iowan Surface & sc
Org: Native

P. persica (L.) Batsch
Com: Peach
Hab: Roads; fencerows
A&D: Rare escape from cult
Org: Not native

P. pumila L.
Syn: *P. susquehanae* Willd.
Com: Sand cherry
Hab: Dry, sandy plains; sand prairies; blowouts
A&D: Rare n & se: ALL, BUC, CG 1946, DEL, DIC 1928, LOU, LYO, MUS & WNS
Org: Native

P. serotina Ehrh.
Com: Wild black cherry
Hab: Moist, wooded slopes; upland woods
A&D: Freq to common thr
Org: Native

P. virginiana L.
Com: Choke cherry
Hab: Open woods; woodland borders; rocky bluffs; fencerows
A&D: Common thr
Org: Native

Pyrus L. see also ***Malus*** & ***Aronia***

P. communis L.
Com: Pear
Hab: Near habitation, apparently self-seeded
A&D: Rare c, ec & se: CLI 1921, DAL, DM, JOH & LEE
Org: Not native

Rosa L. Rose

R. acicularis Lindley [incl. ssp. *sayi* (Schwein.) W. H. Lewis]
Hab: Algific talus slopes
A&D: Rare ne: ALL, CLT, DEL & WNS
Org: Native

R. arkansana Porter var. *suffulta* (Greene) Cockerell
Syn: *R. suffulta* Greene
Com: Sunshine rose
Hab: Dry prairies
A&D: Infreq to freq thr
Org: Native

R. blanda Aiton
Com: Meadow rose
Hab: Prairie remnants; wooded slopes; roadsides
A&D: Infreq to freq thr
Org: Native

R. carolina L. [incl. var. *grandiflora* (Baker) Rehder; var. *villosa* (Best) Rehder]
Com: Pasture rose
Hab: Prairie remnants; open, sandy places; open, upland woods
A&D: Common e 1/2; freq nc; infreq to rare elsewh
Org: Native

R. eglanteria L.
Com: Sweetbriar rose
Hab: Roadsides
A&D: Infreq escape from cult in nc, in lakes area & se
Org: Not native

R. multiflora Thunb. ex Murray
Com: Multiflora rose
Hab: Escape to waste ground; pastures; old fields
A&D: Freq to common s 1/2; rare n
Org: Not native

R. palustris Marsh.
Com: Swamp rose
Hab: Moist thickets
A&D: Rare sw: TAY
Org: Native

R. setigera Michx. [incl. var. *tomentosa* T. & G.]
Com: Prairie rose
Hab: Open woods; fencerows
A&D: Rare sw & se
Org: Native

R. woodsii Lindley [incl. var. *fendleri* (Crepin) Rydb.]
Syn: *R. fendleri* Crepin
Hab: Prairie remnants; sandy soil; calcareous bluffs
A&D: Rare n 1/2
Org: Native

Rubus L. (Iowa taxa need a thorough restudy)

R. allegheniensis Porter ex Bailey [incl. R. ostryifolius Rydb. & R. pensilvanicus Poiret]
Com: Blackberry
Hab: Moist-to-dry woods; woodland edges; roadsides
A&D: Common thr
Org: Native

R. flagellaris Willd.
Com: Dewberry
Hab: Sandy soil
A&D: Infreq to rare n 1/2
Org: Native

R. hispidus L.
Com: Dewberry
Hab: Edges of moist, sandy, prairie swales
A&D: Rare ne: BH
Org: Native

R. idaeus L.
Com: Cultivated red raspberry
Hab: Waste ground; fencerows; woodland edges
A&D: Rare escape from cult in sw, nc & extreme e
Org: Not native

R. occidentalis L.
Com: Black raspberry
Hab: Upland woods; woodland edges; roadsides
A&D: Common thr
Org: Native

R. pubescens Raf.
Syn: *R. triflorus* Gray
Hab: Algific talus slopes; fens
A&D: Rare ne
Org: Native

R. strigosus Michx.
Syn: *R. idaeus* L. var. *strigosus* (Michx.) Maxim.
Syn: *R. idaeus* L. ssp. *sachalinensis* (Levl.) Focke
Com: Wild red raspberry
Hab: Sandy woods; moist, wooded slopes
A&D: Infreq ne, except common in Pal. Plateau
Org: Native

Sanguisorba L.

S. annua (Nutt. ex Hooker) T. & G.
Hab: Disturbed areas
A&D: Rare escape from cult
Org: Not native

Sorbaria (Ser.) A. Br.

S. sorbifolia (L.) A. Br.
Com: False spiraea
Hab: Disturbed ground near dwellings
A&D: Rare escape from cult in ne: ALL
Org: Not native

Sorbus L.

S. aucuparia L.
Com: Mountain ash
Hab: Hedges; woodland margins; sandstone outcrops
A&D: Occasional escape from cult
Org: Not native

Spiraea L.

S. alba Du Roi
Com: Meadowsweet
Hab: Low prairies; marshy ground; fens
A&D: Freq to common ne 1/2; infreq to rare elsewh
Org: Native

RUBIACEAE

Cephalanthus L.

C. occidentalis L.
Com: Buttonbush
Hab: Marshes; lakeshores; moist alluvium
A&D: Common s 1/2 & e; infreq to rare elsewh
Org: Native

Diodia L.

D. teres Walter [incl. var. *setifera* Fern. & Grisc.]
Com: Buttonweed
Hab: Sandy soil; fields; roadsides
A&D: Rare e: CLI, DM, DUB, JAC, LEE, LOU & MUS 1924
Org: Native

Galium L. Bedstraw, madder

G. aparine L.
Com: Cleavers
Hab: Moist woods
A&D: Common thr
Org: Native

G. asprellum Michx.
Com: Rough bedstraw
Hab: Wooded seepage slopes; algific slopes; sandy alluvium
A&D: Rare ne: ALL, CLT, DEL, DUB & WNS
Org: Native

G. boreale L. [incl. var. *intermedium* DC.; var. *hyssopifolium* (Hoffm.) DC.]
Com: Northern bedstraw
Hab: Prairie remnants; limestone ledges; talus slopes; fens
A&D: Common ne 1/4; freq extreme e; infreq nw
Org: Native

G. circaezans Michx. [incl. var. *hypomalacum* Fern.]
Hab: Moist woods
A&D: Freq to common thr
Org: Native

G. concinnum T. & G.
Com: Shining bedstraw
Hab: Upland woods; moist, wooded slopes
A&D: Common thr
Org: Native

G. labradoricum (Wieg.) Wieg.
Com: Bog bedstraw
Hab: Marshes; fens
A&D: Rare nc & ne: CG, CHI, CLT, MIT, WNB & WNS
Org: Native

G. obtusum Bigelow
Com: Wild madder
Hab: Moist prairie remnants; open, alluvial woods; shores
A&D: Freq to infreq thr
Org: Native

G. tinctorium L.
Syn: *G. claytoni* Michx.
Syn: *G. trifidum* L. var. *tinctorium* (L.) T. & G.
Com: Stiff bedstraw
Hab: Open, marshy habitats
A&D: Freq to infreq e 1/2; rare sc
Org: Native

G. trifidum L.
Com: Small bedstraw
Hab: Marshes
A&D: Rare nc & ne: DM lobe & ALL, WNS
Org: Native

G. triflorum Michx.
Com: Sweet-scented bedstraw
Hab: Open woods; moist, wooded slopes; alluvial woods
A&D: Freq nw; infreq nc; common elsewh
Org: Native

G. verum L.
Com: Yellow bedstraw
Hab: Roadsides; edges of woods; dry prairies
A&D: Rare w: CAS 1925, DIC, & GRE 1929
Org: Not native

Hedyotis L.

H. crassifolia Raf.
Syn: *Houstonia minima* Beck
Com: Bluets
Hab: Sandy or rocky lowland prairies
A&D: Infreq e
Org: Native

H. nigricans (Lam.) Fosb.
Syn: *Houstonia nigricans* (Lam.) Fern.
Hab: Loess bluffs
A&D: Freq to common in Loess Hills & sw
Org: Native

Mitchella L.

M. repens L.
Com: Partridge berry
Hab: Rich, upland woods
A&D: Rare ne: DUB 1901 & WNS
Org: Native

RUTACEAE

Ptelea L.

P. trifoliata L.
Com: Wafer ash
Hab: Woods along streams; rocky, wooded bluffs; sandy habitats
A&D: Freq se & extreme e; rare nc
Org: Native

Zanthoxylum L.

Z. americanum P. Miller
Com: Prickly ash
Hab: Open, upland woods; woodland openings; edges
A&D: Common thr
Org: Native

SALICACEAE

Populus L. Poplar

P. alba L.
Com: Silver poplar
Hab: Roadsides; fencerows; fields
A&D: Infreq escape from cult thr
Org: Not native

P. balsamifera L.
Syn: *P. candicans* Aiton
Syn: *P. tacamahacca* P. Miller
Com: Balsam poplar
Hab: Moist woods; woodland edges
A&D: Rare escape from cult n
Org: Not native

P. deltoides Bartram ex Marsh.
Com: Cottonwood
Hab: Moist habitats, usually on alluvium, occasionally on upland slopes
A&D: Common thr
Org: Native

P. deltoides Bartram ex Marsh. ssp. *monilifera* (Aiton) Eckenw.
Syn: *P. deltoides* Bartram ex Marsh. var. *occidentalis* Rydb.
Syn: *P. sargentii* Dode
Hab: Moist habitats, usually on alluvium
A&D: Infreq w
Org: Native

P. grandidentata Michx.
Com: Big-tooth aspen
Hab: Moist-to-dry, usually upland woods
A&D: Freq to common nc, ne & ec; rare se
Org: Native

P. nigra L. var. *italica* Moench
Com: Lombardy poplar
Hab: Waste ground near habitations
A&D: Occasionally persists from cult
Org: Not native

P. X *rouleauiana* Boivin
Syn: *P. alba* X *P. grandidentata*
Hab: Moist, upland woods
A&D: Infreq to rare e 1/2
Org: Hybrid of mixed origin

P. tremuloides Michx.
Syn: *P. tremula* L. ssp. *tremuloides* (Michx.) Love & Love
Com: Quaking aspen
Hab: Open woods; moist prairies; woodland edges
A&D: Freq to common n 1/2; infreq to freq s 1/2
Org: Native

Salix L. Willow

S. alba L.
Com: White willow
Hab: Moist ground; roadsides
A&D: Infreq to rare escape from cult thr
Org: Not native

S. amygdaloides Andersson
Com: Peach-leaved willow
Hab: Along streams
A&D: Freq ne 1/4; common elsewh
Org: Native

S. babylonica L.
Com: Weeping willow
Hab: Moist or sandy habitats near dwellings
A&D: Rarely persists from cult
Org: Not native

S. bebbiana Sarg.
Com: Beaked willow
Hab: Moist ground; n-facing talus slopes; fens
A&D: Infreq ne 1/4; rare nc & extreme e
Org: Native

S. candida Fluegge ex Willd.
Com: Sage willow, hoary willow
Hab: Calcareous aquatic habitats; fens
A&D: Rare ne 1/3
Org: Native

S. discolor Muhl.
Com: Pussy willow
Hab: Streambanks; low prairies; marsh edges
A&D: Common nc & ne; infreq to rare elsewh
Org: Native

S. exigua Nutt. ssp. *interior* (Rowlee) Cronq.
Syn: *S. interior* Rowlee
Com: Sandbar willow
Hab: Streambanks; sandbars; alluvial bottoms
A&D: Common thr
Org: Native

S. fragilis L.
Com: Crack willow
Hab: Lakeshores & other moist habitats
A&D: Infreq to freq escape from cult thr
Org: Not native

S. humilis Marsh. [incl. var. *hyporhysa* Fern.; var. *microphylla* (Andersson) Fern.]
Syn: *S. tristis* Aiton
Com: Prairie willow
Hab: Prairie remnants
A&D: Freq to common thr
Org: Native

S. lucida Muhl.
Com: Shining willow
Hab: Low, moist ground; lakeshores; streambanks; fens
A&D: Rare n
Org: Native

S. nigra Marsh.
Com: Black willow
Hab: Streambanks; lake margins; alluvial woods
A&D: Infreq nw & extreme e; common elsewh
Org: Native

S. pedicellaris Pursh
Com: Bog willow
Hab: Fens; peat lands
A&D: Rare nc & ne
Org: Native

S. pentandra L.
Com: Bay-leaved willow
Hab: Waste ground; disturbed, moist ground near dwellings
A&D: Rarely persists from cult
Org: Not native

S. petiolaris Smith
Syn: *S. gracilis* Andersson var. *textoris* Fern.
Hab: Moist prairie remnants; marsh edges; fens
A&D: Common nc & ne; rare ec & se
Org: Native

S. purpurea L.
Com: Purple willow
Hab: Disturbed soil near dwellings
A&D: Rare escape from cult
Org: Not native

S. rigida Muhl. [incl. var. *angustata* (Pursh) Fern.; var. *watsonii* (Bebb) Cronq.; var. *vestita* Andersson]
Syn: *S. cordata* Michx. var. *angustata* (Pursh) Gray
Syn: *S. cordata* Michx. var. *rigida* (Muhl.) Carey
Syn: *S. eriocephala* Michx.
Hab: Streambanks; wet lowlands; ditches
A&D: Freq to common thr
Org: Native

S. sericea Marsh.
Com: Silky willow
Hab: Streambanks; marsh edges; fens
A&D: Rare e
Org: Native

S. X *subsericea* (Andersson) Schneider
Syn: *S. petiolaris* X *S. sericea*
Hab: Gravelly soil
A&D: Rare nw: EMM
Org: Native

SANTALACEAE

Comandra Nutt.

C. umbellata (L.) Nutt.
Syn: *C. richardsiana* Fern.
Com: Bastard toadflax
Hab: Prairie remnants; openings in upland woods
A&D: Common thr
Org: Native

SAXIFRAGACEAE

Chrysosplenium L.

C. iowense Rydb.
Syn: *C. alternifolium* L. var. *iowense* (Rydb.) Boivin
Syn: *C. tetrandrum* (Lynd.) Fries, misappl.
Com: Golden saxifrage
Hab: Algific talus slopes
A&D: Rare ne & ec: ALL, CLT, DUB, FAY, HOW, JAC & WNS
Org: Native

Heuchera L. Alumroot

H. americana L. var. *hirsuticaulis* (Wheelock) Rosend., Butters & Lak.
Hab: Prairie remnants
A&D: Rare se
Org: Native

H. richardsonii R. Br. [incl. var. *hispidior* Rosend., Butters & Lak.]
Syn: *H.* X *hirsuticaulis* (Wheelock) Rydb.
Com: Alumroot
Hab: Prairies; open, rocky woods; limestone bluffs
A&D: Common ne 1/4 & sw; infreq to freq elsewh
Org: Native

Mitella L. Bishop's cap

M. diphylla L.
Com: Bishop's cap, mitrewort
Hab: Wooded, rocky slopes & bluffs
A&D: Freq to common ne 1/4; infreq nc; rare se & sc
Org: Native

M. nuda L.
Com: Small Bishop's cap
Hab: Mossy, n-facing, wooded slopes
A&D: Rare ne: ALL
Org: Native

Parnassia L.

P. glauca Raf.
Com: Grass of Parnassus
Hab: Fens; wet, calcareous prairies
A&D: Rare ne 1/2
Org: Native

Penthorum L. (Some authors place in Crassulaceae)

P. sedoides L.
Com: Ditch stonecrop
Hab: Marshes; shores; moist prairies; alluvium
A&D: Infreq nw; common elsewh
Org: Native

Philadelphus L.

P. pubescens Loisel
Com: Mock orange
Hab: Upland oak-hickory forest
A&D: Rare ne: DUB
Org: Native of U.S., but not Iowa

Ribes L. Gooseberry, currant

R. americanum P. Miller
Com: Wild black currant
Hab: Moist, open woods; margins of lakes & marshes; fens
A&D: Freq ne 1/4; infreq extreme e & nw; rare elsewh
Org: Native

R. cynosbati L.
Syn: *Grossularia cynosbati* (L.) P. Miller
Com: Prickly gooseberry
Hab: Wooded rocky bluffs; limestone ledges; moist woods
A&D: Infreq to rare nw & s 1/2; freq to common elsewh
Org: Native

R. hirtellum Michx.
Hab: Moist woods; fens
A&D: Rare se: VB
Org: Native

R. hudsonianum Richardson
Com: Northern currant
Hab: Algific talus slopes
A&D: Rare ne: ALL, CLT, DEL & DUB
Org: Native

R. missouriense Nutt. ex T. & G.
Syn: *Grossularia missouriensis* (Nutt.) Cov. & Britton
Com: Wild gooseberry
Hab: Open woods; woodland edges
A&D: Common thr
Org: Native

R. odoratum Wendl.
Com: Buffalo currant
Hab: Thickets; woodland margins
A&D: Rare w & sc
Org: Native

R. sativum (Reichenb.) Syme
Syn: *R. rubrum* L.
Com: Garden currant
Hab: Waste or disturbed ground
A&D: Rare escape from cult
Org: Not native

Saxifraga L.

S. forbesii Vasey
Syn: *S. pensylvanica* L. var. *forbesii* (Vasey) Engl. & Irmsch.
Com: Forbes' saxifrage
Hab: Moist, limestone ledges; algific talus slopes
A&D: Freq in Pal. Plateau
Org: Native

S. pensylvanica L.
Com: Swamp saxifrage
Hab: Low prairies; fens
A&D: Freq ne 1/4; rare se & sc: MRN & MUS
Org: Native

Sullivantia Torrey & Gray

S. sullivantii (T. & G.) Britton
Syn: *S. renifolia* Rosend.
Hab: Moist, shaded, limestone cliffs; algific talus slopes
A&D: Rare ne & ec: ALL, CLT, DEL, DUB, FAY, JAC, JON & LIN
Org: Native

SCROPHULARIACEAE

Agalinis Raf.

A. aspera (Douglas ex Bentham) Britton
Syn: *Gerardia aspera* Douglas
Hab: Dry prairie remnants; loess bluffs; hill prairies
A&D: Freq in Iowan Surface & sw; infreq ne; rare nw
Org: Native

A. gattingeri (Small) Small
Syn: *Gerardia gattingeri* Small
Hab: Dry, sandy prairie openings on bluffs
A&D: Rare c, ec, se & sc: DEC 1903, HEN n.d., JEF 1935, JON, LEE, MUS & WEB 1908
Org: Native

A. paupercula (Gray) Britton
Syn: *Gerardia paupercula* (Gray) Britton
Syn: *Gerardia purpurea* (L.) Pennell var. *parviflora* Bentham of authors
Hab: Moist, open, sandy places; fens
A&D: Infreq to rare nc & e; rare sw: POT 1898
Org: Native

A. purpurea (L.) Pennell
Syn: *Gerardia purpurea* L.
Hab: Moist, open sand
A&D: Absent se & sc; infreq to rare elsewh
Org: Native

A. skinneriana (Wood) Britton
Syn: *Gerardia skinneriana* Wood
Hab: Dry, sandy prairies
A&D: Rare ne & se: ALL, DUB & MUS 1922
Org: Native

A. tenuifolia (Vahl) Raf. [incl. var. *macrophylla* (Bentham) Blake; var. *parviflora* (Nutt.) Pennell]
Syn: *Gerardia tenuifolia* Vahl
Hab: Moist prairies; marshy ground; fens; dry, open woods
A&D: Infreq ne & se; rare nw; common elsewh
Org: Native

Aureolaria Raf.

A. grandiflora (Bentham) Pennell var. *pulchra* Pennell
Syn: *Gerardia grandiflora* Bentham var. *pulchra* (Pennell) Fern.
Com: Yellow false foxglove
Hab: Rocky or sandy soil; openings on dry limestone bluffs
A&D: Freq extreme e; rare se & sc
Org: Native

A. pedicularia (L.) Raf.
Com: Clammy false foxglove
Hab: Dry, sandy woodlands
A&D: Rare ne: ALL
Org: Native

Bacopa Aublet

B. rotundifolia (Michx.) Wettst.
Com: Water hyssop
Hab: Shallow, standing water; muddy shores
A&D: Infreq se & sc; rare nw & ne
Org: Native

Besseya Rydb.

B. bullii (Eaton) Rydb.
Syn: *Synthris bullii* (Eaton) Heller
Syn: *Wulfenia bullii* (Eaton) Barnh.
Com: Kittentails
Hab: Dry, sometimes rocky, prairie ridges
A&D: Rare n & e
Org: Native

Castilleja Mutis ex L. f.

C. coccinea (L.) Sprengel
Com: Indian paintbrush
Hab: Rocky & mesic prairies
A&D: Infreq to rare nc, & in nw: SIO
Org: Native

C. sessiliflora Pursh
Com: Downy painted cup
Hab: Prairie openings on bluffs; dry prairie ridges; tops of loess bluffs
A&D: Infreq n 1/2 & sw
Org: Native

Chaenorrhinum (DC.) Reichenb.

C. minus (L.) Lange
Syn: *Linaria minor* (L.) Desf.
Com: Dwarf snapdragon
Hab: Dry sand or gravel, often along railroads
A&D: Freq to infreq s 1/2; rare n 1/2
Org: Not native

Chelone L.

C. glabra L.
Com: White turtlehead
Hab: Marshes; fens; shores
A&D: Rare thr most of state; not reported from extreme w
Org: Native

C. obliqua L. var. *speciosa* Pennell & Wherry
Com: Pink turtlehead
Hab: Marshy ground
A&D: Rare nc, ec & se: CLI 1930, DM, LEE 1898, MIT 1929, MUS 1894 & SCO
Org: Native

Collinsia Nutt.

C. verna Nutt.
Com: Blue-eyed Mary
Hab: Moist woods
A&D: Rare se: JEF 1896 & WAS
Org: Native

Dasistoma Raf.

D. macrophylla (Nutt.) Raf.
Syn: *Seymeria macrophylla* Nutt.
Hab: Dry, wooded, calcareous bluffs
A&D: Infreq se & sc
Org: Native

Gerardia see ***Agalinis***, ***Tomanthera*** & ***Aureolaria***

Gratiola L. Hedge hyssop

G. neglecta Torrey
Com: Hedge hyssop
Hab: Marshes; low, sandy areas; streambanks; moist prairie remnants
A&D: Freq sc; infreq to rare elsewh
Org: Native

G. virginiana L.
Hab: Muddy shores; shallow, standing water in sandy areas
A&D: Rare se & sc: DEC 1900, LEE & MUS
Org: Not native

Leucospora Nutt.

L. multifida (Michx.) Nutt.
Syn: *Conobea multifida* (Michx.) Bentham
Hab: Moist, sandy soil
A&D: Rare e: FAY 1894, LEE n.d. (probably 1890's), LOU, MUS & SCO
Org: Native

Linaria P. Miller

L. canadensis (L.) Dum.-Cours.
Com: Toadflax
Hab: Dry, open, sandy soil
A&D: Infreq e
Org: Native

L. macedonica Griseb.
Hab: Disturbed areas
A&D: Rare escape from cult in sc: MAD 1942
Org: Not native

L. vulgaris Hill
Com: Butter & eggs
Hab: Roadsides; fields; woodland edges; disturbed soil
A&D: Freq se & sw; infreq elsewh
Org: Not native

Lindernia All. False pimpernel

L. anagallidea (Michx.) Pennell
Syn: *L. dubia* (L.) Pennell var. *anagallidea* (Michx.) Cooperrider
Com: False pimpernel
Hab: Marshes; sandy alluvium
A&D: Rare w 2/3
Org: Native

L. dubia (L.) Pennell
Hab: Clear, shallow pools; wet soil; streambanks
A&D: Common s 1/2 & extreme e; freq in Pal. Plateau; rare elsewh
Org: Native

Mimulus L. Monkey flower

M. alatus Aiton
Com: Winged monkey flower
Hab: Wet alluvium
A&D: Rare se & sc
Org: Native

M. glabratus HBK. var. *fremontii* (Bentham) Grant
Syn: *M. geyeri* Torrey
Com: Yellow monkey flower
Hab: Shallow water of cold springs; slowly flowing streams; fens
A&D: Rare n, e & sw
Org: Native

M. ringens L. [incl. var. *minthodes* (Greene) Grant]
Com: Monkey flower
Hab: Muddy lakeshores; moist, alluvial woods
A&D: Infreq nw; common elsewh
Org: Native

Pedicularis L.

P. canadensis L. [incl. var. *dobbsii* Fern.]
Com: Lousewort
Hab: Prairie remnants; woodland openings
A&D: Infreq to rare w; freq to common elsewh
Org: Native

P. lanceolata Michx.
Com: Swamp lousewort
Hab: Marshes; fens; prairie swales; wet sand
A&D: Freq to common ne 1/4; rare nw & s 1/2
Org: Native

Penstemon Mitchell Beardtongue

P. albidus Nutt.
Hab: Loess bluffs; dry prairies
A&D: Rare nw: LYO, PLY & SIO
Org: Native

P. cobaea Nutt.
Hab: Loess bluffs
A&D: Rare sw: FRE
Org: Native

P. digitalis Nutt.
Com: Foxglove penstemon
Hab: Roadsides; sandy prairies; sandy openings
A&D: Freq se; rare ne, ec, sc & sw
Org: Native

P. gracilis Nutt.
Hab: Dry prairie slopes
A&D: Rare wc & nw: HRR & LYO
Org: Native

P. grandiflorus Nutt.
Syn: *P. bradburii* Pursh
Com: Large-flowered beardtongue
Hab: Sandy soil; loess bluffs; dry slopes
A&D: Freq to common in Loess Hills & sandy areas of c & e
Org: Native

P. pallidus Small
Com: Pale beardtongue
Hab: Open, sandy fields; open, dry woods
A&D: Freq se; rare extreme e & sc
Org: Native

P. tubiflorus Nutt.
Hab: Prairies; dry woods
A&D: Rare c, ec, se & sc: CLR, IOW, JEF 1932, LIN & STO
Org: Native

Scrophularia L. Figwort

S. lanceolata Pursh
Hab: Loess bluffs; dry prairie remnants; openings in upland woods
A&D: Freq to common n & extreme e; infreq to rare elsewh
Org: Native

S. marilandica L.
Hab: Open woods; sandy roadsides
A&D: Infreq nw; freq to common elsewh
Org: Native

Tomanthera Raf.

T. auriculata (Michx.) Raf.
Syn: *Gerardia auriculata* Michx.
Syn: *Agalinis auriculata* (Michx.) Blake
Hab: Moist prairie remnants
A&D: Rare e & sc
Org: Native

Verbascum L. Mullein

V. blattaria L.
Com: Moth mullein
Hab: Roadsides; disturbed prairies; waste places
A&D: Freq nc; infreq se & sc; rare nw
Org: Not native

V. lychnitis L.
Com: White mullein
Hab: Prairie openings
A&D: Rare sc: MAD 1917
Org: Not native

V. phlomoides L.
Hab: Roadsides; pastures; disturbed prairies
A&D: Rare e, & in c & wc: POL & SAC
Org: Not native

V. thapsus L.
Com: Common mullein
Hab: Pastures; roadsides; waste places
A&D: Common thr
Org: Not native

Veronica L. Speedwell

V. agrestis L.
Com: Field speedwell
Hab: Lawns
A&D: Rare nw, & in sw: PAG
Org: Not native

V. americana (Raf.) Schwein. ex Bentham
Com: American brookline
Hab: Margins & shallow water of swiftly flowing streams
A&D: Rare ne & se: ALL, LEE n.d. (ca. 1887), MUS pre-1900 & WNS
Org: Native

V. anagallis-aquatica L.
Com: Water speedwell
Hab: Sandy riverbanks; streambanks; springs
A&D: Rare n & ec
Org: Not native

V. arvensis L.
Com: Corn speedwell
Hab: Fields; roadsides; sandy soil; rocky slopes; pastures
A&D: Freq to common se; freq sw; infreq to rare elsewh
Org: Not native

V. catenata Pennell
Syn: *V. comosa* Richter, misappl.
Syn: *V. connata* Raf., misappl.
Com: Water speedwell
Hab: Shores; shallow water
A&D: Freq in DM lobe; rare or absent elsewh
Org: Native

V. officinalis L.
Com: Common speedwell
Hab: Streambanks
A&D: Rare ec: CLI
Org: Not native

V. peregrina L. [incl. var. *xalapensis* (HBK.) St. John & Warren]
Hab: Roadsides; lawns; yards; sandy alluvium
A&D: Rare nw; freq to common elsewh
Org: Native

V. persica Poiret
Syn: *V. tournefortii* Camel, misappl.
Hab: Lawns; disturbed habitats
A&D: Rare nw & e: CHI 1926, JOH 1926, SIO & VB
Org: Not native

V. scutellata L.
Com: Marsh speedwell
Hab: Marsh edges
A&D: Rare ec: CLI
Org: Native

V. serpyllifolia L.
Hab: Open areas; ravines; open woodlands
A&D: Infreq e
Org: Not native

Veronicastrum Heister ex Fabr.

V. virginicum (L.) Farw.
Com: Culver's root
Hab: Moist prairies; moist, open, upland woods; woodland borders
A&D: Infreq nw; common elsewh
Org: Native

SIMAROUBACEAE

Ailanthus Desf.

A. altissima (P. Miller) Swingle
Com: Tree of heaven
Hab: Disturbed soil in urban areas
A&D: Freq in s 1/2, spreading from cult
Org: Not native

SOLANACEAE

Datura L.

D. stramonium L. [incl. var. *tatula* (L.) Torrey]
Com: Jimsonweed
Hab: Farmyards; often sandy, disturbed areas
A&D: Freq s 1/2; infreq to rare n 1/2
Org: Not native

Lycium L.

L. halimifolium P. Miller
Syn: *L. barbarum* L.
Com: Matrimony vine
Hab: Waste ground; disturbed soil
A&D: Infreq to rare escape in s 1/2
Org: Not native

Lycopersicon P. Miller

L. esculentum P. Miller
Com: Tomato
Hab: Sandy, cultivated field
A&D: Not persisting from cult
Org: Not native

Nicandra Adanson

N. physalodes (L.) Gaertner
Com: Apple of Peru
Hab: Woodland edges
A&D: Rare c, ne & se: ALL, KEO, MUS & STO
Org: Not native

Petunia Juss.

P. axillaris (Lam.) BSP.
Syn: *P. hybrida* Vilm.
Com: Petunia
Hab: Disturbed soil near dwellings
A&D: Rare escape from cult
Org: Not native

Physalis L.

P. heterophylla Nees
Com: Ground cherry
Hab: Disturbed prairies; roadsides; sandy, open habitats
A&D: Freq to common thr
Org: Native

P. ixocarpa Brotero ex Hornem.
Com: Tomatillo
Hab: Disturbed, sandy soil
A&D: Rare escape from cult
Org: Not native

P. pubescens L.
Com: Annual ground cherry
Hab: Waste ground; disturbed soil
A&D: Rare thr
Org: Native

P. pubescens L. var. *integrifolia* (Dunal) Waterfall
Syn: *P. pruinosa* L., misappl.
Com: Strawberry tomato
Hab: Edges of fields
A&D: Rare escape from cult
Org: Not native

P. virginiana P. Miller [incl. var. *subglabrata* (Mack. & Bush) Waterfall; var. *sonorae* (Torrey) Waterfall]
Syn: *P. longifolia* Nutt.
Syn: *P. subglabrata* Mack. & Bush
Com: Ground cherry
Hab: Prairie remnants; disturbed, sandy soil
A&D: Freq to common thr
Org: Native

Solanum L.

S. americanum P. Miller
Syn: *S. nigrum* L., misappl.
Syn: *S. ptycanthum* Dun. ex DC.
Com: Black nightshade
Hab: Roadsides; fields; waste places
A&D: Common thr
Org: Native

S. carolinense L.
Com: Horse nettle
Hab: Fields; roadsides; along railroads; waste ground
A&D: Infreq to rare ne; common elsewh
Org: Native

S. dulcamara L.
Com: European bittersweet
Hab: Roadsides; alluvium; waste ground
A&D: Infreq sc; rare nc, extreme e & se; spreading thr
Org: Not native

S. interius Rydb.
Com: Plains black nightshade
Hab: Floodplain woods
A&D: Rare: HRR
Org: Native

S. rostratum Dunal
Syn: *S. cornutum* Lam.
Com: Buffalo bur
Hab: Farmyards; roadsides; disturbed soil
A&D: Freq to common w 1/2 & se; infreq to rare ne
Org: Native of U.S., but not Iowa

STAPHYLEACEAE

Staphylea L.

S. trifolia L.
Com: Bladdernut
Hab: Moist, rocky, wooded slopes
A&D: Rare nw & nc; freq to common elsewh
Org: Native

THYMELAEACEAE

Dirca L.

D. palustris L.
Com: Leatherwood
Hab: Moist, wooded slopes
A&D: Freq in Pal. Plateau, extreme e & c; rare to absent elsewh
Org: Native

Thymelaea P. Miller

T. passerina (L.) Cosson & Germ.
Syn: *Passerina annua* Wikstr.
Hab: Disturbed prairies; roadsides
A&D: Rare w: HRR, MIL, MNN, PLY, POT & WOO
Org: Not native

TILIACEAE

Tilia L.

T. americana L. [incl. var. *neglecta* (Spach) Fosb.]
Com: Basswood, American linden
Hab: Moist upland woods & slopes; protected bluffs & ravines
A&D: Common thr
Org: Native

T. heterophylla Vent.
Com: White basswood
Hab: Moist, disturbed soil
A&D: Widely cult
Org: Native of U.S., but not Iowa

ULMACEAE

Celtis L.

C. occidentalis L. [incl. var. *pumila* (Pursh) Gray; var. *canina* (Raf.) Sarg.]
Com: Hackberry
Hab: Moist, low woods; open, disturbed soil
A&D: Common thr
Org: Native

Ulmus L.

U. americana L.
Com: American elm
Hab: Woods, especially alluvial flats
A&D: Common thr
Org: Native

U. pumila L.
Com: Siberian elm
Hab: Fencerows; successional fields
A&D: Freq escape from plantings
Org: Not native

U. rubra Muhl.
Syn: *U. fulva* Michx.
Com: Red elm, slippery elm
Hab: Wooded slopes & bluffs
A&D: Infreq nw; freq to common elsewh
Org: Native

U. thomasii Sarg.
Com: Rock elm, cork elm
Hab: Bases of moist, wooded slopes
A&D: Infreq to rare n 1/2, & in se & sc: DEC 1900, LEE 1939, MAH 1928 & VB 1940
Org: Native

URTICACEAE

Boehmeria Jacq.

B. cylindrica (L.) Sw.
Com: Bog hemp
Hab: Marshes; alluvium; low woods; shorelines; fens
A&D: Freq to common sc & extreme e; infreq to rare elsewh
Org: Native

Laportea Gaud.

L. canadensis (L.) Wedd.
Com: Wood nettle
Hab: Moist alluvial woods
A&D: Freq nw; common elsewh
Org: Native

Parietaria L.

P. pensylvanica Muhl. ex Willd.
Com: Pellitory
Hab: Wooded, rocky bluffs & ledges
A&D: Infreq ne; freq to common elsewh
Org: Native

Pilea Lindley   Clearweed

P. fontana (Lunell) Rydb.
Com: Bog clearweed
Hab: Moist, lowland prairies; pond margins; fens
A&D: Rare in lakes area & e
Org: Native

P. pumila (L.) Gray [incl. var. *deamii* (Lunell) Fern.]
Com: Clearweed
Hab: Moist woods; streambanks; alluvium
A&D: Rare nw; freq to common elsewh
Org: Native

Urtica L.

U. dioica L. [incl. ssp. *gracilis* (Aiton) Selander]
Com: Stinging nettle
Hab: Moist, alluvial woods; disturbed soil
A&D: Common thr
Org: Native

U. urens L.
Hab: Waste ground
A&D: Rare wc & ne: ALL 1925 & CAR 1921
Org: Not native

VALERIANACEAE

Valeriana L.

V. edulis Nutt. ex T. & G. ssp. *ciliata* (T. & G.) F. G. Meyer
Syn: *V. ciliata* T. & G.
Com: Valerian
Hab: Wet prairies; fens
A&D: Rare ne 1/3
Org: Native

V. officinalis L.
Com: Garden heliotrope
Hab: Moist, disturbed soil
A&D: Rare escape from cult
Org: Not native

VERBENACEAE

Phyla Lour.

P. lanceolata (Michx.) Greene
Syn: *Lippia lanceolata* Michx.
Com: Fogfruit
Hab: Marshes; pond & stream margins; alluvial woods
A&D: Infreq nw & in Iowan Surface; freq to common elsewh
Org: Native

Verbena L. Vervain

V. X *blanchardi* Moldenke
Syn: *V. hastata* X *V. simplex*
Hab: Prairie
A&D: Rare ne & sw: BH & CAS
Org: Native

V. bracteata Lag. & Rodr.
Com: Creeping vervain
Hab: Farmyards; along railroads; roadsides; loess bluffs
A&D: Infreq ne; freq to common elsewh
Org: Native

V. canadensis (L.) Britton
Hab: Ledges, limestone or rimrock
A&D: Rare ne & sc: DUB, LUC & WAR
Org: Native of U.S., but not Iowa

V. X *deamii* Moldenke
Syn: *V. bracteata* X *V. stricta*
Hab: Dry, sandy pastures; roadsides
A&D: Rare ne: ALL
Org: Native

V. X *engelmannii* Moldenke
Syn: *V. urticifolia* X *V. hastata*
Hab: Moist thickets
A&D: Rare se: LOU, MUS & VB
Org: Native

V. hastata L.
Com: Blue vervain
Hab: Marshes; moist prairies; streambanks
A&D: Common thr
Org: Native

V. X *moechina* Moldenke
Syn: *V. simplex* X *V. stricta*
Hab: Prairie openings on bluffs
A&D: Rare e: BH 1930, CLI, JON & MUS 1929
Org: Native

V. X *rydbergii* Moldenke
Syn: *V. hastata* X *V. stricta*
Hab: Moist or sandy areas
A&D: Rare nw, ne, se & sc: BH, DEC, DIC, LOU 1927 & MUS
Org: Native

V. simplex Lehm.
Syn: *V. angustifolia* Michx.
Hab: Often sandy, dry soil
A&D: Freq ne & extreme e; infreq se; rare c & nw: STO & LYO 1928
Org: Native

V. stricta Vent.
Com: Hoary vervain
Hab: Dry prairies; roadsides; dry pastures; loess bluffs
A&D: Common thr
Org: Native

V. urticifolia L.
Com: White vervain
Hab: Openings in woods; streambanks; low woods; disturbed areas
A&D: Freq to common thr
Org: Native

VIOLACEAE

Hybanthus Jacq.

H. concolor (T. F. Forster) Sprengel
Syn: *Cubellium concolor* (T. F. Forster) Raf.
Com: Green violet
Hab: Algific talus slopes
A&D: Rare c, ne & ec: ALL, BOO, CLT, DUB, JON & WNS
Org: Native

Viola L. Violet

V. adunca J. E. Sm.
Hab: Algific talus slopes
A&D: Rare ne: ALL
Org: Native

V. X *bernardii* Greene
Syn: *V. pedatifida* X *V. sororia*
Hab: Prairies & woodland margins
A&D: Rare c, nc, e & sc
Org: Native

V. canadensis L. var. *rugulosa* (Greene) C. L. Hitchc.
Syn: *V. canadensis* L. var. *corymbosa* Nutt. ex T. & G.
Syn: *V. rugulosa* Greene
Hab: Moist, wooded slopes; algific talus slopes
A&D: Infreq to rare thr most of state
Org: Native

V. incognita Brainerd
Hab: Low, moist woods
A&D: Rare ne & se: ALL, MUS 1935 & WNS
Org: Native

V. lanceolata L.
Com: Lance-leaved violet
Hab: Moist, sandy areas
A&D: Rare e: BEN, BUC, CED, JOH, JON, LIN, SCO & MUS 1923
Org: Native

V. macloskeyi Lloyd ssp. *pallens* (Banks ex DC.) M. S. Baker
Syn: *V. pallens* (Banks ex DC.) Brainerd
Hab: Wet, sandy areas; fens
A&D: Rare e, & in nw: DIC
Org: Native

V. missouriensis Greene
Hab: Moist, often sandy, alluvial woods
A&D: Freq extreme e; infreq to rare in remainder of e 1/2
Org: Native

V. missouriensis Greene X *V. sororia* Willd.
Hab: Moist woods
A&D: Rare c, ec & se: BEN, BOO, CLI, JEF 1933, STO & VB
Org: Native

V. X *napae* House
Syn: *V. pratincola* X *V. sororia*
Hab: Lawns
A&D: Rare c & se: STO 1946 & MUS 1924
Org: Native

V. nephrophylla Greene
Com: Bog violet
Hab: Low prairies; marshes; fens
A&D: Infreq thr much of state; rare nc & sw
Org: Native

V. nephrophylla Greene X *V. sororia* Willd.
Hab: Moist woods
A&D: Rare ec: CLI, JOH
Org: Native

V. pedata L. [incl. var. *lineariloba* DC.]
Com: Bird's-foot violet
Hab: Prairie remnants
A&D: Common in Pal. Plateau; freq sw; infreq elsewh
Org: Native

V. pedatifida G. Don
Com: Prairie violet
Hab: Prairie remnants; dry, rocky ridges
A&D: Common nw & nc; freq to infreq elsewh
Org: Native

V. pratincola Greene
Syn: *V. papilionacea* Pursh
Com: Common blue violet
Hab: Moist woods; roadsides; waste places
A&D: Infreq nw & extreme e; freq to common elsewh
Org: Native

V. pratincola Greene X *V. pedatifida* G. Don
Hab: Sandy, wooded slopes
A&D: Rare c, wc, nw & e
Org: Native

V. pubescens Aiton
Syn: *V. eriocarpa* Schwein.
Syn: *V. pensylvanica* Michx.
Syn: *V. pubescens* Aiton var. *eriocarpa* (Schwein.) Russell
Com: Downy yellow violet
Hab: Moist, wooded slopes; low, sandy woods
A&D: Absent nw & nc; rare to infreq elsewh
Org: Native

V. rafinesquii Greene
Syn: *V. bicolor* Pursh
Syn: *V. kitaibeliana* R. & S. var. *rafinesquii* (Greene) Fern.
Com: Wild pansy
Hab: Usually disturbed, sandy soil
A&D: Rare c, se & sc
Org: Native

V. renifolia Gray
Com: Kidney-leaved violet
Hab: Algific talus slopes
A&D: Rare ne: ALL, CLT, DUB & WNS
Org: Native

V. sagittata Aiton
Com: Arrow-leaved violet
Hab: Moist, low, sandy areas; moist prairie remnants
A&D: Rare to infreq e & sc; rare nw: LYO 1896
Org: Native

V. sagittata Aiton X *V. pedatifida* G. Don
Hab: Moist or sandy areas
A&D: Rare ec & se: JOH & MUS
Org: Native

V. sororia Willd.
Com: Hairy blue violet
Hab: Alluvial woods; moist, upland woods; woodland edges
A&D: Common thr
Org: Native

V. striata Aiton
Hab: Moist woods
A&D: Rare se: JEF & VB
Org: Native

V. X *sublanceolata* House
Syn: *V. lanceolata* X *V. macloskeyi*
Hab: Sandy marshes
A&D: Rare ec & se: JON & MUS 1935
Org: Native

V. tricolor L.
Com: Garden pansy
Hab: Disturbed soil near dwellings
A&D: Rare escape from cult
Org: Not native

V. viarum Pollard
Com: Plains violet
Hab: Sandy soil; loess
A&D: Rare s 1/2
Org: Native

VITACEAE

Ampelopsis Michx.

A. cordata Michx.
Com: Raccoon grape
Hab: Wooded bluffs
A&D: Rare se & sw: FRE 1898 & LEE
Org: Native

Parthenocissus Planchon

P. quinquefolia (L.) Planchon
Com: Virginia Creeper
Hab: Moist-to-dry upland & alluvial woods
A&D: Freq nw; rare nc; common elsewh
Org: Native

P. vitacea (Knerr) A. S. Hitchc.
Syn: *P. inserta* (Kerner) Fritsch
Com: Woodbine
Hab: Wooded slopes; sandy areas; wooded borders
A&D: Freq to common thr most of state
Org: Native

Vitis Adanson

V. aestivalis Michx. [incl. var. *argentifolia* (Munson) Fern.]
Com: Summer grape
Hab: Moist woods; openings
A&D: Rare e: CLT, DUB, FAY, JAC, JON, LEE & LOU
Org: Native

V. cinerea Engelm.
Com: Winter grape, fox grape
Hab: Often sandy, low woods
A&D: Rare s
Org: Native

V. riparia Michx.
Com: Riverbank grape
Hab: Woodland edges; along streams
A&D: Common thr
Org: Native

V. vulpina L.
Com: Frost grape
Hab: Wooded bluffs
A&D: Rare c, se & sc: DEC 1942, LEE, MAH, POW & VB
Org: Native

ZYGOPHYLLACEAE

Tribulis L.

T. terrestris L.
Com: Puncture-weed, caltrop
Hab: Sandy soil
A&D: Infreq s 1/2; rare nw: EMM, PLY & SIO
Org: Not native

ANGIOSPERMS: MONOCOTYLEDONS

AGAVACEAE

Yucca L. (Some authors place in Liliaceae)

Y. glauca Nutt. ex Fraser
Com: Soapweed
Hab: Dry loess bluffs
A&D: Freq to common in Loess Hills
Org: Native

ALISMATACEAE

Alisma L. Water plantain

A. gramineum J. G. Gmelin
Hab: Shores; shallow water
A&D: Rare wc: GRE
Org: Native

A. plantago-aquatica L. [incl. var. *americanum* Schultes; var. *parviflorum* (Pursh) Torrey]
Syn: *A. triviale* Pursh
Syn: *A. parviflorum* Pursh
Syn: *A. subcordatum* Raf.
Hab: Shallow water of lakes, ponds & streams
A&D: Common in most of state
Org: Native

Echinodorus L. C. Rich.

E. cordifolius (L.) Griseb.
Syn: *E. berteroi* (Sprengel) Fassett
Syn: *E. rostratus* (Nutt.) Engelm.
Com: Burhead
Hab: Shallow water; wet sand
A&D: Infreq sw; rare nw, ne & se
Org: Native

Sagittaria L. Arrowhead

S. brevirostra Mack. & Bush
Syn: *S. engelmanniana* J. G. Smith ssp. *brevirostra* (Mack. & Bush) Bogin
Hab: Muddy shores; shallow water
A&D: Rare to infreq e 1/2; infreq to common w 1/2
Org: Native

S. calycina Engelm.
Syn: *Lophotocarpus calycinus* (Engelm.) J. G. Smith
Syn: *S. montevidensis* Cham. & Schlecter ssp. *calycina* (Engelm.) Bogin
Hab: Muddy shores; shallow water
A&D: Infreq sw 2/3
Org: Native

S. cristata Engelm.
Syn: *S. graminea* Michx. var. *cristata* (Engelm.) Bogin
Hab: Muddy shores; shallow water
A&D: Rare se 2/3; freq in lakes area
Org: Native

S. cuneata Sheldon
Hab: Muddy shores; shallow water
A&D: Rare n 1/2 except freq in lakes area
Org: Native

S. graminea Michx.
Hab: Muddy shores; shallow water
A&D: Rare se 2/3; freq in lakes area
Org: Native

S. latifolia Willd. [incl. var. *obtusa* (Engelm.) Wiegand]
Hab: Muddy shores; shallow water
A&D: Common ne 1/2; rare to infreq elsewh
Org: Native

S. rigida Pursh
Hab: Muddy shores; shallow water
A&D: Apparently absent from nw, sw & extreme ne; infreq elsewh
Org: Native

ARACEAE

Acorus L.

A. calamus L.
Syn: *A. americanus* (Raf.) Raf.
Com: Sweetflag
Hab: Marshes; shallow, standing water
A&D: Freq c & in lakes area; rare w & extreme ne
Org: Native

Arisaema Mart.

A. dracontium (L.) Schott
Com: Green dragon
Hab: Moist alluvial woods
A&D: Rare to infreq ne; freq s; rare in lakes area
Org: Native

A. triphyllum (L.) Schott
Syn: *A. atrorubens* (Aiton) Blume
Com: Jack-in-the-pulpit
Hab: Mesic woods
A&D: Common thr
Org: Native

Peltandra Raf.

P. virginica (L.) Schott
Com: Arrow arum
Hab: Muddy shores; shallow, standing water
A&D: Rare wc, ec & se: CED, DM & GRE
Org: Native

Symplocarpus Salisb. ex Nutt.

S. foetidus (L.) Nutt.
Com: Skunk cabbage
Hab: Shaded seeps; moist alluvial woods
A&D: Rare e
Org: Native

COMMELINACEAE

Commelina L. Day-flower

C. communis L.
Hab: Moist, disturbed sites, usually near dwellings
A&D: Absent nw & extreme ne; infreq to freq elsewh
Org: Not native

C. erecta L. var. *angustifolia* (Michx.) Fern.
Hab: Dry, open, sandy areas
A&D: Rare se: LEE 1931, LOU & MUS
Org: Native

Tradescantia L. Spiderwort

T. bracteata Small
Hab: Low, sandy, open areas
A&D: Common w 2/3; rare to freq ne; infreq se
Org: Native

T. occidentalis (Britton) Smyth
Hab: Moist sand
A&D: Rare wc: WOO
Org: Native

T. ohiensis Raf.
Hab: Sandy, open places
A&D: Rare nw but absent in lakes area; freq to common se 2/3
Org: Native

T. virginiana L.
Hab: Open woodlands; disturbed, open sites
A&D: Rare se & sc: DAV 1939, JEF 1935, KEO 1897, MAH 1938, WAP 1902 & WAS
Org: Native

CYPERACEAE

Bulbostylis Kunth

B. capillaris (L.) C. B. Clarke
Syn: *Stenophyllus capillaris* (L.) Britton
Com: hair sedge
Hab: Dry, open, sandy soil
A&D: Rare to infreq e
Org: Native

Carex L. Sedge

C. aggregata Mack.
Syn: *C. sparganioides* Willd. var. *aggregata* (Mack.) Gl.
Hab: Moist, open ground; algific talus slopes
A&D: Rare c, ne & sw: ALL, CLT, PAG & STO
Org: Native

C. albursina Sheldon
Syn: *C. laxiflora* Lam. var. *latifolia* Boott
Hab: Moist, rocky, wooded slopes
A&D: Freq to common e; rare to infreq elsewh
Org: Native

C. alopecoidea Tuckerman
Hab: Low prairies; moist uplands
A&D: Rare in lakes area, se & sc
Org: Native

C. amphibola Steudel var. *turgida* Fern.
Syn: *C. grisea* Wahl.
Hab: Alluvial woods
A&D: Infreq n 1/2; infreq to common s 1/2
Org: Native

C. annectens (Bickn.) Bickn. var. *xanthocarpa* (Bickn.) Wieg.
Syn: *C. brachyglossa* Mack.
Hab: Moist areas; edges of marshes; sedge swales
A&D: Rare to infreq sw 3/4
Org: Native

C. aquatilis Wahl.
Syn: *C. substricta* (Kukenth.) Mack.
Hab: Moist prairies; fens
A&D: Rare nw & c
Org: Native

C. artitecta Mack.
Syn: *C. nigromarginata* Schwein. var. *muhlenbergii* (Gray) Gl.
Hab: Sandy soil along lakeshores
A&D: Rare sw, se & in lakes area
Org: Native

C. assiniboinensis W. Boott
Hab: Moist woods & lake margins
A&D: Rare n
Org: Native

C. atherodes Sprengel
Hab: Marshes; lake margins
A&D: Freq to common c & in lakes area; rare to infreq elsewh
Org: Native

C. backii F. Boott
Hab: Dry, wooded slopes; rocky or sandy soil
A&D: Rare nw & ne: ALL, DUB, EMM & WNS
Org: Native

C. bebbii (Bailey) Fern.
Hab: Prairie swales; moist woods
A&D: Infreq n 1/2; rare s 1/2
Org: Native

C. bicknellii Britton
Hab: Prairies
A&D: Freq w 3/4; rare e
Org: Native

C. blanda Dewey
Syn: *C. laxiflora* Lam. var. *blanda* (Dewey) Boott
Hab: Mesic woodlands
A&D: Common thr
Org: Native

C. brevior (Dewey) Mack. ex Lunell
Hab: Loess bluffs; prairie remnants
A&D: Common w & se; freq elsewh
Org: Native

C. bushii Mack.
Hab: Wet roadsides; moist, sandy areas
A&D: Rare se & sw: DAV 1939, LEE, PAG & WAP 1939
Org: Native

C. buxbaumii Wahl.
Hab: Moist prairies; fens
A&D: Rare to infreq e 3/4
Org: Native

C. careyana Dewey
Hab: Moist, wooded slopes
A&D: Rare ne & ec
Org: Native

C. cephalantha (Bailey) Bickn.
Syn: *C. muricata* L. var. *cephalantha* Bailey
Hab: Fens
A&D: Rare nc: HAN
Org: Native

C. *cephaloidea* (Dewey) Dewey
Syn: C. *sparganioides* Willd. var. *cephaloidea* (Dewey) Carey
Hab: Open, upland woods; wooded slopes
A&D: Rare to infreq e 3/4
Org: Native

C. *cephalophora* Willd.
Hab: Mesic woods; low prairies
A&D: Freq to common se 3/4
Org: Native

C. *chordorrhiza* Ehrh. ex L. f.
Hab: Fens; sphagnum fens
A&D: Rare nw & nc: EMM 1884 & HAN
Org: Native

C. *communis* Bailey
Hab: Wooded slopes
A&D: Rare s 1/2; infreq in Pal. Plateau
Org: Native

C. *comosa* Boott
Hab: Wet prairies
A&D: Freq in lakes area; rare elsewh
Org: Native

C. *conjuncta* Boott
Hab: Alluvial woods
A&D: Rare to infreq thr
Org: Native

C. *conoidea* Schkuhr ex Willd.
Hab: Sandy swales; prairie seeps
A&D: Rare ne & ec
Org: Native

C. *convoluta* Mack.
Syn: C. *flaccidula* Steudel
Syn: C. *rosea* Willd. var. *pusilla* Howe
Hab: Moist, upland woods; wooded slopes
A&D: Common n 1/2
Org: Native

C. *crawei* Dewey
Hab: Dry prairies
A&D: Rare nw, nc & ec: EMM 1904, FLO & JOH
Org: Native

C. *crawfordii* Fern.
Syn: C. *scoparia* Willd. var. *minor* Boott
Hab: Moist sand
A&D: Rare wc & nw
Org: Native

C. *crinita* Lam.
Hab: Low woods; alluvial soils
A&D: Rare ec & se: JEF 1934 & LIN
Org: Native

C. *cristatella* Britton
Hab: Alluvial woods; wet prairies
A&D: Rare nw & e; common sw; infreq to freq elsewh
Org: Native

C. *crus-corvi* Shuttlew. ex Kunze
Hab: Marshes; pond margins
A&D: Rare nw; infreq s 1/2
Org: Native

C. *davisii* Schwein. & Torrey
Hab: Alluvial woods; prairie swales
A&D: Rare n 1/2; freq s 1/2
Org: Native

C. *deweyana* Schwein.
Hab: N-facing, wooded slopes; algific talus slopes
A&D: Infreq in Pal. Plateau; rare in lakes area & c
Org: Native

C. *diandra* Schrank
Hab: Marshes; wet meadows
A&D: Rare c, nw, nc & ec: CG 1917, DIC, EMM 1925, JOH 1941, WEB 1909 & WNB 1899
Org: Native

C. *douglasii* Boott
Hab: Dry prairies
A&D: Rare c: JAS 1904
Org: Native

C. *eburnea* Boott
Hab: Open, rocky, wooded bluffs
A&D: Rare to infreq n 1/2 & sw; freq e
Org: Native

C. eleocharis Bailey
Syn: *C. stenophylla* Wahl. ssp. *eleocharis* (Bailey) Hulten
Hab: Dry prairies; gravel hills
A&D: Freq nw, especially in lakes area
Org: Native

C. emoryi Dewey
Syn: *C. stricta* Lam. var. *elongata* (Boeck.) Gl.
Hab: Sedge meadows; fens
A&D: Rare sw, in lakes area & in Pal. Plateau
Org: Native

C. festucacea Schkuhr ex Willd.
Hab: Sandy, open areas; disturbed ground
A&D: Rare nw & se: DIC & LOU
Org: Native

C. foenea Willd.
Syn: *C. siccata* Dewey
Hab: Dry, rocky prairies
A&D: Rare nw: CLY 1936
Org: Native

C. frankii Kunth
Hab: Marshes; low, wet soil
A&D: Rare se, sc & extreme e
Org: Native

C. gracilescens Steudel
Syn: *C. laxiflora* Lam. var. *gracillima* (Boott) B. L. Robinson & Fern.
Hab: Dry woods; wooded ravines
A&D: Rare se: DM & WAP 1938
Org: Native

C. gracillima Schwein.
Hab: Mesic, wooded slopes; alluvial woods
A&D: Rare n except freq in Pal. Plateau
Org: Native

C. granularis Muhl. ex Willd.
Syn: *C. haleana* Olney
Hab: Moist, wooded ravines
A&D: Rare nc; infreq e 1/2
Org: Native

C. gravida Bailey
Syn: *C. lunelliana* Mack.
Hab: Low woods; thickets; prairies
A&D: Freq to common thr
Org: Native

C. grayi Carey
Hab: Alluvial woods
A&D: Infreq se 2/3
Org: Native

C. haydenii Dewey
Hab: Moist prairies; alluvial woods
A&D: Rare to infreq n 1/2; rare s 1/2
Org: Native

C. heliophila Mack.
Syn: *C. pensylvanica* Lam. var. *digyna* Boeck.
Hab: Dry prairies; plains; loess bluffs
A&D: Infreq thr
Org: Native

C. hirsutella Mack.
Syn: *C. complanata* T. & H. var. *hirsuta* (Bailey) Gl.
Hab: Open, upland woods
A&D: Freq se; rare sc; not reported elsewh
Org: Native

C. hirtifolia Mack.
Hab: Moist, wooded slopes
A&D: Common in Pal. Plateau; infreq to rare ne 3/4
Org: Native

C. hitchcockiana Dewey
Hab: Moist, wooded, calcareous slopes
A&D: Freq in lakes area; rare to infreq elsewh
Org: Native

C. hyalinolepis Steudel
Syn: *C. lacustris* Willd. var. *laxiflora* Dewey
Hab: Railroad right-of-way
A&D: Rare sw: FRE
Org: Native

C. hystericina Muhl. ex Willd.
Syn: *C. hystricina* Muhl. ex Willd. of authors
Hab: Marshy areas; fens; alluvial woods
A&D: Common nc; infreq to freq elsewh
Org: Native

C. interior Bailey
Hab: Marshes; fens; low prairies
A&D: Rare to infreq e 2/3
Org: Native

C. jamesii Schwein.
Hab: Moist, n-facing talus slopes; moist, wooded slopes
A&D: Rare to infreq e 3/4
Org: Native

C. lacustris Willd.
Syn: *C. riparia* Curtis var. *lacustris* (Willd.) Kuek.
Hab: Marshes; sedge swales
A&D: Freq nc; rare nw & se
Org: Native

C. laeviconica Dewey
Syn: *C. atherodes* Sprengel var. *longo-lanceolata* (Dewey) Gilly
Syn: *C. trichocarpa* Schkuhr var. *deweyi* Bailey
Hab: Marsh edges; sedge swales; low prairies
A&D: Rare in much of state; not reported from se
Org: Native

C. laevivaginata (Kuek.) Mack.
Syn: *C. stipata* Muhl. ex Willd. var. *laevivaginata* Kuek.
Hab: Marshes; moist woodlands
A&D: Rare to infreq thr
Org: Native

C. lanuginosa Michx.
Syn: *C. lasiocarpa* Ehrh. var. *latifolia* (Boeck.) Gilly
Hab: Moist prairies
A&D: Common in lakes area; rare extreme e; infreq to freq elsewh
Org: Native

C. lasiocarpa Ehrh. var. *americana* Fern.
Syn: *C. lanuginosa* Michx. var. *americana* (Fern.) Boivin
Syn: *C. lasiocarpa* Ehrh. ssp. *americana* (Fern.) Love & Bernhard
Com: Slender sedge
Hab: Shallow water; prairie swales; fens
A&D: Rare c, nw, ec & se
Org: Native

C. laxiculmis Schwein.
Syn: *C.* X *copulata* (Bailey) Mack.
Syn: *C. digitalis* Willd. var. *copulata* Bailey
Hab: Wooded talus slopes
A&D: Rare se 1/4
Org: Native

C. leavenworthii Dewey
Hab: Prairie openings
A&D: Freq to infreq se; rare ne
Org: Native

C. leptalea Wahl.
Hab: Swales in sandy prairies
A&D: Rare ne & ec: BEN, BH & BUC
Org: Native

C. limosa L.
Hab: Fens
A&D: Rare nw & nc: EMM 1892 & HAN
Org: Native

C. lupuliformis Sartw. ex Dewey
Hab: Pond & lake margins
A&D: Rare se & sc: DEC 1900 & LEE 1931
Org: Native

C. lupulina Muhl. ex Willd.
Hab: Alluvial woods; marshes
A&D: Infreq to freq e; rare nw
Org: Native

C. lurida Wahl.
Hab: Low prairies
A&D: Rare c, se & sc: JEF 1945, LEE 1931, MAH & STO 1886
Org: Native

C. meadii Dewey
Syn: *C. tetanica* Schkuhr var. *meadii* (Dewey) Bailey
Hab: Prairie remnants
A&D: Rare nw & ne; freq to infreq elsewh
Org: Native

C. media R. Br.
Syn: *C. norvegica* Retz., in part
Hab: Algific talus slopes
A&D: Rare ne: CLT & DEL; disjunct from n Wisc.
Org: Native

C. molesta Mack.
Syn: *C.* X *molesta* Mack. of authors
Hab: Prairies; upland woods
A&D: Freq n, sc & sw; rare to infreq elsewh
Org: Native

C. muhlenbergii Schkuhr ex Willd. [incl. var. *enervis* Boott]
Hab: Dry, sandy prairies; dry woodlands
A&D: Freq se; rare to infreq elsewh
Org: Native

C. muskingumensis Schwein.
Hab: Alluvial woods; marsh edges
A&D: Rare n; infreq s
Org: Native

C. normalis Mack.
Hab: Moist woods; prairies
A&D: Freq ne; infreq elsewh
Org: Native

C. oligocarpa Willd.
Hab: Moist, n-facing, wooded slopes
A&D: Freq in Pal. Plateau; rare to infreq elsewh
Org: Native

C. peckii Howe
Syn: *C. nigromarginata* Schwein. var. *elliptica* (Boott) Gl.
Hab: Algific talus slopes
A&D: Freq in Pal. Plateau
Org: Native

C. pedunculata Muhl. ex Willd.
Hab: Wooded talus slopes
A&D: Common in Pal. Plateau; rare to infreq in remainder of ne 1/2
Org: Native

C. pensylvanica Lam.
Hab: Upland woods; wooded slopes
A&D: Common thr
Org: Native

C. plantaginea Lam.
Hab: Moist, n-facing, wooded slopes
A&D: Rare e
Org: Native

C. praegracilis W. Boott
Hab: Moist prairies
A&D: Infreq to rare w 3/4
Org: Native

C. prairea Dewey
Syn: *C. prarisa* Dewey
Hab: Fens
A&D: Freq in lakes area; rare e
Org: Native

C. projecta Mack.
Hab: Alluvial woods; wet prairies
A&D: Rare e 1/2 & nc
Org: Native

C. retroflexa Muhl. ex Willd.
Hab: Moist, open, sandy ground
A&D: Rare ec: JON
Org: Native

C. retrorsa Schwein.
Hab: Wooded bluffs; alluvial woods
A&D: Infreq nc; rare ne
Org: Native

C. richardsonii R. Br.
Hab: Dry, open, rocky places
A&D: Rare c & n
Org: Native

C. rosea Schkuhr ex Willd.
Syn: *C. flaccidula* Steudel in part
Syn: *C. rosea* Willd. var. *radiata* (Wahl.) Dewey
Syn: *C. radiata* (Wahl.) Small
Hab: Alluvial woods
A&D: Freq to common nw & s; rare in lakes area
Org: Native

C. rostrata Stokes ex Willd. var. *utriculata* (Boott) Bailey
Syn: *C. inflata* Hudson var. *utriculata* (Boott) Druce
Hab: Prairie swales; marshes
A&D: Rare in scattered sites thr
Org: Native

C. sartwellii Dewey
Hab: Moist-to-wet prairies; marshes; fens
A&D: Infreq thr
Org: Native

C. saximontana Mack.
Syn: *C. backii* Boott var. *saximontana* (Mack.) Boivin
Hab: Dry woods; prairies
A&D: Rare wc & nw: LYO, PLY & WOO
Org: Native

C. scoparia Schkuhr ex Willd.
Hab: Sedge meadows; marsh margins; alluvial woods
A&D: Common ne 1/4, except rare in Pal. Plateau; infreq to freq elsewh
Org: Native

C. shortiana Dewey
Hab: Low, moist woods
A&D: Freq to infreq se & sc; rare ne
Org: Native

C. sparganioides Muhl. ex Willd.
Hab: Moist woods
A&D: Infreq to freq thr
Org: Native

C. sprengelii Dewey ex Sprengel
Hab: Upland woods; thickets
A&D: Common in Pal. Plateau; rare se; freq to infreq elsewh
Org: Native

C. squarrosa L.
Hab: Moist woodland depressions; alluvial woods
A&D: Rare se
Org: Native

C. sterilis Willd.
Hab: Fens
A&D: Rare ne: BUC, CHI, FAY & WNS
Org: Native

C. stipata Muhl. ex Willd.
Syn: *C.* X *stipata* Muhl. ex Willd. of authors
Hab: Marshes; prairie swales
A&D: Freq nc & ne; rare sc & sw
Org: Native

C. stricta Lam.
Syn: *C. strictior* Dewey
Hab: Alluvial woods; marshes; calcareous fens
A&D: Common sw; rare se & extreme e; infreq to freq elsewh
Org: Native

C. suberecta (Olney) Britton
Hab: Mudflats; prairie swales
A&D: Infreq nc; rare ne, se & sw
Org: Native

C. sychnocephala Carey
Hab: Marshes; sandy areas
A&D: Infreq nw, especially in lakes area; rare se: LOU
Org: Native

C. tenera Dewey
Hab: Wooded slopes
A&D: Not reported ec & se; rare elsewh
Org: Native

C. tetanica Schkuhr
Hab: Wet prairies; marshes
A&D: Rare to infreq n 1/2
Org: Native

C. tonsa (Fern.) Bickn.
Syn: *C. rugospermum* Mack. var. *tonsa* (Fern.) Voss
Syn: *C. umbellata* Schkuhr ex Willd. var. *tonsa* Fern.
Hab: Sandy soil; sand dunes
A&D: Rare e
Org: Native

C. tribuloides Wahl.
Hab: Marshes; wet, sandy areas; fens
A&D: Common s 1/2; infreq extreme e; rare nw
Org: Native

C. trichocarpa Schkuhr
Hab: Wet sands or marshes
A&D: Rare thr most of state
Org: Native

C. tuckermanii Dewey
Hab: Wet soil along rivers
A&D: Rare c: JAS 1897
Org: Native

C. typhina Michx.
Hab: Marshes; alluvial woods
A&D: Rare se 2/3
Org: Native

C. umbellata Schkuhr ex Willd.
Syn: *C. abdita* Bickn.
Hab: Sandy or rocky, dry prairies
A&D: Rare ne: ALL & DUB
Org: Native

C. vesicaria L.
Hab: Sandy marshes; lake margins
A&D: Infreq nc & ne; rare s 1/2
Org: Native

C. vulpinoidea Michx.
Hab: Low, moist ground; alluvial woods
A&D: Common thr
Org: Native

C. woodii Dewey
Syn: *C. tetanica* Schkuhr var. *woodii* (Dewey) Wood
Hab: Cool, n-facing talus slopes; moist, wooded slopes
A&D: Infreq to rare ne
Org: Native

Cyperus L. Nut grass, umbrella sedge

C. acuminatus Torrey & Hooker
Hab: Often sandy, wet areas
A&D: Infreq to rare sw 2/3
Org: Native

C. aristatus Rottb.
Syn: *C. inflexus* Muhl.
Hab: Wet, usually sandy, areas
A&D: Freq nc; infreq sw 1/2; rare e
Org: Native

C. diandrus Torrey
Hab: Wet sandy areas
A&D: Rare thr most of state
Org: Native

C. engelmannii Steudel
Hab: Moist, sandy edges of ponds & lakes
A&D: Rare n 1/2
Org: Native

C. erythrorhizos Muhl.
Hab: Moist, sandy or muddy, margins of streams, ponds & lakes
A&D: Freq s; infreq to rare n 1/2 & e
Org: Native

C. esculentus L.
Com: Yellow nut grass
Hab: Shores; marshes; moist, disturbed soil
A&D: Freq to common s 1/2 & nc; infreq to rare elsewh
Org: Native

C. filiculmis Vahl
Syn: *C. bushii* Britton
Hab: Dry, sandy soil
A&D: Common locally in extreme ne; freq s 1/2; rare elsewh
Org: Native

C. odoratus L. var. *squarrosus* (Britton) Gilly
Syn: *C. ferruginescens* Boeck.
Syn: *C. speciosus* Vahl
Hab: Moist or wet soil
A&D: Freq to common nw; infreq s 1/2; infreq to rare ne 1/4
Org: Native

C. rivularis Kunth
Hab: Moist, open sand; pond margins; fens
A&D: Freq to infreq thr
Org: Native

C. schweinitzii Torrey
Hab: Sandy areas; dry prairies; roadsides
A&D: Freq to infreq ne 1/2
Org: Native

C. strigosus L.
Hab: Moist, sandy shores; marshy places; wet prairies
A&D: Freq to common thr
Org: Native

Dulichium L. C. Rich.

D. arundinaceum (L.) Britton
Com: Three-way sedge
Hab: Sandy, shallow marshes; fens
A&D: Rare nc, ne, se & sc
Org: Native

Eleocharis R. Br. Spike-rush

E. acicularis (L.) R. & S.
Hab: Shallow water; margins of ponds & lakes
A&D: Freq to infreq thr most of state
Org: Native

E. atropurpurea (Retz.) Kunth
Hab: Sandy, moist areas
A&D: Rare se: JEF 1933, LOU & MUS
Org: Native

E. compressa Sulliv.
Syn: *E. elliptica* Kunth var. *compressa* (Sulliv.) Drapalik & Mohlenb.
Hab: Moist, sandy areas; mesic prairies
A&D: Infreq to rare thr most of state
Org: Native

E. engelmannii Steudel
Syn: *E. obtusa* (Willd.) Schultes var. *engelmannii* (Steudel) Gilly
Hab: Sandy or muddy shores; prairie swales
A&D: Common in Pal. Plateau; freq nc & sc; infreq to rare elsewh
Org: Native

E. erythropoda Steudel
Syn: *E. calva* Torrey, invalid name
Syn: *E. palustris* (L.) R. & S. var. *calva* (Torrey) Gray
Hab: Moist, open sand; marshes; margins of lakes
A&D: Freq to common w 1/2; infreq to rare e 1/2
Org: Native

E. macrostachya Britton
Syn: *E. palustris* (L.) R. & S. var. *australis* Nees
Hab: Shallow water; prairie swales
A&D: Freq to common nc & sc; infreq to rare e
Org: Native

E. obtusa (Willd.) Schultes
Hab: Sandy or muddy shores; moist prairies
A&D: Common in Pal. Plateau; infreq to freq elsewh
Org: Native

E. olivacea Torrey
Syn: *E. flavescens* (Poiret) Urban var. *olivacea* (Torrey) Gl.
Hab: Margins of lakes
A&D: Rare ec: JOH
Org: Native

E. ovata (Roth) R. & S.
Syn: *E. obtusa* (Willd.) Schultes var. *ovata* (Roth) Drapalik & Mohlenb.
Hab: Fens
A&D: Rare nc: HAN
Org: Native

E. parvula (R. & S.) Link var. *anachaeta* (Torrey) Svenson
Syn: *E. coloradoensis* (Britton) Gilly
Hab: Muddy or sandy shores
A&D: Rare nw: CLY 1936 & PA 1940
Org: Native

E. pauciflora (Lightf.) Link
Hab: Sandy or muddy margins of lakes or marshes; fens
A&D: Rare nw: DIC & EMM
Org: Native

E. smallii Britton
Syn: *E. palustris* (L.) R. & S. var. *major* Sonder
Hab: Shallow water; prairie swales
A&D: Freq to common nc; infreq to rare ne
Org: Native

E. tenuis (Willd.) Schultes [incl. var. *verrucosa* (Svenson) Svenson]
Syn: *E. verrucosa* (Svenson) Harms
Hab: Wet prairies; marshes
A&D: Rare thr most of state
Org: Native

E. wolfii Gray
Hab: Marshes; seeps
A&D: Rare nw, ec & sw: CED, EMM 1886, JOH & UNI
Org: Native

E. xyridiformis Fern. & Brackett
Hab: Shallow, standing water
A&D: Rare sw: PAG
Org: Native

Eriophorum L. Cotton-grass

E. angustifolium Honck.
Syn: *E. polystachion* L.
Com: Tall cotton-grass
Hab: Fens; wet prairies; sedge meadows
A&D: Infreq n 1/2; rare s
Org: Native

E. gracile W. D. J. Koch
Com: Slender cotton-grass
Hab: Marshes; sedge meadows; fens
A&D: Rare c, nw & nc: CG 1917, DIC, EMM 1893, HAN & WEB 1905
Org: Native

E. virginicum L.
Hab: Fens
A&D: Rare ne: BUC
Org: Native

Fimbristylis Vahl

F. autumnalis (L.) R. & S. [incl. var. *mucronulata* (Michx.) Fern.]
Hab: Sandy or muddy lake margins; vernal pools
A&D: Rare e
Org: Native

Fuirena Rottb. Umbrella grass

F. simplex Vahl
Hab: Moist soil
A&D: Rare sw: FRE 1946
Org: Native

Hemicarpha Nees & Arn.

H. micrantha (Vahl) Pax
Syn: *Scirpus micranthus* Vahl
Hab: Streambanks; lakeshores
A&D: Rare nc & ne; infreq se
Org: Native

Rhynchospora Vahl

R. capillacea Torrey
Com: Beaked rush
Hab: Fens
A&D: Rare n
Org: Native

Scirpus L. Bulrush

S. *acutus* Muhl. ex Bigelow
Com: Hard-stemmed bulrush
Hab: Shallow water; margins of lakes, marshes & streams
A&D: Freq to common thr most of state; rare ne
Org: Native

S. *americanus* Pers.
Com: Threesquare
Hab: Wet, sandy soil; fens
A&D: Freq nc; rare nw; rare to infreq sw 1/2
Org: Native

S. *atrovirens* Willd.
Com: Dark green bulrush
Hab: Wet places, especially margins of lakes, marshes, ponds & streams
A&D: Common thr
Org: Native

S. *cyperinus* (L.) Kunth [incl. var. *brachypodus* (Fern.) Gilly; var. *rubricosus* (Kunth) Gilly; var. *laxus* (Gray) Beetle]
Com: Wooly bulrush
Hab: Sandy wetlands; prairie swales; marshes
A&D: Freq to common ne; infreq to rare s
Org: Native

S. *fluviatilis* (Torrey) Gray
Com: River bulrush
Hab: Marshes; shallow, standing water
A&D: Freq to infreq thr most of state
Org: Native

S. *hallii* Gray
Hab: Wet, sandy soil
A&D: Rare se: LOU & MUS 1890
Org: Native

S. *heterochaetus* Chase
Hab: Marshes; shallow, standing water
A&D: Infreq to rare thr most of state
Org: Native

S. *maritimus* L.
Syn: S. *paludosus* A. Nelson
Com: Prairie bulrush
Hab: Sandy lakeshores; sloughs
A&D: Rare nw: DIC & PA 1943
Org: Native

S. *mucronatus* L.
Hab: Shallow, standing water
A&D: Rare sw: PAG
Org: Not native

S. *pallidus* (Britton) Fern.
Syn: S. *atrovirens* Willd. var. *pallidus* Britton
Com: Pale bulrush
Hab: Prairie swales
A&D: Infreq w 1/2
Org: Native

S. *pedicellatus* Fern.
Syn: S. *cyperinus* (L.) Kunth var. *pedicellatus* (Fern.) Schuyler
Hab: Sandy wetlands; prairie swales; marshes
A&D: Rare e: MUS, SCO & WNS 1933
Org: Native

S. *pendulus* Muhl.
Syn: S. *lineatus* Michx., misappl.
Hab: Edges of marshes; wet prairies; roadsides
A&D: Freq to infreq nc & s; rare ne
Org: Native

S. *smithii* Gray
Hab: Sandy shores
A&D: Rare nc & ne: CG & DEL
Org: Native

S. *torreyi* Olney
Hab: Marshes; lake margins
A&D: Rare ec: CLI 1878
Org: Native

S. validus Vahl var. *creber* Fern.
Syn: *S. tabernaemontanii* K. C. Gmelin
Com: Soft-stemmed bulrush
Hab: Shallow, standing water
A&D: Freq to common thr most of state
Org: Native

Scleria Berg. Nut-rush

S. triglomerata Michx.
Com: Tall nut-rush
Hab: Moist prairies & alluvium
A&D: Infreq to rare e 1/2 & sw
Org: Native

S. verticillata Muhl. ex Willd.
Com: Low nut-rush
Hab: Fens
A&D: Rare c, nw & ne: CHI, CLY, EMM, FAY & GRU
Org: Native

DIOSCOREACEAE

Dioscorea L. Wild yam

D. villosa L.
Hab: Open, upland woods
A&D: Common nw; infreq to rare elsewh
Org: Native

HYDROCHARITACEAE

Elodea Michx.

E. canadensis Michx.
Syn: *Anacharis canadensis* (Michx.) Richardson
Hab: Shallow, standing water; shallow streams
A&D: Common in lakes area; infreq remainder of n 1/2; rare e
Org: Native

E. nuttallii (Planchon) St. John
Syn: *Anacharis nuttallii* Planchon
Hab: Shallow, standing water; shallow streams
A&D: Freq se; infreq to rare elsewh
Org: Native

Vallisneria L. Tape grass, eel grass

V. americana Michx.
Hab: Shallow water
A&D: Freq in Mississippi R.; rare nc & in lakes area
Org: Native

IRIDACEAE

Belamcanda Adanson

B. chinensis (L.) DC.
Com: Blackberry lily
Hab: Roadsides; grazed slopes
A&D: Rare escape from cult
Org: Not native

Iris L.

I. X *germanica* L.
Com: Bearded iris
Hab: Waste or disturbed areas
A&D: Rare: occasionally persists from cult
Org: Not native

I. shrevei Small
Syn: *I. versicolor* L. var. *shrevei* (Small) Boivin
Syn: *I. virginica* L. var. *shrevei* (Small) E. Anderson
Com: Blue flag
Hab: Shallow water of marshes, ponds & lakes; prairie swales
A&D: Freq to common thr most of state; especially common in lakes area & nc
Org: Native

Sisyrinchium L. Blue-eyed grass

S. angustifolium P. Miller
Syn: *S. bermudiana* L.
Hab: Moist woods; moist prairies
A&D: Rare s 1/2
Org: Native

S. campestre Bickn. [incl. var. *kansanum* Bickn.]
Hab: Prairies; clearings in woods
A&D: Common thr
Org: Native

JUNCACEAE

Juncus L. Rush

J. acuminatus Michx.
Hab: Wet, sandy prairies; vernal pools
A&D: Infreq se; rare ne & sw
Org: Native

J. alpinus Vill. var. *fuscescens* Fern.
Hab: Fens; wet, sandy soil
A&D: Rare wc & nw: DIC, HRR 1909 & WOO 1888
Org: Native

J. balticus Willd. var. *littoralis* Engelm.
Com: Bog rush
Hab: Moist prairies; lake margins; fens
A&D: Infreq in lakes area; rare elsewh
Org: Native

J. bufonius L.
Com: Toad rush
Hab: Moist sand; lakeshores
A&D: Rare & scattered w, n & se
Org: Native

J. canadensis J. Gay ex Laharpe
Hab: Wet, sandy areas; marsh edges
A&D: Rare sc & e 1/4
Org: Native

J. dudleyi Wieg.
Syn: *J. tenuis* Willd. var. *dudleyi* (Wieg.) F. J. Harms
Syn: *J. tenuis* Willd. var. *uniflorus* (Farw.) Farw.
Hab: Shorelines; wet prairies; wet sand
A&D: Freq to common nc, sc & in lakes area; infreq elsewh
Org: Native

J. effusus L. [incl. var. *solutus* Fern. & Wieg.]
Hab: Marsh edges; alluvial woods
A&D: Rare e
Org: Native

J. greenei Oakes & Tuckerman
Hab: Moist prairie remnants; vernal pools
A&D: Rare ne & ec
Org: Native

J. interior Wieg.
Hab: Moist, open, sandy soil
A&D: Freq to common s 1/2; infreq n 1/2
Org: Native

J. marginatus Rostk.
Hab: Margins of marshes & ponds
A&D: Rare ec & se: CED, CLI, MUS 1892 & SCO
Org: Native

J. X *nodosiformis* Fern.
Syn: *J. alpinus* X *J. nodosus*
Hab: Fens
A&D: Rare nw: DIC
Org: Native

J. nodosus L.
Hab: Sandy marshes; moist prairies
A&D: Infreq to rare thr
Org: Native

J. tenuis Willd.
Com: Path rush
Hab: Along woodland paths; packed soil; moist habitats
A&D: Rare nw; common elsewh
Org: Native

J. torreyi Cov.
Hab: Low, sandy prairies; marshes; muddy shores
A&D: Freq to common w 1/2; infreq to rare e 1/2
Org: Native

J. vaseyi Engelm.
Hab: Moist to mesic prairie
A&D: Rare ne: BH & HOW
Org: Native

Luzula DC. Woodrush

L. acuminata Raf.
Hab: Cool, moist, wooded slopes; algific talus slopes
A&D: Infreq e
Org: Native

L. multiflora (Retz.) Lej. [incl. var. *bulbosa* Wood]
Syn: *L. campestris* (L.) DC. var. *multiflora* (Ehrh.) Celak.
Hab: Sandy, wooded slopes; prairie remnants; algific talus slopes
A&D: Rare ne 1/2
Org: Native

JUNCAGINACEAE

Scheuchzeria L. (Some authors place in Scheuchzeriaceae)

S. palustris L. var. *americana* Fern.
Syn: *S. americana* (Fern.) G. N. Jones
Hab: Fens
A&D: Rare nw: EMM 1884
Org: Native

Triglochin L. Arrow-grass

T. maritimum L.
Com: Common arrow-grass
Hab: Fens; low prairies
A&D: Rare c & n
Org: Native

T. palustris L.
Com: Slender arrow-grass
Hab: Fens
A&D: Rare nw & ne: CHI, CLY, DIC, EMM, OSC & PA 1948
Org: Native

LEMNACEAE

Lemna L.

L. minor L. [incl. *L. turionifera* Landolt]
Com: Duckweed
Hab: Stagnant water
A&D: Common thr
Org: Native

L. perpusilla Torrey
Hab: Ponds
A&D: Rare ec: JOH 1915
Org: Native

L. trisulca L.
Com: Star duckweed
Hab: Stagnant water
A&D: Common in lakes area; infreq to rare elsewh
Org: Native

Spirodela Schleiden

S. polyrhiza (L.) Schleiden
Com: Greater duckweed
Hab: Stagnant water
A&D: Freq to common thr most of state
Org: Native

Wolffia Horkel ex Schleiden Watermeal

W. columbiana Karsten
Hab: Stagnant water
A&D: Common in lakes area; infreq to rare elsewh
Org: Native

W. punctata Griseb.
Syn: *W. borealis* (Engelm.) Landolt
Hab: Stagnant water
A&D: Infreq to rare ne 1/2
Org: Native

LILIACEAE

Allium L.

A. canadense L.
Com: Wild onion
Hab: Prairie remnants
A&D: Freq to common thr
Org: Native

A. cernuum Roth
Com: Nodding wild onion
Hab: N-facing, wooded talus slopes
A&D: Rare in Pal. Plateau
Org: Native

A. mutabile Michx.
Syn: *A. canadense* L. var. *mobilense* (Regel) M. Ownbey
Com: Wild onion
Hab: Mesic prairie along old railroad
A&D: Rare ne: BH
Org: Native

A. porrum L.
Com: Leek
Hab: Roadside
A&D: Rare sw: MIL
Org: Not native

A. stellatum Nutt. ex Ker-Gawl.
Com: Wild prairie onion
Hab: Prairie remnants
A&D: Freq to common nw 1/4; rare ne
Org: Native

A. tricoccum Aiton [incl. var. *burdickii* Hanes]
Com: Wild leek
Hab: Moist, wooded slopes & ravines
A&D: Freq to common ne; infreq elsewh
Org: Native

A. vineale L.
Com: Field garlic
Hab: Sandy roadsides; sand & gravel pits
A&D: Rare in ec & s, spreading rapidly
Org: Not native

Asparagus L.

A. officinalis L.
Com: Garden asparagus
Hab: Disturbed ground; roadsides
A&D: Freq to common escape from cult
Org: Not native

Camassia Lindley

C. scilloides (Raf.) Cory
Com: Eastern camass
Hab: Woodland margins; prairie remnants
A&D: Infreq to rare s 1/2
Org: Native

Convallaria L.

C. majalis L.
Com: Lily-of-the-valley
Hab: Disturbed ground near dwellings
A&D: Rare escape from cult
Org: Not native

Erythronium L.

E. albidum Nutt. [incl. var. *mesochoreum* (Knerr) Rickett; E. mesochoreum Knerr]
Com: White trout-lily, white dogtooth-violet
Hab: Moist alluvial woods; moist woodlands; shaded bluffs
A&D: Freq thr
Org: Native

E. americanum Ker-Gawl.
Syn: *E. umbilicatum* Parks & Hardin
Com: Yellow trout-lily, yellow dogtooth-violet
Hab: Moist, wooded slopes; alluvial woodlands; algific talus slopes
A&D: Rare nw, ne & sc: ALL, DUB, FAY, LUC, MRN, O'B 1921 & WNS
Org: Native

Hemerocallis L.

H. fulva (L.) L.
Com: Day lily
Hab: Roadsides; sandy fields
A&D: Common escape from cult thr
Org: Not native

Hypoxis L. (Some authors place in Amaryllidaceae)

H. hirsuta (L.) Cov.
Com: Yellow stargrass
Hab: Prairie remnants; openings in woodlands
A&D: Infreq ne; freq to common elsewh
Org: Native

Lilium L.

L. lancifolium Thunb.
Syn: *L. tigrinum* Ker-Gawl.
Com: Tiger lily
Hab: Disturbed ground along railroads & roads
A&D: Rare escape from gardens
Org: Not native

L. michiganense Farw.
Syn: *L. canadense* L. ssp. *michiganense* (Farw.) Boivin & Cody
Syn: *L. superbum* L., misappl.
Com: Michigan lily
Hab: Moist prairies; roadsides
A&D: Freq to infreq thr
Org: Native

L. philadelphicum L. var. *andinum* (Nutt.) Ker-Gawl.
Syn: *L. umbellatum* Pursh
Com: Wood lily
Hab: Moist prairies
A&D: Infreq to rare thr
Org: Native

Maianthemum Wiggers

M. canadense Desf. [incl. var. *interius* Fern.]
Com: Canada mayflower
Hab: Moist, wooded slopes
A&D: Common in Pal. Plateau, rare in remainder of e
Org: Native

Melanthium L.

M. virginicum L.
Syn: *Veratrum virginicum* (L.) Aiton f.
Com: Bunch-flower
Hab: Moist prairies
A&D: Infreq c, se & sc; rare ne
Org: Native

Ornithogalum L.

O. umbellatum L.
Com: Star of Bethlehem
Hab: Disturbed habitats near dwellings; grassy roadsides
A&D: Rare escape from cult
Org: Not native

Polygonatum P. Miller

P. biflorum (Walter) Ell.
Syn: *P. canaliculatum* (Muhl.) Pursh
Syn: *P. commutatum* (Schultes f.) A. Dietr.
Com: Solomon's seal
Hab: Upland woods; woodland borders; roadsides
A&D: Common thr
Org: Native

P. pubescens (Willd.) Pursh
Com: Downy Solomon's seal
Hab: Moist, e- & n-facing wooded slopes
A&D: Rare ne: ALL & WNS
Org: Native

Smilacina Desf.

S. racemosa (L.) Desf.
Com: False Solomon's seal, false spikenard
Hab: Moist woodlands
A&D: Infreq nw; common elsewh
Org: Native

S. stellata (L.) Desf.
Com: Starry false Solomon's seal
Hab: Moist woodlands
A&D: Infreq nw; common elsewh
Org: Native

Smilax L. (Some authors place in Smilacaceae)

S. ecirrhata (Engelm. ex Kunth) S. Watson
Com: Carrion flower
Hab: Moist, upland woods
A&D: Infreq e; freq to common elsewh
Org: Native

S. herbacea L. [incl. var. *lasioneura* (Hooker) A. DC.]
Syn: *S. lasioneura* Hooker
Com: Carrion flower
Hab: Woodlands; woodland borders; roadsides
A&D: Freq to common thr
Org: Native

S. hispida Muhl.
Syn: *S. rotundifolia* L., misappl.
Syn: *S. tamnoides* L. var. *hispida* (Muhl.) Fern.
Com: Greenbrier
Hab: Alluvial woods; moist woods; thickets
A&D: Infreq nw; common elsewh
Org: Native

Streptopus Michx.

S. roseus Michx.
Com: Rosy twisted stalk
Hab: Algific talus slopes
A&D: Rare ne & ec: ALL, CLT, DEL, DUB, FAY, JAC & WNS
Org: Native

Trillium L.

T. cernuum L.
Com: Nodding trillium
Hab: Moist, wooded slopes & ravines
A&D: Infreq nc & in Iowan Surface; rare se
Org: Native

T. flexipes Raf.
Syn: *T. declinatum* (Gray) Gl.
Syn: *T. gleasoni* Fern.
Com: Nodding trillium
Hab: Moist, wooded slopes; shaded hillsides
A&D: Common ne; rare elsewh
Org: Native

T. nivale Riddell
Com: Snow trillium
Hab: Moist woods; calcareous, wooded slopes
A&D: Rare e 1/2; infreq w 1/2
Org: Native

T. recurvatum Beck
Com: Wake Robin
Hab: Alluvial woods
A&D: Infreq to rare e
Org: Native

Uvularia L.

U. grandiflora Small
Syn: *U. perfoliata* L., misappl.
Com: Bellwort
Hab: Moist, upland woods; wooded slopes
A&D: Infreq nw & sc; common elsewh
Org: Native

U. sessilifolia L.
Com: Sessile-leaved bellwort
Hab: Moist, upland woods
A&D: Rare nc, ne & se
Org: Native

Veratrum L.

V. woodii J. W. Robbins
Syn: *Melanthium woodii* (Robbins ex Wood) Bodkin
Com: False hellebore
Hab: Wooded, calcareous slopes
A&D: Rare s
Org: Native

Zigadenus Michx.

Z. elegans Pursh
Syn: *Z. elegans* Pursh ssp. *elegans*
Com: White camass
Hab: Prairies
A&D: Infreq n
Org: Native

Z. glaucus Nutt.
Syn: *Z. elegans* Pursh ssp. *glaucus* (Nutt.) Hulten
Com: White camass
Hab: Thin soil on sandstone or limestone ledges
A&D: Rare ne
Org: Native

NAJADACEAE

Najas L.   Naiad

N. flexilis (Willd.) Rostk. & Schmidt
Hab: Shallow standing water
A&D: Freq se & in lakes area of nw; rare elsewh
Org: Native

N. guadalupensis (Sprengel) Magnus
Hab: Shallow standing water
A&D: Freq to infreq in lakes area of nw, & also nc, se & sc; rare elsewh
Org: Native

ORCHIDACEAE

Aplectrum (Nutt.) Torrey

A. hyemale (Muhl. ex Willd.) Torrey
Com: Putty-root orchid
Hab: Moist, upland woods
A&D: Infreq to rare c & e
Org: Native

Calopogon R. Br.

C. tuberosus (L.) BSP.
Syn: *C. pulchellus* (Salisb.) R. Br.
Com: Grass pink orchid
Hab: Moist, sandy, acidic soils; fens
A&D: Rare e (all pre-1900 except LIN 1951)
Org: Native

Coeloglossum Hartman

C. viride (L.) Hartman var. *virescens* (Muhl. ex Willd.) Luer
Syn: *Habenaria bracteata* (Muhl. ex Willd.) R. Br.
Syn: *Habenaria viridis* (L.) R. Br. var. *bracteata* (Muhl. ex Willd.) Gray
Com: Bracted orchid
Hab: Woodland margins; interiors of upland woods
A&D: Infreq ne 3/4
Org: Native

Corallorhiza Gagnebin

C. maculata (Raf.) Raf.
Com: Spotted coral-root
Hab: Moist, upland woods; sandy, wooded slopes
A&D: Rare ne: ALL, CLT, DUB & WNS
Org: Native

C. odontorhiza (Willd.) Nutt.
Com: Fall coral-root orchid
Hab: Rich, upland woods; moist, sandy, wooded slopes
A&D: Rare & local thr
Org: Native

Cypripedium L.

C. X *andrewsii* Fuller
Syn: *C. calceolus* var. *pubescens* X *C. candidum*
Syn: *C. calceolus* var. *parviflorum* X *C. candidum*
Hab: Woodland seeps; sedge meadows; moist prairies
A&D: Rare ne & sc: BRE, CHI, DEC, FAY & HOW
Org: Native

C. calceolus L. var. *parviflorum* (Salisb.) Fern.
Syn: *C. parviflorum* Salisb.
Com: Small yellow lady's-slipper orchid
Hab: Sedge meadows; wet prairie
A&D: Rare ne: BUC & CHI
Org: Native

C. calceolus L. var. *pubescens* (Willd.) Correll
Syn: *C. pubescens* Willd.
Com: Yellow lady's-slipper orchid
Hab: Moist, upland woods & slopes; moist prairies
A&D: Infreq to rare e 1/2; rare & scattered w 1/2
Org: Native

C. candidum Muhl. ex Willd.
Com: Small white lady's-slipper orchid
Hab: Moist prairies; prairie swales; fens
A&D: Rare & local thr
Org: Native

C. reginae Walter
Com: Showy lady's-slipper orchid
Hab: Moist woods; algific talus slopes; wet prairies
A&D: Rare & local ne; formerly scattered e 2/3
Org: Native

Galearis Raf.

G. spectabilis (L.) Raf.
Syn: *Orchis spectabilis* L.
Com: Showy orchis
Hab: Moist woods
A&D: Freq ne; rare sw; infreq elsewh
Org: Native

Goodyera R. Br.

G. pubescens (Willd.) R. Br.
Com: Rattlesnake plantain
Hab: Moist woods; white pine groves
A&D: Rare & local e
Org: Native

Habenaria see ***Coeloglossum*** or ***Platanthera***

Liparis L. C. Rich.

L. liliifolia (L.) L. C. Rich. ex Lindley
Com: Twayblade
Hab: Moist, upland woods; wooded slopes
A&D: Infreq e 3/4
Org: Native

L. loeselii (L.) L. C. Rich.
Com: Bog twayblade
Hab: Fens & other moist to wet habitats
A&D: Rare wc, n & e
Org: Native

Malaxis Solander ex Sw.

M. unifolia Michx.
Com: Adder's mouth orchid
Hab: Upland woods
A&D: Rare c & e: IOW 1923, JOH 1907, MUS 1893, STO 1897, TAM n.d. (pre-1900) & WNS 1879
Org: Native

Orchis see ***Galearis***

Platanthera L. C. Rich.

P. clavellata (Michx.) Luer
Syn: *Habenaria clavellata* (Michx.) Sprengel
Syn: *P.* X *clavellata* (Michx.) Luer of authors
Com: Wood orchid
Hab: Sandy woods
A&D: Rare e: FAY 1894, LIN, & MUS 1894
Org: Native

P. flava (L.) Lindley var. *herbiola* (R. Br.) Luer
Syn: *Habenaria flava* (L.) Sprengel var. *herbiola* (R. Br.) Ames & Correll
Com: Tubercled orchid
Hab: Moist, low prairies; sedge meadows
A&D: Rare nc & e
Org: Native

P. hookeri (Torrey ex Gray) Lindley
Syn: *Habenaria hookeri* Torrey ex Gray
Com: Round-leaved orchid
Hab: Moist, upland woods; sandy, wooded slopes
A&D: Rare & local ne
Org: Native

P. hyperborea (L.) R. Br. var. *huronensis* (Nutt.) Luer
Syn: *Habenaria hyperborea* (L.) R. Br. var. *huronensis* (Nutt.) Farw.
Com: Leafy northern green orchid
Hab: Fens; seeps; moist woods
A&D: Rare c, nw & ne: CHE, CLY, DIC, EMM, HOW, STO 1890 & WNS n.d. (pre-1900)
Org: Native

P. lacera (Michx.) G. Don ex Sweet
Syn: *Habenaria lacera* (Michx.) R. Br.
Com: Green fringed orchid
Hab: Moist, open ground
A&D: Rare se: DM & LEE 1929
Org: Native

P. leucophaea (Nutt.) Lindley
Syn: *Habenaria leucophaea* (Nutt.) Gray
Com: Eastern prairie fringed orchid
Hab: Prairie swales
A&D: Rare e: BH 1894, CLT, DEL, HEN 1843, IOW 1903, JOH, LIN 1921 & MUS 1908
Org: Native

P. praeclara Sheviak & Bowles
Com: Western prairie fringed orchid
Hab: Prairie swales
A&D: Rare in scattered locations thr
Org: Native

P. psycodes (L.) Lindley
Syn: *Habenaria psycodes* (L.) Sprengel
Com: Purple fringed orchid
Hab: Moist prairies; moist woods; seeps
A&D: Rare & local ne & se
Org: Native

Spiranthes L. C. Rich.

S. cernua (L.) L. C. Rich.
Com: Nodding ladies'-tresses
Hab: Moist prairies; sedge meadows
A&D: Infreq e 2/3; rare wc: HRR & WOO
Org: Native

S. lacera (Raf.) Raf.
Syn: *S. gracilis* (Bigelow) Beck
Com: Slender ladies'-tresses
Hab: Usually sandy, dry prairies
A&D: Rare nc, e & sc
Org: Native

S. lucida (H. H. Eaton) Ames
Com: Yellow-lipped ladies'-tresses
Hab: Fens
A&D: Rare ne: ALL
Org: Native

S. magnicamporum Sheviak
Com: Great plains ladies'-tresses
Hab: Dry prairie hillsides
A&D: Rare nc, ne & sc: ALL, DEL, DUB, FLO & MRN
Org: Native

S. ovalis Lindley
Hab: Woodland openings
A&D: Rare c, ec, se & sc: HEN, JAC, LIN, MRN, MUS & POL
Org: Native

S. romanzoffiana Cham.
Com: Hooded ladies'-tresses
Hab: Fens
A&D: Rare nw: DIC & EMM
Org: Native

S. vernalis Engelm. & Gray
Hab: Low, wet, open places
A&D: Rare wc & sw: FRE 1915, HRR 1918, MNN & WOO
Org: Native

Triphora Nutt.

T. trianthophora (Sw.) Rydb.
Com: Nodding pogonia
Hab: Moist, wooded areas
A&D: Rare & local ne & ec
Org: Native

POACEAE (GRAMINEAE)

Aegilops L.

A. cylindrica Host
Syn: *Triticum cylindricum* (Host) Ces.
Com: Goat grass
Hab: Railroad ballast; roadsides
A&D: Rare c, sc & sw: BOO, DEC, MAH 1938 & TAY 1942
Org: Not native

X Agrohordeum G. Camus ex A. Camus

X A. macounii (Vasey) LePage
Syn: *Agropyron trachycaulum* X *Hordeum jubatum*
Syn: *Elymus macounii* Vasey
Hab: Prairies; roadsides; marsh edges
A&D: Freq nw; rare sw
Org: Native

Agropyron Gaertner

A. cristatum (L.) Gaertner
Com: Crested wheatgrass
Hab: Roadsides
A&D: Rare escape c & w; planted for erosion control
Org: Not native

A. intermedium (Host) Beauv.
Com: Intermediate wheatgrass
Hab: Roadsides; disturbed ground
A&D: Rare escape from experimental plantings in c & se: KEO & STO
Org: Native

A. pectiniforme R. & S.
Syn: *A. desertorum* (Fischer ex Link) Schultes
Hab: Disturbed prairies
A&D: Rare escape from cult in wc, nw & ne: ALL, MNN, PLY & WOO
Org: Not native

A. repens (L.) Beauv.
Com: Quack grass
Hab: Dry, disturbed soil
A&D: Common thr
Org: Not native

A. repens X *A. trachycaulum*
Hab: Dry soil of roadsides; native grasslands
A&D: Rare n 1/4 of state
Org: Not native

A. smithii Rydb.
Com: Western wheatgrass
Hab: Prairie remnants; open sandy areas; disturbed areas
A&D: Infreq ne & ec; freq to common elsewh
Org: Native

A. trachycaulum (Link) Malte [incl. var. *unilaterale* (Vasey) Malte]
Syn: *A. caninum* (L.) Beauv. ssp. *majus* (Vasey) C. L. Hitchc.
Syn: *A. subsecundum* (Link) C. L. Hitchc.
Com: Slender wheatgrass
Hab: Prairies; openings in woods
A&D: Freq to common n; infreq to rare se & sc
Org: Native

Agrostis L. Bentgrass

A. gigantea Roth
Syn: *A. alba* L., misappl.
Syn: *A. stolonifera* L. var. *major* (Gaudin) Farw.
Com: Redtop
Hab: Roadsides; prairies; disturbed areas
A&D: Common thr
Org: Not native

A. hyemalis (Walter) BSP.
Com: Ticklegrass
Hab: Sandy, open areas
A&D: Freq e; infreq to rare w
Org: Native

A. hyemalis (Walter) BSP. var. *tenuis* (Tuckerman) Gl.
Syn: *A. scabra* Willd.
Com: Hairgrass
Hab: Sandy, open areas; prairies
A&D: Freq n 1/2; rare se; absent elsewh
Org: Native

A. perennans (Walter) Tuckerman
Syn: *A. schweinitzii* Trin.
Com: Upland bent
Hab: Open, upland woods; alluvial woods
A&D: Freq s; infreq to rare n
Org: Native

A. stolonifera L. var. *palustris* (Hudson) Farw.
Syn: *A. palustris* Hudson
Syn: *A. stolonifera* L. var. *compacta* Hartman
Com: Creeping bent
Hab: Moist areas, usually near towns
A&D: Rare escape from golf greens
Org: Not native

Alopecurus L.

A. aequalis Sobol.
Com: Foxtail
Hab: Muddy shores; shallow water
A&D: Common in lakes area; infreq to rare elsewh
Org: Native

A. carolinianus Walter
Syn: *A. geniculatus* L., misappl.
Com: Common foxtail
Hab: Muddy shores; shallow water
A&D: Infreq s; rare nw & ne
Org: Native

A. pratensis L.
Com: Meadow foxtail
Hab: Roadsides, disturbed areas
A&D: Rare c & nc: HAN & STO
Org: Not native

Andropogon L. see also ***Schizachyrium***

A. gerardii Vitman
Syn: *A. furcatus* Muhl.
Com: Big bluestem
Hab: Prairie remnants; roadsides
A&D: Common thr
Org: Native

A. hallii Hackel
Syn: *A. gerardii* Vitman var. *paucipilus* (Nash) Fern.
Com: Sand bluestem
Hab: Sandy plains
A&D: Rare wc & se: LOU, MUS & WOO
Org: Native

A. virginicus L.
Com: Broomsedge
Hab: Clay slopes bordering woods
A&D: Rare se
Org: Native

Aristida L. Three-awned grass

A. basiramea Engelm. ex Vasey
Hab: Dry, sandy soil
A&D: Infreq to rare thr
Org: Native

A. curtissii (Gray) Nash
Syn: *A. basiramea* Engelm. ex Vasey var. *curtissii* (Gray) Shinners
Syn: *A. dichotoma* Michx. var. *curtissii* Gray
Hab: Dry, often sandy, open soil
A&D: Common extreme nw; infreq to rare elsewh
Org: Native

A. dichotoma Michx.
Hab: Dry, sandy soil
A&D: Infreq se; rare sw, & in nw: LYO 1949
Org: Native

A. longespica Poiret
Hab: Dry slopes
A&D: Rare se
Org: Native

A. longespica Poiret var. *geniculata* (Raf.) Fern.
Syn: *A. intermedia* Scribner & Ball
Syn: *A. necopina* Shinners
Hab: Dry, sandy soil
A&D: Infreq s 1/2; rare nw: LYO & PA
Org: Native

A. oligantha Michx.
Hab: Open areas; dry soil; railroad embankments; disturbed areas
A&D: Common s 1/2; rare n 1/2
Org: Native

A. purpurea Nutt. var. *longiseta* (Steudel) Vasey
Syn: *A. longiseta* Steudel
Hab: Loess bluffs; prairie hillsides
A&D: Rare nw
Org: Native

A. ramosissima Engelm. ex Gray
Com: Slender three-awn
Hab: Dry, disturbed ground
A&D: Rare se: HEN 1894
Org: Not native

A. tuberculosa Nutt.
Com: Sea-beach grass
Hab: Sand dunes; sandy prairies
A&D: Infreq to rare e 1/4
Org: Native

Arrhenatherum Beauv.

A. elatius (L.) Presl
Com: Tall oatgrass
Hab: Waste ground
A&D: Rare escape from cult in c, nw, ec & sw: DIC, MRS, PAG, SCO & STO
Org: Not native

Avena L.

A. fatua L.
Com: Wild oats
Hab: Roadsides & other disturbed ground
A&D: Rare thr
Org: Not native

A. sativa L.
Com: Cult oats
Hab: Field edges; disturbed ground
A&D: Infreq escape from cult, not persisting
Org: Not native

Beckmannia Host

B. syzigachne (Steudel) Fern.
Com: American slough grass
Hab: Wet ground; shallow water
A&D: Rare nw: CLY, DIC, EMM, LYO, O'B, OSC & PA
Org: Native

Bouteloua Lag.

B. curtipendula (Michx.) Torrey
Com: Side-oats grama
Hab: Sandy or gravelly, dry prairies
A&D: Freq to common thr
Org: Native

B. gracilis (Willd. ex HBK.) Lag. ex Steudel
Com: Blue grama
Hab: Dry, gravelly hilltops; loess bluffs
A&D: Freq w
Org: Native

B. hirsuta Lag.
Com: Hairy grama
Hab: Dry, gravelly prairies; loess bluffs; sand dunes
A&D: Freq to infreq w; rare elsewh
Org: Native

Brachyelytrum Beauv.

B. erectum (Schreber) Beauv.
Syn: *B. erectum* (Schreber) Beauv. var. *septentrionale* Babel
Hab: Upland woods
A&D: Freq to common e; rare elsewh
Org: Native

Bromus L. Brome grass

B. ciliatus L.
Com: Canada brome grass
Hab: Wet ground; rich, upland woods
A&D: Rare in ne 1/4
Org: Native

B. commutatus Schrader
Com: Hairy chess
Hab: Loess bluffs; sandy areas
A&D: Infreq thr much of state
Org: Not native

B. inermis Leysser
Com: Smooth brome
Hab: Roadsides & other disturbed areas
A&D: Common thr
Org: Not native

B. japonicus Thunb. ex Murray
Com: Japanese brome
Hab: Roadsides; waste places
A&D: Freq to common thr
Org: Not native

B. kalmii Gray
Hab: Upland prairies; sparsely wooded slopes; rocky hillsides
A&D: Freq in Pal. Plateau; rare elsewh in e
Org: Native

B. latiglumis (Shear) A. S. Hitchc.
Syn: *B. altissimus* Pursh
Syn: *B. purgans* L., misappl.
Hab: Low prairies; alluvial woods; open, wooded slopes
A&D: Infreq to freq e; rare sw
Org: Native

B. mollis L.
Syn: *B. hordeaceus* L.
Hab: Waste or cult ground
A&D: Rare c & ne: BH 1896 & WEB n.d.
Org: Not native

B. pubescens Muhl. ex Willd.
Syn: *B. purgans* L., misappl.
Com: Canada brome
Hab: Dense or rocky woods
A&D: Freq to infreq thr
Org: Native

B. secalinus L.
Com: Cheat grass
Hab: Waste ground
A&D: Infreq se & sw; rare elsewh
Org: Not native

B. tectorum L.
Com: Downy chess
Hab: Roadsides & other waste places
A&D: Freq to common thr
Org: Not native

Buchloe Engelm.

B. dactyloides (Nutt.) Engelm.
Com: Buffalo grass
Hab: Dry prairies
A&D: Rare, native in wc & nw: LYO, PLY & WOO, introduced elsewh
Org: Native

Calamagrostis Adanson

C. canadensis (Michx.) Beauv.
Com: Bluejoint
Hab: Wet prairies; shallow marshes
A&D: Infreq to rare in westernmost counties; freq to common elsewh
Org: Native

C. inexpansa Gray
Syn: *C. neglecta* (Ehrh.) Gaertner, B. Meyer, & Schreber
Com: Northern reed grass
Hab: Wet prairies; shallow marshes; fens
A&D: Freq in lakes area; rare remainder of n
Org: Native

Calamovilfa (Gray) Hackel ex Scribner & Southworth
Sand reed-grass

C. longifolia (Hooker) Scribner
Com: Prairie sandreed
Hab: Sandy prairies; dry, open, sandy areas
A&D: Infreq to rare thr
Org: Native

C. longifolia (Hooker) Scribner var. *magna* Scribner & Merr.
Hab: Sand dunes; sandy plains
A&D: Rare se: LOU & MUS
Org: Native

Cenchrus L.

C. longispinus (Hackel) Fern.
Syn: *C. pauciflorus* Bentham, misappl.
Com: Sandbur
Hab: Disturbed, sandy soil; roadsides
A&D: Freq to common thr
Org: Native

Chasmanthium Link

C. latifolium (Michx.) H. Yates
Syn: *Uniola latifolia* Michx.
Com: Wild oats
Hab: Low, moist soil; low woods
A&D: Rare se: LEE
Org: Native

Chloris Sw.

C. verticillata Nutt.
Com: Windmill grass
Hab: Disturbed urban areas
A&D: Rare escape from plantings in c & se
Org: Not native

Cinna L.

C. arundinacea L.
Com: Wood reed
Hab: Moist woods; alluvium
A&D: Freq to infreq thr most of state
Org: Native

Dactylis L.

D. glomerata L.
Com: Orchard grass
Hab: Fields; lawns; roadsides; waste places
A&D: Common escape from cult thr
Org: Not native

Danthonia Lam. & DC.

D. spicata (L.) Beauv. ex R. & S.
Com: Poverty oat grass
Hab: Dry, sandy, open, upland woods
A&D: Infreq to rare thr
Org: Native

Diarrhena Beauv.

D. americana Beauv. var. *obovata* Gl.
Hab: Moist woods
A&D: Infreq to rare s 3/4
Org: Native

Dichanthelium (A. S. Hitchc. & Chase) Gould

D. acuminatum (Sw.) Gould & Clark
Syn: *Panicum huachucae* Ashe
Syn: *Panicum tennesseense* Ashe
Hab: Open woods; prairies; sandy habitats
A&D: Rare e 1/4; freq to common elsewh
Org: Native

D. acuminatum (Sw.) Gould & Clark var. *implicatum* (Scribner) Gould & Clark
Syn: *Panicum implicatum* Scribner
Syn: *Panicum lanuginosum* Ell. var. *implicatum* (Scribner) Fern.
Syn: *Panicum meridionale* Ashe
Hab: Open, sandy woods; prairies
A&D: Rare w; freq to common elsewh
Org: Native

D. acuminatum (Sw.) Gould & Clark var. *lindheimeri* (Nash) Gould & Clark
Syn: *Panicum lanuginosum* Ell. var. *lindheimeri* (Nash) Fern.
Syn: *Panicum lindheimeri* Nash
Hab: Sandy or gravelly soils
A&D: Rare e: BRE, CLI, JON, LOU & SCO
Org: Native

D. acuminatum (Sw.) Gould & Clark var. *villosum* (Gray) Gould & Clark
Syn: *Panicum praecocius* A. S. Hitchc. & Chase
Syn: *Panicum lanuginosum* var. *praecocius* (Hitchc. & Chase) Dore
Hab: Dry, upland prairies
A&D: Infreq ne 1/2
Org: Native

D. boreale (Nash) Freckm.
Syn: *Panicum boreale* Nash
Hab: Dry, sandy prairies
A&D: Rare ne: BH, BUC & CLT 1923
Org: Native

D. clandestinum (L.) Gould
Syn: *Panicum clandestinum* L.
Com: Deertongue grass
Hab: Sandy, upland woods; prairie openings
A&D: Infreq to rare se
Org: Native

D. depauperatum (Muhl.) Gould
Syn: *Panicum depauperatum* Muhl.
Hab: Dry, sandy, upland woods; sandy prairies; sandstone ledges
A&D: Rare c, nc & extreme e
Org: Native

D. latifolium (L.) Gould & Clark
Syn: *Panicum latifolium* L.
Com: Broad-leaved panic grass
Hab: Dry, rocky woodlands
A&D: Freq to infreq e 2/3
Org: Native

D. leibergii (Vasey) Freckm.
Syn: *Panicum leibergii* (Vasey) Scribner
Com: Leiberg's panic grass
Hab: Prairies; dry, open woodlands
A&D: Common nc; rare nw & se; infreq elsewh
Org: Native

D. linearifolium (Scribner) Gould
Syn: *Panicum linearifolium* Scribner
Com: Slim-leaved panic grass
Hab: Rocky upland woods; sandstone bluffs; sandy soil
A&D: Rare wc, se & sc: GUT, MRN & WAP
Org: Native

D. oligosanthes (Schultes) Gould
Syn: *Panicum oligosanthes* Schultes
Hab: Grasslands; open woods
A&D: Rare thr
Org: Native

D. oligosanthes (Schultes) Gould var. *scribnerianum* (Nash) Gould
Syn: *Panicum helleri* Nash
Syn: *Panicum oligosanthes* Schultes var. *helleri* (Nash) Fern.
Syn: *Panicum oligosanthes* Schultes var. *scribnerianum* (Nash) Fern.
Syn: *Panicum scribnerianum* Nash
Hab: Dry prairies; sandy areas
A&D: Freq to common thr
Org: Native

D. oligosanthes (Schultes) Gould var. *wilcoxianum* (Vasey) Gould & Clark
Syn: *Panicum wilcoxianum* Vasey
Hab: Dry, upland prairies; loess bluffs
A&D: Freq nw; rare elsewh
Org: Native

D. perlongum (Nash) Freckm.
Syn: *Panicum perlongum* Nash
Hab: Dry sand; gravely upland prairies; Sandy river terraces
A&D: Rare, e 2/3
Org: Native

D. sabulorum (Lam.) Gould & Clark var. *patulum* (Scribner & Merr.) Gould & Clark
Syn: *Panicum commonsianum* Ashe var. *euchlamydeum* (Shinners) Pohl
Syn: *Panicum villosissimum* Nash, misappl.
Hab: Dry, sandy plains; prairies; blowouts
A&D: Infreq to rare e 1/2
Org: Native

D. sabulorum (Lam.) Gould & Clark var. *thinium* (A. S. Hitchc. & Chase) Gould & Clark
Syn: *Panicum columbianum* Scribner
Hab: Sand blowouts
A&D: Rare ne: ALL
Org: Native

Digitaria Heister ex Fabr.

D. ciliaris (Retz.) Koeler
Com: Southern crab grass
Hab: Dry, disturbed sites
A&D: Rare sw: FRE, MIL, PAG, POT
Org: Not native

D. filiformis (L.) Koeler
Com: Finger grass
Hab: Dry hillsides; sterile knolls
A&D: Rare se: DM, JEF 1935, LEE 1923 & MUS 1898
Org: Native

D. ischaemum (Schreber ex Schweigger) Schreber ex Muhl.
Syn: *D. humifusa* Pers.
Com: Smooth crabgrass
Hab: Lawns; yards; disturbed soil
A&D: Freq to common thr
Org: Not native

D. sanguinalis (L.) Scop.
Com: Common crabgrass
Hab: Lawns; yards; disturbed soil
A&D: Common thr
Org: Not native

Distichlis Raf.

D. spicata (L.) Greene var. *stricta* (Torrey) Beetle
Syn: *D. stricta* (Torrey) Rydb.
Com: Salt grass
Hab: Roadsides; along railroads
A&D: Rare w 1/2, & in c: TAM
Org: Native

Echinochloa Beauv. Barnyard grass

E. crusgalli (L.) Beauv.
Hab: Moist, disturbed soil; fields; marshes
A&D: Common thr
Org: Not native

E. muricata (Beauv.) Fern. [incl. var. *microstachya* Wieg.]
Syn: *E. pungens* (Poiret) Rydb., misappl.
Hab: Moist, disturbed soil
A&D: Freq to common thr
Org: Native

E. walteri (Pursh) Heller
Hab: Moist, disturbed soil
A&D: Rare se 1/4
Org: Native

Eleusine Gaertner

E. indica (L.) Gaertner
Com: Goose grass
Hab: Disturbed soils; waste places
A&D: Freq s 1/2; rare n 1/2
Org: Not native

X Elyhordeum Mansf.

X E. iowense Pohl
Syn: *Elymus villosus* X *Hordeum jubatum*
Hab: Grassy roadside ditch
A&D: Rare c: STO
Org: Native

X E. montanense (Scribner) Bowden
Syn: *Elymus virginicus* X *Hordeum jubatum*
Syn: *Hordeum pammelii* Scribner & Ball
Hab: Disturbed ground along railroad
A&D: Rare nc: HUM 1896
Org: Native

Elymus L. Wild rye

E. canadensis L.
Com: Canada wild rye
Hab: Prairies; roadsides
A&D: Common thr
Org: Native

E. interruptus Buckley
Syn: *E. canadensis* L. var. *interruptus* (Buckley) Church
Syn: *E. diversiglumis* Scribner & Ball
Hab: Dry woodlands
A&D: Rare nw: DIC, EMM 1922
Org: Native

E. X *maltei* Bowden
Syn: *E. canadensis* X *E. virginicus*
Hab: Sandy soil
A&D: Rare in scattered locations
Org: Native

E. riparius Wieg.
Hab: Woodlands
A&D: Rare & local c & ne
Org: Native

E. villosus Muhl. ex Willd.
Syn: *E. striatus* Willd.
Com: Slender wild rye
Hab: Moist woods
A&D: Freq to common thr
Org: Native

E. virginicus L.
Com: Virginia wild rye
Hab: Roadsides; prairies; alluvial woods
A&D: Freq to common thr
Org: Native

E. wiegandii Fern.
Syn: *E. canadensis* L. var. *wiegandii* (Fern.) Bowden
Hab: Ungrazed woods, especially alluvial woods
A&D: Rare thr
Org: Native

Eragrostis Von Wolf Love grass

E. capillaris (L.) Nees
Com: Lacegrass
Hab: Dry, disturbed ground; fields
A&D: Rare in Pal. Plateau, nc, se & sc
Org: Native

E. cilianensis (All.) Link ex E. Mosher
Syn: *E. megastachya* (Koeler) Link
Com: Stinkgrass
Hab: Roadsides; waste ground; gardens; fields
A&D: Common thr
Org: Not native

E. frankii C. A. Meyer ex Steudel
Hab: Wet sands; edges of streams
A&D: Rare w; infreq elsewh
Org: Native

E. frankii C. A. Meyer var. *brevipes* Fassett
Hab: Moist sand at margins of streams
A&D: Rare e
Org: Native

E. hypnoides (Lam.) BSP.
Com: Pony grass
Hab: Wet soil along streams; open, muddy habitats
A&D: Freq to common thr
Org: Native

E. pectinacea (Michx.) Nees
Syn: *E. purshii* Schrader
Hab: Roadsides; fields; waste ground; wet sands
A&D: Common thr
Org: Native

E. pilosa (L.) Beauv.
Hab: Fields; disturbed habitats
A&D: Rare s 1/2
Org: Native

E. poaeoides Beauv. ex R. & S.
Syn: *E. minor* Host
Hab: Disturbed soil along railroads
A&D: Rare c & se
Org: Not native

E. reptans (Michx.) Nees
Hab: Roadsides; fields
A&D: Rare c: HRD n.d. (ca. 1905)
Org: Native

E. spectabilis (Pursh) Steudel
Com: Purple lovegrass
Hab: Prairies; roadsides; open sandy areas
A&D: Rare nw; infreq elsewh
Org: Native

E. trichodes (Nutt.) Wood
Com: Sand lovegrass
Hab: Sandy, open ground or thin woods
A&D: Rare: scattered in s 1/2
Org: Native

Eriochloa HBK.

E. villosa (Thunb.) Kunth
Com: Cup grass
Hab: Fields; waste areas
A&D: Rare: becoming established in scattered locations thr
Org: Not native

Festuca L. Fescue grass

F. arundinacea Schreber
Com: Alta fescue
Hab: Lawns; roadsides
A&D: Rare: scattered locations in se 1/4
Org: Not native

F. obtusa Biehler
Com: Nodding fescue
Hab: Moist woods
A&D: Freq to common thr
Org: Native

F. octoflora Walter var. *tenella* (Willd.) Fern.
Syn: *Vulpia octoflora* (Walter) Rydb.
Com: Six-weeks fescue
Hab: Sand plains; gravelly hills; loess bluffs
A&D: Rare se; infreq elsewh
Org: Native

F. ovina L.
Com: Sheep fescue
Hab: Dry, sandy plains; prairies
A&D: Rare thr
Org: Native

F. paradoxa Desv.
Hab: Prairies; dry woods
A&D: Rare se 1/2
Org: Native

F. pratensis Hudson
Syn: *F. elatior* L., nomen confusum
Com: Meadow fescue
Hab: Lawns; roadsides; waste ground
A&D: Infreq thr
Org: Not native

F. rubra L.
Com: Red fescue
Hab: Sandy meadows; yards; waste areas
A&D: Rare ne, ec & sc: ALL, JOH & MAH 1915
Org: Not native

Glyceria R. Br.

G. borealis (Nash) Batchelder
Com: Manna grass
Hab: Shallow water; muddy shores; wet sand
A&D: Infreq in lakes area; rare nc & ec: HAN & LIN
Org: Native

G. grandis S. Watson
Syn: *G. maxima* (Hartman) Holmb. ssp. *grandis* (S. Watson) Hulten
Com: American manna grass
Hab: Marshy ground; shallow water
A&D: Common in lakes area; freq in remainder of n 1/2
Org: Native

G. septentrionalis A. S. Hitchc.
Com: Eastern manna grass
Hab: Shallow water; pond & stream margins
A&D: Infreq c & se
Org: Native

G. striata (Lam.) A. S. Hitchc.
Com: Fowl manna grass
Hab: Marshes; damp woods; shallow water; fens
A&D: Freq to common s 1/2 & in lakes area; infreq elsewh
Org: Native

Heleochloa Host ex Roemer

H. schoenoides (L.) Host
Hab: Railroad tracks
A&D: Rare c: POL
Org: Not native

Hierochloe R. Br.

H. odorata (L.) Beauv.
Com: Holy grass
Hab: Moist prairie remnants; fens
A&D: Infreq n 1/2
Org: Native

Holcus L.

H. lanatus L.
Com: Velvet grass
Hab: Waste ground
A&D: Rare c, ec & se: LIN 1919, LOU 1919 & STO 1898
Org: Not native

Hordeum L.

H. jubatum L.
Com: Squirrel-tail barley
Hab: Disturbed ground
A&D: Common thr
Org: Native

H. pusillum Nutt.
Com: Little barley
Hab: Dry, open, sandy areas; loess bluffs
A&D: Infreq to freq s; rare n
Org: Native of U.S., but not Iowa

H. vulgare L.
Com: Barley
Hab: Waste ground; roadsides
A&D: Infreq escape from cult thr but not persisting
Org: Not native

Hystrix Moench

H. patula Moench
Syn: *Elymus hystrix* L.
Com: Bottlebrush grass
Hab: Moist woods
A&D: Rare nw; common elsewh
Org: Native

Koeleria Pers.

K. macrantha (Ledeb.) Schultes
Syn: *K. cristata* (L.) Pers., illeg. name
Syn: *K. pyramidata* (Lam.) Beauv.
Com: June grass
Hab: Prairies; loess bluffs; sandy plains
A&D: Infreq e; freq to common elsewh
Org: Native

Leersia Sw.

L. lenticularis Michx.
Com: Catchfly grass
Hab: Alluvial woods
A&D: Rare e 1/2
Org: Native

L. oryzoides (L.) Sw.
Com: Rice cut-grass
Hab: Marshes; muddy margins of lakes; alluvial woods
A&D: Rare nw; freq to common elsewh
Org: Native

L. virginica Willd.
Com: Whitegrass
Hab: Moist alluvial woods; margins of marshes & lakes
A&D: Common in Pal. Plateau; infreq to freq elsewh
Org: Native

Leptochloa Beauv.

L. fascicularis (Lam.) Gray [incl. var. *acuminata* (Nash) Gl.]
Syn: *Diplachne fascicularis* (Lam.) Beauv.
Com: Salt meadow grass
Hab: Wet ground; sandy alluvium; disturbed sites
A&D: Rare to infreq nw 2/3 of state
Org: Native

Leptoloma Chase

L. cognatum (Schultes) Chase
Syn: *Digitaria cognatum* (Schultes) Pilger
Com: Fall witchgrass
Hab: Sandy soil
A&D: Freq to common e 1/4; rare sc
Org: Native

Lolium L.

L. perenne L.
Com: Perennial rye grass
Hab: Lawns, spreading to waste ground
A&D: Infreq to rare thr
Org: Not native

L. perenne L. var. *italicum* Parn.
Syn: *L. multiflorum* Lam.
Syn: *L. perenne* L. var. *aristatum* Willd.
Com: Annual rye grass
Hab: Lawns, spreading to fields & roadsides
A&D: Common sw; rare nc & e
Org: Not native

L. temulentum L.
Com: Darnel
Hab: Crop fields
A&D: Rare nc & ne, not collected since 1922
Org: Not native

Melica L.

M. mutica Walter
Com: Two-flowered melic grass
Hab: Dry, rocky woodlands
A&D: Rare sw: UNI 1898
Org: Native

M. nitens (Scribner) Nutt. ex Piper
Com: Three-flowered melic grass
Hab: Wooded, rocky slopes; prairies
A&D: Rare c & e
Org: Native

Milium L.

M. effusum L.
Com: Millet-grass
Hab: Moist, maple-basswood slopes
A&D: Rare ne: ALL
Org: Native

Miscanthus Andersson

M. sacchariflorus (Maxim.) Hackel
Com: Plume grass
Hab: Roadsides; waste ground
A&D: Infreq escape thr, but increasing in abundance
Org: Not native

Muhlenbergia Schreber   Muhly grass

M. asperifolia (Nees & Meyer) Parodi
Com: Scratchgrass
Hab: Fens; lakeshores; along railroads
A&D: Rare c, wc & nw: BOO, CLY 1948, DIC, MNN, STO 1923 & WOO
Org: Native

M. bushii Pohl
Syn: *M. brachyphylla* Bush
Hab: Moist woods
A&D: Rare sw & se 1/4
Org: Native

M. cuspidata (Torrey) Rydb.
Com: Plains muhly
Hab: Dry, gravelly prairies; loess bluffs
A&D: Common in lakes area & in Loess Hills; rare c & ne
Org: Native

M. frondosa (Poiret) Fern.
Syn: *M. mexicana* (L.) Trin., misappl.
Com: Wirestem muhly
Hab: Moist alluvial woods; edges of marshes; waste places
A&D: Infreq to rare w; freq to common elsewh
Org: Native

M. glomerata (Willd.) Trin.
Hab: Fens; marshes
A&D: Rare nc & e
Org: Native

M. mexicana (L.) Trin.
Syn: *M. foliosa* (R. & S.) Trin., misappl.
Hab: Moist prairies; low woods; fens; lake margins
A&D: Common nc; infreq to rare elsewh
Org: Native

M. racemosa (Michx.) BSP.
Com: Marsh muhly
Hab: Dry prairies; loess bluffs; margins of fields; waste ground
A&D: Freq to common thr
Org: Native

M. schreberi J. F. Gmelin
Com: Nimblewill
Hab: Open woods; alluvium
A&D: Freq se 2/3
Org: Native

M. sobolifera (Muhl. ex Willd.) Trin.
Com: Rock muhly
Hab: Dry, upland woods; wooded slopes
A&D: Infreq to rare se 2/3
Org: Native

M. sylvatica (Torrey) Torrey ex Gray
Com: Forest muhly
Hab: Moist to dry, often rocky woods
A&D: Rare e
Org: Native

M. tenuiflora (Willd.) BSP.
Hab: Moist, rocky, wooded slopes
A&D: Rare e & sc
Org: Native

Oryzopsis Michx. Rice-grass

O. asperifolia Michx.
Com: Rough-leaved rice-grass
Hab: Moist, maple-basswood slopes
A&D: Rare ne: ALL, CLT, DEL, DUB & WNS
Org: Native

O. pungens (Torrey ex Sprengel) A. S. Hitchc.
Com: Short-horned rice-grass
Hab: Dry, sandy woods
A&D: Rare ne: ALL & CLT
Org: Native

O. racemosa (Smith) Ricker
Com: Black-seeded rice-grass
Hab: Steep, n- or e-facing, wooded slopes
A&D: Common in Pal. Plateau & extreme e; rare elsewh in ne 2/3
Org: Native

Panicum L. see also ***Dichanthelium***
Panic grass

P. capillare L.
Com: Witchgrass
Hab: Fields; roadsides; waste ground; disturbed soil
A&D: Common thr
Org: Native

P. dichotomiflorum Michx.
Com: Knee grass
Hab: Wet habitats; sandy soils; fields; gardens; disturbed soils
A&D: Infreq w & ne; freq to common elsewh
Org: Native

P. gattingeri Nash
Hab: Marshes
A&D: Rare nw & se: CLY, DIC & LOU
Org: Native

P. hillmanii Chase
Hab: Waste ground
A&D: Rare nw: POC
Org: Not native

P. miliaceum L.
Com: Proso millet
Hab: Cult; escapes to waste places & field edges
A&D: Rare to infreq sw 2/3
Org: Not native

P. philadelphicum Bernh. ex Trin.
Hab: Dry, sandy soil
A&D: Rare w, nc & sc: CLY, DIC 1948, GRE, HAN, MNR & MNT
Org: Native

P. virgatum L.
Com: Switchgrass
Hab: Prairie remnants; streambanks; sandy soil
A&D: Common thr
Org: Native

Paspalum L.

P. setaceum Michx. var. *ciliatifolium* (Michx.) Vasey
Syn: *P. ciliatifolium* Michx.
Syn: *P. pubescens* Muhl. ex Willd.
Com: Bead grass
Hab: Prairie remnants; dry, sandy soil; loess bluffs
A&D: Rare n 1/2; infreq s 1/2
Org: Native

P. setaceum Michx. var. *muhlenbergii* (Nash) D. Banks
Syn: *P. muhlenbergii* Nash
Hab: Dry, sandy soil
A&D: Infreq to rare s 1/2
Org: Native

P. setaceum Michx. var. *stramineum* (Nash) D. Banks
Syn: *P. bushii* Nash
Hab: Dry, sandy soil
A&D: Infreq to rare se 1/2
Org: Native

Pennisetum L. C. Rich ex Pers.

P. petiolare (Hochst.) Chiov.
Hab: Lawn from birdseed
A&D: Rare c: STO
Org: Not native

Phalaris L.

P. arundinacea L.
Com: Reed canary grass
Hab: Marshes; lakeshores; floodplains
A&D: Common thr
Org: Native

P. canariensis L.
Com: Canary grass
Hab: Waste ground near dwellings
A&D: Rare waif thr, from birdseed
Org: Not native

Phleum L.

P. pratense L.
Com: Timothy
Hab: Fields; open, disturbed habitats; roadsides
A&D: Common thr
Org: Not native

Phragmites Adanson

P. australis (Cav.) Trin. ex Steudel
Syn: *P. communis* Trin.
Com: Reed
Hab: Marshes; moist soil along roads; railroads
A&D: Common c & nc; infreq to rare elsewh
Org: Native

Poa L. Bluegrass

P. annua L.
Com: Annual bluegrass
Hab: Shaded lawns; waste ground; wet, disturbed sites
A&D: Freq to common thr, though rarely collected
Org: Not native

P. arida Vasey
Com: Plains bluegrass
Hab: Dry prairies on Sioux Quartzite
A&D: Rare nw: LYO
Org: Native

P. bulbosa L.
Hab: Lawns
A&D: Rare c, nw & se: PLY, MUS 1922 & STO 1929
Org: Not native

P. chapmaniana Scribner
Hab: Fields; sandy, open habitats
A&D: Rare ec & se: JOH 1889, LOU n.d. (pre-1900) & WAP 1899
Org: Native

P. compressa L.
Com: Canadian bluegrass
Hab: Dry, open woods; pastures; loess bluffs; roadsides
A&D: Common thr
Org: Not native

P. languida A. S. Hitchc.
Com: Woodland bluegrass
Hab: Dry, upland woods
A&D: Rare c & e: ALL, SCO n.d. (pre-1900), STO 1897 & MUS
Org: Native

P. nemoralis L.
Hab: Cult in lawns
A&D: Rare c & ec: BOO, SCO, STO
Org: Not native

P. paludigena Fern. & Wieg.
Com: Marsh bluegrass
Hab: Algific talus slopes
A&D: Rare ne: ALL, DUB & WNS
Org: Native

P. palustris L.
Com: Fowl meadow grass
Hab: Moist prairie remnants; marshes; fens
A&D: Common in lakes area & in Pal. Plateau; infreq to rare elsewh
Org: Native

P. pratensis L.
Com: Kentucky bluegrass
Hab: Lawns; pastures; disturbed habitats
A&D: Common thr
Org: Not native

P. sylvestris Gray
Com: Woodland bluegrass
Hab: Moist woods; alluvium
A&D: Rare se 1/2 of state
Org: Native

P. trivialis L.
Com: Meadow grass
Hab: Lawns
A&D: Rare c & ne: ALL, CLT & STO
Org: Not native

P. wolfii Scribner
Com: Meadow bluegrass
Hab: Moist woodlands; steep, n-facing slopes
A&D: Rare: scattered locations in e 1/2
Org: Native

Puccinellia Parl. Alkali grass

P. distans (L.) Parl.
Com: European alkali grass
Hab: Disturbed roadsides
A&D: Rare c: HAM
Org: Not native

Schedonnardus Steudel

S. paniculatus (Nutt.) Trel.
Com: Tumblegrass
Hab: Dry soils; pastures; loess bluffs
A&D: Rare w: GUT 1928, HRR, LYO, PAG, PLY & WOO
Org: Native

Schizachne Hack.

S. purpurascens (Torrey) Swallen
Com: False medic
Hab: Moist, sandy, wooded slopes; algific talus slopes
A&D: Freq in Pal. Plateau; rare elsewh
Org: Native

Schizachyrium Nees

S. scoparium (Michx.) Nash
Syn: *Andropogon scoparius* Michx.
Com: Little bluestem
Hab: Upland prairies
A&D: Common thr
Org: Native

Sclerochloa Beauv.

S. dura (L.) Beauv.
Hab: Dry, disturbed site
A&D: Rare sw: PAG
Org: Not native

Scolochloa Link

S. festucacea (Willd.) Link
Com: Whitetop
Hab: Sedge meadows; lakeshores; shallow water of marshes
A&D: Freq in lakes area; rare nc
Org: Native

Secale L.

S. cereale L.
Com: Cult rye
Hab: Waste ground; roadsides
A&D: Infreq escape from cult thr
Org: Not native

Setaria Beauv. Foxtail grass

S. faberi Herrm.
Com: Giant foxtail
Hab: Fields; roadsides; disturbed ground
A&D: Infreq n 1/2; common s 1/2
Org: Not native

S. geniculata (Lam.) Beauv.
Hab: Moist, sandy alluvium
A&D: Rare ec: JON
Org: Native

S. glauca (L.) Beauv.
Syn: *S. lutescens* (Weigel) Hubb.
Com: Yellow foxtail
Hab: Fields; roadsides; disturbed soil
A&D: Common thr
Org: Not native

S. italica (L.) Beauv.
Com: Foxtail millet
Hab: Fields; roadsides; waste ground
A&D: Rare thr
Org: Not native

S. verticillata (L.) Beauv.
Com: Bristly foxtail
Hab: Fields; disturbed ground
A&D: Rare ne; infreq to freq elsewh
Org: Not native

S. viridis (L.) Beauv.
Com: Green foxtail
Hab: Fields; disturbed ground
A&D: Common thr
Org: Not native

Sorghastrum Nash

S. nutans (L.) Nash
Syn: *S. avenaceum* (Michx.) Nash
Com: Indian grass
Hab: Prairies; roadsides
A&D: Common thr
Org: Native

Sorghum Moench

S. bicolor (L.) Moench
Syn: *S. vulgare* Pers.
Com: Sorghum
Hab: Field edges; waste ground
A&D: Rare escape from cult
Org: Not native

S. halepense (L.) Pers.
Com: Johnson grass
Hab: Roadsides; field edges
A&D: Rare escape from cult in extreme s
Org: Not native

S. sudanense (Piper) Stapf
Syn: *S. bicolor* (L.) Moench in part
Com: Sudan grass
Hab: Roadsides; field edges
A&D: Rare escape from cult
Org: Not native

Spartina Schreber

S. pectinata Link
Com: Slough grass, cord grass
Hab: Prairie swales; edges of marshes; wet roadsides
A&D: Freq to common thr
Org: Native

Sphenopholis Scribner Wedge grass

S. obtusata (Michx.) Scribner
Hab: Prairies; loess bluffs; open woods
A&D: Freq to common nc & sc; infreq to rare elsewh
Org: Native

S. obtusata (Michx.) Scribner var. *major* (Torrey) K. S. Erdman
Syn: *S. intermedia* Rydb.
Hab: Low, moist ground; open woods
A&D: Common se; rare w 1/4; infreq to freq elsewh
Org: Native

Sporobolus R. Br. Dropseed

S. asper (Michx.) Kunth
Com: Dropseed
Hab: Dry prairie slopes; gravelly hills; disturbed prairies
A&D: Infreq to rare ne; freq to common elsewh
Org: Native

S. clandestinus (Biehler) A. S. Hitchc.
Syn: *S. asper* (Michx.) Kunth var. *clandestinus* (Biehler) Shinners
Hab: Sandy prairies
A&D: Rare se: HEN 1935, JEF 1935 & MUS
Org: Native

S. cryptandrus (Torrey) Gray
Com: Sand dropseed
Hab: Loess bluffs; dry, sandy prairies
A&D: Freq to common thr
Org: Native

S. heterolepis (Gray) Gray
Com: Prairie dropseed
Hab: Dry prairies; loess bluffs
A&D: Common nc & sw; infreq elsewh
Org: Native

S. neglectus Nash
Syn: *S. vaginiflorus* (Torrey ex Gray) Wood var. *neglectus* (Nash) Scribner
Hab: Dry prairies; waste ground; lawns; pastures
A&D: Freq nc & sw; infreq to rare elsewh
Org: Native

S. vaginiflorus (Torrey ex Gray) Wood [incl. var. *inaequalis* Fern.]
Com: Poverty grass
Hab: Dry, sandy soil
A&D: Freq to infreq thr
Org: Native

Stipa L.

S. comata Trin. & Rupr.
Com: Needle-and-thread, spear grass
Hab: Dry, gravelly prairies; loess bluffs
A&D: Rare wc & nw: HRR, O'B, OSC & WOO
Org: Native

S. spartea Trin.
Com: Porcupine grass
Hab: Prairie remnants; sandy, open soil
A&D: Freq to common thr
Org: Native

S. viridula Trin.
Com: Green needlegrass
Hab: Loess bluffs; dry, disturbed soil along railroads; pastures
A&D: Rare n 2/3, possibly native only in n Loess Hills
Org: Native

Tridens Roemer & Schultes

T. flavus (L.) A. S. Hitchc.
Com: Purple top
Hab: Sandy prairies; disturbed prairies; alluvium
A&D: Common se; infreq to rare extreme s & along Missouri R.
Org: Native

Triplasis Beauv.

T. purpurea (Walter) Chapman
Com: Sand grass
Hab: Dry, sandy soil
A&D: Freq se & sw; infreq to rare ne & extreme e
Org: Native

Tripsacum L.

T. dactyloides (L.) L.
Com: Gama grass
Hab: Low, moist ground; roadsides
A&D: Infreq s
Org: Native

Triticum L.

T. aestivum L.
Com: Cultivated wheat
Hab: Roadsides; waste ground
A&D: Rare escape from cult, not persisting
Org: Not native

Zea L.

Z. mays L.
Com: Cultivated corn
Hab: Edges of fields; roadsides; disturbed ground
A&D: Infreq escape from cult, not persisting
Org: Not native

Zizania L. Wild rice

Z. aquatica L. [incl. var. *angustifolia* A. S. Hitchc.; var. *interior* Fassett]
Syn: *Z. palustris* L.
Com: Wild rice
Hab: Shallow marshes; margins of streams
A&D: Rare: scattered in n 2/3
Org: Native

PONTEDERIACEAE

Heteranthera Ruiz & Pavon Water star-grass

H. dubia (Jacq.) MacM.
Syn: *Zosterella dubia* (Jacq.) Small
Hab: Shallow water; muddy shores
A&D: Infreq nw & e; rare elsewh
Org: Native

H. limosa (Sw.) Willd.
Hab: Shallow water; muddy shores
A&D: Rare nw, se & sw: FRE 1888, LYO & MUS 1894
Org: Native

H. reniformis R. & P.
Hab: Shallow water
A&D: Rare sc: LUC
Org: Native

Pontederia L.

P. cordata L.
Com: Pickerel-weed
Hab: Marshy shores; shallow water
A&D: Infreq to rare thr
Org: Native

POTAMOGETONACEAE

Potamogeton L. Pondweed

P. amplifolius Tuckerman
Hab: Shallow water of ponds; lakes
A&D: Rare c, nw, nc & se: CG 1896, DIC, FLO 1880's, HAN, MUS 1894 & TAM 1891
Org: Native

P. crispus L.
Com: Curly pondweed
Hab: Shallow water of lakes; backwaters of Mississippi R.; shallow streams of ne
A&D: Rare & local, though spreading
Org: Not native

P. diversifolius Raf.
Syn: *P. capillaceus* Poiret
Hab: Marshes; shallow ponds
A&D: Rare ne, se & sc
Org: Native

P. epihydrus Raf.
Hab: Shallow water in marshes
A&D: Rare nc, ne & se: BRE, FAY 1894, MUS 1896 & WNB 1896
Org: Native

P. foliosus Raf.
Hab: Shallow marshes; ponds; lakes
A&D: Freq to common thr
Org: Native

P. friesii Rupr.
Hab: Shallow water at edges of lakes
A&D: Rare nw, nc & sc
Org: Native

P. gramineus L.
Hab: Shallow water
A&D: Infreq nc & in lakes area
Org: Native

P. illinoensis Morong
Hab: Shallow water of lakes & ponds
A&D: Freq nc & in lakes area; rare se & sw
Org: Native

P. natans L.
Hab: Shallow water at edges of lakes & marshes
A&D: Infreq nc & in lakes area; rare ne & se
Org: Native

P. nodosus Poiret
Syn: *P. americanus* C. & S.
Hab: Shallow water at edges of lakes & marshes
A&D: Common in lakes area & nc; infreq elsewh
Org: Native

P. pectinatus L.
Com: Sago pondweed
Hab: Shallow standing water; backwaters of Mississippi R.
A&D: Common in lakes area; infreq elsewh
Org: Native

P. praelongus Wulfen
Hab: Shallow water of lakes & marshes
A&D: Rare nw & nc: CG 1896, DIC & EMM 1895
Org: Native

P. pusillus L.
Syn: *P. panormitanus* Biv.
Hab: Shallow water of lakes & marshes
A&D: Freq in lakes area & se; infreq to rare sc & sw
Org: Native

P. pusillus L. var. *tenuissimus* Mert. & Koch
Syn: *P. berchtoldii* Fieber
Hab: Shallow water of lakes
A&D: Rare in lakes area, & in wc: GRE
Org: Native

P. richardsonii (A. Benn.) Rydb.
Com: Red-head pondweed
Hab: Shallow water of lakes & marshes
A&D: Common in lakes area; rare remainder of nw & in Pal. Plateau
Org: Native

P. spirillus Tuckerman
Hab: Shallow standing water
A&D: Rare nc & se: HAN 1896, MUS 1896 & WNB 1896
Org: Native

P. strictifolius A. Benn.
Hab: Shallow water of lakes
A&D: Rare nc & in lakes area, last collected in 1917
Org: Native

P. vaseyi Robbins
Hab: Shallow water of marshes
A&D: Rare nc, ec & s: LIN, LOU, LUC, RIN & WOR
Org: Native

P. zosteriformis Fern.
Com: Flat-stemmed pondweed
Hab: Shallow water of ponds, rivers & lakes
A&D: Freq nc & in lakes area; rare ne, & in ec, se & sw: FRE 1905, LIN 1895, LOU & MUS 1895
Org: Native

RUPPIACEAE

Ruppia L. (Some authors place in Potamogetonaceae or Zosteraceae)

R. maritima L.
Com: Widgeon grass
Hab: Moderately shallow water
A&D: Rare nw: DIC
Org: Native

SPARGANIACEAE

Sparganium L. Bur-reed

S. americanum Nutt.
Hab: Shallow water of marsh edges
A&D: Infreq se; rare ne, sc & sw
Org: Native

S. androcladum (Engelm.) Morong
Hab: Shallow water of marshes
A&D: Rare ec & se: JOH, MUS 1922
Org: Native

S. chlorocarpum Rydb.
Hab: Shallow water of marshes
A&D: Infreq nc & in lakes area
Org: Native

S. eurycarpum Engelm.
Hab: Shallow water of marshes
A&D: Rare ne; freq to infreq elsewh
Org: Native

TYPHACEAE

Typha L.

T. angustifolia L.
Com: Narrow-leaved cattail
Hab: Marshy shores; shallow water; wet roadsides; edges of shallow streams
A&D: Freq thr
Org: Native

T. X *glauca* Godron
Syn: *T. angustifolia* X *T. latifolia*
Com: Hybrid cattail
Hab: Shallow water of marshes; wet roadsides
A&D: Freq to common thr
Org: Native

T. latifolia L.
Com: Common cattail
Hab: Marshes; shallow standing water; wet roadsides
A&D: Infreq to freq thr
Org: Native

XYRIDACEAE

Xyris L.

X. torta J. E. Sm.
Syn: *X. flexuosa* Muhl.
Com: Yellow-eyed grass
Hab: Sandy pond margins; vernal pools
A&D: Rare e: BEN, BUC, CED, FAY 1894, LIN & MUS
Org: Native

ZANNICHELLIACEAE

Zannichellia L. (Some authors place in Potamogetonaceae)

Z. palustris L.
Com: Horned pondweed
Hab: Shallow marshes; cold-water streams of ne
A&D: Freq in lakes area; infreq ne 1/4; rare se: MUS 1894
Org: Native

Index of Taxa and Synonyms

The column on the left contains all the taxon names from the checklist in alphabetic order, both accepted names and their synonyms. A binomial in this column in italics indicates that the name is an accepted one and can be found in the family listed in the middle column. If the name in the left column is preceded by an asterisk, it is a synonym for the accepted name which is given in the right column. The letter following the hyphen at the end of the family name is an abbreviation for the major taxon:

P = Pteridophytes
G = Gymnosperms
D = Angiosperms: Dicotyledons
M = Angiosperms: Monocotyledons

BINOMIAL	FAMILY	ACCEPTED BINOMIAL
Abies balsamea	PINACEAE-G	
Abutilon theophrasti	MALVACEAE-D	
Acalypha gracilens	EUPHORBIACEAE-D	
*Acalypha monococca	EUPHORBIACEAE-D	*Acalypha gracilens*
Acalypha ostryifolia	EUPHORBIACEAE-D	
Acalypha rhomboidea	EUPHORBIACEAE-D	
Acalypha virginica	EUPHORBIACEAE-D	
Acer ginnala	ACERACEAE-D	
Acer negundo	ACERACEAE-D	
Acer nigrum	ACERACEAE-D	
Acer rubrum	ACERACEAE-D	
Acer saccharinum	ACERACEAE-D	
Acer saccharum	ACERACEAE-D	
Acer spicatum	ACERACEAE-D	
*Achillea lanulosa	ASTERACEAE-D	*Achillea millefolium* ssp. *lanulosa*
Achillea millefolium ssp. *lanulosa*	ASTERACEAE-D	
*Acnida altissima	AMARANTHACEAE-D	*Amaranthus tuberculatus*
Aconitum noveboracense	RANUNCULACEAE-D	
*Aconitum uncinatum ssp. noveboracense	RANUNCULACEAE-D	*Aconitum noveboracense*
*Acorus americanus	ARACEAE-M	*Acorus calamus*
Acorus calamus	ARACEAE-M	
*Actaea alba	RANUNCULACEAE-D	*Actaea pachypoda*
Actaea pachypoda	RANUNCULACEAE-D	
Actaea rubra	RANUNCULACEAE-D	
Adiantum pedatum	ADIANTACEAE-P	
Adlumia fungosa	PAPAVERACEAE-D	
Adoxa moschatellina	ADOXACEAE-D	
Aegilops cylindrica	POACEAE-M	
Aesculus glabra	HIPPOCASTANACEAE-D	
Aesculus hippocastanum	HIPPOCASTANACEAE-D	
Agalinis aspera	SCROPHULARIACEAE-D	
*Agalinis auriculata	SCROPHULARIACEAE-D	*Tomanthera auriculata*
Agalinis gattingeri	SCROPHULARIACEAE-D	
Agalinis paupercula	SCROPHULARIACEAE-D	
Agalinis purpurea	SCROPHULARIACEAE-D	
Agalinis skinneriana	SCROPHULARIACEAE-D	
Agalinis tenuifolia	SCROPHULARIACEAE-D	
Agastache foeniculum	LAMIACEAE-D	
Agastache nepetoides	LAMIACEAE-D	

Agastache scrophulariifolia	LAMIACEAE-D	
*Ageratina altissima	ASTERACEAE-D	*Eupatorium altissimum*
*Ageratina altissima	ASTERACEAE-D	*Eupatorium rugosum*
*Agoseris cuspidata	ASTERACEAE-D	*Nothocalais cuspidata*
Agrimonia eupatoria	ROSACEAE-D	
Agrimonia gryposepala	ROSACEAE-D	
Agrimonia parviflora	ROSACEAE-D	
Agrimonia pubescens	ROSACEAE-D	
Agrimonia striata	ROSACEAE-D	
*Agropyron caninum ssp. majus	POACEAE-M	*Agropyron trachycaulum*
Agropyron cristatum	POACEAE-M	
*Agropyron desertorum	POACEAE-M	*Agropyron pectiniforme*
Agropyron intermedium	POACEAE-M	
Agropyron pectiniforme	POACEAE-M	
Agropyron repens	POACEAE-M	
Agropyron repens X *A. trachycaulum*	POACEAE-M	
Agropyron smithii	POACEAE-M	
*Agropyron subsecundum	POACEAE-M	*Agropyron trachycaulum*
Agropyron trachycaulum	POACEAE-M	
*Agropyron trachycaulum X Hordeum jubatum	POACEAE-M	X *Agrohordeum macounii*
Agrostemma githago	CARYOPHYLLACEAE-D	
*Agrostis alba	POACEAE-M	*Agrostis gigantea*
Agrostis gigantea	POACEAE-M	
Agrostis hyemalis	POACEAE-M	
Agrostis hyemalis var. *tenuis*	POACEAE-M	
*Agrostis palustris	POACEAE-M	*Agrostis stolonifera* var. *palustris*
Agrostis perennans	POACEAE-M	
*Agrostis scabra	POACEAE-M	*Agrostis hyemalis* var. *tenuis*
*Agrostis schweinitzii	POACEAE-M	*Agrostis perennans*
*Agrostis stolonifera var. compacta	POACEAE-M	*Agrostis stolonifera* var. *palustris*
*Agrostis stolonifera var. major	POACEAE-M	*Agrostis gigantea*
Agrostis stolonifera var. *palustris*	POACEAE-M	
Ailanthus altissima	SIMAROUBACEAE-D	
Alcea rosea	MALVACEAE-D	
Alisma gramineum	ALISMATACEAE-M	
*Alisma parviflorum	ALISMATACEAE-M	*Alisma plantago-aquatica*
Alisma plantago-aquatica	ALISMATACEAE-M	

*Alisma subcordatum	ALISMATACEAE-M	*Alisma plantago-aquatica*
*Alisma triviale	ALISMATACEAE-M	*Alisma plantago-aquatica*
*Alliaria officinalis	BRASSICACEAE-D	*Alliaria petiolata*
Alliaria petiolata	BRASSICACEAE-D	
Allium canadense	LILIACEAE-M	
*Allium canadense var. mobilense	LILIACEAE-M	*Allium mutabile*
Allium cernuum	LILIACEAE-M	
Allium mutabile	LILIACEAE-M	
Allium porrum	LILIACEAE-M	
Allium stellatum	LILIACEAE-M	
Allium tricoccum	LILIACEAE-M	
Allium vineale	LILIACEAE-M	
*Alnus incana ssp. rugosa	BETULACEAE-D	*Alnus rugosa*
Alnus rugosa	BETULACEAE-D	
Alopecurus aequalis	POACEAE-M	
Alopecurus carolinianus	POACEAE-M	
*Alopecurus geniculatus	POACEAE-M	*Alopecurus carolinianus*
Alopecurus pratensis	POACEAE-M	
*Althaea rosea	MALVACEAE-D	*Alcea rosea*
Alyssum alyssoides	BRASSICACEAE-D	
Amaranthus albus	AMARANTHACEAE-D	
Amaranthus arenicola	AMARANTHACEAE-D	
*Amaranthus blitoides	AMARANTHACEAE-D	*Amaranthus graecizans*
Amaranthus graecizans	AMARANTHACEAE-D	
Amaranthus hybridus	AMARANTHACEAE-D	
Amaranthus powellii	AMARANTHACEAE-D	
Amaranthus retroflexus	AMARANTHACEAE-D	
Amaranthus rudis	AMARANTHACEAE-D	
Amaranthus spinosus	AMARANTHACEAE-D	
*Amaranthus tamariscinus	AMARANTHACEAE-D	*Amaranthus rudis*
*Amaranthus torreyi	AMARANTHACEAE-D	*Amaranthus arenicola*
Amaranthus tuberculatus	AMARANTHACEAE-D	
Ambrosia artemisiifolia	ASTERACEAE-D	
Ambrosia bidentata	ASTERACEAE-D	
Ambrosia psilostachya	ASTERACEAE-D	
Ambrosia trifida	ASTERACEAE-D	
Amelanchier alnifolia	ROSACEAE-D	
Amelanchier arborea	ROSACEAE-D	
*Amelanchier canadensis	ROSACEAE-D	*Amelanchier arborea*
Amelanchier humilis	ROSACEAE-D	
Amelanchier interior	ROSACEAE-D	
*Amelanchier laevis	ROSACEAE-D	*Amelanchier arborea*
Amelanchier sanguinea	ROSACEAE-D	
*Amelanchier spicata	ROSACEAE-D	*Amelanchier humilis*

*Amelanchier stolonifera	ROSACEAE-D	*Amelanchier humilis*
*Amelanchier X wiegandii	ROSACEAE-D	*Amelanchier interior*
Ammannia coccinea	LYTHRACEAE-D	
Ammannia robusta	LYTHRACEAE-D	
Amorpha canescens	FABACEAE-D	
Amorpha fruticosa	FABACEAE-D	
*Amorpha microphylla	FABACEAE-D	*Amorpha nana*
Amorpha nana	FABACEAE-D	
*Ampelamus albidus	ASCLEPIADACEAE-D	*Cynanchum laeve*
Ampelopsis cordata	VITACEAE-D	
Amphicarpaea bracteata	FABACEAE-D	
*Anacharis canadensis	HYDROCHARITACEAE-M	*Elodea canadensis*
*Anacharis nuttallii	HYDROCHARITACEAE-M	*Elodea nuttallii*
Anagallis arvensis	PRIMULACEAE-D	
Anaphalis margaritacea	ASTERACEAE-D	
Anchusa azurea	BORAGINACEAE-D	
*Andropogon furcatus	POACEAE-M	*Andropogon gerardii*
Andropogon gerardii	POACEAE-M	
*Andropogon gerardii var. paucipilus	POACEAE-M	*Andropogon hallii*
Andropogon hallii	POACEAE-M	
*Andropogon scoparius	POACEAE-M	*Schizachyrium scoparium*
Andropogon virginicus	POACEAE-M	
Androsace occidentalis	PRIMULACEAE-D	
Anemone canadensis	RANUNCULACEAE-D	
Anemone caroliniana	RANUNCULACEAE-D	
Anemone cylindrica	RANUNCULACEAE-D	
*Anemone patens	RANUNCULACEAE-D	*Pulsatilla patens* ssp. *multifida*
*Anemone patens var. wolfgangiana	RANUNCULACEAE-D	*Pulsatilla patens* ssp. *multifida*
Anemone quinquefolia	RANUNCULACEAE-D	
Anemone virginiana	RANUNCULACEAE-D	
*Anemonella thalictroides	RANUNCULACEAE-D	*Thalictrum thalictroides*
Angelica atropurpurea	APIACEAE-D	
Antennaria neglecta	ASTERACEAE-D	
Antennaria plantaginifolia	ASTERACEAE-D	
Anthemis arvensis	ASTERACEAE-D	
Anthemis cotula	ASTERACEAE-D	
Anthemis tinctoria	ASTERACEAE-D	
Anthyllis vulneraria	FABACEAE-D	
Apios americana	FABACEAE-D	
Aplectrum hyemale	ORCHIDACEAE-M	
Apocynum androsaemifolium	APOCYNACEAE-D	
*Apocynum androsaemifolium X A. sibiricum	APOCYNACEAE-D	*Apocynum* X *medium*

Apocynum cannabinum	APOCYNACEAE-D	
*Apocynum cannabinum var. hypericifolium	APOCYNACEAE-D	*Apocynum sibiricum*
Apocynum sibiricum	APOCYNACEAE-D	
Apocynum X *medium*	APOCYNACEAE-D	
Aquilegia canadensis	RANUNCULACEAE-D	
Arabis canadensis	BRASSICACEAE-D	
Arabis divaricarpa	BRASSICACEAE-D	
Arabis drummondii	BRASSICACEAE-D	
Arabis glabra	BRASSICACEAE-D	
Arabis hirsuta	BRASSICACEAE-D	
Arabis laevigata	BRASSICACEAE-D	
Arabis lyrata	BRASSICACEAE-D	
Arabis missouriensis	BRASSICACEAE-D	
*Arabis perstellata var. shortii	BRASSICACEAE-D	*Arabis shortii*
Arabis shortii	BRASSICACEAE-D	
*Arabis virginica	BRASSICACEAE-D	*Sibara virginica*
*Arabis viridis var. deamii	BRASSICACEAE-D	*Arabis missouriensis*
Aralia nudicaulis	ARALIACEAE-D	
Aralia racemosa	ARALIACEAE-D	
Arctium lappa	ASTERACEAE-D	
Arctium minus	ASTERACEAE-D	
Arctium tomentosum	ASTERACEAE-D	
Arctostaphylos uva-ursi	ERICACEAE-D	
*Arenaria lateriflora	CARYOPHYLLACEAE-D	*Moehringia lateriflora*
Arenaria serpyllifolia	CARYOPHYLLACEAE-D	
*Arenaria stricta	CARYOPHYLLACEAE-D	*Minuartia michauxii*
Argemone albiflora	PAPAVERACEAE-D	
*Argemone intermedia	PAPAVERACEAE-D	*Argemone albiflora*
Argemone mexicana	PAPAVERACEAE-D	
Argemone polyanthemos	PAPAVERACEAE-D	
*Arisaema atrorubens	ARACEAE-M	*Arisaema triphyllum*
Arisaema dracontium	ARACEAE-M	
Arisaema triphyllum	ARACEAE-M	
Aristida basiramea	POACEAE-M	
*Aristida basiramea var. curtissii	POACEAE-M	*Aristida curtissii*
Aristida curtissii	POACEAE-M	
Aristida dichotoma	POACEAE-M	
*Aristida dichotoma var. curtissii	POACEAE-M	*Aristida curtissii*
*Aristida intermedia	POACEAE-M	*Aristida longespica* var. *geniculata*
Aristida longespica	POACEAE-M	

Aristida longespica var. *geniculata*	POACEAE-M	
*Aristida longiseta	POACEAE-M	*Aristida purpurea* var. *longiseta*
*Aristida necopina	POACEAE-M	*Aristida longespica* var. *geniculata*
Aristida oligantha	POACEAE-M	
Aristida purpurea var. *longiseta*	POACEAE-M	
Aristida ramosissima	POACEAE-M	
Aristida tuberculosa	POACEAE-M	
Aristolochia serpentaria	ARISTOLOCHIACEAE-D	
Armoracia aquatica	BRASSICACEAE-D	
*Armoracia lacustris	BRASSICACEAE-D	*Armoracia aquatica*
*Armoracia lapathifolia	BRASSICACEAE-D	*Armoracia rusticana*
Armoracia rusticana	BRASSICACEAE-D	
*Arnoglossum atriplicifolium	ASTERACEAE-D	*Cacalia atriplicifolia*
*Arnoglossum plantagineum	ASTERACEAE-D	*Cacalia plantaginea*
*Arnoglossum reniforme	ASTERACEAE-D	*Cacalia muhlenbergii*
Aronia melanocarpa	ROSACEAE-D	
Arrhenatherum elatius	POACEAE-M	
Artemisia abrotanum	ASTERACEAE-D	
Artemisia absinthium	ASTERACEAE-D	
Artemisia annua	ASTERACEAE-D	
Artemisia biennis	ASTERACEAE-D	
Artemisia campestris ssp. *caudata*	ASTERACEAE-D	
*Artemisia caudata	ASTERACEAE-D	*Artemisia campestris* ssp. *caudata*
*Artemisia dracunculoides	ASTERACEAE-D	*Artemisia dracunculus*
Artemisia dracunculus	ASTERACEAE-D	
Artemisia frigida	ASTERACEAE-D	
*Artemisia glauca	ASTERACEAE-D	*Artemisia dracunculus*
*Artemisia gnaphalodes	ASTERACEAE-D	*Artemisia ludoviciana*
Artemisia ludoviciana	ASTERACEAE-D	
Artemisia serrata	ASTERACEAE-D	
Artemisia vulgaris	ASTERACEAE-D	
Aruncus dioicus	ROSACEAE-D	
Asarum canadense	ARISTOLOCHIACEAE-D	
Asclepias amplexicaulis	ASCLEPIADACEAE-D	
*Asclepias auriculata	ASCLEPIADACEAE-D	*Asclepias engelmanniana*
Asclepias engelmanniana	ASCLEPIADACEAE-D	
Asclepias exaltata	ASCLEPIADACEAE-D	
Asclepias hirtella	ASCLEPIADACEAE-D	
Asclepias incarnata	ASCLEPIADACEAE-D	
Asclepias lanuginosa	ASCLEPIADACEAE-D	

Asclepias meadii	ASCLEPIADACEAE-D	
*Asclepias nuttalliana	ASCLEPIADACEAE-D	*Asclepias lanuginosa*
*Asclepias otarioides	ASCLEPIADACEAE-D	*Asclepias lanuginosa*
Asclepias ovalifolia	ASCLEPIADACEAE-D	
Asclepias purpurascens	ASCLEPIADACEAE-D	
Asclepias quadrifolia	ASCLEPIADACEAE-D	
Asclepias speciosa	ASCLEPIADACEAE-D	
Asclepias stenophylla	ASCLEPIADACEAE-D	
Asclepias sullivantii	ASCLEPIADACEAE-D	
Asclepias syriaca	ASCLEPIADACEAE-D	
Asclepias tuberosa ssp. *interior*	ASCLEPIADACEAE-D	
Asclepias verticillata	ASCLEPIADACEAE-D	
Asclepias viridiflora	ASCLEPIADACEAE-D	
Asimina triloba	ANNONACEAE-D	
Asparagus officinalis	LILIACEAE-M	
Asplenium platyneuron	ASPLENIACEAE-P	
Asplenium rhizophyllum	ASPLENIACEAE-P	
Aster azureus	ASTERACEAE-D	
*Aster borealis	ASTERACEAE-D	*Aster junciformis*
Aster brachyactis	ASTERACEAE-D	
Aster cordifolius	ASTERACEAE-D	
Aster drummondii	ASTERACEAE-D	
Aster dumosus	ASTERACEAE-D	
Aster ericoides	ASTERACEAE-D	
*Aster ericoides X A. novae-angliae	ASTERACEAE-D	*Aster* X *amethystinus*
Aster falcatus ssp. *commutatus*	ASTERACEAE-D	
Aster furcatus	ASTERACEAE-D	
*Aster interior	ASTERACEAE-D	*Aster lanceolatus*
Aster junciformis	ASTERACEAE-D	
Aster laevis	ASTERACEAE-D	
Aster lanceolatus	ASTERACEAE-D	
Aster lateriflorus	ASTERACEAE-D	
Aster linariifolius	ASTERACEAE-D	
*Aster lucidulus	ASTERACEAE-D	*Aster puniceus*
Aster macrophyllus	ASTERACEAE-D	
*Aster nebraskensis	ASTERACEAE-D	*Aster praealtus* var. *nebraskensis*
Aster novae-angliae	ASTERACEAE-D	
Aster oblongifolius	ASTERACEAE-D	
Aster ontarionis	ASTERACEAE-D	
*Aster oolentangiensis	ASTERACEAE-D	*Aster azureus*
Aster parviceps	ASTERACEAE-D	
Aster pilosus	ASTERACEAE-D	

Aster praealtus	ASTERACEAE-D	
Aster praealtus var. *nebraskensis*	ASTERACEAE-D	
Aster prenanthoides	ASTERACEAE-D	
*Aster ptarmicoides	ASTERACEAE-D	*Solidago ptarmicoides*
Aster pubentior	ASTERACEAE-D	
Aster puniceus	ASTERACEAE-D	
Aster sagittifolius	ASTERACEAE-D	
*Aster sagittifolius var. drummondii	ASTERACEAE-D	*Aster drummondii*
Aster schreberi	ASTERACEAE-D	
Aster sericeus	ASTERACEAE-D	
Aster shortii	ASTERACEAE-D	
*Aster simplex	ASTERACEAE-D	*Aster lanceolatus*
*Aster simplex var. ramossimus	ASTERACEAE-D	*Aster lanceolatus*
Aster turbinellus	ASTERACEAE-D	
Aster umbellatus	ASTERACEAE-D	
*Aster umbellatus var. pubens	ASTERACEAE-D	*Aster pubentior*
*Aster vimineus	ASTERACEAE-D	*Aster lateriflorus*
*Aster woldeni	ASTERACEAE-D	*Aster praealtus* var. *nebraskensis*
Aster X *amethystinus*	ASTERACEAE-D	
*Aster X sagittifolius	ASTERACEAE-D	*Aster sagittifolius*
Astragalus adsurgens var. *robustior*	FABACEAE-D	
Astragalus agrestis	FABACEAE-D	
Astragalus canadensis	FABACEAE-D	
*Astragalus caryocarpus	FABACEAE-D	*Astragalus crassicarpus*
Astragalus crassicarpus	FABACEAE-D	
Astragalus distortus	FABACEAE-D	
Astragalus flexuosus	FABACEAE-D	
*Astragalus goniatus	FABACEAE-D	*Astragalus agrestis*
Astragalus lotiflorus	FABACEAE-D	
Astragalus missouriensis	FABACEAE-D	
*Astragalus striatus	FABACEAE-D	*Astragalus adsurgens* var. *robustior*
*Athyrium acrostichoides	ASPLENIACEAE-P	*Athyrium thelypterioides*
*Athyrium angustum	ASPLENIACEAE-P	*Athyrium filix-femina* var. *angustum*
Athyrium filix-femina var. *angustum*	ASPLENIACEAE-P	
Athyrium pycnocarpon	ASPLENIACEAE-P	
Athyrium thelypterioides	ASPLENIACEAE-P	
Atriplex patula	CHENOPODIACEAE-D	

Atriplex rosea	CHENOPODIACEAE-D	
Aureolaria grandiflora var. *pulchra*	SCROPHULARIACEAE-D	
Aureolaria pedicularia	SCROPHULARIACEAE-D	
Avena fatua	POACEAE-M	
Avena sativa	POACEAE-M	
Azolla mexicana	AZOLLACEAE-P	
Bacopa rotundifolia	SCROPHULARIACEAE-D	
Ballota nigra	LAMIACEAE-D	
*Baptisia alba var. macrophylla	FABACEAE-D	*Baptisia lactea*
Baptisia australis var. *minor*	FABACEAE-D	
Baptisia bracteata var. *glabrescens*	FABACEAE-D	
Baptisia lactea	FABACEAE-D	
*Baptisia leucantha	FABACEAE-D	*Baptisia lactea*
*Baptisia leucophaea	FABACEAE-D	*Baptisia bracteata* var. *glabrescens*
*Baptisia minor	FABACEAE-D	*Baptisia australis* var. *minor*
Baptisia tinctoria	FABACEAE-D	
Barbarea vulgaris	BRASSICACEAE-D	
Beckmannia syzigachne	POACEAE-M	
Belamcanda chinensis	IRIDACEAE-M	
Berberis thunbergii	BERBERIDACEAE-D	
Berberis vulgaris	BERBERIDACEAE-D	
Berteroa incana	BRASSICACEAE-D	
Berula erecta var. *incisum*	APIACEAE-D	
*Berula incisa	APIACEAE-D	*Berula erecta* var. *incisum*
*Berula pusilla	APIACEAE-D	*Berula erecta* var. *incisum*
Besseya bullii	SCROPHULARIACEAE-D	
*Betula alba	BETULACEAE-D	*Betula papyrifera*
Betula alleghaniensis	BETULACEAE-D	
*Betula glandulosa var. glandulifera	BETULACEAE-D	*Betula pumila* var. *glandulifera*
*Betula lutea	BETULACEAE-D	*Betula alleghaniensis*
Betula nigra	BETULACEAE-D	
Betula papyrifera	BETULACEAE-D	
Betula pumila var. *glandulifera*	BETULACEAE-D	
Betula pumila X *Betula nigra*	BETULACEAE-D	

Bidens aristosa	ASTERACEAE-D	
*Bidens aristosa var. retrorsa	ASTERACEAE-D	*Bidens polylepis*
*Bidens beckii	ASTERACEAE-D	*Megalodonta beckii*
Bidens bipinnata	ASTERACEAE-D	
Bidens cernua	ASTERACEAE-D	
*Bidens comosa	ASTERACEAE-D	*Bidens tripartita*
Bidens connata	ASTERACEAE-D	
Bidens coronata	ASTERACEAE-D	
Bidens discoidea	ASTERACEAE-D	
Bidens frondosa	ASTERACEAE-D	
Bidens polylepis	ASTERACEAE-D	
*Bidens trichosperma	ASTERACEAE-D	*Bidens coronata*
Bidens tripartita	ASTERACEAE-D	
Bidens vulgata	ASTERACEAE-D	
Blephilia ciliata	LAMIACEAE-D	
Blephilia hirsuta	LAMIACEAE-D	
Boehmeria cylindrica	URTICACEAE-D	
Boltonia asteroides	ASTERACEAE-D	
Botrychium campestre	OPHIOGLOSSACEAE-P	
Botrychium dissectum f. dissectum	OPHIOGLOSSACEAE-P	
Botrychium dissectum f. obliquum	OPHIOGLOSSACEAE-P	
*Botrychium dissectum var. obliquum	OPHIOGLOSSACEAE-P	*Botrychium dissectum f. obliquum*
Botrychium matricariifolium	OPHIOGLOSSACEAE-P	
Botrychium multifidum	OPHIOGLOSSACEAE-P	
*Botrychium multifidum var. intermedium	OPHIOGLOSSACEAE-P	*Botrychium multifidum*
Botrychium simplex	OPHIOGLOSSACEAE-P	
Botrychium virginianum	OPHIOGLOSSACEAE-P	
Bouteloua curtipendula	POACEAE-M	
Bouteloua gracilis	POACEAE-M	
Bouteloua hirsuta	POACEAE-M	
*Brachyactis ciliata	ASTERACEAE-D	*Aster brachyactis*
Brachyelytrum erectum	POACEAE-M	
*Brachyelytrum erectum var. septentrionale	POACEAE-M	*Brachyelytrum erectum*
Brasenia schreberi	NYMPHAEACEAE-D	
Brassica campestris	BRASSICACEAE-D	
*Brassica hirta	BRASSICACEAE-D	*Sinapis alba*
Brassica juncea	BRASSICACEAE-D	
Brassica Kaber	BRASSICACEAE-D	
*Brassica kaber	BRASSICACEAE-D	*Sinapis arvensis*
Brassica napus	BRASSICACEAE-D	

Brassica nigra	BRASSICACEAE-D	
Brassica oleracea	BRASSICACEAE-D	
*Brassica rapa ssp. olifera	BRASSICACEAE-D	*Brassica campestris*
*Breweria pickeringii var. pattersonii	CONVOLVULACEAE-D	*Stylisma pickeringii var. pattersonii*
Brickellia eupatorioides	ASTERACEAE-D	
*Bromus altissimus	POACEAE-M	*Bromus latiglumis*
Bromus ciliatus	POACEAE-M	
Bromus commutatus	POACEAE-M	
*Bromus hordeaceus	POACEAE-M	*Bromus mollis*
Bromus inermis	POACEAE-M	
Bromus japonicus	POACEAE-M	
Bromus kalmii	POACEAE-M	
Bromus latiglumis	POACEAE-M	
Bromus mollis	POACEAE-M	
Bromus pubescens	POACEAE-M	
*Bromus purgans	POACEAE-M	*Bromus latiglumis*
*Bromus purgans	POACEAE-M	*Bromus pubescens*
Bromus secalinus	POACEAE-M	
Bromus tectorum	POACEAE-M	
Buchloe dactyloides	POACEAE-M	
*Buglossoides arvense	BORAGINACEAE-D	*Lithospermum arvense*
Bulbostylis capillaris	CYPERACEAE-M	
Cacalia atriplicifolia	ASTERACEAE-D	
Cacalia muhlenbergii	ASTERACEAE-D	
Cacalia plantaginea	ASTERACEAE-D	
Cacalia suaveolens	ASTERACEAE-D	
*Cacalia tuberosa	ASTERACEAE-D	*Cacalia plantaginea*
Calamagrostis canadensis	POACEAE-M	
Calamagrostis inexpansa	POACEAE-M	
*Calamagrostis neglecta	POACEAE-M	*Calamagrostis inexpansa*
Calamovilfa longifolia	POACEAE-M	
Calamovilfa longifolia var. magna	POACEAE-M	
Callirhoe alcaeoides	MALVACEAE-D	
Callirhoe bushii	MALVACEAE-D	
Callirhoe involucrata	MALVACEAE-D	
Callirhoe triangulata	MALVACEAE-D	
Callitriche heterophylla	CALLITRICHACEAE-D	
*Callitriche palustris	CALLITRICHACEAE-D	*Callitriche verna*
Callitriche verna	CALLITRICHACEAE-D	
*Calopogon pulchellus	ORCHIDACEAE-M	*Calopogon tuberosus*
Calopogon tuberosus	ORCHIDACEAE-M	
Caltha palustris	RANUNCULACEAE-D	
Calylophus serrulatus	ONAGRACEAE-D	

*Calystegia macounii	CONVOLVULACEAE-D	*Calystegia sepium*
Calystegia sepium	CONVOLVULACEAE-D	
Calystegia spithamaea	CONVOLVULACEAE-D	
Camassia scilloides	LILIACEAE-M	
Camelina microcarpa	BRASSICACEAE-D	
Camelina sativa	BRASSICACEAE-D	
Campanula americana	CAMPANULACEAE-D	
Campanula aparinoides	CAMPANULACEAE-D	
Campanula rapunculoides	CAMPANULACEAE-D	
Campanula rotundifolia	CAMPANULACEAE-D	
*Campanula uliginosa	CAMPANULACEAE-D	*Campanula aparinoides*
Campsis radicans	BIGNONIACEAE-D	
*Camptosorus rhizophyllus	ASPLENIACEAE-P	*Asplenium rhizophyllum*
Cannabis sativa	MORACEAE-D	
Capsella bursa-pastoris	BRASSICACEAE-D	
Caragana arborescens	FABACEAE-D	
Cardamine bulbosa	BRASSICACEAE-D	
*Cardamine concatenata	BRASSICACEAE-D	*Dentaria laciniata*
Cardamine douglassii	BRASSICACEAE-D	
Cardamine parviflora var. *arenicola*	BRASSICACEAE-D	
Cardamine pensylvanica	BRASSICACEAE-D	
Cardaria chalapensis	BRASSICACEAE-D	
Cardaria draba	BRASSICACEAE-D	
Carduus acanthoides	ASTERACEAE-D	
Carduus nutans	ASTERACEAE-D	
*Carex abdita	CYPERACEAE-M	*Carex umbellata*
Carex aggregata	CYPERACEAE-M	
Carex albursina	CYPERACEAE-M	
Carex alopecoidea	CYPERACEAE-M	
Carex amphibola var. *turgida*	CYPERACEAE-M	
Carex annectens var. *xanthocarpa*	CYPERACEAE-M	
Carex aquatilis	CYPERACEAE-M	
Carex artitecta	CYPERACEAE-M	
Carex assiniboinensis	CYPERACEAE-M	
Carex atherodes	CYPERACEAE-M	
*Carex atherodes var. longo-lanceolata	CYPERACEAE-M	*Carex laeviconica*
Carex backii	CYPERACEAE-M	
*Carex backii var. saximontana	CYPERACEAE-M	*Carex saximontana*
Carex bebbii	CYPERACEAE-M	
Carex bicknellii	CYPERACEAE-M	
Carex blanda	CYPERACEAE-M	

*Carex brachyglossa	CYPERACEAE-M	*Carex annectens* var. *xanthocarpa*
Carex brevior	CYPERACEAE-M	
Carex bushii	CYPERACEAE-M	
Carex buxbaumii	CYPERACEAE-M	
Carex careyana	CYPERACEAE-M	
Carex cephalantha	CYPERACEAE-M	
Carex cephaloidea	CYPERACEAE-M	
Carex cephalophora	CYPERACEAE-M	
Carex chordorrhiza	CYPERACEAE-M	
Carex communis	CYPERACEAE-M	
Carex comosa	CYPERACEAE-M	
*Carex complanata var. hirsuta	CYPERACEAE-M	*Carex hirsutella*
Carex conjuncta	CYPERACEAE-M	
Carex conoidea	CYPERACEAE-M	
Carex convoluta	CYPERACEAE-M	
Carex crawei	CYPERACEAE-M	
Carex crawfordii	CYPERACEAE-M	
Carex crinita	CYPERACEAE-M	
Carex cristatella	CYPERACEAE-M	
Carex crus-corvi	CYPERACEAE-M	
Carex davisii	CYPERACEAE-M	
Carex deweyana	CYPERACEAE-M	
Carex diandra	CYPERACEAE-M	
*Carex digitalis var. copulata	CYPERACEAE-M	*Carex laxiculmis*
Carex douglasii	CYPERACEAE-M	
Carex eburnea	CYPERACEAE-M	
Carex eleocharis	CYPERACEAE-M	
Carex emoryi	CYPERACEAE-M	
Carex festucacea	CYPERACEAE-M	
*Carex flaccidula	CYPERACEAE-M	*Carex convoluta*
*Carex flaccidula	CYPERACEAE-M	*Carex rosea*
Carex foenea	CYPERACEAE-M	
Carex frankii	CYPERACEAE-M	
Carex gracilescens	CYPERACEAE-M	
Carex gracillima	CYPERACEAE-M	
Carex granularis	CYPERACEAE-M	
Carex gravida	CYPERACEAE-M	
Carex grayi	CYPERACEAE-M	
*Carex grisea	CYPERACEAE-M	*Carex amphibola* var. *turgida*
*Carex haleana	CYPERACEAE-M	*Carex granularis*
Carex haydenii	CYPERACEAE-M	
Carex heliophila	CYPERACEAE-M	

Carex hirsutella	CYPERACEAE-M	
Carex hirtifolia	CYPERACEAE-M	
Carex hitchcockiana	CYPERACEAE-M	
Carex hyalinolepis	CYPERACEAE-M	
Carex hystericina	CYPERACEAE-M	
*Carex hystricina	CYPERACEAE-M	*Carex hystericina*
*Carex inflata var. utriculata	CYPERACEAE-M	*Carex rostrata* var. *utriculata*
Carex interior	CYPERACEAE-M	
Carex jamesii	CYPERACEAE-M	
Carex lacustris	CYPERACEAE-M	
*Carex lacustris var. laxiflora	CYPERACEAE-M	*Carex hyalinolepis*
Carex laeviconica	CYPERACEAE-M	
Carex laevivaginata	CYPERACEAE-M	
Carex lanuginosa	CYPERACEAE-M	
*Carex lanuginosa var. americana	CYPERACEAE-M	*Carex lasiocarpa* var. *americana*
*Carex lasiocarpa ssp. americana	CYPERACEAE-M	*Carex lasiocarpa* var. *americana*
Carex lasiocarpa var. *americana*	CYPERACEAE-M	
*Carex lasiocarpa var. latifolia	CYPERACEAE-M	*Carex lanuginosa*
Carex laxiculmis	CYPERACEAE-M	
*Carex laxiflora var. blanda	CYPERACEAE-M	*Carex blanda*
*Carex laxiflora var. gracillima	CYPERACEAE-M	*Carex gracilescens*
*Carex laxiflora var. latifolia	CYPERACEAE-M	*Carex albursina*
Carex leavenworthii	CYPERACEAE-M	
Carex leptalea	CYPERACEAE-M	
Carex limosa	CYPERACEAE-M	
*Carex lunelliana	CYPERACEAE-M	*Carex gravida*
Carex lupuliformis	CYPERACEAE-M	
Carex lupulina	CYPERACEAE-M	
Carex lurida	CYPERACEAE-M	
Carex meadii	CYPERACEAE-M	
Carex media	CYPERACEAE-M	
Carex molesta	CYPERACEAE-M	
Carex muhlenbergii	CYPERACEAE-M	
*Carex muricata var. cephalantha	CYPERACEAE-M	*Carex cephalantha*
Carex muskingumensis	CYPERACEAE-M	

*Carex nigromarginata var. elliptica	CYPERACEAE-M	*Carex peckii*
*Carex nigromarginata var. muhlenbergii	CYPERACEAE-M	*Carex artitecta*
Carex normalis	CYPERACEAE-M	
*Carex norvegica	CYPERACEAE-M	*Carex media*
Carex oligocarpa	CYPERACEAE-M	
Carex peckii	CYPERACEAE-M	
Carex pedunculata	CYPERACEAE-M	
Carex pensylvanica	CYPERACEAE-M	
*Carex pensylvanica var. digyna	CYPERACEAE-M	*Carex heliophila*
Carex plantaginea	CYPERACEAE-M	
Carex praegracilis	CYPERACEAE-M	
Carex prairea	CYPERACEAE-M	
*Carex prarisa	CYPERACEAE-M	*Carex prairea*
Carex projecta	CYPERACEAE-M	
*Carex radiata	CYPERACEAE-M	*Carex rosea*
Carex retroflexa	CYPERACEAE-M	
Carex retrorsa	CYPERACEAE-M	
Carex richardsonii	CYPERACEAE-M	
*Carex riparia var. lacustris	CYPERACEAE-M	*Carex lacustris*
Carex rosea	CYPERACEAE-M	
*Carex rosea var. pusilla	CYPERACEAE-M	*Carex convoluta*
*Carex rosea var. radiata	CYPERACEAE-M	*Carex rosea*
Carex rostrata var. *utriculata*	CYPERACEAE-M	
*Carex rugospermum var. tonsa	CYPERACEAE-M	*Carex tonsa*
Carex sartwellii	CYPERACEAE-M	
Carex saximontana	CYPERACEAE-M	
Carex scoparia	CYPERACEAE-M	
*Carex scoparia var. minor	CYPERACEAE-M	*Carex crawfordii*
Carex shortiana	CYPERACEAE-M	
*Carex siccata	CYPERACEAE-M	*Carex foenea*
Carex sparganioides	CYPERACEAE-M	
*Carex sparganioides var. aggregata	CYPERACEAE-M	*Carex aggregata*
*Carex sparganioides var. cephaloidea	CYPERACEAE-M	*Carex cephaloidea*
Carex sprengelii	CYPERACEAE-M	
Carex squarrosa	CYPERACEAE-M	

*Carex stenophylla ssp. eleocharis	CYPERACEAE-M	*Carex eleocharis*
Carex sterilis	CYPERACEAE-M	
Carex stipata	CYPERACEAE-M	
*Carex stipata var. laevivaginata	CYPERACEAE-M	*Carex laevivaginata*
Carex stricta	CYPERACEAE-M	
*Carex stricta var. elongata	CYPERACEAE-M	*Carex emoryi*
*Carex strictior	CYPERACEAE-M	*Carex stricta*
Carex suberecta	CYPERACEAE-M	
*Carex substricta	CYPERACEAE-M	*Carex aquatilis*
Carex sychnocephala	CYPERACEAE-M	
Carex tenera	CYPERACEAE-M	
Carex tetanica	CYPERACEAE-M	
*Carex tetanica var. meadii	CYPERACEAE-M	*Carex meadii*
*Carex tetanica var. woodii	CYPERACEAE-M	*Carex woodii*
Carex tonsa	CYPERACEAE-M	
Carex tribuloides	CYPERACEAE-M	
Carex trichocarpa	CYPERACEAE-M	
*Carex trichocarpa var. deweyi	CYPERACEAE-M	*Carex laeviconica*
Carex tuckermanii	CYPERACEAE-M	
Carex typhina	CYPERACEAE-M	
Carex umbellata	CYPERACEAE-M	
*Carex umbellata var. tonsa	CYPERACEAE-M	*Carex tonsa*
Carex vesicaria	CYPERACEAE-M	
Carex vulpinoidea	CYPERACEAE-M	
Carex woodii	CYPERACEAE-M	
*Carex X copulata	CYPERACEAE-M	*Carex laxiculmis*
*Carex X molesta	CYPERACEAE-M	*Carex molesta*
*Carex X stipata	CYPERACEAE-M	*Carex stipata*
Carpinus caroliniana	BETULACEAE-D	
*Carya alba	JUGLANDACEAE-D	*Carya tomentosa*
Carya cordiformis	JUGLANDACEAE-D	
Carya illinoensis	JUGLANDACEAE-D	
Carya laciniosa	JUGLANDACEAE-D	
Carya ovata	JUGLANDACEAE-D	
*Carya pecan	JUGLANDACEAE-D	*Carya illinoensis*
Carya tomentosa	JUGLANDACEAE-D	
*Cassia fasciculata	FABACEAE-D	*Chamaecrista fasciculata*
Cassia marilandica	FABACEAE-D	
Castanea dentata	FAGACEAE-D	

Castilleja coccinea	SCROPHULARIACEAE-D	
Castilleja sessiliflora	SCROPHULARIACEAE-D	
Catalpa bignonioides	BIGNONIACEAE-D	
Catalpa speciosa	BIGNONIACEAE-D	
Caulophyllum thalictroides	BERBERIDACEAE-D	
Ceanothus americanus var. *pitcheri*	RHAMNACEAE-D	
Ceanothus herbaceus var. *pubescens*	RHAMNACEAE-D	
*Ceanothus ovatus	RHAMNACEAE-D	*Ceanothus herbaceus* var. *pubescens*
Celastrus orbiculatus	CELASTRACEAE-D	
Celastrus scandens	CELASTRACEAE-D	
Celtis occidentalis	ULMACEAE-D	
Cenchrus longispinus	POACEAE-M	
*Cenchrus pauciflorus	POACEAE-M	*Cenchrus longispinus*
*Centaurea biebersteinii	ASTERACEAE-D	*Centaurea maculosa*
Centaurea calcitrapa	ASTERACEAE-D	
Centaurea cyanus	ASTERACEAE-D	
Centaurea diffusa	ASTERACEAE-D	
Centaurea jacea	ASTERACEAE-D	
Centaurea maculosa	ASTERACEAE-D	
Centaurea moschata	ASTERACEAE-D	
Centaurea nigra	ASTERACEAE-D	
Centaurea repens	ASTERACEAE-D	
Centaurea scabiosa	ASTERACEAE-D	
Centaurea solstitialis	ASTERACEAE-D	
Cephalanthus occidentalis	RUBIACEAE-D	
Cerastium arvense	CARYOPHYLLACEAE-D	
*Cerastium brachypodum	CARYOPHYLLACEAE-D	*Cerastium nutans*
*Cerastium fontanum	CARYOPHYLLACEAE-D	*Cerastium vulgatum*
Cerastium glomeratum	CARYOPHYLLACEAE-D	
Cerastium nutans	CARYOPHYLLACEAE-D	
*Cerastium velutinum	CARYOPHYLLACEAE-D	*Cerastium arvense*
*Cerastium viscosum	CARYOPHYLLACEAE-D	*Cerastium glomeratum*
Cerastium vulgatum	CARYOPHYLLACEAE-D	
*Ceratocephalus testiculatus	RANUNCULACEAE-D	*Ranunculus testiculatus*
Ceratophyllum demersum	CERATOPHYLLACEAE-D	
Cercis canadensis	FABACEAE-D	
Chaenorrhinum minus	SCROPHULARIACEAE-D	
Chaerophyllum procumbens	APIACEAE-D	
Chamaecrista fasciculata	FABACEAE-D	
*Chamaesyce geyeri	EUPHORBIACEAE-D	*Euphorbia geyeri*
*Chamaesyce glyptosperma	EUPHORBIACEAE-D	*Euphorbia glyptosperma*
*Chamaesyce maculata	EUPHORBIACEAE-D	*Euphorbia maculata*
*Chamaesyce nutans	EUPHORBIACEAE-D	*Euphorbia nutans*

Taxon	Family	Synonym
*Chamaesyce serpens	EUPHORBIACEAE-D	*Euphorbia serpens*
*Chamaesyce serpyllifolia	EUPHORBIACEAE-D	*Euphorbia serpyllifolia*
*Chamaesyce stictospora	EUPHORBIACEAE-D	*Euphorbia stictospora*
*Chamomilla recuita	ASTERACEAE-D	*Matricaria chamomilla*
*Chamomilla suaveolens	ASTERACEAE-D	*Matricaria matricarioides*
Chasmanthium latifolium	POACEAE-M	
Cheilanthes feei	ADIANTACEAE-P	
Chelidonium majus	PAPAVERACEAE-D	
Chelone glabra	SCROPHULARIACEAE-D	
Chelone obliqua var. *speciosa*	SCROPHULARIACEAE-D	
Chenopodium album	CHENOPODIACEAE-D	
Chenopodium ambrosioides	CHENOPODIACEAE-D	
Chenopodium berlandieri	CHENOPODIACEAE-D	
*Chenopodium boscianum	CHENOPODIACEAE-D	*Chenopodium standleyanum*
Chenopodium botrys	CHENOPODIACEAE-D	
Chenopodium bushianum	CHENOPODIACEAE-D	
Chenopodium capitatum	CHENOPODIACEAE-D	
Chenopodium desiccatum	CHENOPODIACEAE-D	
Chenopodium foggii	CHENOPODIACEAE-D	
*Chenopodium gigantospermum	CHENOPODIACEAE-D	*Chenopodium hybridum*
Chenopodium glaucum	CHENOPODIACEAE-D	
Chenopodium hybridum	CHENOPODIACEAE-D	
*Chenopodium leptophyllum var. oblongifolium	CHENOPODIACEAE-D	*Chenopodium desiccatum*
Chenopodium missouriensis	CHENOPODIACEAE-D	
Chenopodium murale	CHENOPODIACEAE-D	
Chenopodium polyspermum	CHENOPODIACEAE-D	
*Chenopodium pratericola ssp. desiccatum	CHENOPODIACEAE-D	*Chenopodium desiccatum*
Chenopodium rubrum	CHENOPODIACEAE-D	
Chenopodium standleyanum	CHENOPODIACEAE-D	
Chenopodium strictum var. *glaucophyllum*	CHENOPODIACEAE-D	
Chenopodium urbicum	CHENOPODIACEAE-D	
Chimaphila umbellata	ERICACEAE-D	
Chloris verticillata	POACEAE-M	
Chorispora tenella	BRASSICACEAE-D	
*Chrysanthemum leucanthemum	ASTERACEAE-D	*Leucanthemum vulgare*
*Chrysopsis villosa	ASTERACEAE-D	*Heterotheca villosa*
*Chrysosplenium alternifolium var. iowense	SAXIFRAGACEAE-D	*Chrysosplenium iowense*
Chrysosplenium iowense	SAXIFRAGACEAE-D	
*Chrysosplenium tetrandrum	SAXIFRAGACEAE-D	*Chrysosplenium iowense*
Cichorium intybus	ASTERACEAE-D	
Cicuta bulbifera	APIACEAE-D	

Cicuta maculata	APIACEAE-D	
Cimicifuga racemosa	RANUNCULACEAE-D	
Cinna arundinacea	POACEAE-M	
Circaea alpina	ONAGRACEAE-D	
Circaea lutetiana ssp. *canadensis*	ONAGRACEAE-D	
*Circaea quadrisulcata var. canadensis	ONAGRACEAE-D	*Circaea lutetiana* ssp. *canadensis*
Cirsium altissimum	ASTERACEAE-D	
Cirsium arvense	ASTERACEAE-D	
Cirsium discolor	ASTERACEAE-D	
Cirsium flodmanii	ASTERACEAE-D	
Cirsium hillii	ASTERACEAE-D	
*Cirsium iowense	ASTERACEAE-D	*Cirsium altissimum*
*Cirsium lanceolatum	ASTERACEAE-D	*Cirsium vulgare*
Cirsium muticum	ASTERACEAE-D	
*Cirsium pumilum	ASTERACEAE-D	*Cirsium hillii*
Cirsium undulatum	ASTERACEAE-D	
Cirsium vulgare	ASTERACEAE-D	
Claytonia virginica	PORTULACACEAE-D	
Clematis occidentalis	RANUNCULACEAE-D	
Clematis pitcheri	RANUNCULACEAE-D	
*Clematis verticillaris	RANUNCULACEAE-D	*Clematis occidentalis*
Clematis virginiana	RANUNCULACEAE-D	
Cleome serrulata	CAPPARIDACEAE-D	
*Clinopodium vulgare	LAMIACEAE-D	*Satureja vulgaris*
Coeloglossum viride var. *virescens*	ORCHIDACEAE-M	
Collinsia verna	SCROPHULARIACEAE-D	
Collomia linearis	POLEMONIACEAE-D	
*Comandra richardsiana	SANTALACEAE-D	*Comandra umbellata*
Comandra umbellata	SANTALACEAE-D	
Commelina communis	COMMELINACEAE-M	
Commelina erecta var. *angustifolia*	COMMELINACEAE-M	
Conium maculatum	APIACEAE-D	
*Conobea multifida	SCROPHULARIACEAE-D	*Leucospora multifida*
Conopholis americana	OROBANCHACEAE-D	
Conringia orientalis	BRASSICACEAE-D	
Consolida ambigua	RANUNCULACEAE-D	
Convallaria majalis	LILIACEAE-M	
*Convolvulus americanus	CONVOLVULACEAE-D	*Calystegia sepium*
Convolvulus arvensis	CONVOLVULACEAE-D	
*Convolvulus repens	CONVOLVULACEAE-D	*Calystegia sepium*
*Convolvulus sepium	CONVOLVULACEAE-D	*Calystegia sepium*
*Convolvulus spithamaeus	CONVOLVULACEAE-D	*Calystegia spithamaea*

Conyza canadensis	ASTERACEAE-D	
Conyza ramosissima	ASTERACEAE-D	
Corallorhiza maculata	ORCHIDACEAE-M	
Corallorhiza odontorhiza	ORCHIDACEAE-M	
Coreopsis grandiflora	ASTERACEAE-D	
Coreopsis lanceolata	ASTERACEAE-D	
Coreopsis palmata	ASTERACEAE-D	
Coreopsis tinctoria	ASTERACEAE-D	
Coreopsis tripteris	ASTERACEAE-D	
Corispermum nitidum	CHENOPODIACEAE-D	
Cornus alternifolia	CORNACEAE-D	
Cornus amomum ssp. *obliqua*	CORNACEAE-D	
*Cornus asperifolia	CORNACEAE-D	*Cornus drummondii*
Cornus canadensis	CORNACEAE-D	
Cornus drummondii	CORNACEAE-D	
Cornus foemina ssp. *racemosa*	CORNACEAE-D	
*Cornus obliqua	CORNACEAE-D	*Cornus amomum* ssp. *obliqua*
*Cornus purpusi	CORNACEAE-D	*Cornus amomum* ssp. *obliqua*
*Cornus racemosa	CORNACEAE-D	*Cornus foemina* ssp. *racemosa*
Cornus rugosa	CORNACEAE-D	
*Cornus sericea	CORNACEAE-D	*Cornus stolonifera*
Cornus stolonifera	CORNACEAE-D	
Coronilla varia	FABACEAE-D	
Corydalis aurea	PAPAVERACEAE-D	
Corydalis curvisiliqua ssp. *grandibracteata*	PAPAVERACEAE-D	
Corydalis micrantha	PAPAVERACEAE-D	
Corydalis sempervirens	PAPAVERACEAE-D	
Corylus americana	BETULACEAE-D	
Corylus cornuta	BETULACEAE-D	
*Corylus rostrata	BETULACEAE-D	*Corylus cornuta*
*Cosmos bipinnatus	ASTERACEAE-D	*Bidens bipinnata*
Crataegus calpodendron	ROSACEAE-D	
Crataegus chrysocarpa	ROSACEAE-D	
*Crataegus chrysocarpa	ROSACEAE-D	*Crataegus coccinea*
*Crataegus chrysocarpa	ROSACEAE-D	*Crataegus margaretta*
Crataegus coccinea	ROSACEAE-D	
Crataegus crus-galli	ROSACEAE-D	
*Crataegus cuneiformis	ROSACEAE-D	*Crataegus disperma*
Crataegus disperma	ROSACEAE-D	
*Crataegus mackenzii	ROSACEAE-D	*Crataegus pruinosa*

Crataegus margaretta	ROSACEAE-D	
Crataegus mollis	ROSACEAE-D	
*Crataegus pedicellata	ROSACEAE-D	*Crataegus coccinea*
Crataegus pruinosa	ROSACEAE-D	
Crataegus punctata	ROSACEAE-D	
*Crataegus rotundifolia	ROSACEAE-D	*Crataegus chrysocarpa*
Crataegus succulenta	ROSACEAE-D	
Crepis runcinata	ASTERACEAE-D	
Crepis tectorum	ASTERACEAE-D	
*Cristatella jamesii	CAPPARIDACEAE-D	*Polanisia jamesii*
Crotalaria sagittalis	FABACEAE-D	
Croton capitatus	EUPHORBIACEAE-D	
Croton glandulosus var. *septentrionalis*	EUPHORBIACEAE-D	
Croton monanthogynus	EUPHORBIACEAE-D	
Croton texensis	EUPHORBIACEAE-D	
Crotonopsis elliptica	EUPHORBIACEAE-D	
Cryptogramma stelleri	ADIANTACEAE-P	
Cryptotaenia canadensis	APIACEAE-D	
*Cubellium concolor	VIOLACEAE-D	*Hybanthus concolor*
Cucurbita foetidissima	CUCURBITACEAE-D	
*Cuphea petiolata	LYTHRACEAE-D	*Cuphea viscosissima*
Cuphea viscosissima	LYTHRACEAE-D	
Cuscuta cephalanthii	CONVOLVULACEAE-D	
Cuscuta coryli	CONVOLVULACEAE-D	
Cuscuta cuspidata	CONVOLVULACEAE-D	
Cuscuta glomerata	CONVOLVULACEAE-D	
Cuscuta gronovii	CONVOLVULACEAE-D	
Cuscuta indecora	CONVOLVULACEAE-D	
Cuscuta pentagona	CONVOLVULACEAE-D	
Cuscuta polygonorum	CONVOLVULACEAE-D	
Cycloloma atriplicifolium	CHENOPODIACEAE-D	
Cynanchum laeve	ASCLEPIADACEAE-D	
Cynoglossum officinale	BORAGINACEAE-D	
Cyperus acuminatus	CYPERACEAE-M	
Cyperus aristatus	CYPERACEAE-M	
*Cyperus bushii	CYPERACEAE-M	*Cyperus filiculmis*
Cyperus diandrus	CYPERACEAE-M	
Cyperus engelmannii	CYPERACEAE-M	
Cyperus erythrorhizos	CYPERACEAE-M	
Cyperus esculentus	CYPERACEAE-M	
*Cyperus ferruginescens	CYPERACEAE-M	*Cyperus odoratus* var. *squarrosus*
Cyperus filiculmis	CYPERACEAE-M	
*Cyperus inflexus	CYPERACEAE-M	*Cyperus aristatus*

Cyperus odoratus var. *squarrosus*	CYPERACEAE-M	
Cyperus rivularis	CYPERACEAE-M	
Cyperus schweinitzii	CYPERACEAE-M	
*Cyperus speciosus	CYPERACEAE-M	*Cyperus odoratus* var. *squarrosus*
Cyperus strigosus	CYPERACEAE-M	
Cypripedium calceolus var. *parviflorum*	ORCHIDACEAE-M	
Cypripedium calceolus var. *pubescens*	ORCHIDACEAE-M	
*Cypripedium calceolus X C. candidum	ORCHIDACEAE-M	*Cypripedium* X *andrewsii*
*Cypripedium calceolus X C. candidum	ORCHIDACEAE-M	*Cypripedium* X *andrewsii*
Cypripedium candidum	ORCHIDACEAE-M	
*Cypripedium parviflorum	ORCHIDACEAE-M	*Cypripedium calceolus* var. *parviflorum*
*Cypripedium pubescens	ORCHIDACEAE-M	*Cypripedium calceolus* var. *pubescens*
Cypripedium reginae	ORCHIDACEAE-M	
Cypripedium X *andrewsii*	ORCHIDACEAE-M	
Cystopteris bulbifera	ASPLENIACEAE-P	
*Cystopteris bulbifera X C. fragilis	ASPLENIACEAE-P	*Cystopteris* X *laurentiana*
*Cystopteris bulbifera X C. protrusa	ASPLENIACEAE-P	*Cystopteris* X *tennesseensis*
Cystopteris fragilis	ASPLENIACEAE-P	
*Cystopteris fragilis var. mackayi	ASPLENIACEAE-P	*Cystopteris tenuis*
*Cystopteris fragilis var. protrusa	ASPLENIACEAE-P	*Cystopteris protrusa*
Cystopteris protrusa	ASPLENIACEAE-P	
Cystopteris tenuis	ASPLENIACEAE-P	
Cystopteris X *laurentiana*	ASPLENIACEAE-P	
Cystopteris X *tennesseensis*	ASPLENIACEAE-P	
Dactylis glomerata	POACEAE-M	
*Dalea alopecuroides	FABACEAE-D	*Dalea leporina*
Dalea candida	FABACEAE-D	
Dalea candida var. *oligophylla*	FABACEAE-D	
Dalea enneandra	FABACEAE-D	
*Dalea laxiflora	FABACEAE-D	*Dalea enneandra*
Dalea leporina	FABACEAE-D	
Dalea purpurea	FABACEAE-D	
Dalea villosa	FABACEAE-D	

Danthonia spicata	POACEAE-M	
Dasistoma macrophylla	SCROPHULARIACEAE-D	
Datura stramonium	SOLANACEAE-D	
Daucus carota	APIACEAE-D	
Decodon verticillatus	LYTHRACEAE-D	
*Delphinium ajacis	RANUNCULACEAE-D	*Consolida ambigua*
Delphinium carolinianum	RANUNCULACEAE-D	
*Delphinium carolinianum ssp. virescens	RANUNCULACEAE-D	*Delphinium virescens*
Delphinium tricorne	RANUNCULACEAE-D	
Delphinium virescens	RANUNCULACEAE-D	
Dentaria laciniata	BRASSICACEAE-D	
*Deparia acrostichoides	ASPLENIACEAE-P	*Athyrium thelypterioides*
Descurainia pinnata var. *brachycarpa*	BRASSICACEAE-D	
Descurainia sophia	BRASSICACEAE-D	
Desmanthus illinoensis	FABACEAE-D	
Desmodium canadense	FABACEAE-D	
Desmodium canescens	FABACEAE-D	
Desmodium cuspidatum	FABACEAE-D	
*Desmodium dillenii	FABACEAE-D	*Desmodium paniculatum*
Desmodium glutinosum	FABACEAE-D	
Desmodium illinoense	FABACEAE-D	
Desmodium nudiflorum	FABACEAE-D	
Desmodium paniculatum	FABACEAE-D	
*Desmodium paniculatum var. dillenii	FABACEAE-D	*Desmodium paniculatum*
*Desmodium perplexum	FABACEAE-D	*Desmodium paniculatum*
Desmodium sessilifolium	FABACEAE-D	
Dianthus armeria	CARYOPHYLLACEAE-D	
Diarrhena americana var. *obovata*	POACEAE-M	
Dicentra canadensis	PAPAVERACEAE-D	
Dicentra cucullaria	PAPAVERACEAE-D	
Dichanthelium acuminatum	POACEAE-M	
Dichanthelium acuminatum var. *implicatum*	POACEAE-M	
Dichanthelium acuminatum var. *lindheimeri*	POACEAE-M	
Dichanthelium acuminatum var. *villosum*	POACEAE-M	
Dichanthelium boreale	POACEAE-M	
Dichanthelium clandestinum	POACEAE-M	
Dichanthelium depauperatum	POACEAE-M	
Dichanthelium latifolium	POACEAE-M	
Dichanthelium leibergii	POACEAE-M	

Dichanthelium linearifolium	POACEAE-M	
Dichanthelium oligosanthes	POACEAE-M	
Dichanthelium oligosanthes var. *scribnerianum*	POACEAE-M	
Dichanthelium oligosanthes var. *wilcoxianum*	POACEAE-M	
Dichanthelium perlongum	POACEAE-M	
Dichanthelium sabulorum var. *patulum*	POACEAE-M	
Dichanthelium sabulorum var. *thinium*	POACEAE-M	
Didiplis diandra	LYTHRACEAE-D	
Diervilla lonicera	CAPRIFOLIACEAE-D	
Digitaria ciliaris	POACEAE-M	
*Digitaria cognatum	POACEAE-M	*Leptoloma cognatum*
Digitaria filiformis	POACEAE-M	
*Digitaria humifusa	POACEAE-M	*Digitaria ischaemum*
Digitaria ischaemum	POACEAE-M	
Digitaria sanguinalis	POACEAE-M	
Diodia teres	RUBIACEAE-D	
Dioscorea villosa	DIOSCOREACEAE-M	
Diospyros virginiana	EBENACEAE-D	
*Diplachne fascicularis	POACEAE-M	*Leptochloa fascicularis*
*Diplazium pycnocarpon	ASPLENIACEAE-P	*Athyrium pycnocarpon*
Diplotaxis muralis	BRASSICACEAE-D	
*Dipsacus fullonum	DIPSACACEAE-D	*Dipsacus sylvestris*
Dipsacus laciniatus	DIPSACACEAE-D	
Dipsacus sylvestris	DIPSACACEAE-D	
Dirca palustris	THYMELAEACEAE-D	
Distichlis spicata var. *stricta*	POACEAE-M	
*Distichlis stricta	POACEAE-M	*Distichlis spicata* var. *stricta*
Dodecatheon amethystinum	PRIMULACEAE-D	
Dodecatheon meadia	PRIMULACEAE-D	
*Dodecatheon pulchellum	PRIMULACEAE-D	*Dodecatheon amethystinum*
*Dodecatheon radicatum	PRIMULACEAE-D	*Dodecatheon amethystinum*
Draba nemorosa	BRASSICACEAE-D	
Draba reptans	BRASSICACEAE-D	
Draba verna	BRASSICACEAE-D	
*Dracocephalum nuttallii	LAMIACEAE-D	*Physostegia parviflora*
Dracocephalum parviflorum	LAMIACEAE-D	
Drosera rotundifolia	DROSERACEAE-D	
Dryopteris carthusiana	ASPLENIACEAE-P	
Dryopteris cristata	ASPLENIACEAE-P	

*Dryopteris cristata X D. carthusiana	ASPLENIACEAE-P	*Dryopteris X uliginosa*
*Dryopteris cristata X D. intermedia	ASPLENIACEAE-P	*Dryopteris X boottii*
Dryopteris goldiana	ASPLENIACEAE-P	
Dryopteris intermedia	ASPLENIACEAE-P	
*Dryopteris intermedia X D. carthusiana	ASPLENIACEAE-P	*Dryopteris X triploidea*
Dryopteris marginalis	ASPLENIACEAE-P	
*Dryopteris spinulosa	ASPLENIACEAE-P	*Dryopteris carthusiana*
*Dryopteris spinulosa var. intermedia	ASPLENIACEAE-P	*Dryopteris intermedia*
*Dryopteris thelypteris	ASPLENIACEAE-P	*Thelypteris palustris* var. *pubescens*
Dryopteris X boottii	ASPLENIACEAE-P	
Dryopteris X triploidea	ASPLENIACEAE-P	
Dryopteris X uliginosa	ASPLENIACEAE-P	
Dulichium arundinaceum	CYPERACEAE-M	
Dyssodia papposa	ASTERACEAE-D	
*E. ciliatum X E. coloratum	ONAGRACEAE-D	*Epilobium X wisconsinense*
Echinacea angustifolia	ASTERACEAE-D	
Echinacea pallida	ASTERACEAE-D	
*Echinacea pallida var. angustifolia	ASTERACEAE-D	*Echinacea angustifolia*
Echinacea purpurea	ASTERACEAE-D	
Echinochloa crusgalli	POACEAE-M	
Echinochloa muricata	POACEAE-M	
*Echinochloa pungens	POACEAE-M	*Echinochloa muricata*
Echinochloa walteri	POACEAE-M	
Echinocystis lobata	CUCURBITACEAE-D	
*Echinodorus berteroi	ALISMATACEAE-M	*Echinodorus cordifolius*
Echinodorus cordifolius	ALISMATACEAE-M	
*Echinodorus rostratus	ALISMATACEAE-M	*Echinodorus cordifolius*
Echinops sphaerocephalus	ASTERACEAE-D	
Echium vulgare	BORAGINACEAE-D	
Eclipta alba	ASTERACEAE-D	
*Eclipta prostrata	ASTERACEAE-D	*Eclipta alba*
Elaeagnus angustifolia	ELAEAGNACEAE-D	
Elaeagnus umbellata	ELAEAGNACEAE-D	
Elatine triandra	ELATINACEAE-D	
Eleocharis acicularis	CYPERACEAE-M	
Eleocharis atropurpurea	CYPERACEAE-M	
*Eleocharis calva	CYPERACEAE-M	*Eleocharis erythropoda*
*Eleocharis coloradoensis	CYPERACEAE-M	*Eleocharis parvula* var. *anachaeta*

Eleocharis compressa	CYPERACEAE-M	
*Eleocharis elliptica var. compressa	CYPERACEAE-M	*Eleocharis compressa*
Eleocharis engelmannii	CYPERACEAE-M	
Eleocharis erythropoda	CYPERACEAE-M	
*Eleocharis flavescens var. olivacea	CYPERACEAE-M	*Eleocharis olivacea*
Eleocharis macrostachya	CYPERACEAE-M	
Eleocharis obtusa	CYPERACEAE-M	
*Eleocharis obtusa var. engelmannii	CYPERACEAE-M	*Eleocharis engelmannii*
*Eleocharis obtusa var. ovata	CYPERACEAE-M	*Eleocharis ovata*
Eleocharis olivacea	CYPERACEAE-M	
Eleocharis ovata	CYPERACEAE-M	
*Eleocharis palustris var. australis	CYPERACEAE-M	*Eleocharis macrostachya*
*Eleocharis palustris var. calva	CYPERACEAE-M	*Eleocharis erythropoda*
*Eleocharis palustris var. major	CYPERACEAE-M	*Eleocharis smallii*
Eleocharis parvula var. *anachaeta*	CYPERACEAE-M	
Eleocharis pauciflora	CYPERACEAE-M	
Eleocharis smallii	CYPERACEAE-M	
Eleocharis tenuis	CYPERACEAE-M	
*Eleocharis verrucosa	CYPERACEAE-M	*Eleocharis tenuis*
Eleocharis wolfii	CYPERACEAE-M	
Eleocharis xyridiformis	CYPERACEAE-M	
Eleusine indica	POACEAE-M	
Ellisia nyctelea	HYDROPHYLLACEAE-D	
Elodea canadensis	HYDROCHARITACEAE-M	
Elodea nuttallii	HYDROCHARITACEAE-M	
Elymus canadensis	POACEAE-M	
*Elymus canadensis var. interruptus	POACEAE-M	*Elymus interruptus*
*Elymus canadensis var. wiegandii	POACEAE-M	*Elymus wiegandii*
*Elymus canadensis X E. virginicus	POACEAE-M	*Elymus* X *maltei*
*Elymus diversiglumis	POACEAE-M	*Elymus interruptus*
*Elymus hystrix	POACEAE-M	*Hystrix patula*
Elymus interruptus	POACEAE-M	
*Elymus macounii	POACEAE-M	X *Agrohordeum macounii*
Elymus riparius	POACEAE-M	
*Elymus striatus	POACEAE-M	*Elymus villosus*

Elymus villosus	POACEAE-M	
*Elymus villosus X Hordeum jubatum	POACEAE-M	X *Elyhordeum iowense*
Elymus virginicus	POACEAE-M	
*Elymus virginicus X Hordeum jubatum	POACEAE-M	X *Elyhordeum montanense*
Elymus wiegandii	POACEAE-M	
Elymus X *maltei*	POACEAE-M	
*Enemion biternatum	RANUNCULACEAE-D	*Isopyrum biternatum*
*Epilobium adenocaulon	ONAGRACEAE-D	*Epilobium ciliatum*
Epilobium angustifolium	ONAGRACEAE-D	
Epilobium ciliatum	ONAGRACEAE-D	
Epilobium coloratum	ONAGRACEAE-D	
*Epilobium densum	ONAGRACEAE-D	*Epilobium leptophyllum*
*Epilobium glandulosum var. adenocaulon	ONAGRACEAE-D	*Epilobium ciliatum*
Epilobium leptophyllum	ONAGRACEAE-D	
*Epilobium lineare	ONAGRACEAE-D	*Epilobium leptophyllum*
Epilobium strictum	ONAGRACEAE-D	
Epilobium X *wisconsinense*	ONAGRACEAE-D	
Equisetum arvense	EQUISETACEAE-P	
*Equisetum arvense X E. fluviatile	EQUISETACEAE-P	*Equisetum* X *litorale*
Equisetum fluviatile	EQUISETACEAE-P	
Equisetum hyemale var. *affine*	EQUISETACEAE-P	
*Equisetum hyemale X E. laevigatum	EQUISETACEAE-P	*Equisetum* X *ferrissii*
*Equisetum kansanum	EQUISETACEAE-P	*Equisetum laevigatum*
Equisetum laevigatum	EQUISETACEAE-P	
Equisetum pratense	EQUISETACEAE-P	
Equisetum scirpoides	EQUISETACEAE-P	
Equisetum sylvaticum	EQUISETACEAE-P	
Equisetum X *ferrissii*	EQUISETACEAE-P	
Equisetum X *litorale*	EQUISETACEAE-P	
Eragrostis capillaris	POACEAE-M	
Eragrostis cilianensis	POACEAE-M	
Eragrostis frankii	POACEAE-M	
Eragrostis frankii var. *brevipes*	POACEAE-M	
Eragrostis hypnoides	POACEAE-M	
*Eragrostis megastachya	POACEAE-M	*Eragrostis cilianensis*
*Eragrostis minor	POACEAE-M	*Eragrostis poaeoides*
Eragrostis pectinacea	POACEAE-M	
Eragrostis pilosa	POACEAE-M	
Eragrostis poaeoides	POACEAE-M	

Taxon	Family	Synonym of
*Eragrostis purshii	POACEAE-M	*Eragrostis pectinacea*
Eragrostis reptans	POACEAE-M	
Eragrostis spectabilis	POACEAE-M	
Eragrostis trichodes	POACEAE-M	
Erechtites hieracifolia	ASTERACEAE-D	
Erigeron annuus	ASTERACEAE-D	
*Erigeron canadensis	ASTERACEAE-D	*Conyza canadensis*
*Erigeron divaricatum	ASTERACEAE-D	*Conyza ramosissima*
Erigeron philadelphicus	ASTERACEAE-D	
Erigeron pulchellus	ASTERACEAE-D	
Erigeron strigosus	ASTERACEAE-D	
Eriochloa villosa	POACEAE-M	
Eriophorum angustifolium	CYPERACEAE-M	
Eriophorum gracile	CYPERACEAE-M	
*Eriophorum polystachion	CYPERACEAE-M	*Eriophorum angustifolium*
Eriophorum virginicum	CYPERACEAE-M	
Erodium cicutarium	GERANIACEAE-D	
*Erophila verna	BRASSICACEAE-D	*Draba verna*
Eruca sativa	BRASSICACEAE-D	
*Eruca vesicaria ssp. sativa	BRASSICACEAE-D	*Eruca sativa*
Erucastrum gallicum	BRASSICACEAE-D	
Eryngium yuccifolium	APIACEAE-D	
Erysimum asperum	BRASSICACEAE-D	
Erysimum cheiranthoides	BRASSICACEAE-D	
Erysimum inconspicuum	BRASSICACEAE-D	
Erysimum repandum	BRASSICACEAE-D	
Erythronium albidum	LILIACEAE-M	
Erythronium americanum	LILIACEAE-M	
*Erythronium umbilicatum	LILIACEAE-M	*Erythronium americanum*
Euonymus alatus	CELASTRACEAE-D	
Euonymus atropurpureus	CELASTRACEAE-D	
*Eupatoriadelphus maculatus	ASTERACEAE-D	*Eupatorium maculatum*
*Eupatoriadelphus purpureus	ASTERACEAE-D	*Eupatorium purpureum*
Eupatorium altissimum	ASTERACEAE-D	
Eupatorium maculatum	ASTERACEAE-D	
Eupatorium perfoliatum	ASTERACEAE-D	
Eupatorium purpureum	ASTERACEAE-D	
Eupatorium rugosum	ASTERACEAE-D	
Eupatorium serotinum	ASTERACEAE-D	
Eupatorium sessilifolium var. *brittonianum*	ASTERACEAE-D	
Euphorbia commutata	EUPHORBIACEAE-D	
Euphorbia corollata	EUPHORBIACEAE-D	
Euphorbia cyathophora	EUPHORBIACEAE-D	
Euphorbia cyparissias	EUPHORBIACEAE-D	

Euphorbia dentata	EUPHORBIACEAE-D	
*Euphorbia dictyosperma	EUPHORBIACEAE-D	*Euphorbia spathulata*
Euphorbia esula	EUPHORBIACEAE-D	
Euphorbia falcata	EUPHORBIACEAE-D	
Euphorbia geyeri	EUPHORBIACEAE-D	
Euphorbia glyptosperma	EUPHORBIACEAE-D	
*Euphorbia heterophylla	EUPHORBIACEAE-D	*Euphorbia cyathophora*
Euphorbia hexagona	EUPHORBIACEAE-D	
Euphorbia maculata	EUPHORBIACEAE-D	
*Euphorbia maculata	EUPHORBIACEAE-D	*Euphorbia nutans*
Euphorbia marginata	EUPHORBIACEAE-D	
Euphorbia missurica	EUPHORBIACEAE-D	
Euphorbia nutans	EUPHORBIACEAE-D	
Euphorbia obtusata	EUPHORBIACEAE-D	
Euphorbia peplus	EUPHORBIACEAE-D	
*Euphorbia podperae	EUPHORBIACEAE-D	*Euphorbia esula*
*Euphorbia preslii	EUPHORBIACEAE-D	*Euphorbia nutans*
Euphorbia prostrata	EUPHORBIACEAE-D	
Euphorbia serpens	EUPHORBIACEAE-D	
Euphorbia serpyllifolia	EUPHORBIACEAE-D	
Euphorbia spathulata	EUPHORBIACEAE-D	
Euphorbia stictospora	EUPHORBIACEAE-D	
*Euphorbia supina	EUPHORBIACEAE-D	*Euphorbia maculata*
Euthamia graminifolia	ASTERACEAE-D	
*Euthamia gymnospermoides	ASTERACEAE-D	*Euthamia graminifolia*
Fagopyrum esculentum	POLYGONACEAE-D	
*Fagopyrum sagittatum	POLYGONACEAE-D	*Fagopyrum esculentum*
Falcaria sioides	APIACEAE-D	
*Falcaria vulgaris	APIACEAE-D	*Falcaria sioides*
Festuca arundinacea	POACEAE-M	
*Festuca elatior	POACEAE-M	*Festuca pratensis*
Festuca obtusa	POACEAE-M	
Festuca octoflora var. *tenella*	POACEAE-M	
Festuca ovina	POACEAE-M	
Festuca paradoxa	POACEAE-M	
Festuca pratensis	POACEAE-M	
Festuca rubra	POACEAE-M	
Filipendula rubra	ROSACEAE-D	
Fimbristylis autumnalis	CYPERACEAE-M	
Floerkea proserpinacoides	LIMNANTHACEAE-D	
*Fragaria americana	ROSACEAE-D	*Fragaria vesca* var. *americana*
Fragaria vesca var. *americana*	ROSACEAE-D	
Fragaria virginiana	ROSACEAE-D	

Fraxinus americana	OLEACEAE-D	
*Fraxinus lanceolata	OLEACEAE-D	_Fraxinus pennsylvanica_ var. _lanceolata_
Fraxinus nigra	OLEACEAE-D	
Fraxinus pennsylvanica	OLEACEAE-D	
Fraxinus pennsylvanica var. _lanceolata_	OLEACEAE-D	
*Fraxinus pennsylvanica var. subintegerrima	OLEACEAE-D	_Fraxinus pennsylvanica_ var. _lanceolata_
Fraxinus quadrangulata	OLEACEAE-D	
Froelichia floridana var. _campestris_	AMARANTHACEAE-D	
Froelichia gracilis	AMARANTHACEAE-D	
Fuirena simplex	CYPERACEAE-M	
Fumaria officinalis	PAPAVERACEAE-D	
Gaillardia pulchella	ASTERACEAE-D	
Galearis spectabilis	ORCHIDACEAE-M	
Galeopsis tetrahit	LAMIACEAE-D	
*Galinsoga ciliata	ASTERACEAE-D	_Galinsoga quadriradiata_
Galinsoga parviflora	ASTERACEAE-D	
Galinsoga quadriradiata	ASTERACEAE-D	
Galium aparine	RUBIACEAE-D	
Galium asprellum	RUBIACEAE-D	
Galium boreale	RUBIACEAE-D	
Galium circaezans	RUBIACEAE-D	
*Galium claytoni	RUBIACEAE-D	_Galium tinctorium_
Galium concinnum	RUBIACEAE-D	
Galium labradoricum	RUBIACEAE-D	
Galium obtusum	RUBIACEAE-D	
Galium tinctorium	RUBIACEAE-D	
Galium trifidum	RUBIACEAE-D	
*Galium trifidum var. tinctorium	RUBIACEAE-D	_Galium tinctorium_
Galium triflorum	RUBIACEAE-D	
Galium verum	RUBIACEAE-D	
*Gamochaeta purpurea	ASTERACEAE-D	_Gnaphalium purpureum_
Gaura biennis	ONAGRACEAE-D	
Gaura coccinea	ONAGRACEAE-D	
*Gaura filiformis	ONAGRACEAE-D	_Gaura biennis_
*Gaura longiflora	ONAGRACEAE-D	_Gaura biennis_
Gaura parviflora	ONAGRACEAE-D	
Gaylussacia baccata	ERICACEAE-D	
Gentiana alba	GENTIANACEAE-D	
Gentiana andrewsii	GENTIANACEAE-D	
*Gentiana andrewsii X G. puberulenta	GENTIANACEAE-D	_Gentiana_ X _billingtonii_

*Gentiana crinita	GENTIANACEAE-D	_Gentianopsis crinita_
*Gentiana flavida	GENTIANACEAE-D	_Gentiana alba_
*Gentiana procera	GENTIANACEAE-D	_Gentianopsis procera_
*Gentiana puberula	GENTIANACEAE-D	_Gentiana puberulenta_
Gentiana puberulenta	GENTIANACEAE-D	
*Gentiana quinquefolia var. occidentalis	GENTIANACEAE-D	_Gentianella quinquefolia_ ssp. _occidentalis_
*Gentiana saponaria	GENTIANACEAE-D	_Gentiana_ X _billingtonii_
Gentiana X _billingtonii_	GENTIANACEAE-D	
Gentianella quinquefolia ssp. _occidentalis_	GENTIANACEAE-D	
Gentianopsis crinita	GENTIANACEAE-D	
Gentianopsis procera	GENTIANACEAE-D	
Geranium bicknellii	GERANIACEAE-D	
Geranium carolinianum	GERANIACEAE-D	
Geranium maculatum	GERANIACEAE-D	
*Geranium sphaerospermum	GERANIACEAE-D	_Geranium carolinianum_
*Gerardia aspera	SCROPHULARIACEAE-D	_Agalinis aspera_
*Gerardia auriculata	SCROPHULARIACEAE-D	_Tomanthera auriculata_
*Gerardia gattingeri	SCROPHULARIACEAE-D	_Agalinis gattingeri_
*Gerardia grandiflora var. pulchra	SCROPHULARIACEAE-D	_Aureolaria grandiflora_ var. _pulchra_
*Gerardia paupercula	SCROPHULARIACEAE-D	_Agalinis paupercula_
*Gerardia purpurea	SCROPHULARIACEAE-D	_Agalinis purpurea_
*Gerardia purpurea var. parviflora	SCROPHULARIACEAE-D	_Agalinis paupercula_
*Gerardia skinneriana	SCROPHULARIACEAE-D	_Agalinis skinneriana_
*Gerardia tenuifolia	SCROPHULARIACEAE-D	_Agalinis tenuifolia_
Geum aleppicum var. _strictum_	ROSACEAE-D	
Geum canadense	ROSACEAE-D	
*Geum ciliatum	ROSACEAE-D	_Geum triflorum_
Geum laciniatum	ROSACEAE-D	
*Geum strictum	ROSACEAE-D	_Geum aleppicum_ var. _strictum_
Geum triflorum	ROSACEAE-D	
Geum vernum	ROSACEAE-D	
*Gilia rubra	POLEMONIACEAE-D	_Ipomopsis rubra_
Glechoma hederacea	LAMIACEAE-D	
Gleditsia triacanthos	FABACEAE-D	
Glyceria borealis	POACEAE-M	
Glyceria grandis	POACEAE-M	
*Glyceria maxima ssp. grandis	POACEAE-M	_Glyceria grandis_
Glyceria septentrionalis	POACEAE-M	
Glyceria striata	POACEAE-M	

Glycine max	FABACEAE-D	
Glycyrrhiza lepidota	FABACEAE-D	
Gnaphalium obtusifolium	ASTERACEAE-D	
Gnaphalium purpureum	ASTERACEAE-D	
Goodyera pubescens	ORCHIDACEAE-M	
Gratiola neglecta	SCROPHULARIACEAE-D	
Gratiola virginiana	SCROPHULARIACEAE-D	
Grindelia squarrosa	ASTERACEAE-D	
*Grossularia cynosbati	SAXIFRAGACEAE-D	*Ribes cynosbati*
*Grossularia missouriensis	SAXIFRAGACEAE-D	*Ribes missouriense*
Gutierrezia dracunculoides	ASTERACEAE-D	
Gymnocarpium dryopteris	ASPLENIACEAE-P	
Gymnocarpium robertianum	ASPLENIACEAE-P	
Gymnocladus dioica	FABACEAE-D	
*Habenaria bracteata	ORCHIDACEAE-M	*Coeloglossum viride* var. *virescens*
*Habenaria clavellata	ORCHIDACEAE-M	*Platanthera clavellata*
*Habenaria flava var. herbiola	ORCHIDACEAE-M	*Platanthera flava* var. *herbiola*
*Habenaria hookeri	ORCHIDACEAE-M	*Platanthera hookeri*
*Habenaria hyperborea var. huronensis	ORCHIDACEAE-M	*Platanthera hyperborea* var. *huronensis*
*Habenaria lacera	ORCHIDACEAE-M	*Platanthera lacera*
*Habenaria leucophaea	ORCHIDACEAE-M	*Platanthera leucophaea*
*Habenaria psycodes	ORCHIDACEAE-M	*Platanthera psycodes*
*Habenaria viridis var. bracteata	ORCHIDACEAE-M	*Coeloglossum viride* var. *virescens*
*Hackelia americana	BORAGINACEAE-D	*Hackelia deflexa* var. *americana*
Hackelia deflexa var. *americana*	BORAGINACEAE-D	
Hackelia virginiana	BORAGINACEAE-D	
Hamamelis virginiana	HAMAMELIDACEAE-D	
*Haplopappus ciliatus	ASTERACEAE-D	*Prionopsis ciliata*
*Haplopappus spinulosus	ASTERACEAE-D	*Machaeranthera spinulosa*
*Hasteola suaveolens	ASTERACEAE-D	*Cacalia suaveolens*
Hedeoma hispidum	LAMIACEAE-D	
Hedeoma pulegioides	LAMIACEAE-D	
Hedyotis crassifolia	RUBIACEAE-D	
Hedyotis nigricans	RUBIACEAE-D	
Helenium amarum	ASTERACEAE-D	
Helenium autumnale	ASTERACEAE-D	
Heleochloa schoenoides	POACEAE-M	
Helianthemum bicknellii	CISTACEAE-D	
Helianthemum canadense	CISTACEAE-D	
Helianthus annuus	ASTERACEAE-D	

Taxon	Family	Accepted name
Helianthus decapetalus	ASTERACEAE-D	
Helianthus divaricatus	ASTERACEAE-D	
Helianthus giganteus	ASTERACEAE-D	
Helianthus grosseserratus	ASTERACEAE-D	
Helianthus hirsutus	ASTERACEAE-D	
*Helianthus laetiflorus	ASTERACEAE-D	*Helianthus rigidus*
Helianthus maximiliani	ASTERACEAE-D	
Helianthus mollis	ASTERACEAE-D	
Helianthus occidentalis	ASTERACEAE-D	
Helianthus petiolaris	ASTERACEAE-D	
Helianthus rigidus	ASTERACEAE-D	
Helianthus rigidus ssp. *subrhomboideus*	ASTERACEAE-D	
Helianthus strumosus	ASTERACEAE-D	
*Helianthus trachelifolius	ASTERACEAE-D	*Helianthus strumosus*
Helianthus tuberosus	ASTERACEAE-D	
Heliopsis helianthoides	ASTERACEAE-D	
Hemerocallis fulva	LILIACEAE-M	
Hemicarpha micrantha	CYPERACEAE-M	
*Hepatica acutiloba	RANUNCULACEAE-D	*Hepatica nobilis* var. *acuta*
*Hepatica americana	RANUNCULACEAE-D	*Hepatica nobilis* var. *obtusa*
Hepatica nobilis var. *acuta*	RANUNCULACEAE-D	
Hepatica nobilis var. *obtusa*	RANUNCULACEAE-D	
Heracleum lanatum	APIACEAE-D	
*Heracleum maximum	APIACEAE-D	*Heracleum lanatum*
*Heracleum spondylium ssp. montanum	APIACEAE-D	*Heracleum lanatum*
Hesperis matronalis	BRASSICACEAE-D	
Heteranthera dubia	PONTEDERIACEAE-M	
Heteranthera limosa	PONTEDERIACEAE-M	
Heteranthera reniformis	PONTEDERIACEAE-M	
*Heterotheca camporum	ASTERACEAE-D	*Heterotheca villosa*
Heterotheca villosa	ASTERACEAE-D	
Heuchera americana var. *hirsuticaulis*	SAXIFRAGACEAE-D	
Heuchera richardsonii	SAXIFRAGACEAE-D	
*Heuchera X hirsuticaulis	SAXIFRAGACEAE-D	*Heuchera richardsonii*
Hibiscus laevis	MALVACEAE-D	
*Hibiscus militaris	MALVACEAE-D	*Hibiscus laevis*
Hibiscus trionum	MALVACEAE-D	
Hieracium aurantiacum	ASTERACEAE-D	
Hieracium canadense	ASTERACEAE-D	

Hieracium longipilum	ASTERACEAE-D	
Hieracium scabrum	ASTERACEAE-D	
Hieracium umbellatum	ASTERACEAE-D	
Hierochloe odorata	POACEAE-M	
Hippuris vulgaris	HIPPURIDACEAE-D	
Holcus lanatus	POACEAE-M	
Holosteum umbellatum	CARYOPHYLLACEAE-D	
Hordeum jubatum	POACEAE-M	
*Hordeum pammelii	POACEAE-M	X Elyhordeum montanense
Hordeum pusillum	POACEAE-M	
Hordeum vulgare	POACEAE-M	
*Houstonia minima	RUBIACEAE-D	Hedyotis crassifolia
*Houstonia nigricans	RUBIACEAE-D	Hedyotis nigricans
Hudsonia tomentosa	CISTACEAE-D	
Humulus japonicus	MORACEAE-D	
Humulus lupulus	MORACEAE-D	
Hybanthus concolor	VIOLACEAE-D	
Hydrastis canadensis	RANUNCULACEAE-D	
Hydrophyllum appendiculatum	HYDROPHYLLACEAE-D	
Hydrophyllum virginianum	HYDROPHYLLACEAE-D	
*Hypericum ascyron	HYPERICACEAE-D	Hypericum pyramidatum
Hypericum boreale	HYPERICACEAE-D	
Hypericum canadense	HYPERICACEAE-D	
Hypericum drummondii	HYPERICACEAE-D	
Hypericum gentianoides	HYPERICACEAE-D	
*Hypericum maculatum	HYPERICACEAE-D	Hypericum punctatum
Hypericum majus	HYPERICACEAE-D	
Hypericum mutilum	HYPERICACEAE-D	
Hypericum perforatum	HYPERICACEAE-D	
Hypericum prolificum	HYPERICACEAE-D	
Hypericum punctatum	HYPERICACEAE-D	
Hypericum pyramidatum	HYPERICACEAE-D	
*Hypericum spathulatum	HYPERICACEAE-D	Hypericum prolificum
Hypericum sphaerocarpum	HYPERICACEAE-D	
*Hypericum virginicum var. fraseri	HYPERICACEAE-D	Triadenum fraseri
*Hypopithys monotropa	ERICACEAE-D	Monotropa hypopithys
Hypoxis hirsuta	LILIACEAE-M	
Hystrix patula	POACEAE-M	
Iberis umbellata	BRASSICACEAE-D	
Ilex verticillata	AQUIFOLIACEAE-D	
*Impatiens biflora	BALSAMINACEAE-D	Impatiens capensis
Impatiens capensis	BALSAMINACEAE-D	
Impatiens pallida	BALSAMINACEAE-D	
Inula helenium	ASTERACEAE-D	
Iodanthus pinnatifidus	BRASSICACEAE-D	

Ipomoea coccinea	CONVOLVULACEAE-D	
Ipomoea hederacea	CONVOLVULACEAE-D	
Ipomoea lacunosa	CONVOLVULACEAE-D	
*Ipomoea nil	CONVOLVULACEAE-D	*Ipomoea hederacea*
Ipomoea pandurata	CONVOLVULACEAE-D	
Ipomoea purpurea	CONVOLVULACEAE-D	
Ipomopsis rubra	POLEMONIACEAE-D	
Iris shrevei	IRIDACEAE-M	
*Iris versicolor var. shrevei	IRIDACEAE-M	*Iris shrevei*
*Iris virginica var. shrevei	IRIDACEAE-M	*Iris shrevei*
Iris X *germanica*	IRIDACEAE-M	
*Isanthus brachiatus	LAMIACEAE-D	*Trichostema brachiatum*
Isoetes melanopoda	ISOETACEAE-P	
Isopyrum biternatum	RANUNCULACEAE-D	
Iva annua	ASTERACEAE-D	
*Iva ciliata	ASTERACEAE-D	*Iva annua*
Iva xanthifolia	ASTERACEAE-D	
Jeffersonia diphylla	BERBERIDACEAE-D	
Juglans cinerea	JUGLANDACEAE-D	
Juglans nigra	JUGLANDACEAE-D	
Juncus acuminatus	JUNCACEAE-M	
Juncus alpinus var. *fuscescens*	JUNCACEAE-M	
*Juncus alpinus X J. nodosus	JUNCACEAE-M	*Juncus* X *nodosiformis*
Juncus balticus var. *littoralis*	JUNCACEAE-M	
Juncus bufonius	JUNCACEAE-M	
Juncus canadensis	JUNCACEAE-M	
Juncus dudleyi	JUNCACEAE-M	
Juncus effusus	JUNCACEAE-M	
Juncus greenei	JUNCACEAE-M	
Juncus interior	JUNCACEAE-M	
Juncus marginatus	JUNCACEAE-M	
Juncus nodosus	JUNCACEAE-M	
Juncus tenuis	JUNCACEAE-M	
*Juncus tenuis var. dudleyi	JUNCACEAE-M	*Juncus dudleyi*
*Juncus tenuis var. uniflorus	JUNCACEAE-M	*Juncus dudleyi*
Juncus torreyi	JUNCACEAE-M	
Juncus vaseyi	JUNCACEAE-M	
Juncus X *nodosiformis*	JUNCACEAE-M	

Juniperus communis var. *depressa*	CUPRESSACEAE-G	
Juniperus horizontalis	CUPRESSACEAE-G	
Juniperus virginiana	CUPRESSACEAE-G	
*Jussiaea repens var. glabrescens	ONAGRACEAE-D	*Ludwigia peploides* ssp. *glabrescens*
Justicia americana	ACANTHACEAE-D	
Kochia scoparia	CHENOPODIACEAE-D	
*Koeleria cristata	POACEAE-M	*Koeleria macrantha*
Koeleria macrantha	POACEAE-M	
*Koeleria pyramidata	POACEAE-M	*Koeleria macrantha*
Krigia biflora	ASTERACEAE-D	
Krigia dandelion	ASTERACEAE-D	
Krigia virginica	ASTERACEAE-D	
*Kuhnia eupatorioides	ASTERACEAE-D	*Brickellia eupatorioides*
Kummerowia stipulacea	FABACEAE-D	
Kummerowia striata	FABACEAE-D	
Lactuca biennis	ASTERACEAE-D	
Lactuca canadensis	ASTERACEAE-D	
Lactuca floridana	ASTERACEAE-D	
Lactuca ludoviciana	ASTERACEAE-D	
*Lactuca oblongifolia	ASTERACEAE-D	*Lactuca tatarica* ssp. *pulchella*
*Lactuca pulchella	ASTERACEAE-D	*Lactuca tatarica* ssp. *pulchella*
Lactuca saligna	ASTERACEAE-D	
*Lactuca scariola	ASTERACEAE-D	*Lactuca serriola*
Lactuca serriola	ASTERACEAE-D	
Lactuca tatarica ssp. *pulchella*	ASTERACEAE-D	
Lamium amplexicaule	LAMIACEAE-D	
Lamium purpureum	LAMIACEAE-D	
Laportea canadensis	URTICACEAE-D	
Lappula echinata	BORAGINACEAE-D	
Lappula redowskii	BORAGINACEAE-D	
*Lappula squarrosa	BORAGINACEAE-D	*Lappula echinata*
*Lappula texana	BORAGINACEAE-D	*Lappula redowskii*
*Lappula virginiana	BORAGINACEAE-D	*Hackelia virginiana*
Lathyrus ochroleucus	FABACEAE-D	
Lathyrus palustris	FABACEAE-D	
Lathyrus tuberosus	FABACEAE-D	
Lathyrus venosus	FABACEAE-D	
Lechea intermedia	CISTACEAE-D	
*Lechea mucronata	CISTACEAE-D	*Lechea villosa*
Lechea racemulosa	CISTACEAE-D	
Lechea stricta	CISTACEAE-D	

Lechea tenuifolia	CISTACEAE-D	
Lechea villosa	CISTACEAE-D	
Leersia lenticularis	POACEAE-M	
Leersia oryzoides	POACEAE-M	
Leersia virginica	POACEAE-M	
Lemna minor	LEMNACEAE-M	
Lemna perpusilla	LEMNACEAE-M	
Lemna trisulca	LEMNACEAE-M	
Leontodon autumnalis	ASTERACEAE-D	
Leonurus cardiaca	LAMIACEAE-D	
Leonurus marrubiastrum	LAMIACEAE-D	
Leonurus sibiricus	LAMIACEAE-D	
Lepidium campestre	BRASSICACEAE-D	
Lepidium densiflorum	BRASSICACEAE-D	
Lepidium perfoliatum	BRASSICACEAE-D	
Lepidium virginicum	BRASSICACEAE-D	
Leptochloa fascicularis	POACEAE-M	
Leptoloma cognatum	POACEAE-M	
Lespedeza capitata	FABACEAE-D	
Lespedeza cuneata	FABACEAE-D	
Lespedeza daurica	FABACEAE-D	
Lespedeza leptostachya	FABACEAE-D	
Lespedeza repens	FABACEAE-D	
*Lespedeza stipulacea	FABACEAE-D	*Kummerowia stipulacea*
*Lespedeza striata	FABACEAE-D	*Kummerowia striata*
Lespedeza violacea	FABACEAE-D	
Lespedeza virginica	FABACEAE-D	
Lesquerella ludoviciana	BRASSICACEAE-D	
Leucanthemum vulgare	ASTERACEAE-D	
Leucospora multifida	SCROPHULARIACEAE-D	
Liatris aspera	ASTERACEAE-D	
Liatris cylindracea	ASTERACEAE-D	
Liatris ligulistylis	ASTERACEAE-D	
Liatris punctata	ASTERACEAE-D	
Liatris pycnostachya	ASTERACEAE-D	
Liatris squarrosa	ASTERACEAE-D	
*Lilium canadense ssp. michiganense	LILIACEAE-M	*Lilium michiganense*
Lilium lancifolium	LILIACEAE-M	
Lilium michiganense	LILIACEAE-M	
Lilium philadelphicum var. *andinum*	LILIACEAE-M	
*Lilium superbum	LILIACEAE-M	*Lilium michiganense*
*Lilium tigrinum	LILIACEAE-M	*Lilium lancifolium*
*Lilium umbellatum	LILIACEAE-M	*Lilium philadelphicum* var. *andinum*

Taxon	Family	Accepted name
Linaria canadensis	SCROPHULARIACEAE-D	
Linaria macedonica	SCROPHULARIACEAE-D	
*Linaria minor	SCROPHULARIACEAE-D	*Chaenorrhinum minus*
Linaria vulgaris	SCROPHULARIACEAE-D	
Lindernia anagallidea	SCROPHULARIACEAE-D	
Lindernia dubia	SCROPHULARIACEAE-D	
*Lindernia dubia var. anagallidea	SCROPHULARIACEAE-D	*Lindernia anagallidea*
*Linnaea americana	CAPRIFOLIACEAE-D	*Linnaea borealis* ssp. *americana*
Linnaea borealis ssp. *americana*	CAPRIFOLIACEAE-D	
Linum medium var. *texanum*	LINACEAE-D	
Linum perenne	LINACEAE-D	
Linum rigidum	LINACEAE-D	
Linum sulcatum	LINACEAE-D	
Linum usitatissimum	LINACEAE-D	
Liparis liliifolia	ORCHIDACEAE-M	
Liparis loeselii	ORCHIDACEAE-M	
*Lippia lanceolata	VERBENACEAE-D	*Phyla lanceolata*
Liriodendron tulipifera	MAGNOLIACEAE-D	
Lithospermum arvense	BORAGINACEAE-D	
Lithospermum canescens	BORAGINACEAE-D	
Lithospermum caroliniense	BORAGINACEAE-D	
*Lithospermum croceum	BORAGINACEAE-D	*Lithospermum caroliniense*
Lithospermum incisum	BORAGINACEAE-D	
Lithospermum latifolium	BORAGINACEAE-D	
Lobelia cardinalis	CAMPANULACEAE-D	
Lobelia inflata	CAMPANULACEAE-D	
Lobelia kalmii	CAMPANULACEAE-D	
Lobelia siphilitica	CAMPANULACEAE-D	
Lobelia spicata	CAMPANULACEAE-D	
Lobularia maritima	BRASSICACEAE-D	
*Lolium multiflorum	POACEAE-M	*Lolium perenne* var. *italicum*
Lolium perenne	POACEAE-M	
*Lolium perenne var. aristatum	POACEAE-M	*Lolium perenne* var. *italicum*
Lolium perenne var. *italicum*	POACEAE-M	
Lolium temulentum	POACEAE-M	
Lomatium foeniculaceum	APIACEAE-D	
Lomatium orientale	APIACEAE-D	
Lonicera dioica var. *glaucescens*	CAPRIFOLIACEAE-D	

Lonicera morrowi	CAPRIFOLIACEAE-D	
Lonicera prolifera	CAPRIFOLIACEAE-D	
Lonicera sempervirens	CAPRIFOLIACEAE-D	
*Lonicera sullivantii	CAPRIFOLIACEAE-D	*Lonicera prolifera*
Lonicera tatarica	CAPRIFOLIACEAE-D	
*Lophotocarpus calycinus	ALISMATACEAE-M	*Sagittaria calycina*
*Lotus americanus	FABACEAE-D	*Lotus purshianus*
Lotus corniculatus	FABACEAE-D	
Lotus purshianus	FABACEAE-D	
Ludwigia alternifolia	ONAGRACEAE-D	
Ludwigia palustris	ONAGRACEAE-D	
Ludwigia peploides ssp. *glabrescens*	ONAGRACEAE-D	
Ludwigia polycarpa	ONAGRACEAE-D	
Lupinus perennis	FABACEAE-D	
Luzula acuminata	JUNCACEAE-M	
*Luzula campestris var. multiflora	JUNCACEAE-M	*Luzula multiflora*
Luzula multiflora	JUNCACEAE-M	
*Lychnis alba	CARYOPHYLLACEAE-D	*Silene pratensis*
*Lycium barbarum	SOLANACEAE-D	*Lycium halimifolium*
Lycium halimifolium	SOLANACEAE-D	
Lycopersicon esculentum	SOLANACEAE-D	
Lycopodium clavatum	LYCOPODIACEAE-P	
*Lycopodium complanatum var. flabelliforme	LYCOPODIACEAE-P	*Lycopodium digitatum*
Lycopodium dendroideum	LYCOPODIACEAE-P	
Lycopodium digitatum	LYCOPODIACEAE-P	
*Lycopodium flabelliforme	LYCOPODIACEAE-P	*Lycopodium digitatum*
Lycopodium inundatum	LYCOPODIACEAE-P	
Lycopodium lucidulum	LYCOPODIACEAE-P	
*Lycopodium lucidulum X L. porophilum	LYCOPODIACEAE-P	*Lycopodium X bartleyi*
*Lycopodium obscurum var. dendroideum	LYCOPODIACEAE-P	*Lycopodium dendroideum*
Lycopodium porophilum	LYCOPODIACEAE-P	
*Lycopodium selago var. patens	LYCOPODIACEAE-P	*Lycopodium porophilum*
Lycopodium X bartleyi	LYCOPODIACEAE-P	
Lycopus americanus	LAMIACEAE-D	
Lycopus asper	LAMIACEAE-D	
Lycopus uniflorus	LAMIACEAE-D	
Lycopus virginicus	LAMIACEAE-D	
Lygodesmia juncea	ASTERACEAE-D	
Lygodesmia rostrata	ASTERACEAE-D	
Lysimachia ciliata	PRIMULACEAE-D	

Taxon	Family	Accepted name
Lysimachia clethroides	PRIMULACEAE-D	
Lysimachia hybrida	PRIMULACEAE-D	
Lysimachia lanceolata	PRIMULACEAE-D	
*Lysimachia lanceolata var. hybrida	PRIMULACEAE-D	*Lysimachia hybrida*
Lysimachia nummularia	PRIMULACEAE-D	
Lysimachia punctata	PRIMULACEAE-D	
Lysimachia quadriflora	PRIMULACEAE-D	
Lysimachia terrestris	PRIMULACEAE-D	
Lysimachia thyrsiflora	PRIMULACEAE-D	
Lythrum alatum	LYTHRACEAE-D	
*Lythrum dacotanum	LYTHRACEAE-D	*Lythrum alatum*
Lythrum salicaria	LYTHRACEAE-D	
*Machaeranthera pinnatifida	ASTERACEAE-D	*Machaeranthera spinulosa*
Machaeranthera spinulosa	ASTERACEAE-D	
Maclura pomifera	MORACEAE-D	
Madia sativa var. *congesta*	ASTERACEAE-D	
Maianthemum canadense	LILIACEAE-M	
Malaxis unifolia	ORCHIDACEAE-M	
*Malus coronaria	ROSACEAE-D	*Malus ioensis*
Malus ioensis	ROSACEAE-D	
Malus sylvestris	ROSACEAE-D	
Malva neglecta	MALVACEAE-D	
Malva parviflora	MALVACEAE-D	
Malva rotundifolia	MALVACEAE-D	
Malva sylvestris	MALVACEAE-D	
Malva verticillata	MALVACEAE-D	
*Malvastrum angustum	MALVACEAE-D	*Malvastrum hispidum*
*Malvastrum coccineum	MALVACEAE-D	*Sphaeralcea coccinea*
Malvastrum hispidum	MALVACEAE-D	
Marrubium vulgare	LAMIACEAE-D	
*Marsilea mucronata	MARSILEACEAE-P	*Marsilea vestita*
Marsilea quadrifolia	MARSILEACEAE-P	
Marsilea vestita	MARSILEACEAE-P	
Matricaria chamomilla	ASTERACEAE-D	
Matricaria maritima	ASTERACEAE-D	
Matricaria matricarioides	ASTERACEAE-D	
Matteuccia struthiopteris var. *pensylvanica*	ASPLENIACEAE-P	
Medicago falcata	FABACEAE-D	
Medicago lupulina	FABACEAE-D	
Medicago sativa	FABACEAE-D	
*Medicago sativa ssp. falcata	FABACEAE-D	*Medicago falcata*
Megalodonta beckii	ASTERACEAE-D	

Melanthium virginicum	LILIACEAE-M	
*Melanthium woodii	LILIACEAE-M	*Veratrum woodii*
Melica mutica	POACEAE-M	
Melica nitens	POACEAE-M	
Melilotus alba	FABACEAE-D	
Melilotus officinalis	FABACEAE-D	
Menispermum canadense	MENISPERMACEAE-D	
*Mentha aquatica X M. spicata	LAMIACEAE-D	*Mentha* X *piperita*
Mentha arvensis	LAMIACEAE-D	
*Mentha arvensis X M. spicata	LAMIACEAE-D	*Mentha* X *gentilis*
*Mentha cardiaca	LAMIACEAE-D	*Mentha* X *gentilis*
Mentha spicata	LAMIACEAE-D	
Mentha X *gentilis*	LAMIACEAE-D	
Mentha X *piperita*	LAMIACEAE-D	
Mentzelia decapetala	LOASACEAE-D	
Menyanthes trifoliata	MENYANTHACEAE-D	
Mertensia paniculata	BORAGINACEAE-D	
Mertensia virginica	BORAGINACEAE-D	
*Microseris cuspidata	ASTERACEAE-D	*Nothocalais cuspidata*
Milium effusum	POACEAE-M	
Mimulus alatus	SCROPHULARIACEAE-D	
*Mimulus geyeri	SCROPHULARIACEAE-D	*Mimulus glabratus* var. *fremontii*
Mimulus glabratus var. *fremontii*	SCROPHULARIACEAE-D	
Mimulus ringens	SCROPHULARIACEAE-D	
Minuartia michauxii	CARYOPHYLLACEAE-D	
Mirabilis albida	NYCTAGINACEAE-D	
Mirabilis hirsuta	NYCTAGINACEAE-D	
Mirabilis nyctaginea	NYCTAGINACEAE-D	
Miscanthus sacchariflorus	POACEAE-M	
Mitchella repens	RUBIACEAE-D	
Mitella diphylla	SAXIFRAGACEAE-D	
Mitella nuda	SAXIFRAGACEAE-D	
Moehringia lateriflora	CARYOPHYLLACEAE-D	
*Moldavica parviflora	LAMIACEAE-D	*Dracocephalum parviflorum*
Mollugo verticillata	AIZOACEAE-D	
Monarda didyma	LAMIACEAE-D	
Monarda fistulosa	LAMIACEAE-D	
Monarda punctata var. *villicaulis*	LAMIACEAE-D	
Monolepis nuttalliana	CHENOPODIACEAE-D	
Monotropa hypopithys	ERICACEAE-D	
Monotropa uniflora	ERICACEAE-D	

Montia chamissoi	PORTULACACEAE-D	
Morus alba	MORACEAE-D	
Morus rubra	MORACEAE-D	
Muhlenbergia asperifolia	POACEAE-M	
*Muhlenbergia brachyphylla	POACEAE-M	*Muhlenbergia bushii*
Muhlenbergia bushii	POACEAE-M	
Muhlenbergia cuspidata	POACEAE-M	
*Muhlenbergia foliosa	POACEAE-M	*Muhlenbergia mexicana*
Muhlenbergia frondosa	POACEAE-M	
Muhlenbergia glomerata	POACEAE-M	
Muhlenbergia mexicana	POACEAE-M	
*Muhlenbergia mexicana	POACEAE-M	*Muhlenbergia frondosa*
Muhlenbergia racemosa	POACEAE-M	
Muhlenbergia schreberi	POACEAE-M	
Muhlenbergia sobolifera	POACEAE-M	
Muhlenbergia sylvatica	POACEAE-M	
Muhlenbergia tenuiflora	POACEAE-M	
Myosotis micrantha	BORAGINACEAE-D	
Myosotis verna	BORAGINACEAE-D	
*Myosotis virginica	BORAGINACEAE-D	*Myosotis verna*
Myosoton aquaticum	CARYOPHYLLACEAE-D	
Myosurus minimus	RANUNCULACEAE-D	
Myriophyllum exalbescens	HALORAGIDACEAE-D	
Myriophyllum heterophylum	HALORAGIDACEAE-D	
Myriophyllum pinnatum	HALORAGIDACEAE-D	
Myriophyllum spicatum	HALORAGIDACEAE-D	
Myriophyllum verticillatum	HALORAGIDACEAE-D	
Najas flexilis	NAJADACEAE-M	
Najas guadalupensis	NAJADACEAE-M	
Napaea dioica	MALVACEAE-D	
Nasturtium officinale	BRASSICACEAE-D	
Navarretia intertexta	POLEMONIACEAE-D	
Nelumbo lutea	NYMPHAEACEAE-D	
Nepeta cataria	LAMIACEAE-D	
Neslia paniculata	BRASSICACEAE-D	
Nicandra physalodes	SOLANACEAE-D	
Nothocalais cuspidata	ASTERACEAE-D	
*Nuphar advena	NYMPHAEACEAE-D	*Nuphar luteum* ssp. *variegatum*
Nuphar luteum ssp. *variegatum*	NYMPHAEACEAE-D	
*Nuphar variegatum	NYMPHAEACEAE-D	*Nuphar luteum* ssp. *variegatum*
*Nymphaea odorata	NYMPHAEACEAE-D	*Nymphaea tuberosa*
Nymphaea tuberosa	NYMPHAEACEAE-D	

Oenothera biennis ssp. *centralis*	ONAGRACEAE-D	
*Oenothera biennis var. canescens	ONAGRACEAE-D	*Oenothera villosa*
*Oenothera clelandii	ONAGRACEAE-D	*Oenothera rhombipetala*
*Oenothera cruciata	ONAGRACEAE-D	*Oenothera parviflora*
Oenothera laciniata	ONAGRACEAE-D	
Oenothera parviflora	ONAGRACEAE-D	
Oenothera perennis	ONAGRACEAE-D	
Oenothera pilosella	ONAGRACEAE-D	
Oenothera rhombipetala	ONAGRACEAE-D	
*Oenothera serrulata	ONAGRACEAE-D	*Calylophus serrulatus*
Oenothera speciosa	ONAGRACEAE-D	
*Oenothera strigosa	ONAGRACEAE-D	*Oenothera villosa*
Oenothera villosa	ONAGRACEAE-D	
Onoclea sensibilis	ASPLENIACEAE-P	
Onopordum acanthium	ASTERACEAE-D	
*Onosmodium hispidissimum	BORAGINACEAE-D	*Onosmodium molle* var. *hispidissimum*
*Onosmodium molle ssp. hispidissimum	BORAGINACEAE-D	*Onosmodium molle* var. *hispidissimum*
*Onosmodium molle ssp. occidentale	BORAGINACEAE-D	*Onosmodium molle* var. *occidentale*
Onosmodium molle var. *hispidissimum*	BORAGINACEAE-D	
Onosmodium molle var. *occidentale*	BORAGINACEAE-D	
*Onosmodium occidentale	BORAGINACEAE-D	*Onosmodium molle* var. *occidentale*
Ophioglossum pusillum	OPHIOGLOSSACEAE-P	
*Ophioglossum vulgatum var. pseudopodum	OPHIOGLOSSACEAE-P	*Ophioglossum pusillum*
*Opuntia compressa	CACTACEAE-D	*Opuntia humifusa*
Opuntia fragilis	CACTACEAE-D	
Opuntia humifusa	CACTACEAE-D	
Opuntia macrorhiza	CACTACEAE-D	
Orbexilum onobrychis	FABACEAE-D	
*Orchis spectabilis	ORCHIDACEAE-M	*Galearis spectabilis*
Ornithogalum umbellatum	LILIACEAE-M	
Orobanche fasciculata	OROBANCHACEAE-D	
Orobanche ludoviciana	OROBANCHACEAE-D	
Orobanche uniflora	OROBANCHACEAE-D	
*Orthilia secunda	ERICACEAE-D	*Pyrola secunda*
Oryzopsis asperifolia	POACEAE-M	
Oryzopsis pungens	POACEAE-M	
Oryzopsis racemosa	POACEAE-M	

Osmorhiza claytonii	APIACEAE-D	
Osmorhiza longistylis	APIACEAE-D	
Osmunda cinnamomea	OSMUNDACEAE-P	
Osmunda claytoniana	OSMUNDACEAE-P	
Osmunda regalis var. *spectabilis*	OSMUNDACEAE-P	
Ostrya virginiana	BETULACEAE-D	
Oxalis dillenii	OXALIDACEAE-D	
*Oxalis europaea	OXALIDACEAE-D	*Oxalis stricta*
Oxalis stricta	OXALIDACEAE-D	
*Oxalis stricta	OXALIDACEAE-D	*Oxalis dillenii*
Oxalis violacea	OXALIDACEAE-D	
*Oxybaphus albidus	NYCTAGINACEAE-D	*Mirabilis albida*
*Oxybaphus hirsutus	NYCTAGINACEAE-D	*Mirabilis hirsuta*
*Oxybaphus nyctagineus	NYCTAGINACEAE-D	*Mirabilis nyctaginea*
Oxypolis rigidior	APIACEAE-D	
Oxytropis lambertii	FABACEAE-D	
Panax quinquefolius	ARALIACEAE-D	
*Panicum boreale	POACEAE-M	*Dichanthelium boreale*
Panicum capillare	POACEAE-M	
*Panicum clandestinum	POACEAE-M	*Dichanthelium clandestinum*
*Panicum columbianum	POACEAE-M	*Dichanthelium sabulorum* var. *thinium*
*Panicum commonsianum var. euchlamydeum	POACEAE-M	*Dichanthelium sabulorum* var. *patulum*
*Panicum depauperatum	POACEAE-M	*Dichanthelium depauperatum*
Panicum dichotomiflorum	POACEAE-M	
Panicum gattingeri	POACEAE-M	
*Panicum helleri	POACEAE-M	*Dichanthelium oligosanthes* var. *scribnerianum*
Panicum hillmanii	POACEAE-M	
*Panicum huachucae	POACEAE-M	*Dichanthelium acuminatum*
*Panicum implicatum	POACEAE-M	*Dichanthelium acuminatum* var. *implicatum*
*Panicum lanuginosum var. implicatum	POACEAE-M	*Dichanthelium acuminatum* var. *implicatum*
*Panicum lanuginosum var. lindheimeri	POACEAE-M	*Dichanthelium acuminatum* var. *lindheimeri*
*Panicum lanuginosum var. praecocius	POACEAE-M	*Dichanthelium acuminatum* var. *villosum*
*Panicum latifolium	POACEAE-M	*Dichanthelium latifolium*
*Panicum leibergii	POACEAE-M	*Dichanthelium leibergii*
*Panicum lindheimeri	POACEAE-M	*Dichanthelium acuminatum* var. *lindheimeri*
*Panicum linearifolium	POACEAE-M	*Dichanthelium linearifolium*

*Panicum meridionale	POACEAE-M	*Dichanthelium acuminatum* var. *implicatum*
Panicum miliaceum	POACEAE-M	
*Panicum oligosanthes	POACEAE-M	*Dichanthelium oligosanthes*
*Panicum oligosanthes var. helleri	POACEAE-M	*Dichanthelium oligosanthes* var. *scribnerianum*
*Panicum oligosanthes var. scribnerianum	POACEAE-M	*Dichanthelium oligosanthes* var. *scribnerianum*
*Panicum perlongum	POACEAE-M	*Dichanthelium perlongum*
Panicum philadelphicum	POACEAE-M	
*Panicum praecocius	POACEAE-M	*Dichanthelium acuminatum* var. *villosum*
*Panicum scribnerianum	POACEAE-M	*Dichanthelium oligosanthes* var. *scribnerianum*
*Panicum tennesseense	POACEAE-M	*Dichanthelium acuminatum*
*Panicum villosissimum	POACEAE-M	*Dichanthelium sabulorum* var. *patulum*
Panicum virgatum	POACEAE-M	
*Panicum wilcoxianum	POACEAE-M	*Dichanthelium oligosanthes* var. *wilcoxianum*
Parietaria pensylvanica	URTICACEAE-D	
Parnassia glauca	SAXIFRAGACEAE-D	
Paronychia canadensis	CARYOPHYLLACEAE-D	
Paronychia fastigiata	CARYOPHYLLACEAE-D	
Parthenium integrifolium	ASTERACEAE-D	
*Parthenocissus inserta	VITACEAE-D	*Parthenocissus vitacea*
Parthenocissus quinquefolia	VITACEAE-D	
Parthenocissus vitacea	VITACEAE-D	
*Paspalum bushii	POACEAE-M	*Paspalum setaceum* var. *stramineum*
*Paspalum ciliatifolium	POACEAE-M	*Paspalum setaceum* var. *ciliatifolium*
*Paspalum muhlenbergii	POACEAE-M	*Paspalum setaceum* var. *muhlenbergii*
*Paspalum pubescens	POACEAE-M	*Paspalum setaceum* var. *ciliatifolium*
Paspalum setaceum var. *ciliatifolium*	POACEAE-M	
Paspalum setaceum var. *muhlenbergii*	POACEAE-M	
Paspalum setaceum var. *stramineum*	POACEAE-M	
*Passerina annua	THYMELAEACEAE-D	*Thymelaea passerina*
Pastinaca sativa	APIACEAE-D	
Pedicularis canadensis	SCROPHULARIACEAE-D	
Pedicularis lanceolata	SCROPHULARIACEAE-D	

Pediomelum argophyllum	FABACEAE-D	
Pediomelum esculentum	FABACEAE-D	
Pellaea atropurpurea	ADIANTACEAE-P	
Pellaea glabella	ADIANTACEAE-P	
Peltandra virginica	ARACEAE-M	
Pennisetum petiolare	POACEAE-M	
Penstemon albidus	SCROPHULARIACEAE-D	
*Penstemon bradburii	SCROPHULARIACEAE-D	*Penstemon grandiflorus*
Penstemon cobaea	SCROPHULARIACEAE-D	
Penstemon digitalis	SCROPHULARIACEAE-D	
Penstemon gracilis	SCROPHULARIACEAE-D	
Penstemon grandiflorus	SCROPHULARIACEAE-D	
Penstemon pallidus	SCROPHULARIACEAE-D	
Penstemon tubiflorus	SCROPHULARIACEAE-D	
Penthorum sedoides	SAXIFRAGACEAE-D	
*Peplis diandra	LYTHRACEAE-D	*Didiplis diandra*
Perilla frutescens	LAMIACEAE-D	
*Petalostemon candidum	FABACEAE-D	*Dalea candida*
*Petalostemon occidentale	FABACEAE-D	*Dalea candida* var. *oligophylla*
*Petalostemon purpureum	FABACEAE-D	*Dalea purpurea*
*Petalostemon villosum	FABACEAE-D	*Dalea villosa*
Petunia axillaris	SOLANACEAE-D	
*Petunia hybrida	SOLANACEAE-D	*Petunia axillaris*
Phalaris arundinacea	POACEAE-M	
Phalaris canariensis	POACEAE-M	
*Phegopteris connectilis	ASPLENIACEAE-P	*Thelypteris phegopteris*
*Phegopteris hexagonoptera	ASPLENIACEAE-P	*Thelypteris hexagonoptera*
Philadelphus pubescens	SAXIFRAGACEAE-D	
Phleum pratense	POACEAE-M	
Phlox bifida	POLEMONIACEAE-D	
Phlox divaricata	POLEMONIACEAE-D	
Phlox maculata	POLEMONIACEAE-D	
Phlox paniculata	POLEMONIACEAE-D	
Phlox pilosa	POLEMONIACEAE-D	
Phlox subulata	POLEMONIACEAE-D	
Phragmites australis	POACEAE-M	
*Phragmites communis	POACEAE-M	*Phragmites australis*
Phryma leptostachya	PHRYMACEAE-D	
Phyla lanceolata	VERBENACEAE-D	
Physalis heterophylla	SOLANACEAE-D	
Physalis ixocarpa	SOLANACEAE-D	
*Physalis longifolia	SOLANACEAE-D	*Physalis virginiana*
*Physalis pruinosa	SOLANACEAE-D	*Physalis pubescens* var. *integrifolia*
Physalis pubescens	SOLANACEAE-D	

Physalis pubescens var. *integrifolia*	SOLANACEAE-D	
*Physalis subglabrata	SOLANACEAE-D	*Physalis virginiana*
Physalis virginiana	SOLANACEAE-D	
Physocarpus opulifolius	ROSACEAE-D	
Physostegia parviflora	LAMIACEAE-D	
*Physostegia speciosa	LAMIACEAE-D	*Physostegia virginiana*
Physostegia virginiana	LAMIACEAE-D	
Phytolacca americana	PHYTOLACCACEAE-D	
Picris echiodes	ASTERACEAE-D	
Pilea fontana	URTICACEAE-D	
Pilea pumila	URTICACEAE-D	
Pinus strobus	PINACEAE-G	
Plantago aristata	PLANTAGINACEAE-D	
Plantago cordata	PLANTAGINACEAE-D	
Plantago indica	PLANTAGINACEAE-D	
Plantago lanceolata	PLANTAGINACEAE-D	
Plantago major	PLANTAGINACEAE-D	
Plantago patagonica	PLANTAGINACEAE-D	
*Plantago purshii	PLANTAGINACEAE-D	*Plantago patagonica*
Plantago rugelii	PLANTAGINACEAE-D	
Plantago virginica	PLANTAGINACEAE-D	
Platanthera clavellata	ORCHIDACEAE-M	
Platanthera flava var. *herbiola*	ORCHIDACEAE-M	
Platanthera hookeri	ORCHIDACEAE-M	
Platanthera hyperborea var. *huronensis*	ORCHIDACEAE-M	
Platanthera lacera	ORCHIDACEAE-M	
Platanthera leucophaea	ORCHIDACEAE-M	
Platanthera praeclara	ORCHIDACEAE-M	
Platanthera psycodes	ORCHIDACEAE-M	
*Platanthera X clavellata	ORCHIDACEAE-M	*Platanthera clavellata*
Platanus occidentalis	PLATANACEAE-D	
Poa annua	POACEAE-M	
Poa arida	POACEAE-M	
Poa bulbosa	POACEAE-M	
Poa chapmaniana	POACEAE-M	
Poa compressa	POACEAE-M	
Poa languida	POACEAE-M	
Poa nemoralis	POACEAE-M	
Poa paludigena	POACEAE-M	
Poa palustris	POACEAE-M	
Poa pratensis	POACEAE-M	
Poa sylvestris	POACEAE-M	
Poa trivialis	POACEAE-M	

Poa wolfii	POACEAE-M	
Podophyllum peltatum	BERBERIDACEAE-D	
*Poinsettia cyathophora	EUPHORBIACEAE-D	*Euphorbia cyathophora*
*Poinsettia dentata	EUPHORBIACEAE-D	*Euphorbia dentata*
Polanisia dodecandra	CAPPARIDACEAE-D	
Polanisia dodecandra ssp. *trachysperma*	CAPPARIDACEAE-D	
*Polanisia graveolens	CAPPARIDACEAE-D	*Polanisia dodecandra*
Polanisia jamesii	CAPPARIDACEAE-D	
*Polanisia trachysperma	CAPPARIDACEAE-D	*Polanisia dodecandra* ssp. *trachysperma*
Polemonium reptans	POLEMONIACEAE-D	
Polygala cruciata	POLYGALACEAE-D	
Polygala incarnata	POLYGALACEAE-D	
Polygala polygama var. *obtusata*	POLYGALACEAE-D	
Polygala sanguinea	POLYGALACEAE-D	
Polygala senega	POLYGALACEAE-D	
Polygala verticillata	POLYGALACEAE-D	
*Polygala viridescens	POLYGALACEAE-D	*Polygala sanguinea*
Polygonatum biflorum	LILIACEAE-M	
*Polygonatum canaliculatum	LILIACEAE-M	*Polygonatum biflorum*
*Polygonatum commutatum	LILIACEAE-M	*Polygonatum biflorum*
Polygonatum pubescens	LILIACEAE-M	
Polygonella articulata	POLYGONACEAE-D	
Polygonum achoreum	POLYGONACEAE-D	
*Polygonum acre	POLYGONACEAE-D	*Polygonum punctatum*
Polygonum amphibium var. *emersum*	POLYGONACEAE-D	
Polygonum amphibium var. *stipulaceum*	POLYGONACEAE-D	
*Polygonum arenastrum	POLYGONACEAE-D	*Polygonum aviculare*
Polygonum aviculare	POLYGONACEAE-D	
*Polygonum bicorne	POLYGONACEAE-D	*Polygonum pensylvanicum* var. *laevigatum*
Polygonum cespitosum var. *longisetum*	POLYGONACEAE-D	
*Polygonum coccineum	POLYGONACEAE-D	*Polygonum amphibium* var. *emersum*
Polygonum convolvulus	POLYGONACEAE-D	
Polygonum cuspidatum	POLYGONACEAE-D	
Polygonum douglasii	POLYGONACEAE-D	
Polygonum erectum	POLYGONACEAE-D	
*Polygonum fluitans	POLYGONACEAE-D	*Polygonum amphibium* var. *stipulaceum*
Polygonum hydropiper	POLYGONACEAE-D	

Polygonum hydropiperoides	POLYGONACEAE-D	
Polygonum lapathifolium	POLYGONACEAE-D	
*Polygonum longistylum	POLYGONACEAE-D	*Polygonum pensylvanicum* var. *laevigatum*
*Polygonum natans	POLYGONACEAE-D	*Polygonum amphibium* var. *stipulaceum*
Polygonum orientale	POLYGONACEAE-D	
Polygonum pensylvanicum var. *laevigatum*	POLYGONACEAE-D	
Polygonum persicaria	POLYGONACEAE-D	
*Polygonum prolificum	POLYGONACEAE-D	*Polygonum ramosissimum*
Polygonum punctatum	POLYGONACEAE-D	
Polygonum ramosissimum	POLYGONACEAE-D	
Polygonum sagittatum	POLYGONACEAE-D	
Polygonum scandens	POLYGONACEAE-D	
Polygonum tenue	POLYGONACEAE-D	
Polygonum virginianum	POLYGONACEAE-D	
Polymnia canadensis	ASTERACEAE-D	
Polypodium virginianum	POLYPODIACEAE-P	
*Polypodium vulgare var. virginianum	POLYPODIACEAE-P	*Polypodium virginianum*
Polystichum acrostichoides	ASPLENIACEAE-P	
Polytaenia nuttallii	APIACEAE-D	
Pontederia cordata	PONTEDERIACEAE-M	
Populus alba	SALICACEAE-D	
*Populus alba X P. grandidentata	SALICACEAE-D	*Populus* X *rouleauiana*
Populus balsamifera	SALICACEAE-D	
*Populus candicans	SALICACEAE-D	*Populus balsamifera*
Populus deltoides	SALICACEAE-D	
Populus deltoides ssp. *monilifera*	SALICACEAE-D	
*Populus deltoides var. occidentalis	SALICACEAE-D	*Populus deltoides* ssp. *monilifera*
Populus grandidentata	SALICACEAE-D	
Populus nigra var. *italica*	SALICACEAE-D	
*Populus sargentii	SALICACEAE-D	*Populus deltoides* ssp. *monilifera*
*Populus tacamahacca	SALICACEAE-D	*Populus balsamifera*
*Populus tremula ssp. tremuloides	SALICACEAE-D	*Populus tremuloides*
Populus tremuloides	SALICACEAE-D	
Populus X *rouleauiana*	SALICACEAE-D	
Portulaca grandiflora	PORTULACACEAE-D	
Portulaca oleracea	PORTULACACEAE-D	

*Potamogeton americanus	POTAMOGETONACEAE-M	*Potamogeton nodosus*
Potamogeton amplifolius	POTAMOGETONACEAE-M	
*Potamogeton berchtoldii	POTAMOGETONACEAE-M	*Potamogeton pusillus* var. *tenuissimus*
*Potamogeton capillaceus	POTAMOGETONACEAE-M	*Potamogeton diversifolius*
Potamogeton crispus	POTAMOGETONACEAE-M	
Potamogeton diversifolius	POTAMOGETONACEAE-M	
Potamogeton epihydrus	POTAMOGETONACEAE-M	
Potamogeton foliosus	POTAMOGETONACEAE-M	
Potamogeton friesii	POTAMOGETONACEAE-M	
Potamogeton gramineus	POTAMOGETONACEAE-M	
Potamogeton illinoensis	POTAMOGETONACEAE-M	
Potamogeton natans	POTAMOGETONACEAE-M	
Potamogeton nodosus	POTAMOGETONACEAE-M	
*Potamogeton panormitanus	POTAMOGETONACEAE-M	*Potamogeton pusillus*
Potamogeton pectinatus	POTAMOGETONACEAE-M	
Potamogeton praelongus	POTAMOGETONACEAE-M	
Potamogeton pusillus	POTAMOGETONACEAE-M	
Potamogeton pusillus var. *tenuissimus*	POTAMOGETONACEAE-M	
Potamogeton richardsonii	POTAMOGETONACEAE-M	
Potamogeton spirillus	POTAMOGETONACEAE-M	
Potamogeton strictifolius	POTAMOGETONACEAE-M	
Potamogeton vaseyi	POTAMOGETONACEAE-M	
Potamogeton zosteriformis	POTAMOGETONACEAE-M	
Potentilla anserina	ROSACEAE-D	
Potentilla argentea	ROSACEAE-D	
Potentilla arguta	ROSACEAE-D	
Potentilla fruticosa	ROSACEAE-D	
Potentilla intermedia	ROSACEAE-D	
*Potentilla nicolletii	ROSACEAE-D	*Potentilla paradoxa*
Potentilla norvegica	ROSACEAE-D	
Potentilla palustris	ROSACEAE-D	
Potentilla paradoxa	ROSACEAE-D	
Potentilla pensylvanica	ROSACEAE-D	
Potentilla recta	ROSACEAE-D	
Potentilla rivalis	ROSACEAE-D	
Potentilla simplex	ROSACEAE-D	
Potentilla tridentata	ROSACEAE-D	
Prenanthes alba	ASTERACEAE-D	
Prenanthes aspera	ASTERACEAE-D	
Prenanthes racemosa	ASTERACEAE-D	
Primula mistassinica	PRIMULACEAE-D	
Prionopsis ciliata	ASTERACEAE-D	
Proboscidea louisianica	MARTYNIACEAE-D	
Proserpinaca palustris	HALORAGIDACEAE-D	

Prunella vulgaris	LAMIACEAE-D	
Prunella vulgaris var. *lanceolata*	LAMIACEAE-D	
Prunus americana	ROSACEAE-D	
Prunus besseyi	ROSACEAE-D	
Prunus hortulana	ROSACEAE-D	
Prunus mexicana	ROSACEAE-D	
Prunus nigra	ROSACEAE-D	
Prunus pensylvanica	ROSACEAE-D	
Prunus persica	ROSACEAE-D	
Prunus pumila	ROSACEAE-D	
*Prunus pumila var. besseyi	ROSACEAE-D	*Prunus besseyi*
Prunus serotina	ROSACEAE-D	
*Prunus susquehanae	ROSACEAE-D	*Prunus pumila*
Prunus virginiana	ROSACEAE-D	
*Psoralea argophylla	FABACEAE-D	*Pediomelum argophyllum*
*Psoralea esculenta	FABACEAE-D	*Pediomelum esculentum*
*Psoralea lanceolata	FABACEAE-D	*Psoralidium lanceolatum*
*Psoralea onobrychis	FABACEAE-D	*Orbexilum onobrychis*
*Psoralea tenuiflora var. floribunda	FABACEAE-D	*Psoralidium batesii*
Psoralidium batesii	FABACEAE-D	
Psoralidium lanceolatum	FABACEAE-D	
Ptelea trifoliata	RUTACEAE-D	
*Pteretis pennsylvanica	ASPLENIACEAE-P	*Matteuccia struthiopteris* var. *pensylvanica*
Pteridium aquilinum var. *latiusculum*	DENNSTAEDTIACEAE-P	
Puccinellia distans	POACEAE-M	
*Pulsatilla nuttalliana	RANUNCULACEAE-D	*Pulsatilla patens* ssp. *multifida*
Pulsatilla patens ssp. *multifida*	RANUNCULACEAE-D	
*Pycnanthemum flexuosum	LAMIACEAE-D	*Pycnanthemum tenuifolium*
Pycnanthemum pilosum	LAMIACEAE-D	
Pycnanthemum tenuifolium	LAMIACEAE-D	
Pycnanthemum virginianum	LAMIACEAE-D	
Pyrola asarifolia	ERICACEAE-D	
Pyrola elliptica	ERICACEAE-D	
Pyrola secunda	ERICACEAE-D	
Pyrrhopappus carolinianus	ASTERACEAE-D	
Pyrus communis	ROSACEAE-D	
*Pyrus ioensis	ROSACEAE-D	*Malus ioensis*
*Pyrus malus	ROSACEAE-D	*Malus sylvestris*
*Pyrus melanocarpa	ROSACEAE-D	*Aronia melanocarpa*

*Quamoclit coccinea	CONVOLVULACEAE-D	*Ipomoea coccinea*
Quercus alba	FAGACEAE-D	
*Quercus alba X Q. macrocarpa	FAGACEAE-D	*Quercus* X *bebbiana*
*Quercus alba X Q. muhlenbergii	FAGACEAE-D	*Quercus* X *deamii*
*Quercus alba X Q. stellata	FAGACEAE-D	*Quercus* X *fernowii*
Quercus bicolor	FAGACEAE-D	
*Quercus bicolor X Q. macrocarpa	FAGACEAE-D	*Quercus* X *schuettei*
Quercus borealis var. *maxima*	FAGACEAE-D	
*Quercus borealis X Q. velutina	FAGACEAE-D	*Quercus* X *hawkinsii*
Quercus ellipsoidalis	FAGACEAE-D	
*Quercus ellipsoidalis X Q. velutina	FAGACEAE-D	*Quercus* X *paleolithicola*
Quercus imbricaria	FAGACEAE-D	
*Quercus imbricaria X Q. palustris	FAGACEAE-D	*Quercus* X *exacta*
*Quercus imbricaria X Q. velutina	FAGACEAE-D	*Quercus* X *leana*
Quercus macrocarpa	FAGACEAE-D	
Quercus marilandica	FAGACEAE-D	
*Quercus marilandica X Q. velutina	FAGACEAE-D	*Quercus* X *bushii*
Quercus muhlenbergii	FAGACEAE-D	
Quercus palustris	FAGACEAE-D	
Quercus prinoides	FAGACEAE-D	
*Quercus prinoides var. acuminata	FAGACEAE-D	*Quercus muhlenbergii*
*Quercus rubra	FAGACEAE-D	*Quercus borealis* var. *maxima*
Quercus stellata	FAGACEAE-D	
Quercus velutina	FAGACEAE-D	
Quercus X *bebbiana*	FAGACEAE-D	
Quercus X *bushii*	FAGACEAE-D	
Quercus X *deamii*	FAGACEAE-D	
Quercus X *exacta*	FAGACEAE-D	
Quercus X *fernowii*	FAGACEAE-D	
Quercus X *hawkinsii*	FAGACEAE-D	
*Quercus X hillii	FAGACEAE-D	*Quercus* X *schuettei*
Quercus X *leana*	FAGACEAE-D	
Quercus X *paleolithicola*	FAGACEAE-D	
Quercus X *schuettei*	FAGACEAE-D	

Ranunculus abortivus	RANUNCULACEAE-D	
Ranunculus acris	RANUNCULACEAE-D	
Ranunculus aquatilis var. *capillaceus*	RANUNCULACEAE-D	
*Ranunculus circinatus	RANUNCULACEAE-D	*Ranunculus longirostris*
Ranunculus circinatus var. *subrigidus*	RANUNCULACEAE-D	
Ranunculus cymbalaria	RANUNCULACEAE-D	
Ranunculus fascicularis	RANUNCULACEAE-D	
Ranunculus flabellaris	RANUNCULACEAE-D	
Ranunculus gmelinii var. *hookeri*	RANUNCULACEAE-D	
*Ranunculus hispidus var. nitidus	RANUNCULACEAE-D	*Ranunculus septentrionalis*
Ranunculus longirostris	RANUNCULACEAE-D	
Ranunculus pensylvanicus	RANUNCULACEAE-D	
*Ranunculus purshii	RANUNCULACEAE-D	*Ranunculus gmelinii* var. *hookeri*
Ranunculus recurvatus	RANUNCULACEAE-D	
Ranunculus repens	RANUNCULACEAE-D	
Ranunculus rhomboideus	RANUNCULACEAE-D	
Ranunculus sceleratus	RANUNCULACEAE-D	
Ranunculus septentrionalis	RANUNCULACEAE-D	
*Ranunculus subrigidus	RANUNCULACEAE-D	*Ranunculus circinatus* var. *subrigidus*
Ranunculus testiculatus	RANUNCULACEAE-D	
*Ranunculus trichophyllus	RANUNCULACEAE-D	*Ranunculus aquatilis* var. *capillaceus*
Raphanus raphanistrum	BRASSICACEAE-D	
Raphanus sativus	BRASSICACEAE-D	
Ratibida columnifera	ASTERACEAE-D	
Ratibida pinnata	ASTERACEAE-D	
Reseda luteola	RESEDACEAE-D	
Rhamnus alnifolia	RHAMNACEAE-D	
Rhamnus cathartica	RHAMNACEAE-D	
Rhamnus davurica	RHAMNACEAE-D	
Rhamnus frangula	RHAMNACEAE-D	
Rhamnus lanceolata	RHAMNACEAE-D	
Rhexia virginica	MELASTOMATACEAE-D	
Rhus aromatica	ANACARDIACEAE-D	
Rhus copallina	ANACARDIACEAE-D	
Rhus glabra	ANACARDIACEAE-D	
*Rhus radicans	ANACARDIACEAE-D	*Toxicodendron radicans* ssp. *negundo*
*Rhus radicans var. rydbergii	ANACARDIACEAE-D	*Toxicodendron rydbergii*

*Rhus toxicodendron	ANACARDIACEAE-D	*Toxicodendron radicans* ssp. *negundo*
*Rhus trilobata var. arenaria	ANACARDIACEAE-D	*Rhus aromatica*
Rhus typhina	ANACARDIACEAE-D	
Rhynchospora capillacea	CYPERACEAE-M	
Ribes americanum	SAXIFRAGACEAE-D	
Ribes cynosbati	SAXIFRAGACEAE-D	
Ribes hirtellum	SAXIFRAGACEAE-D	
Ribes hudsonianum	SAXIFRAGACEAE-D	
Ribes missouriense	SAXIFRAGACEAE-D	
Ribes odoratum	SAXIFRAGACEAE-D	
*Ribes rubrum	SAXIFRAGACEAE-D	*Ribes sativum*
Ribes sativum	SAXIFRAGACEAE-D	
Robinia pseudoacacia	FABACEAE-D	
Rorippa austriaca	BRASSICACEAE-D	
*Rorippa islandica var. fernaldiana	BRASSICACEAE-D	*Rorippa palustris*
*Rorippa islandica var. hispida	BRASSICACEAE-D	*Rorippa palustris*
*Rorippa nasturtium-aquaticum	BRASSICACEAE-D	*Nasturtium officinale*
Rorippa palustris	BRASSICACEAE-D	
Rorippa prostrata	BRASSICACEAE-D	
Rorippa sessiliflora	BRASSICACEAE-D	
Rorippa sinuata	BRASSICACEAE-D	
Rorippa sylvestris	BRASSICACEAE-D	
Rosa acicularis	ROSACEAE-D	
Rosa arkansana var. *suffulta*	ROSACEAE-D	
Rosa blanda	ROSACEAE-D	
Rosa carolina	ROSACEAE-D	
Rosa eglanteria	ROSACEAE-D	
*Rosa fendleri	ROSACEAE-D	*Rosa woodsii*
Rosa multiflora	ROSACEAE-D	
Rosa palustris	ROSACEAE-D	
Rosa setigera	ROSACEAE-D	
*Rosa suffulta	ROSACEAE-D	*Rosa arkansana* var. *suffulta*
Rosa woodsii	ROSACEAE-D	
Rotala ramosior	LYTHRACEAE-D	
Rubus allegheniensis	ROSACEAE-D	
Rubus flagellaris	ROSACEAE-D	
Rubus hispidus	ROSACEAE-D	
Rubus idaeus	ROSACEAE-D	
*Rubus idaeus ssp. sachalinensis	ROSACEAE-D	*Rubus strigosus*

*Rubus idaeus var. strigosus	ROSACEAE-D	*Rubus strigosus*
Rubus occidentalis	ROSACEAE-D	
Rubus pubescens	ROSACEAE-D	
Rubus strigosus	ROSACEAE-D	
*Rubus triflorus	ROSACEAE-D	*Rubus pubescens*
Rudbeckia hirta	ASTERACEAE-D	
Rudbeckia laciniata	ASTERACEAE-D	
*Rudbeckia serotina	ASTERACEAE-D	*Rudbeckia hirta*
Rudbeckia subtomentosa	ASTERACEAE-D	
Rudbeckia triloba	ASTERACEAE-D	
Ruellia humilis	ACANTHACEAE-D	
Ruellia strepens	ACANTHACEAE-D	
Rumex acetosella	POLYGONACEAE-D	
Rumex altissimus	POLYGONACEAE-D	
Rumex crispus	POLYGONACEAE-D	
Rumex maritimus var. *fueginus*	POLYGONACEAE-D	
Rumex mexicanus	POLYGONACEAE-D	
Rumex obtusifolius	POLYGONACEAE-D	
Rumex occidentalis	POLYGONACEAE-D	
Rumex orbiculatus	POLYGONACEAE-D	
Rumex patientia	POLYGONACEAE-D	
*Rumex persicarioides	POLYGONACEAE-D	*Rumex maritimus* var. *fueginus*
*Rumex triangulivalvis	POLYGONACEAE-D	*Rumex mexicanus*
Rumex venosus	POLYGONACEAE-D	
Rumex verticillatus	POLYGONACEAE-D	
Ruppia maritima	RUPPIACEAE-M	
Sabatia campestris	GENTIANACEAE-D	
Sagittaria brevirostra	ALISMATACEAE-M	
Sagittaria calycina	ALISMATACEAE-M	
Sagittaria cristata	ALISMATACEAE-M	
Sagittaria cuneata	ALISMATACEAE-M	
*Sagittaria engelmanniana ssp. brevirostra	ALISMATACEAE-M	*Sagittaria brevirostra*
Sagittaria graminea	ALISMATACEAE-M	
*Sagittaria graminea var. cristata	ALISMATACEAE-M	*Sagittaria cristata*
Sagittaria latifolia	ALISMATACEAE-M	
*Sagittaria montevidensis ssp. calycina	ALISMATACEAE-M	*Sagittaria calycina*
Sagittaria rigida	ALISMATACEAE-M	
Salix alba	SALICACEAE-D	
Salix amygdaloides	SALICACEAE-D	
Salix babylonica	SALICACEAE-D	

Salix bebbiana	SALICACEAE-D	
Salix candida	SALICACEAE-D	
*Salix cordata var. angustata	SALICACEAE-D	*Salix rigida*
*Salix cordata var. rigida	SALICACEAE-D	*Salix rigida*
Salix discolor	SALICACEAE-D	
*Salix eriocephala	SALICACEAE-D	*Salix rigida*
Salix exigua ssp. *interior*	SALICACEAE-D	
Salix fragilis	SALICACEAE-D	
*Salix gracilis var. textoris	SALICACEAE-D	*Salix petiolaris*
Salix humilis	SALICACEAE-D	
*Salix interior	SALICACEAE-D	*Salix exigua* ssp. *interior*
Salix lucida	SALICACEAE-D	
Salix nigra	SALICACEAE-D	
Salix pedicellaris	SALICACEAE-D	
Salix pentandra	SALICACEAE-D	
Salix petiolaris	SALICACEAE-D	
*Salix petiolaris X S. sericea	SALICACEAE-D	*Salix* X *subsericea*
Salix purpurea	SALICACEAE-D	
Salix rigida	SALICACEAE-D	
Salix sericea	SALICACEAE-D	
*Salix tristis	SALICACEAE-D	*Salix humilis*
Salix X *subsericea*	SALICACEAE-D	
Salsola collina	CHENOPODIACEAE-D	
Salsola iberica	CHENOPODIACEAE-D	
*Salsola kali var. tenuifolia	CHENOPODIACEAE-D	*Salsola iberica*
*Salvia azurea	LAMIACEAE-D	*Salvia pitcheri*
*Salvia lanceolata	LAMIACEAE-D	*Salvia reflexa*
Salvia nemorosa	LAMIACEAE-D	
Salvia pitcheri	LAMIACEAE-D	
Salvia reflexa	LAMIACEAE-D	
Salvia sylvestris	LAMIACEAE-D	
*Salvia sylvestris	LAMIACEAE-D	*Salvia nemorosa*
Sambucus canadensis	CAPRIFOLIACEAE-D	
*Sambucus pubens	CAPRIFOLIACEAE-D	*Sambucus racemosa* ssp. *pubens*
Sambucus racemosa ssp. *pubens*	CAPRIFOLIACEAE-D	
Sanguinaria canadensis	PAPAVERACEAE-D	
Sanguisorba annua	ROSACEAE-D	

Sanicula canadensis	APIACEAE-D	
Sanicula gregaria	APIACEAE-D	
Sanicula marilandica	APIACEAE-D	
Sanicula trifoliata	APIACEAE-D	
Saponaria officinalis	CARYOPHYLLACEAE-D	
*Saponaria vaccaria	CARYOPHYLLACEAE-D	*Vaccaria pyramidata*
Sassafras albidum	LAURACEAE-D	
Satureja vulgaris	LAMIACEAE-D	
Saxifraga forbesii	SAXIFRAGACEAE-D	
Saxifraga pensylvanica	SAXIFRAGACEAE-D	
*Saxifraga pensylvanica var. forbesii	SAXIFRAGACEAE-D	*Saxifraga forbesii*
Schedonnardus paniculatus	POACEAE-M	
*Scheuchzeria americana	JUNCAGINACEAE-M	*Scheuchzeria palustris* var. *americana*
Scheuchzeria palustris var. *americana*	JUNCAGINACEAE-M	
Schizachne purpurascens	POACEAE-M	
Schizachyrium scoparium	POACEAE-M	
Schrankia nuttallii	FABACEAE-D	
*Schrankia uncinata	FABACEAE-D	*Schrankia nuttallii*
Scirpus acutus	CYPERACEAE-M	
Scirpus americanus	CYPERACEAE-M	
Scirpus atrovirens	CYPERACEAE-M	
*Scirpus atrovirens var. pallidus	CYPERACEAE-M	*Scirpus pallidus*
Scirpus cyperinus	CYPERACEAE-M	
*Scirpus cyperinus var. pedicellatus	CYPERACEAE-M	*Scirpus pedicellatus*
Scirpus fluviatilis	CYPERACEAE-M	
Scirpus hallii	CYPERACEAE-M	
Scirpus heterochaetus	CYPERACEAE-M	
*Scirpus lineatus	CYPERACEAE-M	*Scirpus pendulus*
Scirpus maritimus	CYPERACEAE-M	
*Scirpus micranthus	CYPERACEAE-M	*Hemicarpha micrantha*
Scirpus mucronatus	CYPERACEAE-M	
Scirpus pallidus	CYPERACEAE-M	
*Scirpus paludosus	CYPERACEAE-M	*Scirpus maritimus*
Scirpus pedicellatus	CYPERACEAE-M	
Scirpus pendulus	CYPERACEAE-M	
Scirpus smithii	CYPERACEAE-M	
*Scirpus tabernaemontanii	CYPERACEAE-M	*Scirpus validus* var. *creber*
Scirpus torreyi	CYPERACEAE-M	
Scirpus validus var. *creber*	CYPERACEAE-M	

Taxon	Family	Accepted name
Scleria triglomerata	CYPERACEAE-M	
Scleria verticillata	CYPERACEAE-M	
Sclerochloa dura	POACEAE-M	
Scolochloa festucacea	POACEAE-M	
Scrophularia lanceolata	SCROPHULARIACEAE-D	
Scrophularia marilandica	SCROPHULARIACEAE-D	
*Scutellaria epilobiifolia	LAMIACEAE-D	*Scutellaria galericulata*
Scutellaria galericulata	LAMIACEAE-D	
Scutellaria incana	LAMIACEAE-D	
Scutellaria lateriflora	LAMIACEAE-D	
Scutellaria leonardii	LAMIACEAE-D	
Scutellaria nervosa	LAMIACEAE-D	
Scutellaria ovata	LAMIACEAE-D	
Scutellaria parvula	LAMIACEAE-D	
*Scutellaria parvula var. leonardii	LAMIACEAE-D	*Scutellaria leonardii*
Secale cereale	POACEAE-M	
Sedum acre	CRASSULACEAE-D	
Sedum ternatum	CRASSULACEAE-D	
*Selaginella apoda	SELAGINELLACEAE-P	*Selaginella eclipes*
Selaginella eclipes	SELAGINELLACEAE-P	
Selaginella rupestris	SELAGINELLACEAE-P	
Senecio aureus	ASTERACEAE-D	
Senecio congestus	ASTERACEAE-D	
Senecio glabellus	ASTERACEAE-D	
Senecio integerrimus	ASTERACEAE-D	
*Senecio palustris	ASTERACEAE-D	*Senecio congestus*
Senecio pauperculus	ASTERACEAE-D	
Senecio plattensis	ASTERACEAE-D	
Senecio pseudaureus var. *semicordatus*	ASTERACEAE-D	
*Senecio semicordatus	ASTERACEAE-D	*Senecio pseudaureus* var. *semicordatus*
Senecio vulgaris	ASTERACEAE-D	
Setaria faberi	POACEAE-M	
Setaria geniculata	POACEAE-M	
Setaria glauca	POACEAE-M	
Setaria italica	POACEAE-M	
*Setaria lutescens	POACEAE-M	*Setaria glauca*
Setaria verticillata	POACEAE-M	
Setaria viridis	POACEAE-M	
*Seymeria macrophylla	SCROPHULARIACEAE-D	*Dasistoma macrophylla*
Shepherdia argentea	ELAEAGNACEAE-D	
*Shinneroseris rostrata	ASTERACEAE-D	*Lygodesmia rostrata*
Sibara virginica	BRASSICACEAE-D	
Sicyos angulatus	CUCURBITACEAE-D	

Sida spinosa	MALVACEAE-D	
*Sidopsis hispida	MALVACEAE-D	*Malvastrum hispidum*
*Sieversia triflorum	ROSACEAE-D	*Geum triflorum*
*Silene alba	CARYOPHYLLACEAE-D	*Silene pratensis*
Silene antirrhina	CARYOPHYLLACEAE-D	
Silene cserei	CARYOPHYLLACEAE-D	
*Silene cucubalus	CARYOPHYLLACEAE-D	*Silene vulgaris*
Silene dichotoma	CARYOPHYLLACEAE-D	
*Silene latifolia	CARYOPHYLLACEAE-D	*Silene pratensis*
Silene nivea	CARYOPHYLLACEAE-D	
Silene noctiflora	CARYOPHYLLACEAE-D	
Silene pratensis	CARYOPHYLLACEAE-D	
Silene stellata	CARYOPHYLLACEAE-D	
Silene virginica	CARYOPHYLLACEAE-D	
Silene vulgaris	CARYOPHYLLACEAE-D	
Silphium integrifolium	ASTERACEAE-D	
Silphium laciniatum	ASTERACEAE-D	
Silphium perfoliatum	ASTERACEAE-D	
Silphium terebinthinaceum	ASTERACEAE-D	
Sinapis alba	BRASSICACEAE-D	
Sinapis arvensis	BRASSICACEAE-D	
Sisymbrium altissimum	BRASSICACEAE-D	
Sisymbrium loeselii	BRASSICACEAE-D	
Sisymbrium officinale	BRASSICACEAE-D	
Sisyrinchium angustifolium	IRIDACEAE-M	
*Sisyrinchium bermudiana	IRIDACEAE-M	*Sisyrinchium angustifolium*
Sisyrinchium campestre	IRIDACEAE-M	
Sium suave	APIACEAE-D	
Smilacina racemosa	LILIACEAE-M	
Smilacina stellata	LILIACEAE-M	
Smilax ecirrhata	LILIACEAE-M	
Smilax herbacea	LILIACEAE-M	
Smilax hispida	LILIACEAE-M	
*Smilax lasioneura	LILIACEAE-M	*Smilax herbacea*
*Smilax rotundifolia	LILIACEAE-M	*Smilax hispida*
*Smilax tamnoides var. hispida	LILIACEAE-M	*Smilax hispida*
Solanum americanum	SOLANACEAE-D	
Solanum carolinense	SOLANACEAE-D	
*Solanum cornutum	SOLANACEAE-D	*Solanum rostratum*
Solanum dulcamara	SOLANACEAE-D	
Solanum interius	SOLANACEAE-D	
*Solanum nigrum	SOLANACEAE-D	*Solanum americanum*
*Solanum ptycanthum	SOLANACEAE-D	*Solanum americanum*
Solanum rostratum	SOLANACEAE-D	
*Solidago altissima	ASTERACEAE-D	*Solidago canadensis*

*Solidago bicolor var. concolor	ASTERACEAE-D	*Solidago hispida*
Solidago canadensis	ASTERACEAE-D	
*Solidago decemflora	ASTERACEAE-D	*Solidago nemoralis*
Solidago flexicaulis	ASTERACEAE-D	
Solidago gigantea	ASTERACEAE-D	
*Solidago graminifolia var. gymnospermoides	ASTERACEAE-D	*Euthamia graminifolia*
Solidago hispida	ASTERACEAE-D	
*Solidago latifolia	ASTERACEAE-D	*Solidago flexicaulis*
*Solidago longipetiolata	ASTERACEAE-D	*Solidago nemoralis*
Solidago missouriensis	ASTERACEAE-D	
Solidago nemoralis	ASTERACEAE-D	
Solidago patula	ASTERACEAE-D	
Solidago ptarmicoides	ASTERACEAE-D	
Solidago riddellii	ASTERACEAE-D	
Solidago rigida	ASTERACEAE-D	
Solidago sciaphila	ASTERACEAE-D	
Solidago speciosa	ASTERACEAE-D	
Solidago uliginosa	ASTERACEAE-D	
Solidago ulmifolia	ASTERACEAE-D	
Sonchus arvensis	ASTERACEAE-D	
Sonchus asper	ASTERACEAE-D	
Sonchus oleraceus	ASTERACEAE-D	
*Sonchus uliginosus	ASTERACEAE-D	*Sonchus arvensis*
Sorbaria sorbifolia	ROSACEAE-D	
Sorbus aucuparia	ROSACEAE-D	
*Sorghastrum avenaceum	POACEAE-M	*Sorghastrum nutans*
Sorghastrum nutans	POACEAE-M	
Sorghum bicolor	POACEAE-M	
*Sorghum bicolor	POACEAE-M	*Sorghum sudanense*
Sorghum halepense	POACEAE-M	
Sorghum sudanense	POACEAE-M	
*Sorghum vulgare	POACEAE-M	*Sorghum bicolor*
Sparganium americanum	SPARGANIACEAE-M	
Sparganium androcladum	SPARGANIACEAE-M	
Sparganium chlorocarpum	SPARGANIACEAE-M	
Sparganium eurycarpum	SPARGANIACEAE-M	
Spartina pectinata	POACEAE-M	
*Specularia leptocarpa	CAMPANULACEAE-D	*Triodanis leptocarpa*
*Specularia perfoliata	CAMPANULACEAE-D	*Triodanis perfoliata*
Spermolepis inermis	APIACEAE-D	
Sphaeralcea coccinea	MALVACEAE-D	
*Sphenopholis intermedia	POACEAE-M	*Sphenopholis obtusata* var. *major*
Sphenopholis obtusata	POACEAE-M	

Sphenopholis obtusata var. *major*	POACEAE-M	
Spiraea alba	ROSACEAE-D	
Spiranthes cernua	ORCHIDACEAE-M	
*Spiranthes gracilis	ORCHIDACEAE-M	*Spiranthes lacera*
Spiranthes lacera	ORCHIDACEAE-M	
Spiranthes lucida	ORCHIDACEAE-M	
Spiranthes magnicamporum	ORCHIDACEAE-M	
Spiranthes ovalis	ORCHIDACEAE-M	
Spiranthes romanzoffiana	ORCHIDACEAE-M	
Spiranthes vernalis	ORCHIDACEAE-M	
Spirodela polyrhiza	LEMNACEAE-M	
Sporobolus asper	POACEAE-M	
*Sporobolus asper var. clandestinus	POACEAE-M	*Sporobolus clandestinus*
Sporobolus clandestinus	POACEAE-M	
Sporobolus cryptandrus	POACEAE-M	
Sporobolus heterolepis	POACEAE-M	
Sporobolus neglectus	POACEAE-M	
Sporobolus vaginiflorus	POACEAE-M	
*Sporobolus vaginiflorus var. neglectus	POACEAE-M	*Sporobolus neglectus*
Stachys aspera	LAMIACEAE-D	
*Stachys hispida	LAMIACEAE-D	*Stachys tenuifolia*
*Stachys hyssopifolia var. ambigua	LAMIACEAE-D	*Stachys aspera*
Stachys palustris	LAMIACEAE-D	
Stachys tenuifolia	LAMIACEAE-D	
Staphylea trifolia	STAPHYLEACEAE-D	
*Stellaria aquatica	CARYOPHYLLACEAE-D	*Myosoton aquaticum*
Stellaria graminea	CARYOPHYLLACEAE-D	
Stellaria longifolia	CARYOPHYLLACEAE-D	
Stellaria media	CARYOPHYLLACEAE-D	
*Stenophyllus capillaris	CYPERACEAE-M	*Bulbostylis capillaris*
Stipa comata	POACEAE-M	
Stipa spartea	POACEAE-M	
Stipa viridula	POACEAE-M	
Streptopus roseus	LILIACEAE-M	
Strophostyles helvula	FABACEAE-D	
Strophostyles leiosperma	FABACEAE-D	
Stylisma pickeringii var. *pattersonii*	CONVOLVULACEAE-D	
*Sullivantia renifolia	SAXIFRAGACEAE-D	*Sullivantia sullivantii*
Sullivantia sullivantii	SAXIFRAGACEAE-D	
Symphoricarpos albus	CAPRIFOLIACEAE-D	
Symphoricarpos occidentalis	CAPRIFOLIACEAE-D	

Taxon	Family	Synonym of
Symphoricarpos orbiculatus	CAPRIFOLIACEAE-D	
Symplocarpus foetidus	ARACEAE-M	
*Synthris bullii	SCROPHULARIACEAE-D	*Besseya bullii*
Syringa vulgaris	OLEACEAE-D	
Taenidia integerrima	APIACEAE-D	
Talinum parviflorum	PORTULACACEAE-D	
Talinum rugospermum	PORTULACACEAE-D	
Tanacetum vulgare	ASTERACEAE-D	
*Taraxacum erythrospermum	ASTERACEAE-D	*Taraxacum laevigatum*
Taraxacum laevigatum	ASTERACEAE-D	
Taraxacum officinale	ASTERACEAE-D	
Taxus canadensis	TAXACEAE-G	
Tephrosia virginiana	FABACEAE-D	
*Teuchrium canadense var. occidentale	LAMIACEAE-D	*Teucrium canadense* var. *boreale*
Teucrium canadense	LAMIACEAE-D	
Teucrium canadense var. *boreale*	LAMIACEAE-D	
Thalictrum dasycarpum	RANUNCULACEAE-D	
Thalictrum dioicum	RANUNCULACEAE-D	
Thalictrum revolutum	RANUNCULACEAE-D	
Thalictrum thalictroides	RANUNCULACEAE-D	
Thaspium barbinode	APIACEAE-D	
Thelypteris hexagonoptera	ASPLENIACEAE-P	
Thelypteris palustris var. *pubescens*	ASPLENIACEAE-P	
Thelypteris phegopteris	ASPLENIACEAE-P	
Thlaspi arvense	BRASSICACEAE-D	
Thuja occidentalis	CUPRESSACEAE-G	
Thymelaea passerina	THYMELAEACEAE-D	
Tilia americana	TILIACEAE-D	
Tilia heterophylla	TILIACEAE-D	
Tomanthera auriculata	SCROPHULARIACEAE-D	
Torilis arvensis	APIACEAE-D	
*Torilis japonica	APIACEAE-D	*Torilis arvensis*
*Tovara virginianum	POLYGONACEAE-D	*Polygonum virginianum*
Toxicodendron radicans ssp. *negundo*	ANACARDIACEAE-D	
Toxicodendron rydbergii	ANACARDIACEAE-D	
Tradescantia bracteata	COMMELINACEAE-M	
Tradescantia occidentalis	COMMELINACEAE-M	
Tradescantia ohiensis	COMMELINACEAE-M	
Tradescantia virginiana	COMMELINACEAE-M	
Tragopogon dubius	ASTERACEAE-D	
*Tragopogon major	ASTERACEAE-D	*Tragopogon dubius*
Tragopogon porrifolius	ASTERACEAE-D	

Tragopogon pratensis	ASTERACEAE-D	
Triadenum fraseri	HYPERICACEAE-D	
*Triadenum virginicum	HYPERICACEAE-D	*Triadenum fraseri*
Tribulis terrestris	ZYGOPHYLLACEAE-D	
Trichostema brachiatum	LAMIACEAE-D	
Trichostema dichotomum	LAMIACEAE-D	
Tridens flavus	POACEAE-M	
*Trifolium agrarium	FABACEAE-D	*Trifolium aureum*
Trifolium arvense	FABACEAE-D	
Trifolium aureum	FABACEAE-D	
Trifolium campestre	FABACEAE-D	
Trifolium dubium	FABACEAE-D	
Trifolium hybridum	FABACEAE-D	
Trifolium incarnatum	FABACEAE-D	
Trifolium pratense	FABACEAE-D	
*Trifolium procumbens	FABACEAE-D	*Trifolium campestre*
Trifolium reflexum	FABACEAE-D	
Trifolium repens	FABACEAE-D	
Trifolium resupinatum	FABACEAE-D	
Triglochin maritimum	JUNCAGINACEAE-M	
Triglochin palustris	JUNCAGINACEAE-M	
Trillium cernuum	LILIACEAE-M	
*Trillium declinatum	LILIACEAE-M	*Trillium flexipes*
Trillium flexipes	LILIACEAE-M	
*Trillium gleasoni	LILIACEAE-M	*Trillium flexipes*
Trillium nivale	LILIACEAE-M	
Trillium recurvatum	LILIACEAE-M	
Triodanis leptocarpa	CAMPANULACEAE-D	
Triodanis perfoliata	CAMPANULACEAE-D	
Triosteum aurantiacum	CAPRIFOLIACEAE-D	
Triosteum perfoliatum	CAPRIFOLIACEAE-D	
*Triosteum perfoliatum var. aurantiacum	CAPRIFOLIACEAE-D	*Triosteum aurantiacum*
Triphora trianthophora	ORCHIDACEAE-M	
Triplasis purpurea	POACEAE-M	
Tripsacum dactyloides	POACEAE-M	
Triticum aestivum	POACEAE-M	
*Triticum cylindricum	POACEAE-M	*Aegilops cylindrica*
Typha angustifolia	TYPHACEAE-M	
*Typha angustifolia X T. latifolia	TYPHACEAE-M	*Typha X glauca*
Typha latifolia	TYPHACEAE-M	
Typha X glauca	TYPHACEAE-M	
Ulmus americana	ULMACEAE-D	
*Ulmus fulva	ULMACEAE-D	*Ulmus rubra*
Ulmus pumila	ULMACEAE-D	

Ulmus rubra	ULMACEAE-D	
Ulmus thomasii	ULMACEAE-D	
*Uniola latifolia	POACEAE-M	*Chasmanthium latifolium*
Urtica dioica	URTICACEAE-D	
Urtica urens	URTICACEAE-D	
Utricularia gibba	LENTIBULARIACEAE-D	
Utricularia intermedia	LENTIBULARIACEAE-D	
*Utricularia macrorhiza	LENTIBULARIACEAE-D	*Utricularia vulgaris*
Utricularia minor	LENTIBULARIACEAE-D	
Utricularia vulgaris	LENTIBULARIACEAE-D	
Uvularia grandiflora	LILIACEAE-M	
*Uvularia perfoliata	LILIACEAE-M	*Uvularia grandiflora*
Uvularia sessilifolia	LILIACEAE-M	
Vaccaria pyramidata	CARYOPHYLLACEAE-D	
*Vaccaria segetalis	CARYOPHYLLACEAE-D	*Vaccaria pyramidata*
Vaccinium angustifolium	ERICACEAE-D	
Vaccinium myrtilloides	ERICACEAE-D	
*Valeriana ciliata	VALERIANACEAE-D	*Valeriana edulis* ssp. *ciliata*
Valeriana edulis ssp. *ciliata*	VALERIANACEAE-D	
Valeriana officinalis	VALERIANACEAE-D	
Vallisneria americana	HYDROCHARITACEAE-M	
*Veratrum virginicum	LILIACEAE-M	*Melanthium virginicum*
Veratrum woodii	LILIACEAE-M	
Verbascum blattaria	SCROPHULARIACEAE-D	
Verbascum lychnitis	SCROPHULARIACEAE-D	
Verbascum phlomoides	SCROPHULARIACEAE-D	
Verbascum thapsus	SCROPHULARIACEAE-D	
*Verbena angustifolia	VERBENACEAE-D	*Verbena simplex*
Verbena bracteata	VERBENACEAE-D	
*Verbena bracteata X V. stricta	VERBENACEAE-D	*Verbena* X *deamii*
Verbena canadensis	VERBENACEAE-D	
Verbena hastata	VERBENACEAE-D	
*Verbena hastata X V. simplex	VERBENACEAE-D	*Verbena* X *blanchardi*
*Verbena hastata X V. stricta	VERBENACEAE-D	*Verbena* X *rydbergii*
Verbena simplex	VERBENACEAE-D	
*Verbena simplex X V. stricta	VERBENACEAE-D	*Verbena* X *moechina*
Verbena stricta	VERBENACEAE-D	
Verbena urticifolia	VERBENACEAE-D	
*Verbena urticifolia X V. hastata	VERBENACEAE-D	*Verbena* X *engelmannii*

Taxon	Family	Synonym of
Verbena X *blanchardi*	VERBENACEAE-D	
Verbena X *deamii*	VERBENACEAE-D	
Verbena X *engelmannii*	VERBENACEAE-D	
Verbena X *moechina*	VERBENACEAE-D	
Verbena X *rydbergii*	VERBENACEAE-D	
Verbesina alternifolia	ASTERACEAE-D	
Verbesina encelioides ssp. *exauriculata*	ASTERACEAE-D	
*Vernonia altissima	ASTERACEAE-D	*Vernonia gigantea*
Vernonia baldwinii	ASTERACEAE-D	
Vernonia fasciculata	ASTERACEAE-D	
Vernonia gigantea	ASTERACEAE-D	
Vernonia missurica	ASTERACEAE-D	
Veronica agrestis	SCROPHULARIACEAE-D	
Veronica americana	SCROPHULARIACEAE-D	
Veronica anagallis-aquatica	SCROPHULARIACEAE-D	
Veronica arvensis	SCROPHULARIACEAE-D	
Veronica catenata	SCROPHULARIACEAE-D	
*Veronica comosa	SCROPHULARIACEAE-D	*Veronica catenata*
*Veronica connata	SCROPHULARIACEAE-D	*Veronica catenata*
Veronica officinalis	SCROPHULARIACEAE-D	
Veronica peregrina	SCROPHULARIACEAE-D	
Veronica persica	SCROPHULARIACEAE-D	
Veronica scutellata	SCROPHULARIACEAE-D	
Veronica serpyllifolia	SCROPHULARIACEAE-D	
*Veronica tournefortii	SCROPHULARIACEAE-D	*Veronica persica*
Veronicastrum virginicum	SCROPHULARIACEAE-D	
Viburnum dentatum	CAPRIFOLIACEAE-D	
Viburnum lentago	CAPRIFOLIACEAE-D	
Viburnum molle	CAPRIFOLIACEAE-D	
Viburnum opulus	CAPRIFOLIACEAE-D	
*Viburnum opulus var. americanum	CAPRIFOLIACEAE-D	*Viburnum trilobum*
Viburnum prunifolium	CAPRIFOLIACEAE-D	
Viburnum rafinesquianum	CAPRIFOLIACEAE-D	
Viburnum trilobum	CAPRIFOLIACEAE-D	
Vicia americana	FABACEAE-D	
Vicia americana var. *minor*	FABACEAE-D	
*Vicia angustifolia	FABACEAE-D	*Vicia sativa* var. *nigra*
*Vicia angustifolia var. segetalis	FABACEAE-D	*Vicia sativa*
Vicia cracca	FABACEAE-D	
Vicia sativa	FABACEAE-D	

Vicia sativa var. *nigra*	FABACEAE-D	
Vicia villosa	FABACEAE-D	
Vinca minor	APOCYNACEAE-D	
Viola adunca	VIOLACEAE-D	
*Viola bicolor	VIOLACEAE-D	*Viola rafinesquii*
*Viola canadensis var. corymbosa	VIOLACEAE-D	*Viola canadensis* var. *rugulosa*
Viola canadensis var. *rugulosa*	VIOLACEAE-D	
*Viola eriocarpa	VIOLACEAE-D	*Viola pubescens*
Viola incognita	VIOLACEAE-D	
*Viola kitaibeliana var. rafinesquii	VIOLACEAE-D	*Viola rafinesquii*
Viola lanceolata	VIOLACEAE-D	
*Viola lanceolata X V. macloskeyi	VIOLACEAE-D	*Viola* X *sublanceolata*
Viola macloskeyi ssp. *pallens*	VIOLACEAE-D	
Viola missouriensis	VIOLACEAE-D	
Viola missouriensis X *V. sororia*	VIOLACEAE-D	
Viola nephrophylla	VIOLACEAE-D	
Viola nephrophylla X *V. sororia*	VIOLACEAE-D	
*Viola pallens	VIOLACEAE-D	*Viola macloskeyi* ssp. *pallens*
*Viola papilionacea	VIOLACEAE-D	*Viola pratincola*
Viola pedata	VIOLACEAE-D	
Viola pedatifida	VIOLACEAE-D	
*Viola pedatifida X V. sororia	VIOLACEAE-D	*Viola* X *bernardii*
*Viola pensylvanica	VIOLACEAE-D	*Viola pubescens*
Viola pratincola	VIOLACEAE-D	
Viola pratincola X *V. pedatifida*	VIOLACEAE-D	
*Viola pratincola X V. sororia	VIOLACEAE-D	*Viola* X *napae*
Viola pubescens	VIOLACEAE-D	
*Viola pubescens var. eriocarpa	VIOLACEAE-D	*Viola pubescens*
Viola rafinesquii	VIOLACEAE-D	
Viola renifolia	VIOLACEAE-D	
*Viola rugulosa	VIOLACEAE-D	*Viola canadensis* var. *rugulosa*
Viola sagittata	VIOLACEAE-D	

Viola sagittata X *V. pedatifida*	VIOLACEAE-D	
Viola sororia	VIOLACEAE-D	
Viola striata	VIOLACEAE-D	
Viola tricolor	VIOLACEAE-D	
Viola viarum	VIOLACEAE-D	
Viola X *bernardii*	VIOLACEAE-D	
Viola X *napae*	VIOLACEAE-D	
Viola X *sublanceolata*	VIOLACEAE-D	
Vitis aestivalis	VITACEAE-D	
Vitis cinerea	VITACEAE-D	
Vitis riparia	VITACEAE-D	
Vitis vulpina	VITACEAE-D	
*Vulpia octoflora	POACEAE-M	*Festuca octoflora* var. *tenella*
Wisteria frutescens	FABACEAE-D	
*Wolffia borealis	LEMNACEAE-M	*Wolffia punctata*
Wolffia columbiana	LEMNACEAE-M	
Wolffia punctata	LEMNACEAE-M	
Woodsia ilvensis	ASPLENIACEAE-P	
Woodsia obtusa	ASPLENIACEAE-P	
Woodsia oregana	ASPLENIACEAE-P	
*Wulfenia bullii	SCROPHULARIACEAE-D	*Besseya bullii*
X *Agrohordeum macounii*	POACEAE-M	
X *Elyhordeum iowense*	POACEAE-M	
X *Elyhordeum montanense*	POACEAE-M	
Xanthium spinosum	ASTERACEAE-D	
Xanthium strumarium	ASTERACEAE-D	
*Xyris flexuosa	XYRIDACEAE-M	*Xyris torta*
Xyris torta	XYRIDACEAE-M	
Yucca glauca	AGAVACEAE-M	
Zannichellia palustris	ZANNICHELLIACEAE-M	
Zanthoxylum americanum	RUTACEAE-D	
Zea mays	POACEAE-M	
Zigadenus elegans	LILIACEAE-M	
*Zigadenus elegans ssp. elegans	LILIACEAE-M	*Zigadenus elegans*
*Zigadenus elegans ssp. glaucus	LILIACEAE-M	*Zigadenus glaucus*
Zigadenus glaucus	LILIACEAE-M	
Zizania aquatica	POACEAE-M	
*Zizania palustris	POACEAE-M	*Zizania aquatica*
Zizia aptera	APIACEAE-D	
Zizia aptera X *Z. aurea*	APIACEAE-D	
Zizia aurea	APIACEAE-D	
*Zosterella dubia	PONTEDERIACEAE-M	*Heteranthera dubia*

Index of Common Names

The column on the left contains, in alphabetic order, all the common names of the species from the checklist. Knowing the common name, one can find the associated species binomial in the right column and the family name in the middle column. The letter following the hyphen at the end of the family name is an abbreviation for the major taxon which includes that family:

P = Pteridophytes
G = Gymnosperms
D = Angiosperms: Dicotyledons
M = Angiosperms: Monocotyledons

With this information, one can find the species description in the annotated checklist since, within the major taxa, the checklist is arranged in alphabetic order by family, genus, and species names.

COMMON NAME	FAMILY	ACCEPTED BINOMIAL
Adder's-tongue, northern	OPHIOGLOSSACEAE-P	*Ophioglossum pusillum*
Agrimony, soft	ROSACEAE-D	*Agrimonia pubescens*
swamp	ROSACEAE-D	*Agrimonia parviflora*
tall	ROSACEAE-D	*Agrimonia gryposepala*
Alder, speckled	BETULACEAE-D	*Alnus rugosa*
Alfalfa	FABACEAE-D	*Medicago sativa*
yellow	FABACEAE-D	*Medicago falcata*
Alkanet	BORAGINACEAE-D	*Anchusa azurea*
Alumroot	SAXIFRAGACEAE-D	*Heuchera richardsonii*
Alyssum, hoary	BRASSICACEAE-D	*Berteroa incana*
sweet	BRASSICACEAE-D	*Lobularia maritima*
Amaranth, green	AMARANTHACEAE-D	*Amaranthus hybridus*
American pennyroyal	LAMIACEAE-D	*Hedeoma pulegioides*
Anemone, Canada	RANUNCULACEAE-D	*Anemone canadensis*
Carolina	RANUNCULACEAE-D	*Anemone caroliniana*
false rue	RANUNCULACEAE-D	*Isopyrum biternatum*
rue	RANUNCULACEAE-D	*Thalictrum thalictroides*
tall	RANUNCULACEAE-D	*Anemone virginiana*
wood	RANUNCULACEAE-D	*Anemone quinquefolia*
Angelica	APIACEAE-D	*Angelica atropurpurea*
Anise root	APIACEAE-D	*Osmorhiza longistylis*
Annual morning glory	CONVOLVULACEAE-D	*Ipomoea purpurea*
Apple	ROSACEAE-D	*Malus sylvestris*
Apple of Peru	SOLANACEAE-D	*Nicandra physalodes*
Apple, hedge	MORACEAE-D	*Maclura pomifera*
wild balsam	CUCURBITACEAE-D	*Echinocystis lobata*
Arbor vitae	CUPRESSACEAE-G	*Thuja occidentalis*
Arrow arum	ARACEAE-M	*Peltandra virginica*
Arrow-grass, common	JUNCAGINACEAE-M	*Triglochin maritimum*
slender	JUNCAGINACEAE-M	*Triglochin palustris*
Arrowwood	CAPRIFOLIACEAE-D	*Viburnum molle*
downy	CAPRIFOLIACEAE-D	*Viburnum rafinesquianum*
southern	CAPRIFOLIACEAE-D	*Viburnum dentatum*
Artichoke, Jerusalem	ASTERACEAE-D	*Helianthus tuberosus*
Ash, black	OLEACEAE-D	*Fraxinus nigra*
blue	OLEACEAE-D	*Fraxinus quadrangulata*
green	OLEACEAE-D	*Fraxinus pennsylvanica* var. *lanceolata*
mountain	ROSACEAE-D	*Sorbus aucuparia*
prickly	RUTACEAE-D	*Zanthoxylum americanum*
red	OLEACEAE-D	*Fraxinus pennsylvanica*
wafer	RUTACEAE-D	*Ptelea trifoliata*

Common name	Family	Scientific name
Ash, cont.		
white	OLEACEAE-D	*Fraxinus americana*
Asparagus, garden	LILIACEAE-M	*Asparagus officinalis*
Aspen, big-tooth	SALICACEAE-D	*Populus grandidentata*
quaking	SALICACEAE-D	*Populus tremuloides*
Aster, aromatic	ASTERACEAE-D	*Aster oblongifolius*
arrow-leaved	ASTERACEAE-D	*Aster sagittifolius*
big-leaved	ASTERACEAE-D	*Aster macrophyllus*
blue wood	ASTERACEAE-D	*Aster cordifolius*
crooked stem	ASTERACEAE-D	*Aster prenanthoides*
Drummond's	ASTERACEAE-D	*Aster drummondii*
false	ASTERACEAE-D	*Boltonia asteroides*
flat-topped	ASTERACEAE-D	*Aster umbellatus*
flax-leaved	ASTERACEAE-D	*Aster linariifolius*
forked	ASTERACEAE-D	*Aster furcatus*
hairy	ASTERACEAE-D	*Aster pilosus*
heath	ASTERACEAE-D	*Aster ericoides*
New England	ASTERACEAE-D	*Aster novae-angliae*
Ontario	ASTERACEAE-D	*Aster ontarionis*
panicled	ASTERACEAE-D	*Aster lanceolatus*
rayless	ASTERACEAE-D	*Aster brachyactis*
ricebutton	ASTERACEAE-D	*Aster dumosus*
rush	ASTERACEAE-D	*Aster junciformis*
Schreber's	ASTERACEAE-D	*Aster schreberi*
side-flowered	ASTERACEAE-D	*Aster lateriflorus*
silky	ASTERACEAE-D	*Aster sericeus*
sky-blue	ASTERACEAE-D	*Aster azureus*
smooth blue	ASTERACEAE-D	*Aster laevis*
swamp	ASTERACEAE-D	*Aster puniceus*
white	ASTERACEAE-D	*Aster umbellatus*
willow	ASTERACEAE-D	*Aster praealtus*
Avens, purple	ROSACEAE-D	*Geum triflorum*
rough	ROSACEAE-D	*Geum laciniatum*
spring	ROSACEAE-D	*Geum vernum*
white	ROSACEAE-D	*Geum canadense*
yellow	ROSACEAE-D	*Geum aleppicum* var. *strictum*
Bachelor's button	ASTERACEAE-D	*Centaurea cyanus*
Bamboo, Japanese	POLYGONACEAE-D	*Polygonum cuspidatum*
Baneberry, red	RANUNCULACEAE-D	*Actaea rubra*
white	RANUNCULACEAE-D	*Actaea pachypoda*
Barberry, European	BERBERIDACEAE-D	*Berberis vulgaris*
Japanese	BERBERIDACEAE-D	*Berberis thunbergii*
Barley	POACEAE-M	*Hordeum vulgare*
little	POACEAE-M	*Hordeum pusillum*

Barley, cont.		
squirrel-tail	POACEAE-M	*Hordeum jubatum*
Basil	LAMIACEAE-D	*Satureja vulgaris*
Basswood	TILIACEAE-D	*Tilia americana*
white	TILIACEAE-D	*Tilia heterophylla*
Beaked hazel	BETULACEAE-D	*Corylus cornuta*
Bearberry	ERICACEAE-D	*Arctostaphylos uva-ursi*
Beardtongue, large-flowered	SCROPHULARIACEAE-D	*Penstemon grandiflorus*
pale	SCROPHULARIACEAE-D	*Penstemon pallidus*
Bedstraw, bog	RUBIACEAE-D	*Galium labradoricum*
northern	RUBIACEAE-D	*Galium boreale*
rough	RUBIACEAE-D	*Galium asprellum*
shining	RUBIACEAE-D	*Galium concinnum*
small	RUBIACEAE-D	*Galium trifidum*
stiff	RUBIACEAE-D	*Galium tinctorium*
sweet-scented	RUBIACEAE-D	*Galium triflorum*
yellow	RUBIACEAE-D	*Galium verum*
Beech, blue	BETULACEAE-D	*Carpinus caroliniana*
Beefsteak plant	LAMIACEAE-D	*Perilla frutescens*
Beggar-ticks	ASTERACEAE-D	*Bidens frondosa*
swamp	ASTERACEAE-D	*Bidens discoidea*
tall	ASTERACEAE-D	*Bidens vulgata*
Beggar's-lice	BORAGINACEAE-D	*Lappula echinata*
Bellflower, marsh	CAMPANULACEAE-D	*Campanula aparinoides*
tall	CAMPANULACEAE-D	*Campanula americana*
Bellwort	LILIACEAE-M	*Uvularia grandiflora*
sessile-leaved	LILIACEAE-M	*Uvularia sessilifolia*
Bent, creeping	POACEAE-M	*Agrostis stolonifera* var. *palustris*
upland	POACEAE-M	*Agrostis perennans*
Bergamot, wild	LAMIACEAE-D	*Monarda fistulosa*
Berry, buffalo	ELAEAGNACEAE-D	*Shepherdia argentea*
partridge	RUBIACEAE-D	*Mitchella repens*
Bindweed, black	POLYGONACEAE-D	*Polygonum convolvulus*
European	CONVOLVULACEAE-D	*Convolvulus arvensis*
low	CONVOLVULACEAE-D	*Calystegia spithamaea*
Birch, canoe	BETULACEAE-D	*Betula papyrifera*
paper	BETULACEAE-D	*Betula papyrifera*
river	BETULACEAE-D	*Betula nigra*
swamp	BETULACEAE-D	*Betula pumila* var. *glandulifera*
yellow	BETULACEAE-D	*Betula alleghaniensis*
Bishop's cap	SAXIFRAGACEAE-D	*Mitella diphylla*
Bittersweet	CELASTRACEAE-D	*Celastrus scandens*
European	SOLANACEAE-D	*Solanum dulcamara*

Bittersweet, cont.		
round-leaved	CELASTRACEAE-D	*Celastrus orbiculatus*
Bitterweed	ASTERACEAE-D	*Helenium amarum*
Black-eyed Susan	ASTERACEAE-D	*Rudbeckia hirta*
Black medic	FABACEAE-D	*Medicago lupulina*
Blackberry	ROSACEAE-D	*Rubus allegheniensis*
Bladder-pod, silvery	BRASSICACEAE-D	*Lesquerella ludoviciana*
Bladdernut	STAPHYLEACEAE-D	*Staphylea trifolia*
Bladderwort, common	LENTIBULARIACEAE-D	*Utricularia vulgaris*
flat-leaved	LENTIBULARIACEAE-D	*Utricularia intermedia*
humped	LENTIBULARIACEAE-D	*Utricularia gibba*
small	LENTIBULARIACEAE-D	*Utricularia minor*
Blanket flower	ASTERACEAE-D	*Gaillardia pulchella*
Blazing star	ASTERACEAE-D	*Liatris aspera*
Blazing star	ASTERACEAE-D	*Liatris cylindracea*
Blazing star	ASTERACEAE-D	*Liatris ligulistylis*
Bloodroot	PAPAVERACEAE-D	*Sanguinaria canadensis*
Blue cohosh	BERBERIDACEAE-D	*Caulophyllum thalictroides*
Blue curls	LAMIACEAE-D	*Trichostema dichotomum*
Blue-eyed Mary	SCROPHULARIACEAE-D	*Collinsia verna*
Blue flag	IRIDACEAE-M	*Iris shrevei*
Bluebell	BORAGINACEAE-D	*Mertensia virginica*
Blueberry, low sweet	ERICACEAE-D	*Vaccinium angustifolium*
velvet-leaf	ERICACEAE-D	*Vaccinium myrtilloides*
Bluegrass, annual	POACEAE-M	*Poa annua*
Canadian	POACEAE-M	*Poa compressa*
Kentucky	POACEAE-M	*Poa pratensis*
marsh	POACEAE-M	*Poa paludigena*
Meadow	POACEAE-M	*Poa wolfii*
plains	POACEAE-M	*Poa arida*
woodland	POACEAE-M	*Poa languida*
woodland	POACEAE-M	*Poa sylvestris*
Bluejoint	POACEAE-M	*Calamagrostis canadensis*
Bluestem, big	POACEAE-M	*Andropogon gerardii*
little	POACEAE-M	*Schizachyrium scoparium*
sand	POACEAE-M	*Andropogon hallii*
Bluets	RUBIACEAE-D	*Hedyotis crassifolia*
Bluevine	ASCLEPIADACEAE-D	*Cynanchum laeve*
Blueweed	BORAGINACEAE-D	*Echium vulgare*
Boneset	ASTERACEAE-D	*Eupatorium perfoliatum*
false	ASTERACEAE-D	*Brickellia eupatorioides*
late	ASTERACEAE-D	*Eupatorium serotinum*
upland	ASTERACEAE-D	*Eupatorium sessilifolium* var. *brittonianum*
Bouncing Bet	CARYOPHYLLACEAE-D	*Saponaria officinalis*
Brier, sensitive	FABACEAE-D	*Schrankia nuttallii*

Brome, Canada	POACEAE-M	*Bromus pubescens*
Japanese	POACEAE-M	*Bromus japonicus*
smooth	POACEAE-M	*Bromus inermis*
Brookline, American	SCROPHULARIACEAE-D	*Veronica americana*
Broomrape	OROBANCHACEAE-D	*Orobanche ludoviciana*
clustered	OROBANCHACEAE-D	*Orobanche fasciculata*
Broomsedge	POACEAE-M	*Andropogon virginicus*
Broomweed	ASTERACEAE-D	*Gutierrezia dracunculoides*
Brown-eyed Susan	ASTERACEAE-D	*Rudbeckia triloba*
Buckbean	MENYANTHACEAE-D	*Menyanthes trifoliata*
Buckbrush	CAPRIFOLIACEAE-D	*Symphoricarpos occidentalis*
Buckbrush	CAPRIFOLIACEAE-D	*Symphoricarpos orbiculatus*
Buckeye, Ohio	HIPPOCASTANACEAE-D	*Aesculus glabra*
Buckthorn, alder	RHAMNACEAE-D	*Rhamnus alnifolia*
common	RHAMNACEAE-D	*Rhamnus cathartica*
glossy	RHAMNACEAE-D	*Rhamnus frangula*
lance-leaved	RHAMNACEAE-D	*Rhamnus lanceolata*
Buckwheat	POLYGONACEAE-D	*Fagopyrum esculentum*
climbing false	POLYGONACEAE-D	*Polygonum scandens*
Bugbane	RANUNCULACEAE-D	*Cimicifuga racemosa*
Bugleweed, northern	LAMIACEAE-D	*Lycopus uniflorus*
Bulrush, dark green	CYPERACEAE-M	*Scirpus atrovirens*
hard-stemmed	CYPERACEAE-M	*Scirpus acutus*
pale	CYPERACEAE-M	*Scirpus pallidus*
prairie	CYPERACEAE-M	*Scirpus maritimus*
river	CYPERACEAE-M	*Scirpus fluviatilis*
soft-stemmed	CYPERACEAE-M	*Scirpus validus* var. *creber*
wooly	CYPERACEAE-M	*Scirpus cyperinus*
Bunch-flower	LILIACEAE-M	*Melanthium virginicum*
Bunchberry	CORNACEAE-D	*Cornus canadensis*
Bur-cucumber	CUCURBITACEAE-D	*Sicyos angulatus*
Bur, buffalo	SOLANACEAE-D	*Solanum rostratum*
Burdock, common	ASTERACEAE-D	*Arctium minus*
great	ASTERACEAE-D	*Arctium lappa*
Burhead	ALISMATACEAE-M	*Echinodorus cordifolius*
Burning bush	CELASTRACEAE-D	*Euonymus alatus*
Burning bush	CELASTRACEAE-D	*Euonymus atropurpureus*
Butter & eggs	SCROPHULARIACEAE-D	*Linaria vulgaris*
Buttercup, creeping	RANUNCULACEAE-D	*Ranunculus repens*
early	RANUNCULACEAE-D	*Ranunculus fascicularis*
hooked	RANUNCULACEAE-D	*Ranunculus recurvatus*
prairie	RANUNCULACEAE-D	*Ranunculus rhomboideus*
swamp	RANUNCULACEAE-D	*Ranunculus septentrionalis*
Butterfly weed	ASCLEPIADACEAE-D	*Asclepias tuberosa* ssp. *interior*

Butternut	JUGLANDACEAE-D	*Juglans cinerea*
Butterweed	ASTERACEAE-D	*Senecio glabellus*
Buttonbush	RUBIACEAE-D	*Cephalanthus occidentalis*
Buttonweed	RUBIACEAE-D	*Diodia teres*
Caltrop	ZYGOPHYLLACEAE-D	*Tribulis terrestris*
Camass, eastern	LILIACEAE-M	*Camassia scilloides*
white	LILIACEAE-M	*Zigadenus elegans*
white	LILIACEAE-M	*Zigadenus glaucus*
Campion, bladder	CARYOPHYLLACEAE-D	*Silene vulgaris*
starry	CARYOPHYLLACEAE-D	*Silene stellata*
white	CARYOPHYLLACEAE-D	*Silene pratensis*
Cancer-root	OROBANCHACEAE-D	*Conopholis americana*
one-flowered	OROBANCHACEAE-D	*Orobanche uniflora*
Candy tuft	BRASSICACEAE-D	*Iberis umbellata*
Cardinal flower	CAMPANULACEAE-D	*Lobelia cardinalis*
Carpetweed	AIZOACEAE-D	*Mollugo verticillata*
Carrion flower	LILIACEAE-M	*Smilax ecirrhata*
Carrion flower	LILIACEAE-M	*Smilax herbacea*
Catalpa, common	BIGNONIACEAE-D	*Catalpa bignonioides*
Catchfly	CARYOPHYLLACEAE-D	*Silene dichotoma*
night-flowering	CARYOPHYLLACEAE-D	*Silene noctiflora*
sleepy	CARYOPHYLLACEAE-D	*Silene antirrhina*
Catnip	LAMIACEAE-D	*Nepeta cataria*
Cattail, common	TYPHACEAE-M	*Typha latifolia*
hybrid	TYPHACEAE-M	*Typha X glauca*
narrow-leaved	TYPHACEAE-M	*Typha angustifolia*
Cedar, eastern white	CUPRESSACEAE-G	*Thuja occidentalis*
ground	LYCOPODIACEAE-P	*Lycopodium digitatum*
red	CUPRESSACEAE-G	*Juniperus virginiana*
Celandine	PAPAVERACEAE-D	*Chelidonium majus*
Chamomile, field	ASTERACEAE-D	*Anthemis arvensis*
wild	ASTERACEAE-D	*Matricaria chamomilla*
Charlock	BRASSICACEAE-D	*Sinapis arvensis*
Cheeses	MALVACEAE-D	*Malva neglecta*
Cherry, annual ground	SOLANACEAE-D	*Physalis pubescens*
choke	ROSACEAE-D	*Prunus virginiana*
dwarf	ROSACEAE-D	*Prunus besseyi*
ground	SOLANACEAE-D	*Physalis heterophylla*
ground	SOLANACEAE-D	*Physalis virginiana*
pin	ROSACEAE-D	*Prunus pensylvanica*
sand	ROSACEAE-D	*Prunus pumila*
wild black	ROSACEAE-D	*Prunus serotina*
Chervil	APIACEAE-D	*Chaerophyllum procumbens*
Chess, downy	POACEAE-M	*Bromus tectorum*
hairy	POACEAE-M	*Bromus commutatus*

Chestnut, American	FAGACEAE-D	*Castanea dentata*
horse	HIPPOCASTANACEAE-D	*Aesculus hippocastanum*
Chickweed, clammy	CARYOPHYLLACEAE-D	*Cerastium glomeratum*
common	CARYOPHYLLACEAE-D	*Stellaria media*
field	CARYOPHYLLACEAE-D	*Cerastium arvense*
giant	CARYOPHYLLACEAE-D	*Myosoton aquaticum*
jagged	CARYOPHYLLACEAE-D	*Holosteum umbellatum*
low forked	CARYOPHYLLACEAE-D	*Paronychia fastigiata*
mouse-ear	CARYOPHYLLACEAE-D	*Cerastium vulgatum*
nodding	CARYOPHYLLACEAE-D	*Cerastium nutans*
tall forked	CARYOPHYLLACEAE-D	*Paronychia canadensis*
Chicory	ASTERACEAE-D	*Cichorium intybus*
Chokeberry, black	ROSACEAE-D	*Aronia melanocarpa*
Cigar tree	BIGNONIACEAE-D	*Catalpa speciosa*
Cinquefoil, brook	ROSACEAE-D	*Potentilla rivalis*
bushy	ROSACEAE-D	*Potentilla paradoxa*
common	ROSACEAE-D	*Potentilla simplex*
marsh	ROSACEAE-D	*Potentilla palustris*
Norwegian	ROSACEAE-D	*Potentilla norvegica*
shrubby	ROSACEAE-D	*Potentilla fruticosa*
sulphur	ROSACEAE-D	*Potentilla recta*
three-toothed	ROSACEAE-D	*Potentilla tridentata*
Clammy weed	CAPPARIDACEAE-D	*Polanisia dodecandra*
Clammy weed	CAPPARIDACEAE-D	*Polanisia dodecandra* ssp. *trachysperma*
Clearweed	URTICACEAE-D	*Pilea pumila*
bog	URTICACEAE-D	*Pilea fontana*
Cleavers	RUBIACEAE-D	*Galium aparine*
Cliff-brake, purple	ADIANTACEAE-P	*Pellaea atropurpurea*
smooth	ADIANTACEAE-P	*Pellaea glabella*
Clover, alsike	FABACEAE-D	*Trifolium hybridum*
buffalo	FABACEAE-D	*Trifolium reflexum*
creeping bush	FABACEAE-D	*Lespedeza repens*
crimson	FABACEAE-D	*Trifolium incarnatum*
Japanese	FABACEAE-D	*Kummerowia striata*
Korean	FABACEAE-D	*Kummerowia stipulacea*
Persian	FABACEAE-D	*Trifolium resupinatum*
pin	GERANIACEAE-D	*Erodium cicutarium*
prairie bush	FABACEAE-D	*Lespedeza leptostachya*
purple prairie	FABACEAE-D	*Dalea purpurea*
rabbit-foot	FABACEAE-D	*Trifolium arvense*
red	FABACEAE-D	*Trifolium pratense*
round-headed bush	FABACEAE-D	*Lespedeza capitata*
silky bush	FABACEAE-D	*Lespedeza cuneata*
silky prairie	FABACEAE-D	*Dalea villosa*
slender bush	FABACEAE-D	*Lespedeza virginica*

Clover, cont.		
stinking	CAPPARIDACEAE-D	*Cleome serrulata*
violet bush	FABACEAE-D	*Lespedeza violacea*
white	FABACEAE-D	*Trifolium repens*
white prairie	FABACEAE-D	*Dalea candida*
white sweet	FABACEAE-D	*Melilotus alba*
yellow sweet	FABACEAE-D	*Melilotus officinalis*
Clubmoss, bog	LYCOPODIACEAE-P	*Lycopodium inundatum*
rock	LYCOPODIACEAE-P	*Lycopodium porophilum*
shining	LYCOPODIACEAE-P	*Lycopodium lucidulum*
tree	LYCOPODIACEAE-P	*Lycopodium dendroideum*
Coast blite	CHENOPODIACEAE-D	*Chenopodium rubrum*
Cocklebur	ASTERACEAE-D	*Xanthium strumarium*
spiny	ASTERACEAE-D	*Xanthium spinosum*
Columbine	RANUNCULACEAE-D	*Aquilegia canadensis*
Common orach	CHENOPODIACEAE-D	*Atriplex patula*
Compass plant	ASTERACEAE-D	*Silphium laciniatum*
Coneflower, fragrant	ASTERACEAE-D	*Rudbeckia subtomentosa*
gray-headed	ASTERACEAE-D	*Ratibida pinnata*
long-headed	ASTERACEAE-D	*Ratibida columnifera*
pale	ASTERACEAE-D	*Echinacea pallida*
purple	ASTERACEAE-D	*Echinacea angustifolia*
purple	ASTERACEAE-D	*Echinacea purpurea*
tall	ASTERACEAE-D	*Rudbeckia laciniata*
Coontail	CERATOPHYLLACEAE-D	*Ceratophyllum demersum*
Coral-root, spotted	ORCHIDACEAE-M	*Corallorhiza maculata*
Coralberry	CAPRIFOLIACEAE-D	*Symphoricarpos orbiculatus*
Coreopsis, golden	ASTERACEAE-D	*Coreopsis tinctoria*
large-flowered	ASTERACEAE-D	*Coreopsis grandiflora*
prairie	ASTERACEAE-D	*Coreopsis palmata*
tickseed	ASTERACEAE-D	*Coreopsis lanceolata*
Corn cockle	CARYOPHYLLACEAE-D	*Agrostemma githago*
Corn-gromwell	BORAGINACEAE-D	*Lithospermum arvense*
Corn, cultivated	POACEAE-M	*Zea mays*
squirrel	PAPAVERACEAE-D	*Dicentra canadensis*
Cornel, dwarf	CORNACEAE-D	*Cornus canadensis*
Cornflower	ASTERACEAE-D	*Centaurea cyanus*
Corydalis, golden	PAPAVERACEAE-D	*Corydalis aurea*
pink	PAPAVERACEAE-D	*Corydalis sempervirens*
Cotton-grass, slender	CYPERACEAE-M	*Eriophorum gracile*
tall	CYPERACEAE-M	*Eriophorum angustifolium*
Cottonweed	AMARANTHACEAE-D	*Froelichia floridana* var. *campestris*
Cottonweed	AMARANTHACEAE-D	*Froelichia gracilis*
Cottonwood	SALICACEAE-D	*Populus deltoides*
Cow cockle	CARYOPHYLLACEAE-D	*Vaccaria pyramidata*

Cowbane	APIACEAE-D	*Oxypolis rigidior*
Cowherb	CARYOPHYLLACEAE-D	*Vaccaria pyramidata*
Crab, wild	ROSACEAE-D	*Malus ioensis*
Crabgrass, common	POACEAE-M	*Digitaria sanguinalis*
smooth	POACEAE-M	*Digitaria ischaemum*
Cranberry, highbush	CAPRIFOLIACEAE-D	*Viburnum trilobum*
Cranesbill	GERANIACEAE-D	*Geranium carolinianum*
northern	GERANIACEAE-D	*Geranium bicknellii*
Creeper, trumpet	BIGNONIACEAE-D	*Campsis radicans*
Virginia	VITACEAE-D	*Parthenocissus quinquefolia*
Creeping Charlie	LAMIACEAE-D	*Glechoma hederacea*
Creeping Jenny	CONVOLVULACEAE-D	*Convolvulus arvensis*
Cress, Austrian field	BRASSICACEAE-D	*Rorippa austriaca*
bitter	BRASSICACEAE-D	*Cardamine pensylvanica*
creeping yellow	BRASSICACEAE-D	*Rorippa sylvestris*
field	BRASSICACEAE-D	*Lepidium campestre*
hoary	BRASSICACEAE-D	*Cardaria draba*
lake	BRASSICACEAE-D	*Armoracia aquatica*
marsh	BRASSICACEAE-D	*Rorippa palustris*
penny	BRASSICACEAE-D	*Thlaspi arvense*
purple	BRASSICACEAE-D	*Cardamine douglassii*
purple rock	BRASSICACEAE-D	*Arabis divaricarpa*
rock	BRASSICACEAE-D	*Arabis canadensis*
rock	BRASSICACEAE-D	*Arabis drummondii*
rock	BRASSICACEAE-D	*Arabis shortii*
small-flowered bitter	BRASSICACEAE-D	*Cardamine parviflora* var. *arenicola*
spring	BRASSICACEAE-D	*Cardamine bulbosa*
Croton, Texas	EUPHORBIACEAE-D	*Croton texensis*
Crowfoot, bristly	RANUNCULACEAE-D	*Ranunculus pensylvanicus*
cursed	RANUNCULACEAE-D	*Ranunculus sceleratus*
seaside	RANUNCULACEAE-D	*Ranunculus cymbalaria*
small-flowered	RANUNCULACEAE-D	*Ranunculus abortivus*
white water	RANUNCULACEAE-D	*Ranunculus longirostris*
yellow water	RANUNCULACEAE-D	*Ranunculus flabellaris*
Cucumber, wild	CUCURBITACEAE-D	*Echinocystis lobata*
Cudweed, early	ASTERACEAE-D	*Gnaphalium purpureum*
Culver's root	SCROPHULARIACEAE-D	*Veronicastrum virginicum*
Cup plant	ASTERACEAE-D	*Silphium perfoliatum*
Currant, buffalo	SAXIFRAGACEAE-D	*Ribes odoratum*
garden	SAXIFRAGACEAE-D	*Ribes sativum*
northern	SAXIFRAGACEAE-D	*Ribes hudsonianum*
wild black	SAXIFRAGACEAE-D	*Ribes americanum*
Cut-grass, rice	POACEAE-M	*Leersia oryzoides*
Cypress, standing	POLEMONIACEAE-D	*Ipomopsis rubra*
summer	CHENOPODIACEAE-D	*Kochia scoparia*

Daisy, ox-eye	ASTERACEAE-D	*Leucanthemum vulgare*
Peruvian	ASTERACEAE-D	*Galinsoga parviflora*
Peruvian	ASTERACEAE-D	*Galinsoga quadriradiata*
Dalea, foxtail	FABACEAE-D	*Dalea leporina*
Dame's rocket	BRASSICACEAE-D	*Hesperis matronalis*
Dandelion, common	ASTERACEAE-D	*Taraxacum officinale*
dwarf	ASTERACEAE-D	*Krigia virginica*
false	ASTERACEAE-D	*Krigia biflora*
false	ASTERACEAE-D	*Pyrrhopappus carolinianus*
prairie	ASTERACEAE-D	*Nothocalais cuspidata*
red-seeded	ASTERACEAE-D	*Taraxacum laevigatum*
Darnel	POACEAE-M	*Lolium temulentum*
Dewberry	ROSACEAE-D	*Rubus flagellaris*
Dewberry	ROSACEAE-D	*Rubus hispidus*
Dock, bitter	POLYGONACEAE-D	*Rumex obtusifolius*
curly	POLYGONACEAE-D	*Rumex crispus*
prairie	ASTERACEAE-D	*Silphium terebinthinaceum*
Dog fennel	ASTERACEAE-D	*Anthemis cotula*
Dogbane, intermediate	APOCYNACEAE-D	*Apocynum X medium*
spreading	APOCYNACEAE-D	*Apocynum androsaemifolium*
Dogtooth-violet, white	LILIACEAE-M	*Erythronium albidum*
yellow	LILIACEAE-M	*Erythronium americanum*
Dogwood, alternate-leaved	CORNACEAE-D	*Cornus alternifolia*
gray	CORNACEAE-D	*Cornus foemina* ssp. *racemosa*
pagoda	CORNACEAE-D	*Cornus alternifolia*
red-osier	CORNACEAE-D	*Cornus stolonifera*
rough-leaved	CORNACEAE-D	*Cornus drummondii*
round-leaved	CORNACEAE-D	*Cornus rugosa*
silky	CORNACEAE-D	*Cornus amomum* ssp. *obliqua*
speckled	CORNACEAE-D	*Cornus rugosa*
Downy painted cup	SCROPHULARIACEAE-D	*Castilleja sessiliflora*
Dragonhead	LAMIACEAE-D	*Dracocephalum parviflorum*
false	LAMIACEAE-D	*Physostegia virginiana*
small-flowered false	LAMIACEAE-D	*Physostegia parviflora*
Dropseed	POACEAE-M	*Sporobolus asper*
prairie	POACEAE-M	*Sporobolus heterolepis*
sand	POACEAE-M	*Sporobolus cryptandrus*
Duckweed	LEMNACEAE-M	*Lemna minor*
greater	LEMNACEAE-M	*Spirodela polyrhiza*
star	LEMNACEAE-M	*Lemna trisulca*
Dutchman's breeches	PAPAVERACEAE-D	*Dicentra cucullaria*
Dyer's rocket	RESEDACEAE-D	*Reseda luteola*
Elder, box	ACERACEAE-D	*Acer negundo*

Elder, cont.		
common	CAPRIFOLIACEAE-D	*Sambucus canadensis*
marsh	ASTERACEAE-D	*Iva xanthifolia*
red-berried	CAPRIFOLIACEAE-D	*Sambucus racemosa* ssp. *pubens*
Elderberry	CAPRIFOLIACEAE-D	*Sambucus canadensis*
Elecampane	ASTERACEAE-D	*Inula helenium*
Elm, American	ULMACEAE-D	*Ulmus americana*
cork	ULMACEAE-D	*Ulmus thomasii*
red	ULMACEAE-D	*Ulmus rubra*
rock	ULMACEAE-D	*Ulmus thomasii*
Siberian	ULMACEAE-D	*Ulmus pumila*
slippery	ULMACEAE-D	*Ulmus rubra*
Everlasting	ASTERACEAE-D	*Gnaphalium obtusifolium*
False heather	CISTACEAE-D	*Hudsonia tomentosa*
False medic	POACEAE-M	*Schizachne purpurascens*
False pennyroyal	LAMIACEAE-D	*Trichostema brachiatum*
Fameflower	PORTULACACEAE-D	*Talinum rugospermum*
prairie	PORTULACACEAE-D	*Talinum parviflorum*
Fern, Boott's wood	ASPLENIACEAE-P	*Dryopteris X boottii*
bracken	DENNSTAEDTIACEAE-P	*Pteridium aquilinum* var. *latiusculum*
broad beech	ASPLENIACEAE-P	*Thelypteris hexagonoptera*
bulblet bladder	ASPLENIACEAE-P	*Cystopteris bulbifera*
Christmas	ASPLENIACEAE-P	*Polystichum acrostichoides*
cinnamon	OSMUNDACEAE-P	*Osmunda cinnamomea*
common polypody	POLYPODIACEAE-P	*Polypodium virginianum*
creeping fragile	ASPLENIACEAE-P	*Cystopteris protrusa*
crested wood	ASPLENIACEAE-P	*Dryopteris cristata*
dissected grape	OPHIOGLOSSACEAE-P	*Botrychium dissectum* f. *dissectum*
fragile	ASPLENIACEAE-P	*Cystopteris fragilis*
fragile	ASPLENIACEAE-P	*Cystopteris tenuis*
glandular wood	ASPLENIACEAE-P	*Dryopteris intermedia*
Goldie's wood	ASPLENIACEAE-P	*Dryopteris goldiana*
hybrid wood	ASPLENIACEAE-P	*Dryopteris X triploidea*
interrupted	OSMUNDACEAE-P	*Osmunda claytoniana*
leathery grape	OPHIOGLOSSACEAE-P	*Botrychium multifidum*
limestone oak	ASPLENIACEAE-P	*Gymnocarpium robertianum*
little grape	OPHIOGLOSSACEAE-P	*Botrychium simplex*
long beech	ASPLENIACEAE-P	*Thelypteris phegopteris*
marginal shield	ASPLENIACEAE-P	*Dryopteris marginalis*
marsh	ASPLENIACEAE-P	*Thelypteris palustris* var. *pubescens*
mosquito	AZOLLACEAE-P	*Azolla mexicana*

Fern, cont.		
northern fragile	ASPLENIACEAE-P	*Cystopteris X laurentiana*
northern lady	ASPLENIACEAE-P	*Athyrium filix-femina* var. *angustum*
northern maidenhair	ADIANTACEAE-P	*Adiantum pedatum*
oak	ASPLENIACEAE-P	*Gymnocarpium dryopteris*
oblique grape	OPHIOGLOSSACEAE-P	*Botrychium dissectum* f. *obliquum*
ostrich	ASPLENIACEAE-P	*Matteuccia struthiopteris* var. *pensylvanica*
rattlesnake	OPHIOGLOSSACEAE-P	*Botrychium virginianum*
royal	OSMUNDACEAE-P	*Osmunda regalis* var. *spectabilis*
sensitive	ASPLENIACEAE-P	*Onoclea sensibilis*
slender lip	ADIANTACEAE-P	*Cheilanthes feei*
slender rockbrake	ADIANTACEAE-P	*Cryptogramma stelleri*
southern bladder	ASPLENIACEAE-P	*Cystopteris X tennesseensis*
spinulose wood	ASPLENIACEAE-P	*Dryopteris carthusiana*
walking	ASPLENIACEAE-P	*Asplenium rhizophyllum*
Fescue, alta	POACEAE-M	*Festuca arundinacea*
Meadow	POACEAE-M	*Festuca pratensis*
nodding	POACEAE-M	*Festuca obtusa*
red	POACEAE-M	*Festuca rubra*
sheep	POACEAE-M	*Festuca ovina*
six-weeks	POACEAE-M	*Festuca octoflora* var. *tenella*
Feverfew	ASTERACEAE-D	*Parthenium integrifolium*
Fir, balsam	PINACEAE-G	*Abies balsamea*
Firepink	CARYOPHYLLACEAE-D	*Silene virginica*
Fireweed	ASTERACEAE-D	*Erechtites hieracifolia*
Fireweed	ONAGRACEAE-D	*Epilobium angustifolium*
Flax	LINACEAE-D	*Linum perenne*
cultivated	LINACEAE-D	*Linum usitatissimum*
false	BRASSICACEAE-D	*Camelina sativa*
small-fruited false	BRASSICACEAE-D	*Camelina microcarpa*
stiff	LINACEAE-D	*Linum rigidum*
wild	LINACEAE-D	*Linum medium* var. *texanum*
wild	LINACEAE-D	*Linum sulcatum*
Fleabane	ASTERACEAE-D	*Erigeron philadelphicus*
annual	ASTERACEAE-D	*Erigeron annuus*
daisy	ASTERACEAE-D	*Erigeron strigosus*
marsh	ASTERACEAE-D	*Senecio congestus*
Flower-of-an-hour	MALVACEAE-D	*Hibiscus trionum*
Fogfruit	VERBENACEAE-D	*Phyla lanceolata*
Forget-me-not	BORAGINACEAE-D	*Myosotis verna*

Four-o'clock, hairy	NYCTAGINACEAE-D	*Mirabilis hirsuta*
pale	NYCTAGINACEAE-D	*Mirabilis albida*
wild	NYCTAGINACEAE-D	*Mirabilis nyctaginea*
Foxglove, clammy false	SCROPHULARIACEAE-D	*Aureolaria pedicularia*
yellow false	SCROPHULARIACEAE-D	*Aureolaria grandiflora* var. *pulchra*
Foxtail	POACEAE-M	*Alopecurus aequalis*
bristly	POACEAE-M	*Setaria verticillata*
common	POACEAE-M	*Alopecurus carolinianus*
giant	POACEAE-M	*Setaria faberi*
green	POACEAE-M	*Setaria viridis*
Meadow	POACEAE-M	*Alopecurus pratensis*
yellow	POACEAE-M	*Setaria glauca*
Frost weed	ASTERACEAE-D	*Aster ericoides*
Fumewort, slender	PAPAVERACEAE-D	*Corydalis micrantha*
Fumitory	PAPAVERACEAE-D	*Fumaria officinalis*
Gaillardia, rose-ring	ASTERACEAE-D	*Gaillardia pulchella*
Garden rocket	BRASSICACEAE-D	*Eruca sativa*
Garlic, field	LILIACEAE-M	*Allium vineale*
Gentian, bottle	GENTIANACEAE-D	*Gentiana andrewsii*
closed	GENTIANACEAE-D	*Gentiana andrewsii*
downy	GENTIANACEAE-D	*Gentiana puberulenta*
fringed	GENTIANACEAE-D	*Gentianopsis crinita*
pale	GENTIANACEAE-D	*Gentiana alba*
prairie rose	GENTIANACEAE-D	*Sabatia campestris*
small fringed	GENTIANACEAE-D	*Gentianopsis procera*
soapwort	GENTIANACEAE-D	*Gentiana X billingtonii*
stiff	GENTIANACEAE-D	*Gentianella quinquefolia* ssp. *occidentalis*
yellow	GENTIANACEAE-D	*Gentiana alba*
Geranium, wild	GERANIACEAE-D	*Geranium maculatum*
Germander	LAMIACEAE-D	*Teucrium canadense* var. *boreale*
American	LAMIACEAE-D	*Teucrium canadense*
Giant-hyssop, blue	LAMIACEAE-D	*Agastache foeniculum*
purple	LAMIACEAE-D	*Agastache scrophulariifolia*
yellow	LAMIACEAE-D	*Agastache nepetoides*
Ginseng	ARALIACEAE-D	*Panax quinquefolius*
Goat's-beard	ASTERACEAE-D	*Tragopogon dubius*
Goat's-beard	ASTERACEAE-D	*Tragopogon pratensis*
Goat's beard	ROSACEAE-D	*Aruncus dioicus*
Goat's-rue	FABACEAE-D	*Tephrosia virginiana*
Golden alexanders	APIACEAE-D	*Zizia aurea*
Goldenrod, cliff	ASTERACEAE-D	*Solidago sciaphila*
elm-leaved	ASTERACEAE-D	*Solidago ulmifolia*

Goldenrod, cont.		
field	ASTERACEAE-D	*Solidago nemoralis*
Missouri	ASTERACEAE-D	*Solidago missouriensis*
Riddell's	ASTERACEAE-D	*Solidago riddellii*
showy	ASTERACEAE-D	*Solidago speciosa*
smooth	ASTERACEAE-D	*Solidago gigantea*
stiff	ASTERACEAE-D	*Solidago rigida*
swamp	ASTERACEAE-D	*Solidago uliginosa*
tall	ASTERACEAE-D	*Solidago canadensis*
zig-zag	ASTERACEAE-D	*Solidago flexicaulis*
Gooseberry, prickly	SAXIFRAGACEAE-D	*Ribes cynosbati*
wild	SAXIFRAGACEAE-D	*Ribes missouriense*
Goosefoot, many-seeded	CHENOPODIACEAE-D	*Chenopodium polyspermum*
maple-leaved	CHENOPODIACEAE-D	*Chenopodium hybridum*
narrow-leaved	CHENOPODIACEAE-D	*Chenopodium desiccatum*
woodland	CHENOPODIACEAE-D	*Chenopodium standleyanum*
Gourd, Missouri	CUCURBITACEAE-D	*Cucurbita foetidissima*
Grama, blue	POACEAE-M	*Bouteloua gracilis*
hairy	POACEAE-M	*Bouteloua hirsuta*
side-oats	POACEAE-M	*Bouteloua curtipendula*
Grape, fox	VITACEAE-D	*Vitis cinerea*
frost	VITACEAE-D	*Vitis vulpina*
raccoon	VITACEAE-D	*Ampelopsis cordata*
riverbank	VITACEAE-D	*Vitis riparia*
summer	VITACEAE-D	*Vitis aestivalis*
winter	VITACEAE-D	*Vitis cinerea*
Grass of Parnassus	SAXIFRAGACEAE-D	*Parnassia glauca*
Grass, American manna	POACEAE-M	*Glyceria grandis*
American slough	POACEAE-M	*Beckmannia syzigachne*
annual rye	POACEAE-M	*Lolium perenne* var. *italicum*
bead	POACEAE-M	*Paspalum setaceum* var. *ciliatifolium*
bottlebrush	POACEAE-M	*Hystrix patula*
broad-leaved panic	POACEAE-M	*Dichanthelium latifolium*
buffalo	POACEAE-M	*Buchloe dactyloides*
Canada brome	POACEAE-M	*Bromus ciliatus*
canary	POACEAE-M	*Phalaris canariensis*
catchfly	POACEAE-M	*Leersia lenticularis*
cheat	POACEAE-M	*Bromus secalinus*
cord	POACEAE-M	*Spartina pectinata*
cup	POACEAE-M	*Eriochloa villosa*
deertongue	POACEAE-M	*Dichanthelium clandestinum*
eastern manna	POACEAE-M	*Glyceria septentrionalis*
European alkali	POACEAE-M	*Puccinellia distans*
finger	POACEAE-M	*Digitaria filiformis*

Grass, cont.		
fowl manna	POACEAE-M	*Glyceria striata*
fowl meadow	POACEAE-M	*Poa palustris*
gama	POACEAE-M	*Tripsacum dactyloides*
goat	POACEAE-M	*Aegilops cylindrica*
goose	POACEAE-M	*Eleusine indica*
holy	POACEAE-M	*Hierochloe odorata*
Indian	POACEAE-M	*Sorghastrum nutans*
Johnson	POACEAE-M	*Sorghum halepense*
June	POACEAE-M	*Koeleria macrantha*
knee	POACEAE-M	*Panicum dichotomiflorum*
Leiberg's panic	POACEAE-M	*Dichanthelium leibergii*
manna	POACEAE-M	*Glyceria borealis*
Meadow	POACEAE-M	*Poa trivialis*
northern reed	POACEAE-M	*Calamagrostis inexpansa*
orchard	POACEAE-M	*Dactylis glomerata*
perennial rye	POACEAE-M	*Lolium perenne*
plume	POACEAE-M	*Miscanthus sacchariflorus*
pony	POACEAE-M	*Eragrostis hypnoides*
porcupine	POACEAE-M	*Stipa spartea*
poverty	POACEAE-M	*Sporobolus vaginiflorus*
poverty oat	POACEAE-M	*Danthonia spicata*
quack	POACEAE-M	*Agropyron repens*
reed canary	POACEAE-M	*Phalaris arundinacea*
salt	POACEAE-M	*Distichlis spicata* var. *stricta*
salt meadow	POACEAE-M	*Leptochloa fascicularis*
sand	POACEAE-M	*Triplasis purpurea*
sea-beach	POACEAE-M	*Aristida tuberculosa*
slim-leaved panic	POACEAE-M	*Dichanthelium linearifolium*
slough	POACEAE-M	*Spartina pectinata*
southern crab	POACEAE-M	*Digitaria ciliaris*
spear	POACEAE-M	*Stipa comata*
Sudan	POACEAE-M	*Sorghum sudanense*
three-flowered melic	POACEAE-M	*Melica nitens*
two-flowered melic	POACEAE-M	*Melica mutica*
velvet	POACEAE-M	*Holcus lanatus*
vernal whitlow	BRASSICACEAE-D	*Draba verna*
whitlow	BRASSICACEAE-D	*Draba reptans*
widgeon	RUPPIACEAE-M	*Ruppia maritima*
windmill	POACEAE-M	*Chloris verticillata*
yellow nut	CYPERACEAE-M	*Cyperus esculentus*
yellow-eyed	XYRIDACEAE-M	*Xyris torta*
Green dragon	ARACEAE-M	*Arisaema dracontium*
Greenbrier	LILIACEAE-M	*Smilax hispida*
Gromwell, American	BORAGINACEAE-D	*Lithospermum latifolium*

Gromwell, cont.		
false	BORAGINACEAE-D	*Onosmodium molle* var. *hispidissimum*
false	BORAGINACEAE-D	*Onosmodium molle* var. *occidentale*
Ground-nut	FABACEAE-D	*Apios americana*
Ground pine	LYCOPODIACEAE-P	*Lycopodium clavatum*
Groundsel, common	ASTERACEAE-D	*Senecio vulgaris*
Guelder-rose	CAPRIFOLIACEAE-D	*Viburnum opulus*
Gum plant	ASTERACEAE-D	*Grindelia squarrosa*
Hackberry	ULMACEAE-D	*Celtis occidentalis*
Hairgrass	POACEAE-M	*Agrostis hyemalis* var. *tenuis*
Harebell	CAMPANULACEAE-D	*Campanula rotundifolia*
Haw, black	CAPRIFOLIACEAE-D	*Viburnum prunifolium*
Hawksbeard	ASTERACEAE-D	*Crepis runcinata*
Hawkweed	ASTERACEAE-D	*Hieracium canadense*
Hawkweed	ASTERACEAE-D	*Hieracium longipilum*
rough	ASTERACEAE-D	*Hieracium scabrum*
Hawthorn, cockspur	ROSACEAE-D	*Crataegus crus-galli*
Hazelnut	BETULACEAE-D	*Corylus americana*
Heliotrope, garden	VALERIANACEAE-D	*Valeriana officinalis*
Hellebore, false	LILIACEAE-M	*Veratrum woodii*
Hemlock, bulblet water	APIACEAE-D	*Cicuta bulbifera*
poison	APIACEAE-D	*Conium maculatum*
water	APIACEAE-D	*Cicuta maculata*
Hemp	MORACEAE-D	*Cannabis sativa*
bog	URTICACEAE-D	*Boehmeria cylindrica*
Indian	APOCYNACEAE-D	*Apocynum cannabinum*
water	AMARANTHACEAE-D	*Amaranthus tuberculatus*
Henbit	LAMIACEAE-D	*Lamium amplexicaule*
Hickory, bitternut	JUGLANDACEAE-D	*Carya cordiformis*
kingnut	JUGLANDACEAE-D	*Carya laciniosa*
mockernut	JUGLANDACEAE-D	*Carya tomentosa*
shagbark	JUGLANDACEAE-D	*Carya ovata*
Hog peanut	FABACEAE-D	*Amphicarpaea bracteata*
Hollyhock	MALVACEAE-D	*Alcea rosea*
Honewort	APIACEAE-D	*Cryptotaenia canadensis*
Honeysuckle, bush	CAPRIFOLIACEAE-D	*Diervilla lonicera*
Morrow's	CAPRIFOLIACEAE-D	*Lonicera morrowi*
Tartarian	CAPRIFOLIACEAE-D	*Lonicera tatarica*
trumpet	CAPRIFOLIACEAE-D	*Lonicera sempervirens*
wild	CAPRIFOLIACEAE-D	*Lonicera dioica* var. *glaucescens*
wild	CAPRIFOLIACEAE-D	*Lonicera prolifera*

Common name	Family	Scientific name
Hop-clover	FABACEAE-D	*Trifolium aureum*
little	FABACEAE-D	*Trifolium dubium*
low	FABACEAE-D	*Trifolium campestre*
Hops, common	MORACEAE-D	*Humulus lupulus*
Japanese	MORACEAE-D	*Humulus japonicus*
Horehound, black	LAMIACEAE-D	*Ballota nigra*
water	LAMIACEAE-D	*Lycopus americanus*
Hornbeam, hop	BETULACEAE-D	*Ostrya virginiana*
Hornwort	CERATOPHYLLACEAE-D	*Ceratophyllum demersum*
Horsemint	LAMIACEAE-D	*Monarda fistulosa*
spotted	LAMIACEAE-D	*Monarda punctata* var. *villicaulis*
Horseradish	BRASSICACEAE-D	*Armoracia rusticana*
Horsetail, common	EQUISETACEAE-P	*Equisetum arvense*
hybrid shore	EQUISETACEAE-P	*Equisetum X litorale*
Meadow	EQUISETACEAE-P	*Equisetum pratense*
swamp	EQUISETACEAE-P	*Equisetum fluviatile*
woodland	EQUISETACEAE-P	*Equisetum sylvaticum*
Horseweed	ASTERACEAE-D	*Conyza canadensis*
low	ASTERACEAE-D	*Conyza ramosissima*
Hound's-tongue	BORAGINACEAE-D	*Cynoglossum officinale*
Huckleberry, black	ERICACEAE-D	*Gaylussacia baccata*
Hyssop, hedge	SCROPHULARIACEAE-D	*Gratiola neglecta*
water	SCROPHULARIACEAE-D	*Bacopa rotundifolia*
Illinois bundle flower	FABACEAE-D	*Desmanthus illinoensis*
Indian paintbrush	SCROPHULARIACEAE-D	*Castilleja coccinea*
Indian pipe	ERICACEAE-D	*Monotropa uniflora*
Indigo bush	FABACEAE-D	*Amorpha fruticosa*
Indigo, blue wild	FABACEAE-D	*Baptisia australis* var. *minor*
cream wild	FABACEAE-D	*Baptisia bracteata* var. *glabrescens*
false	FABACEAE-D	*Amorpha fruticosa*
fragrant false	FABACEAE-D	*Amorpha nana*
white wild	FABACEAE-D	*Baptisia lactea*
yellow wild	FABACEAE-D	*Baptisia tinctoria*
Iris, bearded	IRIDACEAE-M	*Iris X germanica*
Ironweed	ASTERACEAE-D	*Vernonia fasciculata*
Baldwin's	ASTERACEAE-D	*Vernonia baldwinii*
Missouri	ASTERACEAE-D	*Vernonia missurica*
tall	ASTERACEAE-D	*Vernonia gigantea*
Ironwood	BETULACEAE-D	*Ostrya virginiana*
Ivy, ground	LAMIACEAE-D	*Glechoma hederacea*
poison	ANACARDIACEAE-D	*Toxicodendron radicans* ssp. *negundo*

Common name	Family	Scientific name
Ivy, cont.		
Rydberg's poison	ANACARDIACEAE-D	*Toxicodendron rydbergii*
Jack-in-the-pulpit	ARACEAE-M	*Arisaema triphyllum*
Jacob's ladder	POLEMONIACEAE-D	*Polemonium reptans*
Jasmine, rock	PRIMULACEAE-D	*Androsace occidentalis*
Jewel weed	BALSAMINACEAE-D	*Impatiens pallida*
Jeweled shooting star	PRIMULACEAE-D	*Dodecatheon amethystinum*
Jimsonweed	SOLANACEAE-D	*Datura stramonium*
Joe-pye-weed, purple	ASTERACEAE-D	*Eupatorium purpureum*
spotted	ASTERACEAE-D	*Eupatorium maculatum*
Jumpseed	POLYGONACEAE-D	*Polygonum virginianum*
Juniper, common	CUPRESSACEAE-G	*Juniperus communis* var. *depressa*
creeping	CUPRESSACEAE-G	*Juniperus horizontalis*
Kentucky coffee tree	FABACEAE-D	*Gymnocladus dioica*
King-devil	ASTERACEAE-D	*Hieracium aurantiacum*
Kittentails	SCROPHULARIACEAE-D	*Besseya bullii*
Knapweed, black	ASTERACEAE-D	*Centaurea nigra*
Knotweed	POLYGONACEAE-D	*Polygonum aviculare*
bushy	POLYGONACEAE-D	*Polygonum ramosissimum*
Lacegrass	POACEAE-M	*Eragrostis capillaris*
Ladies'-tobacco	ASTERACEAE-D	*Antennaria plantaginifolia*
Ladies'-tresses, great plains	ORCHIDACEAE-M	*Spiranthes magnicamporum*
hooded	ORCHIDACEAE-M	*Spiranthes romanzoffiana*
nodding	ORCHIDACEAE-M	*Spiranthes cernua*
slender	ORCHIDACEAE-M	*Spiranthes lacera*
yellow-lipped	ORCHIDACEAE-M	*Spiranthes lucida*
Lady's thumb	POLYGONACEAE-D	*Polygonum persicaria*
Lamb's quarters	CHENOPODIACEAE-D	*Chenopodium album*
Lambert's crazy weed	FABACEAE-D	*Oxytropis lambertii*
Larkspur, dwarf	RANUNCULACEAE-D	*Delphinium tricorne*
prairie	RANUNCULACEAE-D	*Delphinium virescens*
Lead plant	FABACEAE-D	*Amorpha canescens*
Leaf, velvet	MALVACEAE-D	*Abutilon theophrasti*
Leafcup	ASTERACEAE-D	*Polymnia canadensis*
Leather flower	RANUNCULACEAE-D	*Clematis pitcheri*
Leatherwood	THYMELAEACEAE-D	*Dirca palustris*
Leek	LILIACEAE-M	*Allium porrum*
wild	LILIACEAE-M	*Allium tricoccum*
Lettuce, blue	ASTERACEAE-D	*Lactuca floridana*
glaucous white	ASTERACEAE-D	*Prenanthes racemosa*
prairie	ASTERACEAE-D	*Lactuca ludoviciana*

Lettuce, cont.		
prickly	ASTERACEAE-D	*Lactuca serriola*
rough white	ASTERACEAE-D	*Prenanthes aspera*
tall blue	ASTERACEAE-D	*Lactuca biennis*
white	ASTERACEAE-D	*Prenanthes alba*
wild	ASTERACEAE-D	*Lactuca canadensis*
Licorice, wild	FABACEAE-D	*Glycyrrhiza lepidota*
Lilac	OLEACEAE-D	*Syringa vulgaris*
Lily-of-the-valley	LILIACEAE-M	*Convallaria majalis*
Lily, blackberry	IRIDACEAE-M	*Belamcanda chinensis*
day	LILIACEAE-M	*Hemerocallis fulva*
Michigan	LILIACEAE-M	*Lilium michiganense*
sand	LOASACEAE-D	*Mentzelia decapetala*
tiger	LILIACEAE-M	*Lilium lancifolium*
white water	NYMPHAEACEAE-D	*Nymphaea tuberosa*
wood	LILIACEAE-M	*Lilium philadelphicum* var. *andinum*
yellow water	NYMPHAEACEAE-D	*Nuphar luteum* ssp. *variegatum*
Linden, American	TILIACEAE-D	*Tilia americana*
Liverleaf	RANUNCULACEAE-D	*Hepatica nobilis* var. *acuta*
round-lobed	RANUNCULACEAE-D	*Hepatica nobilis* var. *obtusa*
Lobelia, great	CAMPANULACEAE-D	*Lobelia siphilitica*
Kalm's	CAMPANULACEAE-D	*Lobelia kalmii*
spiked	CAMPANULACEAE-D	*Lobelia spicata*
Locoweed	FABACEAE-D	*Oxytropis lambertii*
Locust, black	FABACEAE-D	*Robinia pseudoacacia*
honey	FABACEAE-D	*Gleditsia triacanthos*
Loosestrife, clustered	MALVACEAE-D	*Callirhoe triangulata*
false	ONAGRACEAE-D	*Ludwigia polycarpa*
fringed	PRIMULACEAE-D	*Lysimachia ciliata*
purple	LYTHRACEAE-D	*Lythrum salicaria*
swamp	LYTHRACEAE-D	*Decodon verticillatus*
swamp	PRIMULACEAE-D	*Lysimachia terrestris*
winged	LYTHRACEAE-D	*Lythrum alatum*
Lopseed	PHRYMACEAE-D	*Phryma leptostachya*
Lotus, American	NYMPHAEACEAE-D	*Nelumbo lutea*
Lousewort	SCROPHULARIACEAE-D	*Pedicularis canadensis*
swamp	SCROPHULARIACEAE-D	*Pedicularis lanceolata*
Lovegrass, purple	POACEAE-M	*Eragrostis spectabilis*
sand	POACEAE-M	*Eragrostis trichodes*
Lungwort, northern	BORAGINACEAE-D	*Mertensia paniculata*
Lupine, wild	FABACEAE-D	*Lupinus perennis*

Madder, wild	RUBIACEAE-D	*Galium obtusum*
Mallow, glade	MALVACEAE-D	*Napaea dioica*
halberd-leaved rose	MALVACEAE-D	*Hibiscus laevis*
high	MALVACEAE-D	*Malva sylvestris*
little	MALVACEAE-D	*Malva parviflora*
prickly	MALVACEAE-D	*Sida spinosa*
purple poppy	MALVACEAE-D	*Callirhoe involucrata*
round-leaved	MALVACEAE-D	*Malva rotundifolia*
scarlet	MALVACEAE-D	*Sphaeralcea coccinea*
Maple, Amur	ACERACEAE-D	*Acer ginnala*
black	ACERACEAE-D	*Acer nigrum*
mountain	ACERACEAE-D	*Acer spicatum*
red	ACERACEAE-D	*Acer rubrum*
silver	ACERACEAE-D	*Acer saccharinum*
sugar	ACERACEAE-D	*Acer saccharum*
Mare's-tail	HIPPURIDACEAE-D	*Hippuris vulgaris*
Marigold, fetid	ASTERACEAE-D	*Dyssodia papposa*
marsh	RANUNCULACEAE-D	*Caltha palustris*
nodding bur	ASTERACEAE-D	*Bidens cernua*
swamp	ASTERACEAE-D	*Bidens aristosa*
water	ASTERACEAE-D	*Megalodonta beckii*
Marijuana	MORACEAE-D	*Cannabis sativa*
Matrimony vine	SOLANACEAE-D	*Lycium halimifolium*
Mayapple	BERBERIDACEAE-D	*Podophyllum peltatum*
Mayflower, Canada	LILIACEAE-M	*Maianthemum canadense*
Meadow beauty	MELASTOMATACEAE-D	*Rhexia virginica*
Meadow-rue, early	RANUNCULACEAE-D	*Thalictrum dioicum*
purple	RANUNCULACEAE-D	*Thalictrum dasycarpum*
waxy	RANUNCULACEAE-D	*Thalictrum revolutum*
Meadowsweet	ROSACEAE-D	*Spiraea alba*
Mermaid weed	HALORAGIDACEAE-D	*Proserpinaca palustris*
Mermaid, false	LIMNANTHACEAE-D	*Floerkea proserpinacoides*
Mexican tea	CHENOPODIACEAE-D	*Chenopodium ambrosioides*
Milfoil, American	HALORAGIDACEAE-D	*Myriophyllum exalbescens*
rough water	HALORAGIDACEAE-D	*Myriophyllum pinnatum*
spiked water	HALORAGIDACEAE-D	*Myriophyllum spicatum*
water	HALORAGIDACEAE-D	*Myriophyllum heterophylum*
Milkweed, common	ASCLEPIADACEAE-D	*Asclepias syriaca*
eared	ASCLEPIADACEAE-D	*Asclepias engelmanniana*
green	ASCLEPIADACEAE-D	*Asclepias viridiflora*
Mead's	ASCLEPIADACEAE-D	*Asclepias meadii*
narrow-leaved	ASCLEPIADACEAE-D	*Asclepias stenophylla*
oval	ASCLEPIADACEAE-D	*Asclepias ovalifolia*
poke	ASCLEPIADACEAE-D	*Asclepias exaltata*
prairie	ASCLEPIADACEAE-D	*Asclepias sullivantii*
purple	ASCLEPIADACEAE-D	*Asclepias purpurascens*

Common name	Family	Scientific name
Milkweed, cont.		
sand	ASCLEPIADACEAE-D	*Asclepias amplexicaulis*
showy	ASCLEPIADACEAE-D	*Asclepias speciosa*
swamp	ASCLEPIADACEAE-D	*Asclepias incarnata*
tall green	ASCLEPIADACEAE-D	*Asclepias hirtella*
whorled	ASCLEPIADACEAE-D	*Asclepias quadrifolia*
whorled	ASCLEPIADACEAE-D	*Asclepias verticillata*
wooly	ASCLEPIADACEAE-D	*Asclepias lanuginosa*
Milkwort	POLYGALACEAE-D	*Polygala cruciata*
field	POLYGALACEAE-D	*Polygala sanguinea*
pink	POLYGALACEAE-D	*Polygala incarnata*
purple	POLYGALACEAE-D	*Polygala polygama* var. *obtusata*
whorled	POLYGALACEAE-D	*Polygala verticillata*
Millet-grass	POACEAE-M	*Milium effusum*
Millet, foxtail	POACEAE-M	*Setaria italica*
proso	POACEAE-M	*Panicum miliaceum*
Mimosa, prairie	FABACEAE-D	*Desmanthus illinoensis*
Mint, common mountain	LAMIACEAE-D	*Pycnanthemum virginianum*
hairy mountain	LAMIACEAE-D	*Pycnanthemum pilosum*
slender mountain	LAMIACEAE-D	*Pycnanthemum tenuifolium*
wild	LAMIACEAE-D	*Mentha arvensis*
wood	LAMIACEAE-D	*Blephilia hirsuta*
Mitrewort	SAXIFRAGACEAE-D	*Mitella diphylla*
Mock orange	SAXIFRAGACEAE-D	*Philadelphus pubescens*
Moneywort	PRIMULACEAE-D	*Lysimachia nummularia*
Monkey flower	SCROPHULARIACEAE-D	*Mimulus ringens*
winged	SCROPHULARIACEAE-D	*Mimulus alatus*
yellow	SCROPHULARIACEAE-D	*Mimulus glabratus* var. *fremontii*
Monkshood, northern wild	RANUNCULACEAE-D	*Aconitum noveboracense*
Moonseed	MENISPERMACEAE-D	*Menispermum canadense*
Moonwort, daisy-leaved	OPHIOGLOSSACEAE-P	*Botrychium matricariifolium*
prairie	OPHIOGLOSSACEAE-P	*Botrychium campestre*
Moschatel	ADOXACEAE-D	*Adoxa moschatellina*
Moss-pink	POLEMONIACEAE-D	*Phlox subulata*
Moss-rose	PORTULACACEAE-D	*Portulaca grandiflora*
Motherwort	LAMIACEAE-D	*Leonurus cardiaca*
Mousetail	RANUNCULACEAE-D	*Myosurus minimus*
Mugwort, common	ASTERACEAE-D	*Artemisia vulgaris*
Muhly, forest	POACEAE-M	*Muhlenbergia sylvatica*
marsh	POACEAE-M	*Muhlenbergia racemosa*
plains	POACEAE-M	*Muhlenbergia cuspidata*
rock	POACEAE-M	*Muhlenbergia sobolifera*
wirestem	POACEAE-M	*Muhlenbergia frondosa*
Mulberry, Chinese	MORACEAE-D	*Morus alba*

Common name	Family	Scientific name
Mulberry, cont.		
red	MORACEAE-D	*Morus rubra*
white	MORACEAE-D	*Morus alba*
Muletail	ASTERACEAE-D	*Conyza canadensis*
Mullein, common	SCROPHULARIACEAE-D	*Verbascum thapsus*
moth	SCROPHULARIACEAE-D	*Verbascum blattaria*
white	SCROPHULARIACEAE-D	*Verbascum lychnitis*
Muskroot	ADOXACEAE-D	*Adoxa moschatellina*
Mustard, ball	BRASSICACEAE-D	*Neslia paniculata*
black	BRASSICACEAE-D	*Brassica nigra*
Chinese	BRASSICACEAE-D	*Brassica juncea*
dog	BRASSICACEAE-D	*Erucastrum gallicum*
field	BRASSICACEAE-D	*Brassica campestris*
garlic	BRASSICACEAE-D	*Alliaria petiolata*
hare's-ear	BRASSICACEAE-D	*Conringia orientalis*
tansy	BRASSICACEAE-D	*Descurainia pinnata* var. *brachycarpa*
tower	BRASSICACEAE-D	*Arabis glabra*
tumble	BRASSICACEAE-D	*Sisymbrium altissimum*
white	BRASSICACEAE-D	*Sinapis alba*
wormseed	BRASSICACEAE-D	*Erysimum cheiranthoides*
Nannyberry	CAPRIFOLIACEAE-D	*Viburnum lentago*
Needle-and-thread	POACEAE-M	*Stipa comata*
Needlegrass, green	POACEAE-M	*Stipa viridula*
Nettle, dead	LAMIACEAE-D	*Lamium amplexicaule*
hemp	LAMIACEAE-D	*Galeopsis tetrahit*
horse	SOLANACEAE-D	*Solanum carolinense*
purple dead	LAMIACEAE-D	*Lamium purpureum*
stinging	URTICACEAE-D	*Urtica dioica*
wood	URTICACEAE-D	*Laportea canadensis*
New Jersey tea	RHAMNACEAE-D	*Ceanothus americanus* var. *pitcheri*
Nightshade, black	SOLANACEAE-D	*Solanum americanum*
enchanter's	ONAGRACEAE-D	*Circaea alpina*
enchanter's	ONAGRACEAE-D	*Circaea lutetiana* ssp. *canadensis*
plains black	SOLANACEAE-D	*Solanum interius*
Nimblewill	POACEAE-M	*Muhlenbergia schreberi*
Ninebark	ROSACEAE-D	*Physocarpus opulifolius*
Nits and lice	HYPERICACEAE-D	*Hypericum drummondii*
Nut-rush, low	CYPERACEAE-M	*Scleria verticillata*
tall	CYPERACEAE-M	*Scleria triglomerata*
Oak, black	FAGACEAE-D	*Quercus velutina*
blackjack	FAGACEAE-D	*Quercus marilandica*

Oak, cont.		
bur	FAGACEAE-D	*Quercus macrocarpa*
chinquapin	FAGACEAE-D	*Quercus muhlenbergii*
dwarf chinquapin	FAGACEAE-D	*Quercus prinoides*
hill's	FAGACEAE-D	*Quercus ellipsoidalis*
Jerusalem	CHENOPODIACEAE-D	*Chenopodium botrys*
northern pin	FAGACEAE-D	*Quercus ellipsoidalis*
northern red	FAGACEAE-D	*Quercus borealis* var. *maxima*
pin	FAGACEAE-D	*Quercus palustris*
post	FAGACEAE-D	*Quercus stellata*
shingle	FAGACEAE-D	*Quercus imbricaria*
swamp white	FAGACEAE-D	*Quercus bicolor*
white	FAGACEAE-D	*Quercus alba*
yellow chestnut	FAGACEAE-D	*Quercus muhlenbergii*
Oatgrass, tall	POACEAE-M	*Arrhenatherum elatius*
Oats, cult	POACEAE-M	*Avena sativa*
wild	POACEAE-M	*Avena fatua*
wild	POACEAE-M	*Chasmanthium latifolium*
Obedient plant	LAMIACEAE-D	*Physostegia parviflora*
Olive, autumn	ELAEAGNACEAE-D	*Elaeagnus umbellata*
Russian	ELAEAGNACEAE-D	*Elaeagnus angustifolia*
Onion, nodding wild	LILIACEAE-M	*Allium cernuum*
wild	LILIACEAE-M	*Allium canadense*
wild	LILIACEAE-M	*Allium mutabile*
wild prairie	LILIACEAE-M	*Allium stellatum*
Orchid, adder's mouth	ORCHIDACEAE-M	*Malaxis unifolia*
bracted	ORCHIDACEAE-M	*Coeloglossum viride* var. *virescens*
eastern prairie fringed	ORCHIDACEAE-M	*Platanthera leucophaea*
fall coral-root	ORCHIDACEAE-M	*Corallorhiza odontorhiza*
grass pink	ORCHIDACEAE-M	*Calopogon tuberosus*
green fringed	ORCHIDACEAE-M	*Platanthera lacera*
leafy northern green	ORCHIDACEAE-M	*Platanthera hyperborea* var. *huronensis*
purple fringed	ORCHIDACEAE-M	*Platanthera psycodes*
putty-root	ORCHIDACEAE-M	*Aplectrum hyemale*
round-leaved	ORCHIDACEAE-M	*Platanthera hookeri*
showy lady's-slipper	ORCHIDACEAE-M	*Cypripedium reginae*
small white lady's-slipper	ORCHIDACEAE-M	*Cypripedium candidum*
small yellow lady's-slipper	ORCHIDACEAE-M	*Cypripedium calceolus* var. *parviflorum*
tubercled	ORCHIDACEAE-M	*Platanthera flava* var. *herbiola*
western prairie fringed	ORCHIDACEAE-M	*Platanthera praeclara*

Orchid, cont.		
wood	ORCHIDACEAE-M	*Platanthera clavellata*
yellow lady's-slipper	ORCHIDACEAE-M	*Cypripedium calceolus* var. *pubescens*
Orchis, showy	ORCHIDACEAE-M	*Galearis spectabilis*
Osage orange	MORACEAE-D	*Maclura pomifera*
Oswego tea	LAMIACEAE-D	*Monarda didyma*
Ox-eye	ASTERACEAE-D	*Heliopsis helianthoides*
Ox-tongue	ASTERACEAE-D	*Picris echiodes*
Oyster plant	ASTERACEAE-D	*Tragopogon porrifolius*
Pagoda plant	LAMIACEAE-D	*Blephilia ciliata*
Pansy, garden	VIOLACEAE-D	*Viola tricolor*
wild	VIOLACEAE-D	*Viola rafinesquii*
Parsley, hedge	APIACEAE-D	*Torilis arvensis*
prairie	APIACEAE-D	*Polytaenia nuttallii*
Parsnip, cow	APIACEAE-D	*Heracleum lanatum*
heart-leaved meadow	APIACEAE-D	*Zizia aptera*
Meadow	APIACEAE-D	*Thaspium barbinode*
water	APIACEAE-D	*Berula erecta* var. *incisum*
water	APIACEAE-D	*Sium suave*
wild	APIACEAE-D	*Pastinaca sativa*
Pasque flower	RANUNCULACEAE-D	*Pulsatilla patens* ssp. *multifida*
Paw paw	ANNONACEAE-D	*Asimina triloba*
Pea, partridge	FABACEAE-D	*Chamaecrista fasciculata*
scurfy	FABACEAE-D	*Psoralidium batesii*
veiny	FABACEAE-D	*Lathyrus venosus*
wild	FABACEAE-D	*Lathyrus ochroleucus*
Peach	ROSACEAE-D	*Prunus persica*
Pear	ROSACEAE-D	*Pyrus communis*
Pearly everlasting	ASTERACEAE-D	*Anaphalis margaritacea*
Pecan	JUGLANDACEAE-D	*Carya illinoensis*
Pellitory	URTICACEAE-D	*Parietaria pensylvanica*
Penstemon, foxglove	SCROPHULARIACEAE-D	*Penstemon digitalis*
Peppergrass	BRASSICACEAE-D	*Lepidium densiflorum*
perfoliate	BRASSICACEAE-D	*Lepidium perfoliatum*
Peppermint	LAMIACEAE-D	*Mentha X piperita*
Periwinkle, common	APOCYNACEAE-D	*Vinca minor*
Persimmon	EBENACEAE-D	*Diospyros virginiana*
Petunia	SOLANACEAE-D	*Petunia axillaris*
wild	ACANTHACEAE-D	*Ruellia humilis*
Phlox, blue	POLEMONIACEAE-D	*Phlox divaricata*
cleft	POLEMONIACEAE-D	*Phlox bifida*
garden	POLEMONIACEAE-D	*Phlox paniculata*

Phlox, cont.		
prairie	POLEMONIACEAE-D	*Phlox pilosa*
Pickerel-weed	PONTEDERIACEAE-M	*Pontederia cordata*
Pigweed	AMARANTHACEAE-D	*Amaranthus albus*
Pigweed	AMARANTHACEAE-D	*Amaranthus retroflexus*
prostrate	AMARANTHACEAE-D	*Amaranthus graecizans*
smooth	AMARANTHACEAE-D	*Amaranthus powellii*
spiny	AMARANTHACEAE-D	*Amaranthus spinosus*
winged	CHENOPODIACEAE-D	*Cycloloma atriplicifolium*
Pimpernel, false	SCROPHULARIACEAE-D	*Lindernia anagallidea*
yellow	APIACEAE-D	*Taenidia integerrima*
Pine-sap	ERICACEAE-D	*Monotropa hypopithys*
Pineapple weed	ASTERACEAE-D	*Matricaria matricarioides*
Pineweed	HYPERICACEAE-D	*Hypericum gentianoides*
Pink, deptford	CARYOPHYLLACEAE-D	*Dianthus armeria*
Pinweed, hairy	CISTACEAE-D	*Lechea villosa*
slender-leaved	CISTACEAE-D	*Lechea tenuifolia*
Plantain, bracted	PLANTAGINACEAE-D	*Plantago aristata*
buckhorn	PLANTAGINACEAE-D	*Plantago lanceolata*
common	PLANTAGINACEAE-D	*Plantago rugelii*
great Indian	ASTERACEAE-D	*Cacalia muhlenbergii*
Indian	ASTERACEAE-D	*Cacalia atriplicifolia*
prairie Indian	ASTERACEAE-D	*Cacalia plantaginea*
rattlesnake	ORCHIDACEAE-M	*Goodyera pubescens*
robin's	ASTERACEAE-D	*Erigeron pulchellus*
Rugel's	PLANTAGINACEAE-D	*Plantago rugelii*
sweet Indian	ASTERACEAE-D	*Cacalia suaveolens*
Plum, big-tree	ROSACEAE-D	*Prunus mexicana*
Canada	ROSACEAE-D	*Prunus nigra*
ground	FABACEAE-D	*Astragalus crassicarpus*
hortulan	ROSACEAE-D	*Prunus hortulana*
wild	ROSACEAE-D	*Prunus americana*
Pogonia, nodding	ORCHIDACEAE-M	*Triphora trianthophora*
Poinsettia, wild	EUPHORBIACEAE-D	*Euphorbia cyathophora*
Pokeweed	PHYTOLACCACEAE-D	*Phytolacca americana*
Pondweed, curly	POTAMOGETONACEAE-M	*Potamogeton crispus*
flat-stemmed	POTAMOGETONACEAE-M	*Potamogeton zosteriformis*
horned	ZANNICHELLIACEAE-M	*Zannichellia palustris*
red-head	POTAMOGETONACEAE-M	*Potamogeton richardsonii*
sago	POTAMOGETONACEAE-M	*Potamogeton pectinatus*
Poor-man's pepper	BRASSICACEAE-D	*Lepidium virginicum*
Poplar, balsam	SALICACEAE-D	*Populus balsamifera*
lombardy	SALICACEAE-D	*Populus nigra* var. *italica*
silver	SALICACEAE-D	*Populus alba*
yellow	MAGNOLIACEAE-D	*Liriodendron tulipifera*

Poppy, Mexican	PAPAVERACEAE-D	*Argemone mexicana*
prickly	PAPAVERACEAE-D	*Argemone albiflora*
Prairie blazing star	ASTERACEAE-D	*Liatris pycnostachya*
Prairie smoke	ROSACEAE-D	*Geum triflorum*
Prairie sundrops	ONAGRACEAE-D	*Oenothera pilosella*
Prairie tea	EUPHORBIACEAE-D	*Croton monanthogynus*
Prairie turnip	FABACEAE-D	*Pediomelum esculentum*
Prickly pear	CACTACEAE-D	*Opuntia macrorhiza*
eastern	CACTACEAE-D	*Opuntia humifusa*
little	CACTACEAE-D	*Opuntia fragilis*
Primrose, bird's-eye	PRIMULACEAE-D	*Primula mistassinica*
gray evening	ONAGRACEAE-D	*Oenothera villosa*
ragged evening	ONAGRACEAE-D	*Oenothera laciniata*
sand	ONAGRACEAE-D	*Oenothera rhombipetala*
showy evening	ONAGRACEAE-D	*Oenothera speciosa*
toothed evening	ONAGRACEAE-D	*Calylophus serrulatus*
Prince's pine	ERICACEAE-D	*Chimaphila umbellata*
Puccoon, fringed	BORAGINACEAE-D	*Lithospermum incisum*
hairy	BORAGINACEAE-D	*Lithospermum caroliniense*
hoary	BORAGINACEAE-D	*Lithospermum canescens*
Puncture-weed	ZYGOPHYLLACEAE-D	*Tribulis terrestris*
Purple rocket	BRASSICACEAE-D	*Iodanthus pinnatifidus*
Purple top	POACEAE-M	*Tridens flavus*
Purse, shepherd's	BRASSICACEAE-D	*Capsella bursa-pastoris*
Purslane, common	PORTULACACEAE-D	*Portulaca oleracea*
water	LYTHRACEAE-D	*Didiplis diandra*
water	ONAGRACEAE-D	*Ludwigia palustris*
Pussytoes	ASTERACEAE-D	*Antennaria neglecta*
Pyrola, one-sided	ERICACEAE-D	*Pyrola secunda*
pink	ERICACEAE-D	*Pyrola asarifolia*
Queen Anne's lace	APIACEAE-D	*Daucus carota*
Queen of the prairie	ROSACEAE-D	*Filipendula rubra*
Quillwort, black-footed	ISOETACEAE-P	*Isoetes melanopoda*
Quinine, wild	ASTERACEAE-D	*Parthenium integrifolium*
Radish	BRASSICACEAE-D	*Raphanus sativus*
wild	BRASSICACEAE-D	*Raphanus raphanistrum*
Ragweed, common	ASTERACEAE-D	*Ambrosia artemisiifolia*
giant	ASTERACEAE-D	*Ambrosia trifida*
western	ASTERACEAE-D	*Ambrosia psilostachya*
Ragwort, golden	ASTERACEAE-D	*Senecio aureus*
prairie	ASTERACEAE-D	*Senecio pauperculus*
prairie	ASTERACEAE-D	*Senecio plattensis*
Raspberry, black	ROSACEAE-D	*Rubus occidentalis*
cultivated red	ROSACEAE-D	*Rubus idaeus*

Raspberry, cont.		
wild red	ROSACEAE-D	*Rubus strigosus*
Rattle box	FABACEAE-D	*Crotalaria sagittalis*
Rattlesnake master	APIACEAE-D	*Eryngium yuccifolium*
Rattlesnake-root	ASTERACEAE-D	*Prenanthes alba*
Red morning glory	CONVOLVULACEAE-D	*Ipomoea coccinea*
Red orach	CHENOPODIACEAE-D	*Atriplex rosea*
Redbud	FABACEAE-D	*Cercis canadensis*
Redroot	RHAMNACEAE-D	*Ceanothus herbaceus* var. *pubescens*
Redtop	POACEAE-M	*Agrostis gigantea*
Reed	POACEAE-M	*Phragmites australis*
wood	POACEAE-M	*Cinna arundinacea*
Rice-grass, black-seeded	POACEAE-M	*Oryzopsis racemosa*
rough-leaved	POACEAE-M	*Oryzopsis asperifolia*
short-horned	POACEAE-M	*Oryzopsis pungens*
Rice, wild	POACEAE-M	*Zizania aquatica*
Rockrose	CISTACEAE-D	*Helianthemum bicknellii*
Rose, Meadow	ROSACEAE-D	*Rosa blanda*
multiflora	ROSACEAE-D	*Rosa multiflora*
pasture	ROSACEAE-D	*Rosa carolina*
prairie	ROSACEAE-D	*Rosa setigera*
sunshine	ROSACEAE-D	*Rosa arkansana* var. *suffulta*
swamp	ROSACEAE-D	*Rosa palustris*
sweetbriar	ROSACEAE-D	*Rosa eglanteria*
Rosinweed	ASTERACEAE-D	*Silphium integrifolium*
Rosy twisted stalk	LILIACEAE-M	*Streptopus roseus*
Rough pennyroyal	LAMIACEAE-D	*Hedeoma hispidum*
Ruellia, smooth	ACANTHACEAE-D	*Ruellia strepens*
Rush, beaked	CYPERACEAE-M	*Rhynchospora capillacea*
bog	JUNCACEAE-M	*Juncus balticus* var. *littoralis*
path	JUNCACEAE-M	*Juncus tenuis*
toad	JUNCACEAE-M	*Juncus bufonius*
Rye, Canada wild	POACEAE-M	*Elymus canadensis*
cult	POACEAE-M	*Secale cereale*
slender wild	POACEAE-M	*Elymus villosus*
Virginia wild	POACEAE-M	*Elymus virginicus*
Sage, pitcher's	LAMIACEAE-D	*Salvia pitcheri*
rocky mountain	LAMIACEAE-D	*Salvia reflexa*
white	ASTERACEAE-D	*Artemisia ludoviciana*
wood	LAMIACEAE-D	*Teucrium canadense* var. *boreale*
Sagewort, prairie	ASTERACEAE-D	*Artemisia frigida*

Common name	Family	Scientific name
Sagewort, cont.		
western	ASTERACEAE-D	*Artemisia campestris* ssp. *caudata*
Salsify	ASTERACEAE-D	*Tragopogon porrifolius*
Salvia, lance-leaved	LAMIACEAE-D	*Salvia reflexa*
Sandbur	POACEAE-M	*Cenchrus longispinus*
Sandreed, prairie	POACEAE-M	*Calamovilfa longifolia*
Sandwort	CARYOPHYLLACEAE-D	*Moehringia lateriflora*
rock	CARYOPHYLLACEAE-D	*Minuartia michauxii*
thyme-leaved	CARYOPHYLLACEAE-D	*Arenaria serpyllifolia*
Sarsaparilla, wild	ARALIACEAE-D	*Aralia nudicaulis*
Sassafras	LAURACEAE-D	*Sassafras albidum*
Saxifrage, Forbes'	SAXIFRAGACEAE-D	*Saxifraga forbesii*
golden	SAXIFRAGACEAE-D	*Chrysosplenium iowense*
swamp	SAXIFRAGACEAE-D	*Saxifraga pensylvanica*
Scouring-rush, common	EQUISETACEAE-P	*Equisetum hyemale* var. *affine*
dwarf	EQUISETACEAE-P	*Equisetum scirpoides*
hybrid	EQUISETACEAE-P	*Equisetum X ferrissii*
smooth	EQUISETACEAE-P	*Equisetum laevigatum*
Scratchgrass	POACEAE-M	*Muhlenbergia asperifolia*
Scullcap, downy	LAMIACEAE-D	*Scutellaria incana*
Scurf-pea, silvery	FABACEAE-D	*Pediomelum argophyllum*
Seal, golden	RANUNCULACEAE-D	*Hydrastis canadensis*
Sedge, hair	CYPERACEAE-M	*Bulbostylis capillaris*
slender	CYPERACEAE-M	*Carex lasiocarpa* var. *americana*
three-way	CYPERACEAE-M	*Dulichium arundinaceum*
Seedbox	ONAGRACEAE-D	*Ludwigia alternifolia*
Self heal	LAMIACEAE-D	*Prunella vulgaris*
Self heal	LAMIACEAE-D	*Prunella vulgaris* var. *lanceolata*
Senna, wild	FABACEAE-D	*Cassia marilandica*
Serviceberry	ROSACEAE-D	*Amelanchier arborea*
Shinleaf	ERICACEAE-D	*Pyrola elliptica*
Shooting star	PRIMULACEAE-D	*Dodecatheon meadia*
Siberian pea tree	FABACEAE-D	*Caragana arborescens*
Sickle pod	BRASSICACEAE-D	*Arabis canadensis*
Sickleweed	APIACEAE-D	*Falcaria sioides*
Silverweed	ROSACEAE-D	*Potentilla anserina*
Skeletonweed	ASTERACEAE-D	*Lygodesmia juncea*
annual	ASTERACEAE-D	*Lygodesmia rostrata*
Skullcap, mad-dog	LAMIACEAE-D	*Scutellaria lateriflora*
Skunk cabbage	ARACEAE-M	*Symplocarpus foetidus*
Small Bishop's cap	SAXIFRAGACEAE-D	*Mitella nuda*
Small sundrops	ONAGRACEAE-D	*Oenothera perennis*

Smartweed, creeping	POLYGONACEAE-D	*Polygonum cespitosum* var. *longisetum*
water	POLYGONACEAE-D	*Polygonum amphibium* var. *emersum*
water	POLYGONACEAE-D	*Polygonum punctatum*
Snakeroot, black	APIACEAE-D	*Sanicula canadensis*
black	APIACEAE-D	*Sanicula marilandica*
common	APIACEAE-D	*Sanicula gregaria*
large-fruited black	APIACEAE-D	*Sanicula trifoliata*
seneca	POLYGALACEAE-D	*Polygala senega*
Virginia	ARISTOLOCHIACEAE-D	*Aristolochia serpentaria*
white	ASTERACEAE-D	*Eupatorium rugosum*
Snapdragon, dwarf	SCROPHULARIACEAE-D	*Chaenorrhinum minus*
Sneezeweed	ASTERACEAE-D	*Helenium autumnale*
Snow-on-the-mountain	EUPHORBIACEAE-D	*Euphorbia marginata*
Snowberry	CAPRIFOLIACEAE-D	*Symphoricarpos albus*
Soapweed	AGAVACEAE-M	*Yucca glauca*
Soapwort	CARYOPHYLLACEAE-D	*Saponaria officinalis*
Solomon's seal	LILIACEAE-M	*Polygonatum biflorum*
downy	LILIACEAE-M	*Polygonatum pubescens*
false	LILIACEAE-M	*Smilacina racemosa*
starry false	LILIACEAE-M	*Smilacina stellata*
Sorghum	POACEAE-M	*Sorghum bicolor*
Sorrel, lady's	OXALIDACEAE-D	*Oxalis stricta*
red	POLYGONACEAE-D	*Rumex acetosella*
violet wood	OXALIDACEAE-D	*Oxalis violacea*
yellow wood	OXALIDACEAE-D	*Oxalis dillenii*
yellow wood	OXALIDACEAE-D	*Oxalis stricta*
Soybean	FABACEAE-D	*Glycine max*
Spanish needles	ASTERACEAE-D	*Bidens bipinnata*
Spearmint	LAMIACEAE-D	*Mentha spicata*
Spearscale	CHENOPODIACEAE-D	*Atriplex patula*
Speedwell, common	SCROPHULARIACEAE-D	*Veronica officinalis*
corn	SCROPHULARIACEAE-D	*Veronica arvensis*
field	SCROPHULARIACEAE-D	*Veronica agrestis*
marsh	SCROPHULARIACEAE-D	*Veronica scutellata*
water	SCROPHULARIACEAE-D	*Veronica anagallis-aquatica*
water	SCROPHULARIACEAE-D	*Veronica catenata*
Spikemoss, Meadow	SELAGINELLACEAE-P	*Selaginella eclipes*
rock	SELAGINELLACEAE-P	*Selaginella rupestris*
Spikenard	ARALIACEAE-D	*Aralia racemosa*
false	LILIACEAE-M	*Smilacina racemosa*
Spiraea, false	ROSACEAE-D	*Sorbaria sorbifolia*
Spleenwort, ebony	ASPLENIACEAE-P	*Asplenium platyneuron*
narrow-leaved	ASPLENIACEAE-P	*Athyrium pycnocarpon*
silvery	ASPLENIACEAE-P	*Athyrium thelypterioides*

Spring beauty	PORTULACACEAE-D	*Claytonia virginica*
Spurge, blunt-leaved	EUPHORBIACEAE-D	*Euphorbia obtusata*
carpet	EUPHORBIACEAE-D	*Euphorbia maculata*
cypress	EUPHORBIACEAE-D	*Euphorbia cyparissias*
falcate	EUPHORBIACEAE-D	*Euphorbia falcata*
flowering	EUPHORBIACEAE-D	*Euphorbia corollata*
leafy	EUPHORBIACEAE-D	*Euphorbia esula*
nodding	EUPHORBIACEAE-D	*Euphorbia nutans*
petty	EUPHORBIACEAE-D	*Euphorbia peplus*
toothed	EUPHORBIACEAE-D	*Euphorbia dentata*
warty	EUPHORBIACEAE-D	*Euphorbia obtusata*
wood	EUPHORBIACEAE-D	*Euphorbia commutata*
Squaw-root	OROBANCHACEAE-D	*Conopholis americana*
St. John's wort, Canadian	HYPERICACEAE-D	*Hypericum canadense*
common	HYPERICACEAE-D	*Hypericum perforatum*
giant	HYPERICACEAE-D	*Hypericum pyramidatum*
marsh	HYPERICACEAE-D	*Triadenum fraseri*
northern	HYPERICACEAE-D	*Hypericum boreale*
round-fruited	HYPERICACEAE-D	*Hypericum sphaerocarpum*
shrubby	HYPERICACEAE-D	*Hypericum prolificum*
spotted	HYPERICACEAE-D	*Hypericum punctatum*
weak	HYPERICACEAE-D	*Hypericum mutilum*
Star of Bethlehem	LILIACEAE-M	*Ornithogalum umbellatum*
Stargrass, yellow	LILIACEAE-M	*Hypoxis hirsuta*
Stickseed	BORAGINACEAE-D	*Hackelia deflexa* var. *americana*
Stickseed	BORAGINACEAE-D	*Hackelia virginiana*
Stinkgrass	POACEAE-M	*Eragrostis cilianensis*
Stitchwort	CARYOPHYLLACEAE-D	*Stellaria longifolia*
common	CARYOPHYLLACEAE-D	*Stellaria graminea*
Stonecrop, ditch	SAXIFRAGACEAE-D	*Penthorum sedoides*
mossy	CRASSULACEAE-D	*Sedum acre*
wild	CRASSULACEAE-D	*Sedum ternatum*
Stork's bill	GERANIACEAE-D	*Erodium cicutarium*
Strawberry blite	CHENOPODIACEAE-D	*Chenopodium capitatum*
Strawberry, wild	ROSACEAE-D	*Fragaria virginiana*
woodland	ROSACEAE-D	*Fragaria vesca* var. *americana*
Sumac, dwarf	ANACARDIACEAE-D	*Rhus copallina*
fragrant	ANACARDIACEAE-D	*Rhus aromatica*
smooth	ANACARDIACEAE-D	*Rhus glabra*
staghorn	ANACARDIACEAE-D	*Rhus typhina*
Sumpweed	ASTERACEAE-D	*Iva annua*
Sundew	DROSERACEAE-D	*Drosera rotundifolia*
Sunflower, bristly	ASTERACEAE-D	*Helianthus hirsutus*
common	ASTERACEAE-D	*Helianthus annuus*

Sunflower, cont.		
Maximillian's	ASTERACEAE-D	*Helianthus maximiliani*
pale	ASTERACEAE-D	*Helianthus decapetalus*
pale-leaved	ASTERACEAE-D	*Helianthus strumosus*
petioled	ASTERACEAE-D	*Helianthus petiolaris*
prairie	ASTERACEAE-D	*Helianthus rigidus*
saw-tooth	ASTERACEAE-D	*Helianthus grosseserratus*
tall	ASTERACEAE-D	*Helianthus giganteus*
tickseed	ASTERACEAE-D	*Bidens coronata*
western	ASTERACEAE-D	*Helianthus occidentalis*
woodland	ASTERACEAE-D	*Helianthus divaricatus*
Swallow-wort	PAPAVERACEAE-D	*Chelidonium majus*
Swamp candle	PRIMULACEAE-D	*Lysimachia terrestris*
Sweet cicely	APIACEAE-D	*Osmorhiza claytonii*
Sweet William	POLEMONIACEAE-D	*Phlox divaricata*
Sweetflag	ARACEAE-M	*Acorus calamus*
Switchgrass	POACEAE-M	*Panicum virgatum*
Sycamore	PLATANACEAE-D	*Platanus occidentalis*
Tansy	ASTERACEAE-D	*Tanacetum vulgare*
Tarragon, false	ASTERACEAE-D	*Artemisia dracunculus*
Tarweed	ASTERACEAE-D	*Madia sativa* var. *congesta*
Tearthumb	POLYGONACEAE-D	*Polygonum sagittatum*
Teasel, common	DIPSACACEAE-D	*Dipsacus sylvestris*
cut-leaved	DIPSACACEAE-D	*Dipsacus laciniatus*
Thimbleweed	RANUNCULACEAE-D	*Anemone cylindrica*
Thistle, bull	ASTERACEAE-D	*Cirsium vulgare*
Canada	ASTERACEAE-D	*Cirsium arvense*
common sow	ASTERACEAE-D	*Sonchus oleraceus*
field	ASTERACEAE-D	*Cirsium discolor*
globe	ASTERACEAE-D	*Echinops sphaerocephalus*
musk	ASTERACEAE-D	*Carduus nutans*
perennial sow	ASTERACEAE-D	*Sonchus arvensis*
plumeless	ASTERACEAE-D	*Carduus acanthoides*
Russian	CHENOPODIACEAE-D	*Salsola iberica*
Scotch	ASTERACEAE-D	*Onopordum acanthium*
spiny-leaved sow	ASTERACEAE-D	*Sonchus asper*
star	ASTERACEAE-D	*Centaurea maculosa*
swamp	ASTERACEAE-D	*Cirsium muticum*
tall	ASTERACEAE-D	*Cirsium altissimum*
yellow star	ASTERACEAE-D	*Centaurea solstitialis*
Thoroughwort, tall	ASTERACEAE-D	*Eupatorium altissimum*
Three-awn, slender	POACEAE-M	*Aristida ramosissima*
Three-seeded mercury	EUPHORBIACEAE-D	*Acalypha ostryifolia*
Three-seeded mercury	EUPHORBIACEAE-D	*Acalypha rhomboidea*

Threesquare	CYPERACEAE-M	*Scirpus americanus*
Tick-trefoil, bare-stemmed	FABACEAE-D	*Desmodium nudiflorum*
bracted	FABACEAE-D	*Desmodium cuspidatum*
hoary	FABACEAE-D	*Desmodium canescens*
Illinois	FABACEAE-D	*Desmodium illinoense*
panicled	FABACEAE-D	*Desmodium paniculatum*
pointed	FABACEAE-D	*Desmodium glutinosum*
sessile-leaved	FABACEAE-D	*Desmodium sessilifolium*
showy	FABACEAE-D	*Desmodium canadense*
Ticklegrass	POACEAE-M	*Agrostis hyemalis*
Tickseed	ASTERACEAE-D	*Coreopsis palmata*
tall	ASTERACEAE-D	*Coreopsis tripteris*
Timothy	POACEAE-M	*Phleum pratense*
Toadflax	SCROPHULARIACEAE-D	*Linaria canadensis*
bastard	SANTALACEAE-D	*Comandra umbellata*
Tobacco, Indian	CAMPANULACEAE-D	*Lobelia inflata*
Tomatillo	SOLANACEAE-D	*Physalis ixocarpa*
Tomato	SOLANACEAE-D	*Lycopersicon esculentum*
strawberry	SOLANACEAE-D	*Physalis pubescens* var. *integrifolia*
wild	HYDROPHYLLACEAE-D	*Ellisia nyctelea*
Toothcup	LYTHRACEAE-D	*Ammannia coccinea*
Toothcup	LYTHRACEAE-D	*Rotala ramosior*
Toothwort	BRASSICACEAE-D	*Dentaria laciniata*
Touch-me-not, pale	BALSAMINACEAE-D	*Impatiens pallida*
spotted	BALSAMINACEAE-D	*Impatiens capensis*
Tree of heaven	SIMAROUBACEAE-D	*Ailanthus altissima*
Trefoil, bird's-foot	FABACEAE-D	*Lotus corniculatus*
Trillium, nodding	LILIACEAE-M	*Trillium cernuum*
nodding	LILIACEAE-M	*Trillium flexipes*
snow	LILIACEAE-M	*Trillium nivale*
Trout-lily, white	LILIACEAE-M	*Erythronium albidum*
yellow	LILIACEAE-M	*Erythronium americanum*
Tulip tree	MAGNOLIACEAE-D	*Liriodendron tulipifera*
Tumblegrass	POACEAE-M	*Schedonnardus paniculatus*
Turnip	BRASSICACEAE-D	*Brassica napus*
Turtlehead, pink	SCROPHULARIACEAE-D	*Chelone obliqua* var. *speciosa*
white	SCROPHULARIACEAE-D	*Chelone glabra*
Twayblade	ORCHIDACEAE-M	*Liparis liliifolia*
bog	ORCHIDACEAE-M	*Liparis loeselii*
Twinflower	CAPRIFOLIACEAE-D	*Linnaea borealis* ssp. *americana*
Twinleaf	BERBERIDACEAE-D	*Jeffersonia diphylla*

Unicorn plant	MARTYNIACEAE-D	*Proboscidea louisianica*
Valerian	VALERIANACEAE-D	*Valeriana edulis* ssp. *ciliata*
Venus' looking-glass	CAMPANULACEAE-D	*Triodanis perfoliata*
Vervain, blue	VERBENACEAE-D	*Verbena hastata*
creeping	VERBENACEAE-D	*Verbena bracteata*
hoary	VERBENACEAE-D	*Verbena stricta*
white	VERBENACEAE-D	*Verbena urticifolia*
Vetch	FABACEAE-D	*Vicia americana*
bent milk	FABACEAE-D	*Astragalus distortus*
common	FABACEAE-D	*Vicia sativa*
cow	FABACEAE-D	*Vicia cracca*
crown	FABACEAE-D	*Coronilla varia*
milk	FABACEAE-D	*Astragalus canadensis*
narrow-leaved	FABACEAE-D	*Vicia sativa* var. *nigra*
Vetchling	FABACEAE-D	*Lathyrus ochroleucus*
marsh	FABACEAE-D	*Lathyrus palustris*
Violet, arrow-leaved	VIOLACEAE-D	*Viola sagittata*
bird's-foot	VIOLACEAE-D	*Viola pedata*
bog	VIOLACEAE-D	*Viola nephrophylla*
common blue	VIOLACEAE-D	*Viola pratincola*
downy yellow	VIOLACEAE-D	*Viola pubescens*
green	VIOLACEAE-D	*Hybanthus concolor*
hairy blue	VIOLACEAE-D	*Viola sororia*
kidney-leaved	VIOLACEAE-D	*Viola renifolia*
lance-leaved	VIOLACEAE-D	*Viola lanceolata*
plains	VIOLACEAE-D	*Viola viarum*
prairie	VIOLACEAE-D	*Viola pedatifida*
Virgin's bower	RANUNCULACEAE-D	*Clematis virginiana*
Wahoo	CELASTRACEAE-D	*Euonymus atropurpureus*
winged	CELASTRACEAE-D	*Euonymus alatus*
Wake Robin	LILIACEAE-M	*Trillium recurvatum*
Wall rocket	BRASSICACEAE-D	*Diplotaxis muralis*
Wallflower, western	BRASSICACEAE-D	*Erysimum asperum*
Walnut, black	JUGLANDACEAE-D	*Juglans nigra*
Water-clover, European	MARSILEACEAE-P	*Marsilea quadrifolia*
hairy	MARSILEACEAE-P	*Marsilea vestita*
Watercress	BRASSICACEAE-D	*Nasturtium officinale*
Waterleaf, appendaged	HYDROPHYLLACEAE-D	*Hydrophyllum appendiculatum*
Virginia	HYDROPHYLLACEAE-D	*Hydrophyllum virginianum*
Waterpod	HYDROPHYLLACEAE-D	*Ellisia nyctelea*
Watershield	NYMPHAEACEAE-D	*Brasenia schreberi*
Waterwort	ELATINACEAE-D	*Elatine triandra*

Waxweed	LYTHRACEAE-D	*Cuphea viscosissima*
Wheat, cultivated	POACEAE-M	*Triticum aestivum*
Wheatgrass, crested	POACEAE-M	*Agropyron cristatum*
intermediate	POACEAE-M	*Agropyron intermedium*
slender	POACEAE-M	*Agropyron trachycaulum*
western	POACEAE-M	*Agropyron smithii*
Whitegrass	POACEAE-M	*Leersia virginica*
Whitetop	POACEAE-M	*Scolochloa festucacea*
White pine, eastern	PINACEAE-G	*Pinus strobus*
Wild cabbage	BRASSICACEAE-D	*Brassica oleracea*
Wild ginger	ARISTOLOCHIACEAE-D	*Asarum canadense*
Wild sweet potato	CONVOLVULACEAE-D	*Ipomoea pandurata*
Willow, bay-leaved	SALICACEAE-D	*Salix pentandra*
beaked	SALICACEAE-D	*Salix bebbiana*
black	SALICACEAE-D	*Salix nigra*
bog	SALICACEAE-D	*Salix pedicellaris*
crack	SALICACEAE-D	*Salix fragilis*
hoary	SALICACEAE-D	*Salix candida*
peach-leaved	SALICACEAE-D	*Salix amygdaloides*
prairie	SALICACEAE-D	*Salix humilis*
purple	SALICACEAE-D	*Salix purpurea*
pussy	SALICACEAE-D	*Salix discolor*
sage	SALICACEAE-D	*Salix candida*
sandbar	SALICACEAE-D	*Salix exigua* ssp. *interior*
shining	SALICACEAE-D	*Salix lucida*
silky	SALICACEAE-D	*Salix sericea*
water	ACANTHACEAE-D	*Justicia americana*
weeping	SALICACEAE-D	*Salix babylonica*
white	SALICACEAE-D	*Salix alba*
Willowherb, bog	ONAGRACEAE-D	*Epilobium leptophyllum*
cinnamon	ONAGRACEAE-D	*Epilobium coloratum*
Windflower	RANUNCULACEAE-D	*Anemone cylindrica*
Wingstem	ASTERACEAE-D	*Verbesina alternifolia*
Winterberry	AQUIFOLIACEAE-D	*Ilex verticillata*
Witch hazel	HAMAMELIDACEAE-D	*Hamamelis virginiana*
Witchgrass	POACEAE-M	*Panicum capillare*
fall	POACEAE-M	*Leptoloma cognatum*
Wolfberry	CAPRIFOLIACEAE-D	*Symphoricarpos occidentalis*
Woodbine	VITACEAE-D	*Parthenocissus vitacea*
Woodsia, blunt-lobed	ASPLENIACEAE-P	*Woodsia obtusa*
Oregon	ASPLENIACEAE-P	*Woodsia oregana*
rusty	ASPLENIACEAE-P	*Woodsia ilvensis*
Wormwood, annual	ASTERACEAE-D	*Artemisia annua*
biennial	ASTERACEAE-D	*Artemisia biennis*
Woundwort	LAMIACEAE-D	*Stachys palustris*

Yarrow, western	ASTERACEAE-D	*Achillea millefolium* ssp. *lanulosa*
Yellow rocket	BRASSICACEAE-D	*Barbarea vulgaris*
Yerbo-de-Tajo	ASTERACEAE-D	*Eclipta alba*
Yew, American	TAXACEAE-G	*Taxus canadensis*

Selected References

Aikman, J. M., and R. F. Thorne. 1956. The Cayler Prairie: an ecological and taxonomic study of a northwest Iowa prairie. Proc. Iowa Acad. Sci. 63: 177–200.

Arthur, J. C. 1876. Contributions to the flora of Iowa: a catalogue of the phanerogamous plants. Charles City, Iowa, Intelligencer.

Arthur, J. C. 1877. Contributions to the flora of Iowa, No. 2. Proc. Davenport Acad. Nat. Sci. 2: 126.

Arthur, J. C. 1878. Contributions to the flora of Iowa, No. 3. Proc. Davenport Acad. Nat. Sci. 2: 258–261.

Arthur, J. C. 1882. Contributions to the flora of Iowa, No. 4. Proc. Davenport Acad. Nat. Sci. 3: 169–172.

Arthur, J. C. 1884a. Contributions to the flora of Iowa, No. 5. Proc. Davenport Acad. Nat. Sci. 4: 27–30.

Arthur, J. C. 1884b. Contributions to the flora of Iowa, No. 6. Proc. Davenport Acad. Nat. Sci. 4: 64–75.

Baker, R. G., C. A. Chumbley, P. M. Witinok, and H. K. Kim. 1990. Holocene vegetational changes in eastern Iowa. J. Iowa Acad. Sci. 97: 167–177.

Baker, R. G., D. G. Horton, H. K. Kim, A. E. Sullivan, D. M. Roosa, P. M. Witinok, and W. P. Pusateri. 1987. Late Holocene paleoecology of southeastern Iowa: development of riparian vegetation at Nichols Marsh. Proc. Iowa Acad. Sci. 92: 51–70.

Baker, R. G., L. J. Maher, C. A. Chumbley, and K. L. Van Zant. 1992. Patterns of Holocene environmental changes in the midwestern United States. Quaternary Res. 37: 379–389.

Baker, R. G., and K. L. Van Zant. 1978. The history of prairie in northwest Iowa: the pollen and macrofossil record. Pp. 8–11 in D. C. Glenn-Lewin and R. Q. Landers, eds., Proc. Fifth Midwest Prairie Conference, Iowa State Univ. Extension Serv., Ames.

Beal, E. O., and P. H. Monson. 1954. Marsh and aquatic angiosperms of Iowa. Univ. Iowa Studies Nat. Hist. 19(5): 1–95.

Beal, E. O., J. W. Wooten, and R. B. Kaul. 1982. Review of the *Sagittaria engelmannia* complex with environmental correlations. Syst. Bot. 7: 417–432.

Bessey, C. E. 1871. Contributions to the flora of Iowa. Iowa Agric. Coll. 4th Bienn. Rept., pp. 90–127.

Bettis, E. A., J. C. Prior, G. R. Hallberg, and R. L. Handy. 1986. Geology of the Loess Hills region. Proc. Iowa Acad. Sci. 93: 78–85.

Bishop, R. A. 1981. Iowa's wetlands. Proc. Iowa Acad. Sci. 88: 11–16.

Boot, D. H. 1901. Comparison of field and forest floras of Monona County, Iowa. Botanical Laboratory, Univ. of Iowa, Iowa City.

Boot, D. H. 1917. Plant studies in Lyon County, Iowa. Proc. Iowa Acad. Sci. 60: 82–85.

Boufford, D. E. 1982. The systematics and evolution of Circaea (Onagraceae). Ann.

Missouri Bot. Gard. 69: 804–994.
Braun, E. L. 1950. Deciduous forests of eastern North America. Hafner Press, New York.
Brotherson, J. D. 1969. Species composition, distribution, and phytosociology of Kalsow Prairie, a mesic tallgrass prairie in Iowa. Ph.D. dissertation, Iowa State Univ., Ames.
Brown, M. E., and R. G. Brown. 1939. Preliminary list of the plants of the sand mounds of Muscatine and Louisa counties. Proc. Iowa Acad. Sci. 46: 167–178.
Cahayla-Wynne, R., and D. C. Glenn-Lewin. 1978. The forest vegetation of the Driftless Area, northeast Iowa. Am. Midl. Nat. 100: 307–319.
Carroll, S., R. L. Miller, and P. D. Whitson. 1984. Status of four orchid species at Silver Lake Fen complex. Proc. Iowa Acad. Sci. 91: 132–139.
Carter, J. L. 1960. The flora of northwestern Iowa. Ph.D. dissertation, Univ. of Iowa, Iowa City.
Carter, J. L. 1963. The flora of Cherokee County. Proc. Iowa Acad. Sci. 69: 60–70.
Christiansen, P. A. 1992. Distribution maps of Iowa prairie plants. Iowa Dept. of Transportation, Ames.
Clambey, G. K., and R. Q. Landers. 1978. A survey of wetland vegetation in north-central Iowa. Pp. 32–35 in D. C. Glenn-Lewin and R. Q. Landers, eds., Proc. Fifth Midwest Prairie Conference, Iowa State Univ. Extension Serv., Ames.
Clayton, W. D. 1968. The correct name of the common reed. Taxon 17: 168–169.
Coffey, V. J. The Scrophulariaceae of Iowa. M.S. thesis, Univ. of Iowa, Iowa City.
Coleman, V. W. 1950. The Liliaceae of Iowa. M.S. thesis, Univ. of Iowa, Iowa City.
Conard, H. S. 1938. The fir forests of Iowa. Proc. Iowa Acad. Sci. 45: 69–72.
Conard, H. S. 1951. Plants of Iowa. 7th ed. Iowa City.
Conard, H. S. 1952. The vegetation of Iowa. Univ. Iowa Studies Nat. Hist. 19(4): 1–166.
Cooperrider, T. S. 1959. The ferns and other pteridophytes of Iowa. Univ. Iowa Studies Nat. Hist. 20(1): 1–66.
Cooperrider, T. S. 1962. The vascular plants of Clinton, Jackson, and Jones counties, Iowa. Univ. Iowa Studies Nat. Hist. 20(5): 1–80.
Cratty, R. I. 1933. The Iowa flora: an annotated list of the ferns, fern allies and the native and introduced flowering plants of the state represented in the Iowa State College herbarium. Iowa State Coll. J. Sci. 7: 177–252.
Crawford, D. J. 1970. The Umbelliferae of Iowa. Univ. Iowa Studies Nat. Hist. 21(4): 1–36.
Crins, W. J., and P. W. Ball. 1983. The taxonomy of the *Carex pensylvanica* complex (Cyperaceae) in North America. Can. J. Bot. 61: 1692–1717.
Crist, A. M., and D. C. Glenn-Lewin. 1978. The structure of community and environmental gradients in a northern Iowa prairie. Pp. 57–64 in D. C. Glenn-Lewin and R. Q. Landers, eds., Proc. Fifth Midwest Prairie Conference, Iowa State Univ. Extension Serv., Ames.
Crum, G. H., and J. I. Knapp. 1976. The Elatinaceae in Iowa. Proc. Iowa Acad. Sci. 83: 63.
Curtis, J. T. 1959. The vegetation of Wisconsin. Univ. of Wisconsin Press, Madison.
D'arcy, W. G. 1978. Names in *Agalinis* for some plants that were called *Gerardia* and *Virgularia* (Scrophulariaceae). Ann. Missouri Bot. Gard. 65: 769–771.
Davidson, R. A. 1959. The vascular flora of southeastern Iowa. Univ. Iowa Studies Nat. Hist. 20(2): 1–102.
Davidson, R. A. 1960. Plant communities of southeastern Iowa. Proc. Iowa Acad. Sci. 67: 162–173.
Davis, R. J. 1966. The North American perennial species of *Claytonia*. Brittonia 18: 285–303.
Deevy, E. S., and R. F. Flint. 1957. Postglacial hypsithermal interval. Science 125: 182–184.
Dick-Peddie, W. A. 1955. Presettlement forest types in Iowa. Ph.D. dissertation, Iowa State Univ., Ames.
Dietrich, W., and P. H. Raven. 1976. An earlier name for *Oenothera strigosa* (Onagraceae). Ann. Missouri Bot. Gard. 63: 382–383.
Dorn, R. D. 1988. *Chenopodium simplex*, an earlier name for *C. gigantospermum* (Chenopodiaceae). Madrono 35: 162.
Dorr, L. J. 1990. A revision of the North America genus *Callirhoe* (Malvaceae). Mem. New York Bot. Gard. 56: 1–74.
Duritsa, M. F. 1983. A natural areas inventory of

Black Hawk County, Iowa. M.S. thesis, Univ. of Northern Iowa, Cedar Falls.

Eilers, L. J. 1963. The vegetation of the glacial border during the Wisconsin maximum. Proc. Iowa Acad. Sci. 70: 60–64.

Eilers, L. J. 1965. The postglacial phytogeography of the Iowan Lobe. Proc. Iowa Acad. Sci. 72: 84–98.

Eilers, L. J. 1971. The vascular flora of the Iowan area. Univ. Iowa Studies Nat. Hist. 21(5): 1–137.

Eilers, L. J. 1974. A flora of Brush Creek Canyon State Preserve. Proc. Iowa Acad. Sci. 81: 150–157.

Eilers, L. J. 1975. History of studies on the Iowa flora. Proc. Iowa Acad. Sci. 82: 59–64.

Eilers, L. J. 1979. BIOBANK, a computerized data storage and processing system for the vascular flora of Iowa. Proc. Iowa Acad. Sci. 86: 15–18.

Espenshade, E. B., ed. 1964. Goode's world atlas. 12th ed. Rand McNally Co., Chicago.

Farrar, D. R. 1985. Pteridophytes of Iowa's Loess Hills: adaptations to dry habitats. Proc. Iowa Acad. Sci. 92: 196–198.

Fay, M. J. 1951. The flora of Cedar County, Iowa. Proc. Iowa Acad. Sci. 58: 107–131.

Fay, M. J. 1953. The flora of southwestern Iowa. Ph.D. dissertation, Univ. of Iowa, Iowa City.

Fernald, M. L. 1953. Gray's manual of botany. 8th ed. American Book Co., New York.

Fitzpatrick, T. J., and M. F. L. Fitzpatrick. 1897. The flora of southern Iowa. Proc. Iowa Acad. Sci. 5: 134–173.

Freckmann, R. W. 1978. New combinations in *Dichanthelium* (Poaceae). Phytologia 39: 268–270.

Freese, E. L., and W. J. Platt. 1991. Vascular flora of Arend's Kettle, Freda Haffner Kettlehole State Preserve, Dickinson County, Iowa. J. Iowa Acad. Sci. 98: 102–107.

Frest, T. J. 1981. Iowa Pleistocene snail. Final report on project SE-1-4 submitted to the U.S. Fish and Wildlife Service and Iowa Dept. of Natural Resources.

Fults, J. L. 1934. A botanical survey of Lee County, Iowa. Iowa State Coll. J. Sci. 8: 251–293.

Gabel, M. 1984. A biosystematic study of the genus *Elymus* (Gramineae: Triticae) in Iowa. Proc. Iowa Acad. Sci. 79: 140–146.

Gilly, C. L. 1946. The Cyperaceae of Iowa. Iowa State Coll. J. Sci. 21: 55–151.

Gilly, C. L. 1947. The flora of Iowa: a progress report based on past contributions. Proc. Iowa Acad. Sci. 54: 99–106.

Gilly, C. L., and M. E. MacDonald. 1936. Rare and unusual plants from southeastern Iowa. Proc. Iowa Acad. Sci. 43: 143–149.

Gilly, C. L., and M. E. MacDonald. 1947. A preliminary report on the flora of southeastern Iowa, Part 1. Proc. Iowa Acad. Sci. 54: 107–126.

Gilly, C. L., and M. E. MacDonald. 1948. Preliminary report on the flora of southeastern Iowa, Part 2. Proc. Iowa Acad. Sci. 55: 115–133.

Gleason, H. A., and A. Cronquist. 1963. Manual of vascular plants of northeastern United States and adjacent Canada. D. van Nostrand Co., New York.

Glenn-Lewin, D. C. 1976. The vegetation of Stinson Prairie, Kossuth County, Iowa. Proc. Iowa Acad. Sci. 83: 88–93.

Glenn-Lewin, D. C., R. H. Laushman, and P. D. Whitson. 1984. The vegetation of the Paleozoic Plateau, northeastern Iowa. Proc. Iowa Acad. Sci. 91: 22–27.

Goodman, G. J. 1939. Plants new to Iowa. Proc. Iowa Acad. Sci. 46: 105–106.

Goodman, G. J. 1942. Notes on Iowa plants. Proc. Iowa Acad. Sci. 49: 207–209.

Gould, F. W. 1974. Nomenclatural changes in the Poaceae. Brittonia 26: 59–60.

Gould, F. W., and C. A. Clark. 1978. *Dichanthelium* (Poaceae) in the United States and Canada. Ann. Missouri Bot. Gard. 65: 1088–1132.

Graham, S. A. 1979. The origin of *Ammania* X *coccinea* Rottboell. Taxon 28: 169–178.

Graham, S. A. 1985. A revision of *Ammania* (Lythraceae) in the western hemisphere. J. Arnold Arbor. 66: 395–420.

Grant, M. L. 1950. Dickinson County flora. Proc. Iowa Acad. Sci. 57: 91–129.

Grant, M. L., and R. F. Thorne. 1955. Discovery and description of a sphagnum bog in Iowa, with notes on the distribution of bog plants in the state. Proc. Iowa Acad. Sci. 62: 197–210.

Great Plains Flora Association. 1977. Atlas of the flora of the Great Plains. Univ. Press of Kansas, Lawrence.

Great Plains Flora Association. 1986. Flora of the Great Plains. Univ. Press of Kansas, Lawrence.

Greene, W., ed. 1907. Plants of Iowa: a preliminary list of the native and introduced plants of the state not under cultivation. Bull. State Hort. Soc.: 1–264.

Guldner, L. F. 1960. The vascular plants of Scott and Muscatine counties. Davenport Publ. Mus. Publs. in Botany, No. 1.

Hallberg, G. R., E. A. Bettis, and J. C. Prior. 1984. Geologic overview of the Paleozoic Plateau region of northeastern Iowa. Proc. Iowa Acad. Sci. 91: 12–15.

Hartley, T. H. 1966. The flora of the Driftless Area. Univ. Iowa Studies Nat. Hist. 21(1): 1–174.

Hayden, A. 1940. A supplement to the catalogue of Iowa plants in the Iowa State College herbarium. Iowa State Coll. J. Sci. 14: 199–213.

Hayden, A. 1943. A botanical survey in the Iowa lake region of Clay and Palo Alto counties. Iowa State Coll. J. Sci. 17: 277–415.

Hayden, A. 1945. A second supplement to the catalogue of Iowa plants in the Iowa State College herbarium. Iowa State Coll. J. Sci. 19: 111–132.

Hayden, A. 1946. A progress report on the preservation of prairie. Proc. Iowa Acad. Sci. 53: 45–82.

Hinton, W. F. 1976. The systematics of *Physalis pumila*. Syst. Bot. 1: 188–193.

Hippler, M. I., Sr. 1951. An annotated bibliography of the taxonomic and ecological literature of the vascular plants of Iowa. M.S. thesis, Univ. of Iowa, Iowa City.

Hoch, P. C., and P. H. Raven. 1977. New combinations in *Epilobium* (Onagraceae). Ann. Missouri Bot. Gard. 64: 136.

Holte, K. E., and R. F. Thorne. 1962. Discovery of a calcareous fen complex in northwest Iowa. Proc. Iowa Acad. Sci. 69: 54–60.

Isely, D. 1962. Leguminosae of the north-central states, IV: Psoraleae. Iowa State J. Sci. 37: 103–162.

Isely, D. 1973. Leguminosae of the United States, I: subfamily Mimosoideae. Mem. New York Bot. Gard. 25(1): 1–152.

Isely, D. 1975. Leguminosae of the United States, II: subfamily Caesalpinioideae. Mem. New York Bot. Gard. 25(2): 1–128.

Isely, D. 1984. *Astragalus* L. (Leguminosae: Papilionoideae) II: species summary A–E. Iowa State J. Res. 59: 97–216.

Isely, D. 1985. Leguminosae of the United States, *Astragalus* L., III: species summary F–M. Iowa State J. Res. 60: 179–322.

Isely, D. 1990. Vascular flora of the southeastern United States, vol. 3, pt. 3, Leguminosae (Fabaceae). Univ. of North Carolina Press, Chapel Hill.

Johnson-Groh, C. L., and D. R. Farrar. 1985. Flora and phytogeographical history of Ledges State Park, Boone County, Iowa. Proc. Iowa Acad. Sci. 92: 137–144.

Johnson-Groh, C. L., D. Q. Lewis, and J. F. Shearer. 1987. Vegetation communities and flora of Dolliver State Park, Webster County, Iowa. Proc. Iowa Acad. Sci. 94: 84–88.

Jones, A. G. 1984. Nomenclatural notes on *Aster* (Asteraceae), II: new combinations and some transfers. Phytologia 55: 373–388.

Kartesz, J. T., and K. N. Gandhi. 1989. Nomenclatural notes for the North American flora, I. Phytologia 67: 461–467.

Kartesz, J. T., and K. N. Gandhi. 1990. Nomenclatural notes for the North American flora, II. Phytologia 68: 421–427.

Kartesz, J. T., and R. Kartesz. 1980. A synonymized checklist of the vascular flora of the United States, Canada, and Greenland. Univ. of North Carolina Press, Chapel Hill.

Kellogg, G. E. 1946. The asters of Iowa. Proc. Iowa Acad. Sci. 53: 153–166.

Knapp, J. L. 1983. The erosional cycle of upland wetlands created by eolian sands. M.S. thesis, Univ. of Northern Iowa, Cedar Falls.

Koch, D. 1969. The Sioux Quartzite formation in Gitchie Manitou State Preserve. Development Series Report 8. State Preserves Advisory Board, Iowa City.

Kwang, Yao-Wen. 1951. The Polemoniales of Iowa (Convolvulaceae to Verbenaceae). M.S. thesis, Univ. of Iowa, Iowa City.

Lammers, T. G. 1980. The vascular flora of Starr's Cave State Preserve. Proc. Iowa Acad.

Sci. 87: 148–158.
Lammers, T. G. 1983a. The vascular flora of Des Moines County, Iowa. Proc. Iowa Acad. Sci. 90: 55–71.
Lammers, T. G. 1983b. The vascular flora of Roggman Boreal Slopes State Preserve, Clayton County, Iowa. Proc. Iowa Acad. Sci. 90: 107–111.
Lammers, T. G., and A. G. Van Der Valk. 1977. A checklist of the aquatic and wetland vascular plants of Iowa, I: ferns, fern allies, and dicotyledons. Proc. Iowa Acad. Sci. 84: 41–88.
Lammers, T. G., and A. G. Van Der Valk. 1978. A checklist of the aquatic and wetland vascular plants of Iowa, II: monocotyledons. Proc. Iowa Acad. Sci. 85: 121–163.
Landolt, E. 1960. Biosystematics of the family of duckweeds (Lemnaceae), vol. 1. Veroff. Geobot. Inst. Eth, Stiftung Rubel. Zurich 70: 1–247.
Lehmann, J. W. 1983. The vascular flora of Dubuque County, Iowa. M.S. thesis, Univ. of Northern Iowa, Cedar Falls.
Lellinger, D. B. 1985. A field manual of the ferns and fern allies of the United States and Canada. Smithsonian Institution, Washington, D.C.
Lewis, W. H. 1961. Merger of the North American *Houstonia* and *Oldenlandia* under *Hedyotis*. Rhodora 63: 216–223.
Loomis, W. E., and A. L. McComb. 1943. Recent advances in the forest in Iowa. Proc. Iowa Acad. Sci. 51: 217–224.
McComb, A. L., and W. E. Loomis. 1944. Subclimax prairie. Bull. Torr. Bot. Club 71: 46–76.
Mohlenbrock, R. H. 1986. Guide to the vascular flora of Illinois. Southern Illinois Univ. Press, Carbondale.
Monson, P. H. 1959. Spermatophytes of the Des Moines Lobe in Iowa. Ph.D. dissertation, Iowa State Univ., Ames.
Morrill, J. B. 1953. Prairie flora of the Missouri River bluffs of western Iowa. M.S. thesis, Iowa State Univ., Ames.
Mutel, C. F. 1991. Fragile giants: a natural history of the Loess Hills. Univ. of Iowa Press, Iowa City.
Nekola, J. C. 1990. Rare Iowa plant notes from the R. V. Drexler herbarium. J. Iowa Acad. Sci. 97: 55–73.
Nicholson, D., and N. H. Russell. 1955. The genus *Asclepias* in Iowa. Proc. Iowa Acad. Sci. 62: 211–215.
Niemann, D. A. 1986. The distribution of orchids in Iowa. Proc. Iowa Acad. Sci. 93: 24–34.
Niemeier, P. E., and W. A. Hubert. 1984. The aquatic vascular flora of Clear Lake, Cerro Gordo County, Iowa. Proc. Iowa Acad. Sci. 91: 57–66.
Novacek, J. M. 1985. The Loess Hills of western Iowa: a problem in phytogeography. Proc. Iowa Acad. Sci. 92: 213–219.
Novacek, J. M., D. M. Roosa, and W. P. Pusateri. 1985. The vegetation of the Loess Hills landform along the Missouri River. Proc. Iowa Acad. Sci. 92: 192–212.
Ownbey, G. B., and T. Morley. 1991. Vascular plants of Minnesota, a checklist and atlas. Univ. of Minnesota Press, Minneapolis.
Pammel, L. H. 1899. The forest flora of Hardin County, Iowa. Iowa Geol. Survey Ann. Rept. 10: 306–313.
Pammel, L. H. 1924. The occurrence of *Juniperus horizontalis* in Floyd County near Rockford. Proc. Iowa Acad. Sci. 30: 297–300.
Parry, C. C. 1852. Systematic catalogue of plants of Wisconsin and Minnesota, Art. V. Pp. 606–622 in D. D. Owen, Report of a geological survey of Wisconsin, Iowa, and Minnesota. Lippencott, Grambo & Co., Philadelphia.
Pearson, J. A., and M. L. Leoschke. 1992. Floristic composition and conservation status of fens in Iowa. J. Iowa Acad. Sci. 99: 41–52.
Peck, J. H. 1976. The pteridophyte flora of Iowa. Proc. Iowa Acad. Sci. 83: 143–160.
Peck, J. H. 1980. Life history and reproductive biology of the ferns of Woodman Hollow, Webster County, Iowa. Ph.D. dissertation, Iowa State Univ., Ames.
Peck, J. H. 1982. Ferns and fern allies of the Driftless Area of Illinois, Iowa, Minnesota, and Wisconsin. Milwaukee Publ. Mus. Contr. in Biol. and Geol. 53: 1–140.
Peck, J. H. 1989. Additions to the Iowa pteridophyte flora, III. J. Iowa Acad. Sci. 96: 54–56.
Peck, J. H., and W. R. Buck. 1978. The *Selaginella apoda* complex in Iowa. Am. Fern J.

68: 29.
Peck, J. H., L. J. Eilers, and D. M. Roosa. 1978. The vascular plants of Fremont County, Iowa. Iowa Bird Life 48: 3–18.
Peck, J. H., B. W. Haglan, L. J. Eilers, D. M. Roosa, and D. Vander Zee. 1984. Checklist of the vascular flora of Lyon and Sioux counties, Iowa. Proc. Iowa Acad. Sci. 91: 92–97.
Peck, J. H., T. G. Lammers, B. W. Haglan, D. M. Roosa, and L. J. Eilers. 1981. A checklist of the vascular flora of Lee County, Iowa. Proc. Iowa Acad. Sci. 88: 159–171.
Peck, J. H., J. C. Nekola, and D. R. Farrar. 1989. Five pteridophytes new to Iowa. Amer. Fern J. 79: 28–29.
Peck, J. H., and D. M. Roosa. 1983. Bibliography of Iowa aquatic and wetland plant literature. Proc. Iowa Acad. Sci. 90: 72–77.
Peck, J. H., D. M. Roosa, and L. J. Eilers. 1980. A checklist of the vascular flora of Allamakee County. Proc. Iowa Acad. Sci. 87: 62–75.
Peck, J. H., and M. M. Smart. 1985. Bibliography to upper Mississippi River aquatic and wetland plant literature. Proc. Iowa Acad. Sci. 92: 78–84.
Peck, M. 1904. The flowering plants of Hardin County. Proc. Iowa Acad. Sci. 12: 193–214.
Phillips, M. N. 1977. Systematics of *Saxifraga pensylvanica* and a putative segregate species, *S. forbesii* (Saxifragaceae). M.S. thesis, Univ. of Wisconsin, Madison.
Pike, Z. M. 1810. Sources of the Mississippi and the western Louisiana Territory. March of America Facsimile Series No. 57. University Microfilms, Ann Arbor.
Plouffe, M. E. 1977. An autecological study of *Betula papyrifera* in the Iowa River greenbelt in Hardin County, Iowa, with notes on the vegetation. M.S. thesis, Iowa State Univ., Ames.
Pohl, R. W. 1966. The grasses of Iowa. Iowa State J. Sci. 40: 341–573.
Prior, J. C. 1991. Landforms of Iowa. Univ. of Iowa Press, Iowa City.
Pusateri, W. P., D. M. Roosa, and D. R. Farrar. 1993. Habitat and distribution of plants special to Iowa's Driftless Area. J. Iowa Acad. Sci. 100: 29–53.
Raven, P. H., W. Dietrich, and W. Stubbe. 1979. An outline of the systematics of *Oenothera* subsect. *Euoenothera* (Onagraceae). Syst. Bot. 4(3): 242–251.
Raven, P. H., and D. P. Gregory. 1972. A revision of the genus *Gaura* (Onagraceae). Mem. Torr. Bot. Club 23: 1–96.
Rickey, M. D. 1964. A floristic survey of Delaware County, Iowa. M.S. thesis, Univ. of Iowa, Iowa City.
Roosa, D. M. 1981. Marsh vegetation dynamics at Goose Lake, Hamilton County, Iowa: the role of historical, cyclical, and annual events. Ph.D. dissertation, Iowa State Univ., Ames.
Roosa, D. M., L. J. Eilers, and S. Zager. 1991. An annotated checklist of the vascular plant flora of Guthrie County, Iowa. J. Iowa Acad. Sci. 98(1): 14–30.
Roosa, D. M., M. J. Leoschke, and L. J. Eilers. 1989. Distribution of Iowa's endangered and threatened vascular plants. Dept. of Nat. Resources, Des Moines.
Roosa, D. M., and J. H. Peck. 1986. Annotated bibliography of Iowa prairie literature. Proc. Iowa Acad. Sci. 93: 54–69.
Rosburg, T. R. 1992. A new record for falcate spurge in the midwest. Prairie Nat. 24(1): 41–42.
Salsbury, N. E., and J. C. Knox. 1969. Glacial landforms of the Big Kettle locality, Dickinson County, Iowa. Development Series Report 6. State Preserves Advisory Board, Iowa City.
Sanders, D. R. 1968. Vegetation of slope forests along the Des Moines River. Proc. Iowa Acad. Sci. 75: 78–84.
Scholtes, W. H. 1955. Properties and classification of the paha-derived soils in northeastern Iowa. Iowa State Coll. J. Sci. 30: 163–209.
Sears, P. 1942. Xerothermic theory. Bot. Rev. 8: 708–736.
Sheviak, C. 1977. A new species of *Spiranthes* from the grasslands of central North America. Bot. Mus. Leafl. Harvard Univ. 23: 285–297.
Sheviak, C., and M. L. Bowles. 1986. The prairie fringed orchids: a pollinator-isolated species pair. Rhodora 88: 267–290.
Shimek, B. 1896. The flora of the Sioux Quartzite in Iowa. Proc. Iowa Acad. Sci. 4: 72–77.

Shimek, B. 1899. The flora of Lyon County. Iowa Geol. Surv. Ann. Rept. 10: 157–184. Bull. Lab. Nat. Hist. Univ. Iowa 5(2): 145–170.
Shimek, B. 1910. The geology of Harrison and Monona counties, Iowa. Iowa Geol. Surv. Ann. Rept. 20: 271–485.
Shimek, B. 1915. Early Iowa locality records. Proc. Iowa Acad. Sci. 22: 105–119.
Shimek, B. 1917. The sand flora of Iowa. Bull. Lab. Nat. Hist. Univ. Iowa 7(4): 6–24.
Shimek, B. 1924. The prairie of the Mississippi River bluffs. Proc. Iowa Acad. Sci. 31: 205–212.
Shimek, B. 1948. (H. S. Conard, ed.). The plant geography of Iowa. Univ. Iowa Studies Nat. Hist. 19(4): 1–178.
Smith, D. D. 1981. Iowa prairie: an endangered ecosystem. Proc. Iowa Acad. Sci. 88: 7–10.
Smith, P. E., and R. V. Bovbjerg. 1958. Pilot Knob bog as a habitat. Proc. Iowa Acad. Sci. 65: 546–553.
Spence, W. L. 1959. The Salicaceae of Iowa. M.S. thesis, Univ. of Iowa, Iowa City.
State Planning Board. 1925. The Iowa twenty-five-year plan. Des Moines.
Thompson, C. A., E. A. Bettis, and R. G. Baker. 1992. Geology of Iowa fens. J. Iowa Acad. Sci. 99: 53–59.
Thomson, G. W., and H. G. Hertel. 1981. The forest resources of Iowa in 1980. Proc. Iowa Acad. Sci. 88: 2–6.
Thorne, R. F. 1953. Notes on rare Iowa plants. Proc. Iowa Acad. Sci. 60: 260–274.
Thorne, R. F. 1954. Present status of our knowledge of the vascular flora of Iowa. Proc. Iowa Acad. Sci. 61: 177–183.
Thorne, R. F. 1955. Flora of Johnson County, Iowa. Proc. Iowa Acad. Sci. 62: 155–227.
Thorne, R. F . 1956. Notes on rare Iowa plants, II. Proc. Iowa Acad. Sci. 63: 214–227.
Thorne, R. F. 1964. Relict nature of the flora of White Pine Hollow Forest Preserve, Dubuque County, Iowa. Univ. Iowa Studies Nat. Hist. 20(2): 1–33.
Tuttle, F. M. 1919. Flora of Mitchell County. Proc. Iowa Acad. Sci. 26: 269–299.
Ugarte, E. 1987. The hill prairies of northeast Iowa: vegetation and dynamics. Ph.D. dissertation, Iowa State Univ., Ames.
United States Department of Agriculture. 1941. Climate and man: yearbook of agriculture. U.S. Govt. Printing Office, Washington, D.C.
United States Department of Agriculture. 1982a. National list of scientific plant names, vol. 1: list of plant names. U.S. Govt. Printing Office, Washington, D.C.
United States Department of Agriculture. 1982b. National list of scientific plant names, vol. 2: synonymy. U.S. Govt. Printing Office, Washington, D.C.
Van Bruggen, T. 1958. The flora of south-central Iowa. Ph.D. dissertation, Univ. of Iowa, Iowa City.
Van Bruggen, T. 1985. The vascular plants of South Dakota. 2nd ed. Iowa State Univ. Press, Ames.
Van Der Linden, P., and D. R. Farrar. 1984. Forest and shade trees of Iowa. Iowa State Univ. Press, Ames.
Van Der Valk, A. G. 1975. Floristic composition and structure of fen communities in northwest Iowa. Proc. Iowa Acad. Sci. 82: 109–117.
Vander Zee, D. 1979. The vascular flora of Gitchie Manitou State Preserve. Proc. Iowa Acad. Sci. 86: 66–75.
Van Norman, K. 1987. The vascular flora of Black Hawk County, Iowa. M.S. thesis, Univ. of Northern Iowa, Cedar Falls.
Volker, R., and S. G. Smith. 1975. Changes in the aquatic vascular flora of Lake East Okoboji in historic times. Proc. Iowa Acad. Sci. 72: 65–72.
Voss, E. G. 1966. Nomenclatural notes on monocots. Rhodora 68: 435–463.
Voss, E. G. 1972. Michigan flora, Part 1: gymnosperms and monocots. Cranbrook Institute of Science, Bloomfield Hills, Mich.
Voss, E. G. 1985. Michigan flora, Part 2: dicots (Sauraceae-Cornaceae). Cranbrook Institute of Science, Bloomfield Hills, Mich.
Wagenknecht, B. L. 1954. The flora of Washington County, Iowa. Proc. Iowa Acad. Sci. 61: 184–204.
Wagner, W. L. 1983. New species and combinations in the genus *Oenothera* (Onagraceae). Ann. Missouri Bot. Gard. 70: 194–196.
Walker, P. H. 1966. Postglacial environments in relation to landscape and soils on the Cary Drift, Iowa. Iowa Agric. Exp. Stn. Res. Bull.

549: 838–875.
Webber, J. M., and P. W. Ball. 1979. Proposals to reject *Carex rosea* and *Carex radiata* of eastern North America (Cyperaceae). Taxon 28: 611–616.
Webber, J. M., and P. W. Ball. 1984. The taxonomy of the *Carex rosea* group (section Phaestoglochin) in Canada. Can. J. Bot. 62: 2058–2073.
Welsh, S. L. 1960. Legumes of the north-central states: galegeae. Iowa State J. Sci. 35: 111–250.
Wemple, D. K. 1970. Revision of the genus *Petalostemon* (Leguminosae). Iowa State J. Sci. 45: 1–102.
White, J. A., and D. C. Glenn-Lewin. 1984. Regional and local variation in tallgrass prairies of Iowa and Nebraska. Vegetation 57: 65–78.
Wilson, B. L. 1992. Checklist of the vascular flora of Page County, Iowa. J. Iowa Acad. Sci. 99: 23–33.
Wilson, B. L. 1993. Some significant Iowa plant records from the herbarium of University of Nebraska at Omaha. J. Iowa Acad. Sci. 100: 87–89.
Yatskievych, G., and J. Turner. 1991. Catalogue of the flora of Missouri. Braun-Brumfield, Ann Arbor, Mich.

Bur Oak Books

"All Will Yet Be Well": The Diary of Sarah Gillespie Huftalen, 1873–1952
By Suzanne L. Bunkers

A Cook's Tour of Iowa
By Susan Puckett

A Country So Full of Game: The Story of Wildlife in Iowa
By James J. Dinsmore

The Folks
By Ruth Suckow

Fragile Giants: A Natural History of the Loess Hills
By Cornelia F. Mutel

An Iowa Album: A Photographic History, 1860–1920
By Mary Bennett

Iowa Birdlife
By Gladys Black

Landforms of Iowa
By Jean C. Prior

Land of the Fragile Giants: Landscapes, Environments, and Peoples of the Loess Hills
Edited by Cornelia F. Mutel and Mary Swander

More han Ola og han Per
By Peter J. Rosendahl

Neighboring on the Air: Cooking with the KMA Radio Homemakers
By Evelyn Birkby

Nineteenth Century Home Architecture of Iowa City: A Silver Anniversary Edition
By Margaret N. Keyes

Nothing to Do but Stay: My Pioneer Mother
By Carrie Young

Old Capitol: Portrait of an Iowa Landmark
By Margaret N. Keyes

Parsnips in the Snow: Talks with Midwestern Gardeners
By Jane Anne Staw and Mary Swander

A Place of Sense: Essays in Search of the Midwest
Edited by Michael Martone

Prairie Cooks: Glorified Rice, Three-Day Buns, and Other Reminiscences
By Carrie Young with Felicia Young

Prairies, Forests, and Wetlands: The Restoration of Natural Landscape Communities in Iowa
By Janette R. Thompson

Restoring the Tallgrass Prairie: An Illustrated Manual for Iowa and the Upper Midwest
By Shirley Shirley

A Ruth Suckow Omnibus
By Ruth Suckow

"A Secret to Be Burried": The Diary and Life of Emily Hawley Gillespie, 1858–1888
By Judy Nolte Lensink

Tales of an Old Horsetrader: The First Hundred Years
By Leroy Judson Daniels

The Tattooed Countess
By Carl Van Vechten

"This State of Wonders": The Letters of an Iowa Frontier Family, 1858–1861
Edited by John Kent Folmar

Townships
Edited by Michael Martone

Up a Country Lane Cookbook
By Evelyn Birkby

Vandemark's Folly
By Herbert Quick

The Vascular Plants of Iowa: An Annotated Checklist and Natural History
By Lawrence J. Eilers and Dean M. Roosa

The Wedding Dress: Stories from the Dakota Plains
By Carrie Young